PHOTOSHOP®

RESTORATION & RETOUCHING

THIRD EDITION

KATRIN EISMANN

with WAYNE PALMER

Foreword by JOHN McINTOSH

New Riders

Berkeley, California

Adobe Photoshop Restoration & Retouching
Third Edition
Katrin Eismann with Wayne Palmer

New Riders
1249 Eighth Street
Berkeley, CA 94710
510/524-2178
800/283-9444
510/524-2221 (fax)

Find us on the World Wide Web at: www.newriders.com

To report errors, please send a note to errata@peachpit.com

New Riders is an imprint of Peachpit, a division of Pearson Education

ISBN 0-321-31627-4

9 8 7 6 5 4 3 2 1

Printed in the United States of America

PROJECT EDITOR
Beth Millett

PRODUCTION EDITOR
Hilal Sala

COPY EDITOR
Douglas Adrianson

TECH EDITORS
Victor Gavenda
Jeffrey M. Greene

COMPOSITOR
Kim Scott

PROOFREADERS
Alison Kelley
Evan Pricco

INDEXER
James Minkin

COVER DESIGN
Anne Jones
Aren Howell

INTERIOR DESIGN
Anne Jones

Contents at a Glance

Table of Contents

3

EXPOSURE CORRECTION

4

WORKING WITH COLOR

PART III:
ESSENTIAL RESTORATION, REPAIRING, AND REBUILDING TECHNIQUES

5

DUST, MOLD, AND TEXTURE REMOVAL

6

DAMAGE CONTROL AND REPAIR

PART IV:
PUTTING THE BEST FACE FORWARD

10

GLAMOUR RETOUCHING

APPENDIX

INDEX

DEDICATION

To the memory of the people in the photographs and to the countless retouching artists whose talent ensures that they will not be forgotten.

—Katrin

To my late mother, Hazel, for the right half of my brain, to my father, Ramon, for the left. To my dear wife Pam, whose support has been immeasurable even when the left and right halves were misfiring. And last but not least, to my new daughter, Amanda, who makes an old man feel young again.

—Wayne

ABOUT THE AUTHORS

Katrin Eismann is an internationally respected lecturer and teacher on the subject of imaging, restoration, retouching, and the impact of emerging technologies on professional photographers, artists, and educators. Her clients include Eastman Kodak, Apple, Adobe Systems, International Center of Photography, Professional Photography Association, and Warner Brothers. She received her Bachelor of Fine Arts degree in photographic illustration with a concentration in electronic still imaging from the Rochester Institute of Technology and her Masters of Fine Arts degree in design at the School of Visual Arts in New York City. Katrin is also the author of *Photoshop Masking & Compositing* and *Real World Digital Photography, 2nd edition*. She serves on the advisory council of the Sewall Belmont House and Museum, has recently been inducted into the Photoshop Hall of Fame, and is a card-carrying member of www.binge-golfers.com.

Katrin hopes someday to take photographs that require no color correction, retouching, cropping, dodging and burning, or enhancement of any kind, but in the meantime she'll keep learning (and teaching) Photoshop. To learn more about Katrin please visit www.katrineismann.com. To learn more about this book, please visit www.digitalretouch.org.

Wayne Palmer has had a passion for photography all his life. He has a degree in education from Bloomsburg State College, but his interest in photography kept him in the darkroom as much as the classroom. After graduation, he worked for Guardian Photo, Inc. for 13 years in the marketing of photofinishing services on a national level.

Wayne started his own business, Palmer Multimedia Imaging, in 1994, offering custom photographic, videographic, and digital photo restoration services. He has worked with Photoshop since version 3, and previously used Aldus PhotoStyler. A self-described AV nerd, Wayne enjoys sharing his knowledge of photography, digital imaging, and computers. He teaches Photoshop, Photoshop Elements, and digital photography in the continuing education department of the Pennsylvania College of Technology, and volunteers his time to instruct seniors in computer literacy through the James V. Brown Library.

ACKNOWLEDGMENTS

Writing a book initially seems like a secluded undertaking, but the very task of researching and seeking expert insights into any topic changes the process from solitary to collaborative. Over the years, I have learned from countless Photoshop experts, engineers, artists, students, and especially my readers, whose questions and comments always challenge me to be clearer and remain relevant. Thank you to Ken Allen, Mark Beckelman, Carrie Beene, Russell Brown, Shan Canfield, Jane Conner-ziser, Douglas Dubler, Seán Duggan, Bruce Fraser, Greg Gorman, Mark Hamburg, Gregory Heisler, Art Johnson, Scott Kelby, Julieanne Kost, Schecter Lee, Dan Margulis, Andrew Matusik, Pedro Meyer, Bert Monroy, Myke Ninness, Marc Pawliger, Phil Pool, Andrew Rodney, Jeff Schewe, Eddie Tapp, Chris Tarantino, Leigh-Anne Tompkins, Lee Varis, John Warner, Lloyd Weller, Ben Willmore, and Lorie Zirbes for putting up with last-minute emails, phone calls, and questions from me.

Creating a book is an undertaking where more work is done behind the curtain than in front. My backbone in this project remains Beth Millett, who took two years to convince me to write the first edition, and now I can't believe that she let me convince her to fill her little free time with this update. Beth, I wouldn't and couldn't have done it without you.

Thank you to the numerous contributors who make this third edition so valuable. Readers, photo enthusiasts, and imaging professionals from all around the world are featured in these pages and listed in the "Contributors" appendix. You were all wonderful to work with, generous with your images and techniques, and understanding of my production deadlines. Merci, vielen dank, gracias, and thank you! In addition, JupiterImages allowed me to feature and post images from their collections—most of which are in Chapter 9, "Portrait Retouching." Anyone who knows my photography knows that if it's not moldy and decrepit, I won't photograph it, so I rely on the generosity of others for portrait examples.

Thank you to the numerous readers who emailed since the release of the first and second editions. I sincerely enjoyed hearing from you, seeing the images you worked on, and reading your questions, which showed me what was unclear or missing in the first two editions. A technique that is overly complicated or poorly explained is worthless, and I listened to your ideas and addressed your questions while preparing this third edition. In fact, calling this book a third edition is not accurate—this really is a brand-new book. We reviewed every single technique, substituted many images with better examples, and increased the number of advanced techniques throughout the entire book. Our primary goal was to write a book that readers of the first and second editions would find valuable enough to purchase and feel they got their money's worth. Please let me know if we've accomplished this.

—Katrin

FOREWORD

On the occasion of the third edition of *Photoshop Restoration & Retouching*, I am pleased to renew the foreword to this book. Much has happened since the second edition was released in 2002—the world has witnessed wars and countless suffering caused by natural disasters including the tsunami of 2004 and the vicious destruction of hurricanes. On a personal note, you and your family may have experienced the joy of a birth, wedding, or anniversary or, as many of us have, mourned the loss of a friend, parent, sibling, or spouse.

With every event comes a practical and emotional need for portraits and family pictures. It is not disasters alone that prompt our need. We have come to an age where the baby boomers of the 1950s are facing the inevitable loss of our now-aging parents. We are the sons and daughters of the so-called "greatest generation." We are fixated on this group and the great challenges they faced. We also long for our personal histories, our connection to our parents, grandparents, and great-grandparents. We have come of age and we have been given everything on a silver platter, except that often the information of how we got here has been lost, damaged, or forgotten.

We baby boomers are one of the last generations whose lives were documented primarily by photography. We are the generation of the still image, the snapshot, the photo album, and the formal family portrait. These are the documents of our lives, and we are not about to let them go. When we discover or are given old family photographs we relish every memory as we sort through the images. When the best of these images are damaged or lost, we are universally sad. In fact, it is common knowledge that if we have to leave home in an emergency, the two items we are most likely to grab (after children and pets) are family photographs and personal documents.

My mother recently told me about a trend at funerals in our hometown. She told me how nice it was to see a montage of images taken throughout her friend's life at the viewing. The nostalgia for images certainly is natural and based in the fundamental emotional need to not only remember but to be reminded of the past. It is extremely upsetting to my mother that all our family snapshots were lost years ago and there will not be a montage of her life at her funeral.

These are the emotions that inspire a groundswell of interest in image retouching and restoration. Of course, these skills were once the province of the experienced airbrush artist; today it is a Photoshop project. With a computer, Photoshop, a flatbed or film scanner, and an ink-jet printer you have every tool you need. The rest is up to your level of interest, enthusiasm, and persistence.

It is mind-boggling to see the relentless efforts and the clever solutions retouchers find when they make the commitment to restore an image. Limbs are borrowed from other photographs, backgrounds are replaced or simplified, and the cloning tool evaporates divorced spouses in seconds! Remember, we once had to cut these offending persons out of images with scissors or tear the print in two.

The Authors

For this third edition, Katrin shared the update process with Wayne Palmer, whose expertise, insights, and humor insure that this edition is the best book possible. Wayne and Katrin have worked on numerous books and imaging projects together and she has come to trust him with her "baby"—the first book she authored as a solo writer.

Katrin is a photographer, imaging artist, educator, wife, and author. She works harder then anyone I know and she is extremely disciplined. She is also very generous with her skills and her time. Her workshop students use her as a knowledge base for everything Photoshop. Her undergraduate and graduate students at the School of VISUAL ARTS are often intimidated by her expectations and passionate demand for hard work and the highest quality images. She is challenging and every bit a great and highly respected teacher.

Finally, as an author, Katrin uses a relaxed, conversational style to effectively convey complex Photoshop techniques. Her secret lies in her ability to use relevant examples, explain concepts, and create screen captures that actually make sense to the reader. This is practiced skill. In this edition, every example has been checked, double-checked, updated, and improved by Katrin and Wayne. Her personal expectations are extremely high and her goal is to reach her readers at a personal as well as professional level. This is a unique and successful approach. When readers write email to Katrin, many are shocked when she responds personally. This is not a tactic or a strategy—this is Katrin.

John McIntosh

Chair, Computer Art
School of Visual Arts
New York City
Fall, 2005

INTRODUCTION

I haven't gone to a photo lab to drop off or pick up a roll of film since September 2001, and a few months ago I packed up my last film camera and shipped it off to an eBay buyer. Our household is now 100 percent film camera-free, and we have a lot more room in the refrigerator for food and beer, space that used to be taken up by film. But I cannot join in the chorus that loudly proclaims the death of film. Due to the billions—if not trillions—of existing film-based images, film is not dead. In fact, as more and more people reach into the proverbial family shoebox to restore images and recall family memories, film is proving itself to be as alive as ever. Even though many photographers may no longer use film as a capture technology, your (and my) family photographs still carry a tremendous amount of information that no one can negate the value of—regardless of what technology was used to capture the fleeting photons.

Film is not dead—it is all around us, holding within it the lives and histories of our families and communities. But keep in mind: While the essence, the meaning of the film image is not dead, the actual medium is dying a slow death as it fades, degrades, and is eaten by pests. Save the photos; get them out of the damp basement or dry, hot attic; take them out of those corrosive cardboard boxes and into archival storage sleeves and boxes. Do your best to store them somewhere cool and dry (relative humidity of 20 to 50 percent). If you really want to be all digital, scan the film to create digital masters. You may be surprised how beautiful and compelling that old, dying film really is.

THE IMPORTANCE OF IMAGES

Our photographs contain our memories and our legacy, and they connect us to our family and friends. Even if they are cracked, yellowed, or damaged, we don't throw them away. No matter how tattered or faded a photograph is, it still helps us remember and learn about the past. The combination of image, emotion, and memory fascinates me. With the addition of one component to this mixture—Photoshop—you can make faded colors rich again, remove damage, and clean up mold, making images as clear and crisp as the day they were taken. With the skilled use of Adobe Photoshop as presented in this book, you can fight the ravages of time and, more importantly, share the memories with your family and friends.

I started working with an early version of Photoshop 1.0 in 1989, and since 1992 have been teaching digital imaging at workshops and schools around the world. My students and readers always surprise me with questions, challenges, and examples of taking what I've taught them and going much further than I imagined possible. Take a look at what Alan, a reader of the first two editions and an imaging professional, started with in figure 1, which is a photograph of his mother as a young girl in Atlantic City in 1939. Figure 2 shows the final results, which Alan created with the careful use of layers, cloning, healing, and sharpening. More important than any of the Photoshop techniques is the joy of being together that these women share, which bursts from the frame. This photo echoes countless summer vacation photos that we all share and cherish. (But thankfully we don't need to wear high heels when we go swimming anymore!) Our photographs are our legacy and they need to be protected and preserved.

figure 1

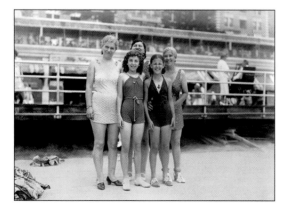

figure 2

As you can see by paging through this book, not all the pictures and examples featured here are historical. Many of the examples are images captured with the latest digital cameras or that came from leading photo studios. As a photographer, I always try to get the picture right before hitting the shutter, instead of relying on Photoshop to rescue a bad photograph. In other words, if I can create a better picture by fixing the lighting, hiring a professional makeup artist, or changing camera lenses or position, I'll always opt to make the extra effort to get the picture right in front of the lens.

THE IMPORTANCE OF LEARNING

Time, practice, and patience—you can't be good at a sport, cook a gourmet meal, or restore an image without them. There will be frustration, anger, and muttering, generally along the lines of "Why do I even bother… this looks terrible… I might as well just stop right now." Please turn off that noisy, no-good critic (whom we all have in our heads). Shut the voice down and keep practicing. Just as you learned to master a hobby, sport, or language, you'll learn to master and enjoy Photoshop restoration and retouching.

While I was updating this book, but especially Chapter 10, "Glamour Retouching," which shows the true insider secrets used by the best New York retouchers, my contributors said things like, "Why am I telling you all of this?" and "I'm giving away all of my secrets!" Well, yes, they have, and you and I are very fortunate to learn from them. But what you need to know is that every single person whose work is featured in these pages has lost a lot of sleep, neglected family and friends, and sometimes been accused of being social outcasts as they passionately work in Photoshop. There is no magic pill, instant quality button, or make-it-better keystroke. It takes time, dedication, curiosity, and a hint of stubbornness to get past the missteps and misclicks. Every image you work on today teaches you strategy and skills for the image you'll open tomorrow.

IS THIS BOOK RIGHT FOR YOU?

This book is right for you if you love images or work with photographs as a dedicated amateur or full-time professional. You may be a historian, photographer, librarian, teacher, multimedia artist, designer, artist, or the grandmother who wants to share the best photos with the rest of the family. This book addresses salvaging historical images and righting the contemporary images that have gone wrong—the missed exposures, the poor color balance, the busy and distracting background, or the inevitable wrinkle, pimple, or extra pounds that just drive you crazy every time you look at that photo.

This book is *not* for you if you don't have the time, curiosity, and patience to read through the examples, try them out, and then—just as I push my students—take the techniques further by applying them to your own images.

You have three ways to learn the techniques presented in this book:

- By reading the examples and looking at the images.

- By downloading the images from the book's Web site, www.digitalretouch.org, and with the book in hand, re-creating my steps.

- By taking the techniques shown here and applying them to your own images. As you work, you'll need to adjust some of the tool or filter settings to achieve optimal results. It is exactly at that moment, when you are working with your own images, that you're really learning how to restore and retouch images.

This is not an introductory book. To get the most out of it, you should be comfortable with the fundamentals of Photoshop, know where the tools are and what they do, and be familiar with common tasks, such as how to activate a layer or save a selection.

THE STRUCTURE OF THE BOOK AND THE WEB SITE

This book is divided into three primary areas:

- Improving tone, contrast, exposure, and color

- Removing dust and mold, and repairing damage

- Professional portrait and glamour retouching

In fact, the book is structured in the same way you should work with your images, starting with a brief overview of Photoshop essentials, file organization, and the tools a retoucher needs. It then works through tonal and color correction (the first things to focus on when retouching an image), followed by chapters on dust and damage removal, adding creative effects, portrait retouching, and the techniques professional retouchers use in the fashion and glamour business.

Each chapter starts with a brief overview of what will be covered in the chapter. I always start with a straightforward example that leads to more advanced examples. You may be tempted to jump to the more advanced sections right away, but I don't recommend it. My teaching and chapter structure serve the purpose of building up the tools and techniques in which the introductory examples serve as the foundation for the advanced examples. Similarly, the chapters on tonal and color correction serve as the foundation for the portrait and glamour retouching chapters. Do I expect you to sit down right now in the bookstore and read the book from cover to cover? Of course not—you should really pay for it first! Rather, take the book home, page through the chapters so you can see how the book and retouching workflow is structured, and then work your way through the book.

Instead of including a CD with the book, I designed and maintain a supplemental Web site, www.digitalretouch.org where you can download images, view the reader gallery, and follow links to additional retouching resources. Each chapter (except for Chapter 1, "Photoshop Essentials") has JPEG images that you can download. For those of you with a fast Internet connection (or a lot of patience), I've also included self-extracting image archives for each chapter, and one huge file that contains all of the support materials for the entire book.

Note

The images on the book's companion Web site are for your personal use only and should not be distributed by any other means or used to promote any business of any kind.

Numerous professional retouchers, teachers, photographers, and JupiterImages have generously shared many of their images and examples, many of which are posted on the Web site. Throughout the book, I did feature some images for which we were not able to procure permission to post the files, so these have not be posted on the Web. Call me old-fashioned, but I respect international and U.S. copyright laws—the copyright of all images remains with the originator, as noted throughout the book. Please do not email the publisher or me to request images that are not posted. I will not send them to you. You really don't want me to go to jail, do you?

In the cases where I didn't have permission to post specific images on the book's Web site, you can use similar images from your own photo albums or collections to follow along. Although you won't have the exact image I am using in the book, the problems being corrected are so universal that I am sure you'll be able to learn the techniques by working with similar images. After all, I'm sure you will be branching out to your own problem files sooner rather than later.

FOR INSTRUCTORS

This book was built around techniques I have taught over the years to the numerous students in my digital and creative imaging classes. As a teacher yourself, I'm sure you can appreciate how much time and work this represents. My hope is that this book and the examples and images I have provided will help you both learn and demonstrate the concepts and techniques of Photoshop retouching and restoration, but I also ask that you respect my work and that of the many other professionals whose work I've featured. Please do not copy pages of the book, distribute any of the images from the Web site, or otherwise reproduce or paraphrase the information without proper attribution and permission. Of course, each student who owns a copy of the book can can freely download and use the images from the Web site.

For information about educational sales of the book, please call 800-445-6991 for college sales, 800-848-9500 for K-12.

I would love to hear from you. Please email your comments about the book and Web site to me at katrin@digitalretouch.org. Show me how you've taken the techniques in these pages and gone further with them. If you send me before-and-after files of the retouched image, I'll post them in the readers' gallery. (Please keep them small, 1MB in total as JPEGs.) Great examples of restoration and retouching may be fodder for the next edition of the book; be sure to include your contact information so I can get your permission.

IS THIS BOOK APPLICABLE TO PHOTOSHOP ELEMENTS?

I've received numerous emails asking me whether this book is worthwhile for a Photoshop Elements user. Photoshop Elements is a terrific program; it includes a surprising number of Photoshop features and is often included with the sale of a scanner or digital camera. My co-author, Wayne Palmer, calls it "75 percent of Photoshop for around $75."

Photoshop Elements does have its limits, but it is definitely capable of tackling a great number of restoration tasks presented in this book.

First, the limitations:

- Only RGB and grayscale color modes are supported
- Curves, Color Balance, Channel Mixer, and Photo Filters are missing from the adjustment options
- No History snapshot features
- No access to channels
- No access to paths
- Layer masking available only with adjustment layers

Second, the possibilities:

- Spot Healing Brush and Healing Brush
- Supports Adjustment Layers and layer Blend Modes
- Supports the Sample All Layers feature, so you can clone onto a separate layer
- Most filters are included—sharpening, blurring, and high pass
- Selections can be saved
- Supports layer masking—indirectly (You must define your layer as a pattern and use a pattern adjustment layer.)
- You do have a History palette and can simulate the snapshot feature by saving your work at different stages as "copy merged" layers.

A reader wrote to me regarding my book and Photoshop Elements. "I am using your book with Photoshop Elements. What your book does that others don't is discuss the reasons for making certain adjustments, and the theory behind making certain adjustments, so I think it is applicable to Elements, but I also have PaintShop Pro and I find it helpful for that as well. There are many books that are highly rated that give the reader examples and exercises, and tell the reader exactly how to make adjustments to suit a specific photo. It's hard to take that info and make it work for the readers in their own photos. For example, a book that tells me to set Unsharp Mask for a specific photo to 143, 2, 12 does not help me learn the best way to sharpen my own photos, so I think your book does a good job of explaining much more the theory of retouching, not just the mechanics of correcting a sample photo."

Although this book was an ambitious project from the very start, there is a lot of Photoshop that I do not cover. I concentrated on Photoshop CS2, which is the latest version. If you are still working with version 6.0 or later, you will still learn a lot from this book, because the most important tools for retouching—layers, adjustment layers, and blending modes—all go back that far. (And this book probably will still be useful long after the next release of Photoshop.) I do not address Photoshop basics; I don't go down the toolbox, which would just bore you to death; and I don't cover complex selections or masking. Please see my separate book, *Photoshop Masking and Compositing*, for an in-depth coverage of that topic.

Last but certainly not least, let me introduce my co-author, Wayne Palmer. Wayne is the owner of Palmer Multimedia Imaging and has been doing digital photo restoration for over 10 years and is a photographer in his own right. Over the years, I have called upon him for his expertise in the field. Because of his practical experience and involvement with the first two editions of this book, I asked him to co-author this project. Wayne added valuable insights about the business of restoration and made sure that the featured techniques were practical, productive, and applicable to a variety of restoration challenges.

We wish you a lot of fun as you bring back image memories and take your contemporary photographs to a higher level.

Best regards,

Katrin Eismann
katrin@digitalretouch.org
The Big Apple, New York City

1

Photoshop for Retouching

PHOTOSHOP ESSENTIALS

Put three people in a room, give them each a computer and 30 minutes, and I bet that they'll each come up with at least three different ways to solve the same Photoshop problem. The variety of approaches that Photoshop allows can at times be frustrating or invigorating, depending on how much you like to explore and experiment. So what separates a casual Photoshop user from a power user? In most cases, it's experience and the ability to visualize the final outcome of the project. To power users, Photoshop is transparent—the interface practically disappears as they work to create the retouched or restored image. For novices, Photoshop can be so overwhelming that they get lost finding tools, commands, and controls. Even though they might get the image done, it will have taken them a lot longer than necessary.

Learning to move quickly through Photoshop helps you be a better retoucher because you can concentrate on the image and not the software. In this chapter, you will learn to be more efficient with Photoshop and, in the same vein, be a better Photoshop retoucher by

- Working efficiently with shortcuts

- Using file navigation

- Discovering the importance of layers

- Developing file organization and workflow methods

- Designing an efficient work area

Restoration and retouching takes more than being a fast mouse clicker. Good retouchers understand that the images they are working with are very important to the client, a family member, or the person in the picture. Before you start a retouching project, take a moment to consider that the pixels represent real people and real events—they're more than a collection of dark and light specks of digital information. It's your job to bring back memories from faded, cracked, and damaged originals. This is a weighty responsibility, and keeping that in mind throughout the retouching process helps you see the image with empathy and care.

Note

Preferences, Color Settings, and Color Management Policies

Improve Photoshop's efficiency by setting the application preferences and color settings. On an Apple computer, you'll find these settings under Photoshop > Preferences > General and Edit > Color Settings. On a PC, they are under Edit > Preferences and Edit > Color Settings. There is an article in the Additional Information section of the book's web site, www.digitalre-touch.com, that addresses these topics. Included are how to increase your number of undos, how to speed up Photoshop, and what to do with all those color profile mismatch warnings.

WORKING EFFICIENTLY WITH KEYBOARD SHORTCUTS

Photoshop was developed from the ground up to be used with two hands: one on the keyboard and one on the mouse. The time you save by using keyboard equivalents to access a tool or command, and to navigate through a file will make you a more efficient retoucher. Additionally, using the keyboard rather than the mouse reduces the total number of repetitive mouse clicks that can add up to the pain, aggravation, and lost productivity of repetitive-motion injury.

Knowing the keyboard shortcuts to access tools, change settings, and control palettes enables you to concentrate on the image and be a better retoucher. For example, imagine that you're retouching a file and need to access the Clone Stamp tool, increase the brush size, and change the brush opacity to 40%. The manual method involves selecting the Clone Stamp tool, dragging to the brush size required, highlighting the Opacity value, and typing 40. The shortcut-key method entails tapping the letter S, tapping the right bracket to increase the brush size, and typing in the desired opacity with either the numerals on the top of your keyboard or on the extended keypad to the right of your keyboard. It's a much faster way to get the same results!

Photoshop offers numerous methods to navigate through a file and a plethora of shortcut keys to choose tools and open menus. Do you need to know them all? Of course not. There are over 600 of them! Should you learn how to activate the tools that you'll be using everyday? Absolutely. If you use a Photoshop tool or command three or more times a day, learning its keyboard shortcut saves time and makes sense. Additionally, if you access a filter or sequence of commands more than three times a day, learning how to create an action or a custom keyboard command is also a good idea.

Tip

Go to Edit > Keyboard Shortcuts and Menus to view any established keyboard shortcut or to create your own custom shortcuts. As Adobe has used up practically every possible keyboard combination, you will probably bump an existing command to create your own. But don't worry; you can always change the keyboard shortcuts back to their default settings.

For all intents and purposes, Photoshop is identical on both the Macintosh and Windows platforms. Throughout this book I have used both commands, with Macintosh before Windows. For example, undoing the last step would read Cmd-Z/Ctrl-Z. In general, the Macintosh Command (Cmd) key would be used where the Windows Control (Ctrl) key is, and you'll find that the Mac Option key maps to the Windows Alt key. Where the right mouse button is used on Windows, Control is used on the Mac.

The following section covers the primary navigational shortcuts and shortcut keys used throughout this book that will help you be a more efficient retoucher.

The Toolbox

Tapping the appropriate letter on the keyboard activates a specific tool in the Photoshop Toolbox. In most cases, the first letter of the tool's name is the letter to tap, such as B for Brush and M for the Marquee tool. Of course, there are exceptions to the first-letter rule, such as J for the Spot Healing Brush and V for the Move tool. **Figure 1.1** spells out the letter commands you use to access each tool.

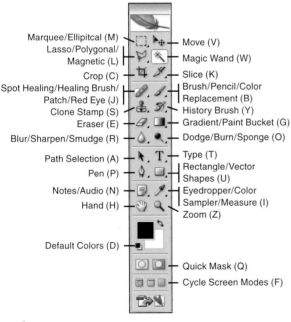

figure 1.1

The Photoshop Toolbox with keyboard commands.

 T i p

To see and learn the tool tips, hold your mouse over a tool and a tool tip will appear listing the name of the tool along with its keyboard shortcut, as shown in **figure 1.2**. By default, the Show Tool Tips option is turned on. If you don't see them choose Cmd-K/Ctrl-K and turn on Show Tool Tips.

figure 1.2

Use the tool tips to learn the most important keyboard quick keys.

As you can see in **figure 1.3**, some tools are nested. For example, the Dodge, Burn, and Sponge tools all share one spot in the Toolbox. You can cycle through the tools by holding the Shift key as you press the shortcut key until you reach the desired tool. **Table 1.1** lists all the nested shortcuts you'll need for retouching and restoration

figure 1.3

The Dodge, Burn, and Sponge tool share the same square on the Toolbox.

If you would rather just press the key (without holding Shift) to cycle through a nested tool, select Cmd-K/Ctrl-K and uncheck Use Shift Key for Tool Switch.

table 1.1
Nested Retouching Tools

Marquee	*Shift-M cycles between the Rectangular and Elliptical Marquee tools.*
Lasso	*Shift-L cycles through the Lasso, Polygonal Lasso, and Magnetic Lasso tools.*
Spot Healing Brush	*Shift-J cycles through the Spot Healing Brush, Healing Brush, Patch, and Red Eye tools.*

continues

table 1.1 (continued)
Nested Retouching Tools

Brush	Shift-B cycles through the Brush, Pencil, and Color Replacement tools.
Clone Stamp	Shift-S cycles through the Clone Stamp and Pattern Stamp tools.
History Brush	Shift-Y cycles between the History Brush and Art History Brush tools.
Eraser tool	Shift-E cycles through the Eraser, Background Eraser, and Magic Eraser tools. (Think E for evil; more on that later.)
Gradient	Shift-G cycles between the Gradient and Paint Bucket tools.
Blur	Shift-R cycles through the Blur, Sharpen, and Smudge tools.
Dodge	Shift-O cycles through the Dodge, Burn, and Sponge tools.
Path Selection	Shift-A cycles between the Path Selection and Direct Selection tools.
Pen	Shift-P cycles through the Pen and Freeform Pen tools.
Eyedropper	Shift-I cycles through the Eyedropper, Color Sampler, and Measure tools.

Brushes

When using the Brush, Clone Stamp, History Brush, and Eraser tools, change the opacity by simply typing the required value; you don't need to highlight the Opacity box. Just type a number from 1 to 9, and the brush opacity or pressure will change to the corresponding value between 10% and 90%. Typing 0 will set it to 100%, and you can set even finer values by quickly typing the precise percentage you want. To change the Flow, which is how fast the "paint" builds up to the selected opacity, use the Shift key plus the desired number. When using the Exposure and Blur tools, the opacity settings are respectively represented by exposure and strength. Thankfully, the same command to dial in a setting applies.

To change brush size or hardness for any of the painting, exposure, or blur tools use these shortcuts:

- Left bracket ([) decreases brush size while maintaining hardness and spacing settings.

- Right bracket (]) increases brush size while maintaining hardness and spacing settings.

- Shift-left bracket ([) decreases brush hardness while maintaining size and spacing.

- Shift-right bracket (]) increases brush hardness while maintaining size and spacing.

Hint

Another way of changing opacity and flow settings is to use the scrubby sliders, as seen in **figure 1.4**. Just click on the Menu Item and drag with your mouse to quickly change settings.

figure 1.4

Scrubby sliders are a faster way to change opacity, exposure, and strength settings.

Saving Tool Presets

How often have you set the Crop tool to 5×7 inches or defined a soft-edged, white brush with 5% opacity set to Overlay blending mode? OK—maybe the Crop tool example rings true but trust me, as you delve into fine portrait retouching, the second example of the finely tuned brush will also come in very handy.

Wouldn't it be great if you could just save a library of all the tools you use often and, with a single click, have access to them without having to enter values or percentages ever again? With Tool Presets you can load, edit, and create libraries of tool presets using the Tool Preset picker in the options bar, the Tool Presets palette, and the Preset Manager.

In the following example, I will create a commonly used Crop tool setting. Work along and repeat the steps, making changes to the dimensions to create your own useful library of crop settings, and you'll never have to set your Crop tool again.

To create a Crop tool preset:

1. Choose the Crop tool and set the options you want in the options bar, as seen in **figure 1.5**. In this example, I entered 5 in and 7 in. To

use pixels, type px after the numbers; for centimeters, type cm; and for millimeters, type mm. If desired, enter a resolution in the Resolution box. I prefer to leave that blank so I don't inadvertently scale an image as I crop it.

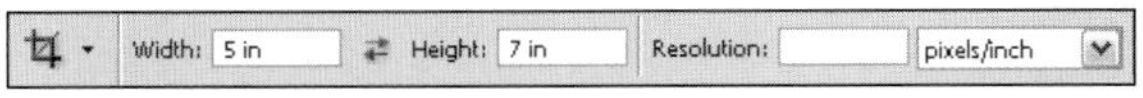

figure 1.5

Determining the settings for the Crop tool.

2. Click the Tool button on the left side of the options bar and click the Create New Tool Preset button (it looks like a little piece of paper) to save one specific tool preset. Or click on the fly-out menu arrow of the Tool Presets palette (see **figure 1.6**) to access the entire tool present manager menu, and select New Tool Preset.

figure 1.6

Select the New Tool preset to name and save tool settings.

3. Name the tool preset, as shown in **figure 1.7**, and click OK. Taking a few minutes to create useful tool presets is a fantastic way to speed up your retouching work. To view and access the tool presets, either click the Tool Preset button on the left side of the options bar or use the Tool Presets palette, as shown in **figure 1.8**.

figure 1.7

Name the tool preset with meaningful information.

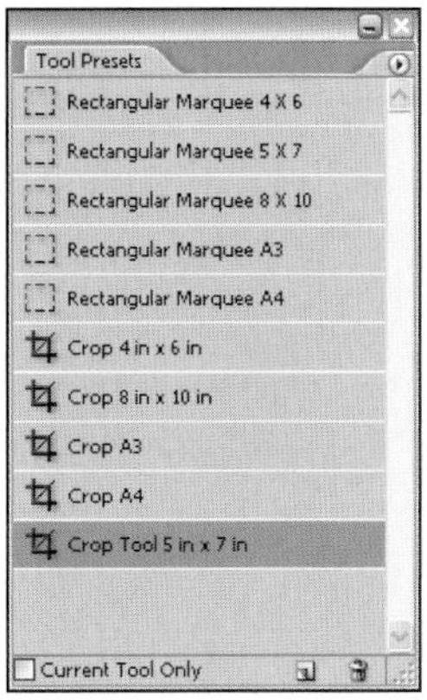

figure 1.8

The Tool Presets palette with all saved tool settings.

Notice that in **figure 1.9** the Current Tool Only checkbox is checked in the lower-left corner. This shows only the presets for the active tool, which keeps your list of visible presets a little more manageable.

After creating a series of Tool Presets, select the Save Tool Presets in the Tool Presets palette menu to insure that your tool settings are saved even if Photoshop unexpectedly crashes. To manage all your tool presets and libraries, select Edit > Preset Manager to see the myriad of brushes, swatches, and patterns you can create, save, load, and share with other Photoshop users.

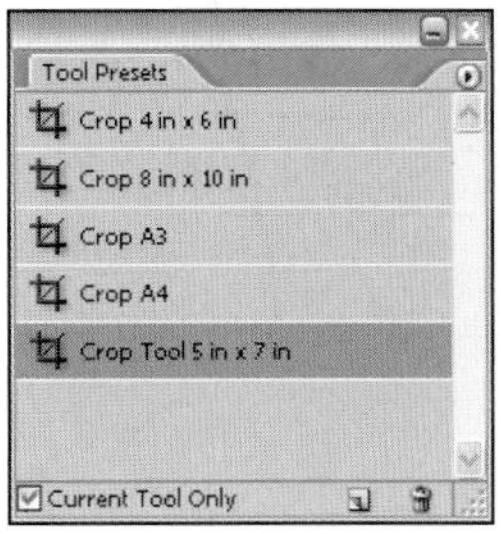

figure 1.9

The Tool Presets palette with only the active tool settings visible.

PALETTES, MENUS, AND CUSTOM WORKSPACES

Hiding, showing, and rearranging palette position while working is irritating, inefficient, and worst of all, adds unnecessary wear and tear to your mousing muscles. Learning the essential keyboard shortcuts and F keys to hide and reveal palettes along with creating custom workspaces is helpful to keep the Photoshop interface out of the way, allowing you to concentrate on the image at hand.

The Palettes and Function Keys

Adobe has assigned function keys to the most important palettes (listed in table 1.2). The function keys are the topmost row of buttons on your keyboard and they begin with the letter F—hence the nickname F keys. You can use them to hide and reveal palettes. I keep my palettes either on a second monitor (see figure 1.10) or, when working on a laptop or single-monitor system, I'll position the palettes to be as far out of the way as possible.

figure 1.10

A side-by-side dual-monitor display arrangement.

Tip

Windows users, if you have assigned an F key function to a task outside of Photoshop, it will override the default Photoshop F key setting.

table 1.2
F Keys to Show and Hide Palettes

Brush palette	F5
Color palette	F6
Layer palette	F7
Info palette	F8
Actions palette	Option-F9/Alt-F9

Not every palette has an assigned function key. You can dock palettes that don't have a function key, like the Histogram, with the Info palette, which uses F8. That will give you access to every palette quickly. For example, dock the Histogram and Info palettes together and then use F8 to open the Info palette, and click the Histogram palette tab to bring it to the forefront. To dock a palette, click the tab heading and drag it to another palette.

Taking a few moments to arrange the palettes and learn the function keys is similar to setting up your workspace in a traditional studio: Brushes go over here and camera equipment goes over there. Position the palettes in relation to how often you use them, with the more important ones—Layers, Channels, and Info—close at hand.

Depending upon your particular work preferences, use the palette well (see figures 1.11 and 1.12) to store the more (or in my case less) frequently used palettes. To drag a palette into the palette well, click and hold its tab and drag up to the palette well and release when the well is highlighted. Drag palettes out by grabbing the specific palette tab and dragging down to the work area.

figure 1.11

The palette well keeps palettes accessible without taking up valuable screen space.

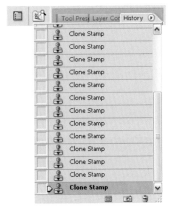

figure 1.12

A *quick click on the palette tab reveals the palette.*

Palette Tips

- When working with a single-monitor workstation, have as few palettes open as possible.

- Press the Tab key to hide and show all palettes and the Toolbox at once.

- Shift-Tab hides all palettes while keeping the Toolbox on screen.

- Pull unnecessary nested palettes out of their groups and close them. For example, the Navigation palette is redundant if you use the navigational tips discussed later in this chapter. If you separate and close it, it won't pop up with the other docked palettes.

- If you close a palette and forget which F key to use to make it appear again, use the Window menu to select the palette you want to see.

- Decide on an ideal palette placement for your workflow. This saves time when hiding and showing palettes, because they will reappear exactly where you positioned them. Save this workspace (discussed in the next section) with a logical name so you can recall it easily later.

- Create actions to assign custom commands to your most often used workspaces to recall them even more quickly than using the Window Workspace menu.

Workspace Settings

Every time you quit Photoshop, the palette positions are remembered and the palettes will be in the same place when you launch Photoshop the next day. If you're like me—working late into the night moving palettes about to get the work done—the last position of the palettes probably aren't the best positions for getting back to work the next morning. To reduce the messy workspace syndrome, take advantage of the ability to save and recall any number of custom workspaces to save time and reduce frustration.

Setting up and saving custom workspaces that reflect the task at hand is well worth the effort. For example, I have one workspace set up for tone and color correction (where all I need to have visible are the Layers, Channels, Info, and Histogram palettes), and one for creative image editing, which places all palettes on the secondary monitor to free up the primary monitor for images (as seen in figure 1.10). And, if you share your computer, different users can have their favorite workspaces without disrupting anyone else's workspace and workflow.

To create a custom workspace:

1. Arrange and size your palettes as desired.

2. Select Window > Workspace > Save Workspace.

3. Name your workspace and Photoshop will save the workspace setting file into the Adobe Photoshop CS2 Settings > Workspace folder.

4. After creating additional workspaces, you can access the different workspaces by selecting one from the Window > Workspace menu.

Adobe also included Delete Workspace and Reset Palette Locations in the Window > Workspace menu. Reset Palette Locations can be very handy if you can't locate a palette or simply want to return to the default Photoshop palette position.

New in Photoshop CS2 are predefined workspaces created for particular types of work including

Painting and Retouching. These predefined workspaces color-code commonly used menu items as well as create custom keyboard shortcuts.

The Workspace View

Your monitor is your worktable. Keeping it organized and neat will pay off with time saved and frustration reduced. Learning to use every bit of your monitor's real estate can make a small monitor seem a lot larger and make a large monitor seem even more expansive.

- Take advantage of your monitor's real estate by working in either Full Screen Mode with Menu Bar or Full Screen Mode. Tap F to cycle through the viewing modes.

- Consider working with a two-monitor system. This requires either a special "dual-head" video card or the installation of a second video card. If you install a second card, you'll need to specify a primary monitor in your system settings. Because you won't be doing any critical color correction or retouching on the second monitor, it can be less expensive—or even used.

- Experiment with changing the display of your video card. If you can comfortably read the menus at a higher resolution, you can greatly expand your working space.

Adobe Bridge

With Photoshop CS2, the File Browser was replaced with the stand-alone application Adobe Bridge (as seen in **figure 1.13**) for image management. Use it to preview, rotate, rename, sort, rank, organize, and open files. You can also automate making contact sheets, web galleries, and Picture Packages. Select Tools > Photoshop > Batch to apply Photoshop actions to batches of images.

The two primary attributes of Bridge I recommend you spend a few minutes configuring are the panel position and the workspace. The panels are tabbed palette content areas for folder hierarchy, favorites, metadata, keywords, and large image preview. Nest, position, and size the panels' to fit your workflow. Bridge comes with four useful workspaces you can test out by clicking the view buttons in the lower right corner of the Bridge window. I find the first two the most useful—thumbnails view to quickly review a photo shoot and filmstrip view to see large previews. If you work with a dual-display monitor system, you can have Bridge open on one monitor and Photoshop on the other, which is very convenient when working with many images.

© Allure West Studios

figure 1.13

Adobe Bridge is a separate application for easy file previewing, navigation, and management.

I find Bridge essential for editing, organizing, and renaming digital camera files. As my students know, I can rave on and on about the Bridge for hours, but rather than taking up a lot of space here, I highly recommend Bruce Fraser's book "Real World Camera RAW for Photoshop CS2" published by Peachpit Press.

QUICK IMAGE NAVIGATION

Learning the most useful Photoshop shortcut keys and navigation techniques takes 15 minutes. To get the most out of the time, go to your computer, launch Photoshop, and open a file that is at least 10MB. The reason I suggest practicing with a 10MB file is that you will really appreciate the ease of navigation when you are working with an image that is larger than your monitor can display.

Moving through a file and zooming in and out quickly are essential skills for an efficient retoucher. Critical retouching is done at a 100% or 200% view (as shown in **figure 1.14**, which means that you are seeing only a small part of the entire file. Zooming in and out of a file allows you to see how the retouched area is blending in with the entire image.

Use any one of the following techniques to navigate through a file.

To go to 100% view to see the full resolution of the file:

- Double-click the Zoom tool (magnifying glass) in the Toolbox.

- Cmd-Option-0/Ctrl-Alt-0. Note: That's a zero, not the letter O.

- Space-Control/Space-right-click and choose Actual Pixels.

- Type 100 in the zoom percentage window in the lower-left corner of the file and press the Enter key.

To see the entire image:

- Double-click the Hand tool in the Toolbox.

- Cmd-0/Ctrl-0. Note: Again, this is a zero, not the letter O.

- Space-Control/Space-right-click and choose Fit on Screen.

© Phil Pool, Omni Photography

figure 1.14

Professional retouchers work at 100% view or 200% view.

To zoom in or out on an image:

- Cmd-"+"/Ctrl-"+" to zoom in and Cmd-"–"/Ctrl-"–" to zoom out.

- Cmd-Space/Ctrl-Space-click to quickly access zoom up and Opt-Space/Alt-Space-click to zoom out.

- To simultaneously zoom in or out on multiple images, add the Shift key to the previous commands.

To zoom in on a specific area:

- Cmd-Space/Ctrl-Space and drag over the area you want to zoom into.

- Select the Zoom tool and drag over the area you want to zoom.

To pan through an image:

- In both Windows and Macintosh, holding down the space bar converts any tool (except the Type tool, if you are actively entering text) into the Hand tool, which enables you to pan through an image. This works only if the image is larger than your monitor can display.

- To scroll through all images at once hold down the Shift-Space. The cursor will become the Hand tool and you can synchronize scroll though all open documents.

To navigate in and compare multiple open files:

- Select Window > Arrange > Tile Horizontally or Tile Vertically

- Activate one file and zoom in to the area or detail you are interested in.

- Select Window > Arrange > Match Zoom and Location and all files will jump to the exact same location and zoom.

- Press Shift-Space to scroll through all open images simultaneously.

You can review an image that is too large to fit entirely on your monitor using only the keyboard. This is very useful when inspecting a file for dust or scratches or when inspecting a high resolution glamour portrait. To see every detail, start by

zooming to 100% view and use these shortcuts to adjust the viewing area one screen width or height at a time:

- Tap the Home key to jump to the upper-left corner.

- Tap the End key to jump to the lower-right corner.

- Tap Page Down to move down one full screen.

- Tap Page Up to move up one full screen.

- Tap Cmd-Page Down/Ctrl-Page Down to move one screen width to the right.

- Tap Cmd-Page Up/Ctrl-Page Up to move one screen width to the left.

Getting into the Corners

When working in full-screen mode, you can pull the image anywhere on the desktop. This is a fantastic feature for restoration work to get into the corners to easily repair them. To move the corner of a picture into the center of the screen, press the letter F key (not a function key) once, zoom to 100% view, and use the Hand tool reposition the image as seen in **figures 1.15** and **1.16**.

figure 1.15

Tap F to enter full screen mode.

figure 1.16

After zooming to 100% view, use the Hand tool to position the corner of the image in the center of the monitor.

If all these navigational tips are starting to get jumbled, remember that you don't need to sit down and memorize them all at once. Just learn the ones you use all the time—including the most often used tools and how to hide and show palettes—you'll be working like a power user in no time.

CONTEXT MENUS

Every Photoshop tool includes context-sensitive menus that you access by Control/right-clicking directly on the image. These menus give you tremendous control over each tool. Rather than going through the menu of every tool here, I suggest you open an image and go through the context menus of each tool. In exchange for that, I'll review the most important context menus you should be aware of. Note that pressing Shift brings up different context menus. For some tools, the context menu will change depending on the state of the tool or file at the time. For example, notice the difference of the context menu for any selection tool with and without an active selection (as shown in figures 1.17 and 1.18, respectively) and after using a filter (as seen in figure 1.19).

figure 1.17

Context menu for any selection tool when there is not an active selection.

figure 1.18

Context menu for any selection tool when there is an active selection.

figure 1.19

Context menu for any selection tool when there is an active selection and after applying a filter.

Brush Context and Controls

While you are using the painting, exposure, and sharpening tools, Control/right-clicking brings up the Brush Presets picker to edit brush size quickly, as shown in **figure 1.20** when the Small Thumbnail option is selected. Shift-Control/Shift-right-clicking brings up the Blending Modes context menu (see **figure 1.21**).

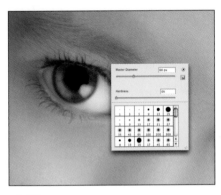

figure 1.20

The context menu of the Painting tools.

figure 1.21

Accessing the blending modes of the paint, exposure, and sharpening tools.

The context menus for the healing tools differ from the painting tools. With the Spot Healing Brush active, Control/right-click to access the Healing tool's specific brush settings menu (see **figure 1.22**). Pressing Shift-Control/Shift-right-click lets you choose the Blend Modes, as you see in **figure 1.23**.

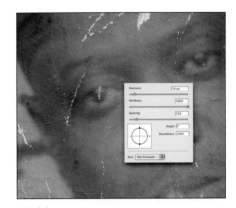

figure 1.22

The context menu of the Spot Healing Brush.

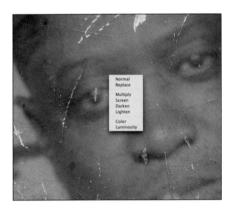

figure 1.23

The Spot and Healing Brush require fewer blending modes to be effective.

LEARNING THE IMPORTANCE OF LAYERS

With the introduction of layers in Photoshop 3.0, Adobe truly entered the world of professional image enhancement. For a retoucher, layers are the most important feature in Photoshop, and throughout this book you will be working with nine different types of layers:

- Background layer: This is your original data and should be treated as carefully as your original prints or film. Never, ever retouch directly on the Background layer. It should remain as pristine as the day you scanned or photographed it. Do I sound adamant about this? You bet. The Background layer is your reference, your guide, your before and after.

Do not touch it. To maintain the Background layer's integrity, either duplicate it or do a Save As to back up the original file before undertaking any color correction, retouching, or restoration.

- Duplicate layers: Duplicating any layer by dragging the layer to the New Layer icon creates an exact copy, in perfect registration, on which you can work and retouch without affecting the original data. Use the short-cut keys Cmd-J/Ctrl-J to duplicate a layer quickly.

- Copied layers: Many times you don't want or need to duplicate the entire Background layer because you need only a portion of a layer to work on. In those cases, select the part of the image you want to use and select Layer > New > Layer via Copy or press Cmd-J/Ctrl-J. Photoshop copies and pastes the selection onto its own layer and keeps the newly created layer information in perfect registration with the original data.

- Adjustment Layers: Adjustment Layers enable you to apply global and selective tonal and color corrections. We will use them extensively in Chapters 2, 3, and 4 to improve images and in Chapter 8 to apply creative effects.

- Empty layers: Photoshop represents empty layers with a grid pattern. Think of these empty layers as a clear sheet of acetate on which you paint, clone, heal, and blur without affecting the pixel data of the layers underneath.

- Neutral layers: Photoshop doesn't show the Blending Mode neutral colors of white, gray, or black when used in combination with specific layer Blending Modes. We'll be using neutral layers to apply subtle and dramatic tonal improvements and sharpening effects throughout the retouching process.

- Fill layers: Fill layers enable you to add solid, gradient, or patterned fills as a separate layer. The solid color fill layer is useful when you are coloring and toning an image.

- Merged layers: As the number of layers increases, it is often easier to work on a Work in Progress (WIP) layer, which is a flattened layer created with all visible layers you have been retouching. To create a new merged layer with image information, press Cmd-Opt-Shift-E/Ctrl-Alt-Shift-E.

- Smart Objects Layer: Photoshop CS2 introduces Smart Objects, a new way of working with composited images. In previous versions of Photoshop, when you added an element to your image—for example, a face with a better expression to replace a face with closed eyes—you threw away pixels if you downsized or transformed the new element. If you changed your mind, realizing you really needed the face larger, Photoshop would interpolate—or make up—the data to fill the new size requirements and the resulting image would not be very sharp.

  After turning a layer into a Smart Object, you can transform and scale the image element to your heart's content as many times as you like. The Smart Object references data from the original file rather than interpolating pixels, which allows both flexibility and quality. Consider turning your images into Smart Objects by selecting Layer > Smart Object > Group into New Smart Object before transforming layers or cropping images.

We will be working with Smart Objects in Chapters 3, 8, and 9.

The best aspect of layers is that they all (with the exception of the Background layer) support layer masks, Blending Modes, opacity and fill changes, and Advanced Blending Options—features you'll be working with throughout the book to retouch and restore images.

Layer Naming and Navigation

Layers enable you to build up a retouch. In many cases, a retouching project can take 5, 10, 20, or more layers to finish. Relying on the generic Photoshop name such as Layer 1 or Layer 1 Copy to identify layers is a sure way to be confused and frustrated as you try to find the layer you need to work on. It only takes a moment, but naming your layers as you build up a retouch enables you to identify and activate the correct layer quickly and easily.

Look at the difference between the two layer stacks in **figure 1.24**. The layers on the left have generic names, and the layers on the right have useful names. Which would you rather work with? Additionally, the context menu of the Move tool gives you instant access to all the layers at the pointer position that have non-transparent pixels. As shown in **figure 1.25**, Control/right-clicking reveals all layer names that have pixel information at the exact point where the mouse is. Best of all, you can then select a specific layer name and activate it—even if the Layers palette is not open at the time.

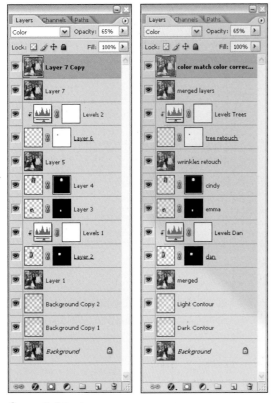

figure 1.24

The generic layer names in the palette on the left won't help you through a complex retouch, but the ones on the right prove that naming your layers is a good habit to adopt.

To name a layer, simply double-click the existing name in the Layers palette and type a meaningful name. It only takes a moment to name a layer, and it will save you countless minutes of frustration.

figure 1.25

The context menu of the Move tool shows you the layers that have pixel information at the cursor location.

Working with Layer Groups

In Photoshop, you can create up to a total of 8,000 layers and layer effects, something that requires a way to organize and manage layers more efficiently. Layer groups, shown in **figure 1.26**, are folders in which you can place related layers. The folders can be expanded or collapsed, the layers moved around within the group, and the layer group moved around within the layer stack.

There are two ways to create a layer group:

• Select New Group from the Layers palette menu, name the layer group, and then drag the desired layers into the group.

• On the Layers palette, select all the layers you would like in a layer group by Shift-clicking to highlight adjacent layers, or Cmd/Ctrl-clicking the layers that are not directly next to each other. Then select New Group from

Layers in the Layers palette menu to place all the selected layers into the new layer group. Add additional layers to a layer group by dragging them into the desired layer group.

figure 1.26

The many layers you create when retouching become much more manageable when they are grouped as layer groups.

There are three ways to delete a layer group:

- Drag the layer group to the trash can on the Layers palette to delete the entire layer group without showing a warning dialog box.

- Cmd/Ctrl-drag the layer group to the trash can to delete the layer group folder without deleting the contents of the layer set. The layers in the group remain in the document in the order they appeared in the set.

- Select Delete Group from the Layers palette menu. The dialog box in figure 1.27 then gives you choices to cancel the operation, delete the group, or delete the group and the group's contents.

figure 1.27

You can delete the group and the contents or just the group (the folder).

You can color-code layers to identify layer relationships quickly and lock layers to prevent accidental edits to image data, transparency settings, and layer position. All in all, organizing, naming, or color-coding layers and layer groups takes only a moment, but it can save you a lot of time in hunting for the layer you want to work on.

Creating and using consistent layers and layer group naming conventions is imperative to an efficient workflow. If you work with a partner, on a team, or as part of a production workflow, you'll especially need to use layer names. Imagine that you're working on a complicated retouching project and, for some reason, you can't come to work to finish the retouch. If the layers are well named, someone else on your team will be able to open the file, find the layers that need additional work, and finish the project. However, if the layers are all over the place, not named, or not in layer groups, it will take a while for someone else to simply figure out where to begin. In the worst-case scenario, a very important layer might be ruined or deleted. Enough said—name your layers!

Flattening and Discarding Layers

I'm a conservative Photoshop retoucher with a large hard drive and a lot of RAM. I don't throw away layers unless I know that they are absolutely wrong or unnecessary. Keep all production layers with a file because you never know whether a mask or tidbit of information from a layer will be useful later in the project or when the client changes his or her mind. By clicking the eyeball in the view column on the left side of the Layers palette, you can hide a layer whenever you like. I flatten an image only after doing a Save As and only as the very last step before sending a file to the printer or taking a file into a page layout program.

FILE ORGANIZATION AND WORKFLOW ISSUES

Taking a few moments to organize your folders and files helps you work more efficiently by saving you time searching for files and projects, and it also reduces the likelihood of deleting important files. For each project I work on, I create a Master Folder, and in that folder I make three folders—Originals, WIP (Work in Progress), and Finals. As you can imagine, the scans go into the Scans folder and those originals are not changed. The WIP folder contains all the layered files and versions of the retouch in progress. The third folder is where only flattened, sized, and sharpened files go. The Finals folder contains only one version of the final file and not files that are obviously not completed, such as "retouch_3_little_better_like_it_more_I_think_maybe_4b.tif."

The Retouching Workflow

Each retouching project is unique, requiring a sensitive eye and sympathetic mouse. An equally sympathetic and patient ear is also helpful when a client tells you the importance of the image as well as how it came to its current state or her or his hopes and dreams for the image.

Of course, each retoucher is just as unique, and over time you will devise your own retouching workflow.

The primary steps in my retouching workflow are shown here:

- Assess the original: Study the original and identify the problems or areas that need enhancement, repair, or replacement. Never lift the mouse without first taking a few minutes to identify the character of either the image or the person in the photograph.

- One thing to determine is whether the image is really salvageable. Not all are. If the key elements of an image are missing and you cannot borrow them from some other image, there probably is not a lot that can be done. Some images can be saved but only with a considerable amount of time investment. Be sure to prepare your client for a bill commensurate with your time.

- Assess your own abilities and be realistic. If the job looks to be too tough for your current skills, you might be better off passing on the job than wasting time and resources.

- Prepare yours client for actual results. Their expectations might be higher than what can be accomplished.

- Make notes on what is to be done and use a work order. Whether the customer wanted the print in B&W or sepia is not something you want to guess later.

- Input: Scan or photograph the original. Use a professional service bureau if you don't have the capability to input the original. For additional information on image scanning, go to www.digitalretouch.org and download Scanning & Resolution.pdf in the "Additional Information" section.

- Develop a strategy: Make a plan to outline the steps to do the retouch. Start with the big problems—exposure, color, and contrast—and then move on to repairing problems, such as dust, mold, and scratches, or removing lines, wrinkles, or blemishes. Make notes on paper or on the file, as described in Chapter 10, "Glamour Retouching." The structure of this book reflects my retouching strategy; it starts with the big problems and then moves into ever-finer nuances of restoration and retouching.

- Retouch: Do the planned retouch. As mentioned, work on a duplicate of the original scan and use layers to build up your work.

- Print a proof: A proof print from a desktop inkjet printer can show areas that need more work or that are poorly retouched.

- Output and deliver: Make a print and deliver the file to the client. Use an archival printer to avoid fading, which would jeopardize your reputation.

- Archive: Make a backup of all files involved in a project. Burning a CD or DVD is an inexpensive and reliable method to make backups. Confirm the files are readable before deleting the files from your hard drive. I recommend burning two identical disks and storing them separately. Use an asset management program, such as Canto Cumulus, Extensis Portfolio, or iView Media Pro to organize your files and backups.

 T i p

The invisible step is to collect payment from the client in exchange for the completed work. Wayne says, "I keep all originals until the client has paid for the job. That way I have something of value, which often motivates the client to pay more quickly."

The Retoucher's Workplace

Your retouching studio or work area is a place you'll be spending a lot of time, so it makes sense to invest the time and money to make it as comfortable and productive as possible. You do not need to remodel your home or build an addition; I'm just suggesting you consider a few improvements that can make your workplace a nicer and more efficient place to be.

Environment and Lighting

The retouching environment should be a quiet area away from distractions and foot traffic. Ideally, a room without windows would be good choice. Windows allow the light levels in your work environment to change through the day, which can affect your perception of the image. Paint the walls a neutral gray and set up the lighting so that there aren't any reflections showing in the monitor. In figure 1.28, you see a retouching work area that is built into a corner. The L-shaped configuration enables the retoucher to get a lot of work done without having to get up and down to make a scan or print. As you can see in figure 1.29, the daylight balanced GTI Graphic Technology lightbox (www.gtilite.com) and 5,000° Kelvin task lamp (www.ottlite.com) provide an area to study originals. To make the retouching area more focused, keep your bookkeeping, paperwork, and business phone on a separate desk.

figure 1.28

My retouching area, with both Macintosh and Windows equipment.

figure 1.29

Controlled lighting is essential when evaluating prints and slides.

Furniture

It always amazes me that people will spend thousands of dollars on computer equipment and then put it all on a cheap folding table that wobbles and bows in the center under all the weight. Even worse are some of the rickety chairs people sit in to work on the computer. After a few hours they wonder why their necks or lower backs are so sore. I prefer a chair with armrest support—and, as Wayne points out, if you use a chair with arms, the arms must be able to slide under the desk. If the chair's arms keep you away from the desk, you have to reach for the keyboard and mouse. After a few hours of this, you will develop muscle aches.

A good table without harsh edges, preferably one that angles down to the point where your arms rest on the table, and a chair with lower-back and arm support are essential retouching equipment. Just think of it: Over the course of a few years, you'll probably replace your computer a few times. How often do you need to replace a good working table and professional chair? Not very often, so making the investment in good furniture will pay off in health and well-being for years to come.

Speaking of health, you should know that uninterrupted, intensive computer use can be bad for your eyes, back, wrists, and more. But it doesn't have to be if you watch your posture, vary your computing activities, and take frequent breaks. An important tip for retouchers is to use these frequent breaks to focus your eyes on something in the distance. For more information about steps you can take to make your work area and work habits as healthy as possible, visit www.healthycomputing.com.

As Patrick O'Connell wrote to me, "Over the course of a week, I spent about 25 hours restoring this image (see **figures 1.30** and **1.31**), and if there's a secret to it at all, I'd say the key was to realize when I was starting to get tired and sloppy, and quit for the day." You need to take breaks and return to your work with a fresh eye.

figure 1.30

Before image restoration.

figure 1.31

After image restoration, which included taking breaks.

Computer Equipment

Adobe has done a fantastic job in developing and releasing Photoshop for both Macintosh and Windows. So does it matter which computer platform you use? Yes, it does. It should be the operating system that you're most comfortable with. My first computer experience was on a Mac, and since then I've come to appreciate its interface, operating system, and how easy it is to maintain. On the other hand, for every one person who prefers a Mac, I'm sure there are many, many people who swear by Windows. Photoshop is Photoshop is Photoshop. The few differences in Photoshop on a Mac or Windows are not going to alter the skills and techniques you need to know to do retouching magic.

Spending money on computer equipment requires research and planning. If you are about to build a workstation for Photoshop work, consider these variables:

- CPU speed: The higher the speed, the faster the computer. Be careful to watch the internal bus speed as well; the fastest CPU will not produce the performance increases you expect if the internal bus speed is slow.

- Bus Speed: Think of the bus as the pipeline that transfers information between the CPU and RAM. The larger the pipe, the faster the data can be transferred between the two.

- RAM: Photoshop is a RAM-hungry program, and the more you have allocated to Photoshop, the better it will run. How much RAM do you need? As much as you can afford! Take into account that often you'll have more than one image open and that as you add layers, your RAM requirements will increase. So how much is enough? Take your average image size and multiply it by five, and then use that figure as your starting point. Adding more RAM to a machine is the easiest way to increase Photoshop performance.

Tip

You can see how efficiently your computer system is running by selecting Efficiency from the status bar found at the bottom of the document window. A reading of less than 100% tells you that the functions you are performing are being written to the scratch disk, which is always slower than working in RAM.

- Hard-drive space: This is a classic "bigger is better" proposition as long as you are choosing from the highest-performance drives. Photoshop wants fast hard drives to write data to when it runs out of RAM so, given the choice, go with speed of at least 7200 rpm (rotations per second) over excessive gigabytes.

- Scratch disk: The scratch disk is free hard-drive space that Photoshop uses as temporary memory after it fills the RAM with image processing. The scratch disk needs to be at least twice the size of the RAM allocated to Photoshop and, more importantly, the space needs to be contiguous; that is, a scratch disk needs to be unfragmented and free of clutter. You can set up partitions on your drive to keep certain areas from being fragmented, or you can use additional software to optimize your drive over time. If you have more than one hard drive, use one for Photoshop and your image files, and the other for your scratch disk. Setting the scratch disk to a drive other than the drive that contains your OS will help to optimize the speed of your computer.

- Monitor: This is the visual component of your system, and no matter how fast or sexy your CPU is, if you are not happy with the image your monitor produces, you will not be happy with your workstation. A good monitor will outlast one to two upgrades of your CPU. The only limitation on the effective life of a monitor is the accuracy of the color it produces—something which is usually in the three- to-five year range.

If you choose a traditional CRT display, 17 inches is minimum and 21 inches is desired. Be careful to match the size of monitor to the amount of video RAM installed in your computer. You must work with millions of colors. Flat-panel LCD displays are much easier on your eyes but a bit harder on your pocketbook.

Monitor calibration is tremendously important. No matter how good the monitor is, it will not be an accurate representation of your image unless it is calibrated. Fortunately you can do a basic calibration with your existing software. For Windows users, a new program called Adobe Gamma was added to your control panels when you installed Photoshop. On the Mac, use Apple Display Calibrator Assistant, found under System Preferences > Displays > Color. Both programs use the judgment of the person calibrating the monitor in the evaluative process. For more accurate profiling, invest in a monitor calibration system such as the GretagMacbeth Eye One Display, which is a hardware and software package to physically and accurately calibrate the monitor. I calibrate my monitors a minimum of once a month or before starting an important project.

T i p

To have two monitors running on the same computer, your computer needs to be able to support a second video card, or you can replace your existing card with one that supports dual display. Install the new card and use the control settings to determine which monitor will be your primary monitor. You can just drag images and palettes back and forth between them.

To use one monitor on two computers: IOGEAR makes a switcher to run up to four computers with one monitor, keyboard, and mouse. Macintosh users may need to purchase an additional adapter from IOGEAR that makes the pin conversion possible.

- CD-R or DVD-R: This is a usability and compatibility issue. In either case, make sure that you have a writeable, not a read-only, CD or DVD drive. In most instances, a writeable CD/DVD will be the most practical and usable media to create disks for your clients.

- Pressure-sensitive tablet: An absolute must. A pressure-sensitive tablet lets you work with a stylus, and it feels just like working with a pencil or brush. The harder you push, the thicker the stroke. Wacom is the leader in this technology, and their progressive improvements with these devices continue to be impressive. Wacom tablets range in size from miniature (4×5 inches) to huge (12×18 inches). Most photographers work best with the smaller (6×8 inch tablets), which is also the size I use when traveling.

T i p

To decrease reflections and distractions, build a monitor hood with black quarter-inch foamcore board, as shown in **figure 1.32**, or visit www.photodon.com to purchase monitor hoods.

figure 1.32

A homemade monitor hood cuts down on reflections.

- Backup or archive system: This is another critical issue as you take on more and more work. You should always back up your work, as well as your system settings. This is a personal discipline that will make you feel very smart when you need the backup or very stupid if you did not back up your files. I have heard many a sad story from my readers, including my co-author, on the loss of data when using removable media, such as CD-Rs or DVDs. So ultimately, redundant USB2 drives or Firewire drives, which are extremely fast, may be best option for backups.

- Scanners: Look at the originals you will be scanning. If most of them are prints, purchasing a good flatbed scanner makes sense; if the majority of your work stems from film originals, a film scanner would be a better choice.

It is difficult to make a general recommendation on scanners because they vary from very poor to very good and from cheap to expensive. Most retouchers have a mid-level flatbed scanner that is capable of scanning 11×17 inch prints. Look for a scanner that captures at least 10 bits of data, and keep an eye on the optical resolution of the scanner—it should be 600 pixels per inch for scanning prints.

If you envision scanning old film, consider a scanner that has a transparency adapter option. Be sure that it comes with a variety of film holders for the different possible sizes of film. If you will be retouching newer images captured on film, consider a separate film scanner for sharper scans and finer detail.

I find myself scanning prints less and less as the actual scanning introduces glare and reflections, which are impossible to retouch out. Rather I am using a digital camera as described in the following section to input delicate and reflective originals.

- Copy work: In many cases, antique originals are too large, too fragile, or too three-dimensional to scan with a standard flatbed scanner. In **figure 1.33**, you see medium-format slides Wayne made to restore a series of antique photographic images that were mounted inside convex, glass bowl frames. Because the originals were three-dimensional, he couldn't just lay them on a flatbed scanner, so he made copy slides and scanned those. A 6 megapixel camera did not provide the detail need for the size of image to be printed so he returned to film and a high-resolution scan for a starting point.

- Professional digital cameras: As digital cameras get both better and cheaper, they are becoming a great input option. Numerous professional museums and historical collections are working with high-resolution scanning cameras, such as the Better Light 6000 or 8000, to digitize their sensitive artwork and archives. **Figures 1.34** and **1.35** show an example from the Dallas Museum of Fine Art, which is using the Better Light Super 6K to catalog fine art. Brad Flowers, the head photographer for the museum, says this unit provides 5 times the resolution and much greater accuracy than 4×5 inch film.

© Wayne Palmer

figure 1.33

It's the unique challenges that make the job interesting. The originals were mounted inside convex glass bowls.

Images © Dallas Museum of Art

figure 1.34

Professional digital cameras offer incredible resolution and color fidelity when inputting artwork.

figure 1.35

Close-up view of painting.

- Prosumer digital cameras are now a viable copying solution. $800 to $1,500 can buy a 6- to 8-megapixel digital camera capable of very respectable image quality. Look for one that can capture uncompressed RAW files and compare their highest non-interpolated resolution (the most important feature for copy purposes). **Figure 1.36** shows Wayne's copystand with a Canon EOS 10D. Depending on the image size required, Wayne will shoot copy files with either the Canon EOS 10D or medium-format film. With the new breed of higher-end digital cameras in the 12- to 16-megapixel range, the resolution captured can match or exceed that of medium-format film.

© Wayne Palmer

figure 1.36

A *professional copystand and a prosumer-level digital camera.*

Tip

Having a service bureau or professional photo lab do scanning and printing for you can be a good alternative, especially when you're just starting out and need to stagger your equipment expenses. Working with a service bureau also gives you access to high-end equipment and services that you may need only once in a while.

- Printers: The quality of inkjet printers is skyrocketing while the costs are nose-diving. Issues to consider before buying a printer include the size of the prints you need and how long the prints will last once you've printed them. Henry Wilhelm does extensive research on inkjet print permanence, and you can read the latest information at www.wilhelm-research.com.

- RIP Software: "A Raster Image Processor, or RIP, is software that allows you to accurately print what you see on your working calibrated monitor. However, it goes beyond that. A well-developed RIP allows you to expand the printable range of color by maximizing the printer's native color space," says Marcia Dolgin of Marcia Dolgin Fine Images (www.dolginimaging.com), who highly recommends using this type of software if you do critical printing and want to print truly neutral black-and-whites images on the same sheet next to color images.

- Additional software: As you do more and more retouching, you may want to consider investing in software that can help you file, track, organize, and most importantly find your files (such as Canto Cumulus or Extensis Portfolio). Other purchases to consider include color management packages, such as the GretagMacbeth EyeOne Pro, and production and special effects filters. For color management information, visit Andrew Rodney's web site at www.digitaldog.net and www.adobe.com.

BEFORE YOU BEGIN: A WORD TO THE WISE

Photoshop is a powerful tool that can either work wondrous magic or wreak havoc on image data. To ensure the best results in your restoration, always start with the best image data possible:

- Professional photographers always shoot more than one exposure of an image. Although the exposure difference may seem minimal, believe me, starting with a properly exposed piece of film or digital file will minimize many a headache.

- Start with the best digital data possible. Investing in a quality scanner or digital camera is something you will seldom regret. If your scanner or digital camera captures high-bit data, take advantage of it as discussed in the in Chapter 2, "Improving Tone and Contrast," in the section "The Benefits of High-Bit Data."

- Try to get the best scan possible. Don't have an "I can always make it better in Photoshop" attitude. If shooting with a digital camera, use the RAW file format for an optimum image.

- Always work on a copy of your original scan.

- Use Adjustment Layers as described throughout the book. (You'll find a concentration of examples in Chapters 2, 3, and 4.) Because you can double-click an Adjustment Layer to open it for further finessing, you have much more control and freedom with your tonal, contrast, and color changes.

- Learn to work nondestructively— if you can perform a task on a layer above your image, do it. For example, the Eraser tool is destructive; pixels are permanently deleted when used. The same effect can be accomplished through layer masks, which we will use in later chapters and does not permanently delete pixels.

- Respect copyrights! Possession of a print is not an automatic right to reproduce it. Copyrights currently can extend many years past the life of the photographer, so don't assume that simply because the photographer has died or the studio is out of business, the photo is legal to copy. Many studios, including the modern larger ones, may grant permission to work on images if they no longer have the negatives or files, or if the studio does not do the type of work you want to do.

- Handle originals with care. One of the questions I frequently receive is how to handle prints that are stuck to glass, and there isn't a simple one-size-fits-all answer. Images stuck to glass might be better served if they remain behind the glass. The task of attempting to remove the print may damage it more than it already is. There are times when soaking an image will release it from glass. I cannot emphasize enough that this should only be done to modern-type print papers and as a very last resort.

- Prints that will not lie flat can become more cooperative if you gently lay them between sheets of cardboard rubber-banded together. It may take weeks or months for the image to become manageable. Wayne, with customer permission, has used tacks in the corners of images mounted to a board long enough to shoot the image. If the tack would do any damage to the actual image, it is usually a simple fix in Photoshop. Again use extreme caution, as you don't want to make a bad situation worse.

- Be a problem solver! Photo restoration and retouching requires you to be resourceful. For example, if your image won't fit your scanner, consider scanning it in segments to reassemble in Photoshop or shoot the image with a digital camera. Learn to beg, borrow, and steal body parts and image elements from related files to rebuild missing sections as described in Chapter 7, "Rebuilding and Re-creating Images."

CLOSING THOUGHTS

The one thing that no computer, book, or class can give you is the passion to practice, learn, and experiment with the skills and techniques it takes to be a good retoucher. Retouching is more than removing dust or covering up a wrinkle here or there. Retouching enables you to give someone cherished memories that have faded over time. Retouching and restoration is a fantastic hobby and a challenging profession, so let's dive in and get to work.

Correcting Tone, Exposure, and Color

II

2

IMPROVING TONE AND CONTRAST

If you had a choice of walking into two unfamiliar rooms—one with the lights on and one without lights—which one would you choose? Unless you're a horror film aficionado, I imagine you'd choose the room with the lights. Working with the tonality and contrast of an image is similar to lighting a room to influence the atmosphere. Finessing the lights and darks of an image can transform a flat, uninteresting photograph into an image that pops off the page and is a pleasure to look at.

Adjusting an image's tone and contrast is a very important step to bringing an image back to life. Although it may not be as sexy or dramatic as replacing a person's head or removing a bothersome telephone pole, adjusting an image's tone and contrast with Levels and Curves is an essential skill.

In this chapter, you'll work with grayscale and color images and learn to

- Appreciate the advantages of high-bit data
- Use levels to improve highlights and shadows
- Use curves to adjust image contrast
- Use blending modes to save time
- Share adjustment layers to save effort
- Apply selective tonal improvements to specific image areas

THE BENEFITS OF HIGH-BIT DATA

The highest possible number of shades of gray that a standard 8-bit grayscale file can contain is 256. An RGB image uses three channels and is a 24-bit image. A CMYK image uses four channels and is often referred to as a 32-bit image. Oddly enough, this doesn't mean that the CMYK file contains more shades of gray or more tonal information, because each channel is still made up of a maximum of 256 shades of gray.

For very critical, high-quality tonal and color correction, 256 shades of gray per channel do not offer you a lot of editing room to change tone and color. Working with high-bit data—files that contain more than 256 shades of gray per channel (see table 2.1)—gives you more tonal values to enhance the tonal and color character of an image.

table 2.1

Bit-Depth per Channel	Shades of Gray
8-bit	256
10-bit	1,024
12-bit	4,096
16-bit	65,536

If you work with scanners or digital cameras that capture high-bit data, I recommend you take advantage of the additional tonal information high-bit data provides, especially for grayscale images. Wouldn't you rather have up to 65,536 shades of gray to work with compared to only 256? At the very least, perform all tonal and color corrections and clean up dust on the high-bit file before converting to 8-bit data. Better yet would be to keep the file in high-bit for the entire restoration or retouching process. Working in hi-bit does require large hard drives and a lot of RAM, as high-bit files are twice the size of 8-bit files—something

which can become very apparent, actually painful, when working with a lot of layers. Additionally not all the filters work on high-bit files. I work with the high-bit information as long as manageability of file size and processing time allow. Then I choose Image > Duplicate and check "Duplicate Merged Layers Only" to flatten the duplicate file, which I convert to 8-bit and save with a new name.

Figure 2.1 shows you the histograms for two images. The image on top was scanned at 8-bit, and the image on the bottom was scanned at 16-bit; otherwise, the two scans are identical.

After bringing the files into Photoshop, I made the identical Levels adjustment to apply the same subtle tonal and color correction to both files. The top histogram in **figure 2.2** reveals the information loss the 8-bit file suffered, even when making such a small tonal and color move. The white gaps in the histogram show where tonal information is missing. Imagine what would happen if I needed to apply an extreme change to an 8-bit file—the histogram would be full of white gaps. In the high-bit file at the bottom of figure 2.2, the same changes improve the file, and the histogram shows that I still have plenty of data to work with. Ideally, you want to avoid leaving gaps in the histogram because image areas with the areas with the gaps may show banding or posterization when printing.

Don't Try to Trick Photoshop

Trying to trick Photoshop into thinking it is working with a high-bit file by converting an 8-bit scan to 16-bit, applying changes, and then converting back to 8-bit doesn't work. This voodoo maneuver is a waste of time and doesn't improve the actual image information. Remember, your goal isn't to produce attractive histograms but to produce good images.

figure 2.1

Before tonal changes, the 8- and 16-bit histograms are
identical.

figure 2.2

After tonal changes, even such a subtle change as I applied
here, the histograms show that the 16-bit image (bottom)
withstood the adjustment far better than the 8-bit image.

EVALUATING IMAGE TONE AND PREVISUALIZING THE FINAL IMAGE

Taking a moment to evaluate the tone of an image is tremendously important. In that moment, you should identify the tonal character of the image and imagine what the image ideally would look like after you're finished editing it. This technique, called previsualization, was developed by the black-and-white photographers Ansel Adams and Edward Weston. By imagining the final image, you create a goal to work toward. For example, in Photoshop you open a dark file. Your previsualization would be, "I want the image to be lighter." Having a visual goal in mind helps you stay focused and not get distracted with the many options that Photoshop offers.

An image's tonal character can be light, dark, or average, also called high-key, low-key, or medium-key. Subject matter and how much light was in the original scene determine the tonal character of the image. If you're not sure which tonal-type image you're looking at, select Window > Histogram to open the Histogram palette, which is addressed in greater detail in this chapter.

A histogram is a graphical representation of the pixels in the image, plotting them from black (on the left) to white (on the right). The greater the number of pixels in the image at a specific level, the taller the histogram is at that point. Knowing this, you can look at the histogram of any image and can tell where the majority of the pixel information falls.

As seen in figure 2.3, the high-key image histogram is bunched to the right because the image is primarily made up of lighter pixels. The low-key histogram falls more to the left because the image is primarily made up of darker pixels (see figure 2.4). The medium-key histogram is spread out, with most of the information falling in the middle (see figure 2.5). Of course, there are images that defy labels, as illustrated in figure 2.6, in which the histogram's two clumps reveal an image with a tonal split personality.

figure 2.3

Although the chair and the young woman's hair are dark, the majority of the image is very light, making this a high-key image.

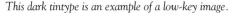

figure 2.4

This dark tintype is an example of a low-key image.

figure 2.5

This image has a full tonal range, from the dark shadows to the white sides of the building.

When editing the tones, it is helpful to recognize which tonal type of image you're working with so you don't apply extreme tonal corrections. For example, if you are working with a high-key image in which the histogram is biased to the right, it wouldn't make any sense to darken the image just so that the histogram looks more balanced. By becoming familiar with what the tonal values represent—the shadows, midtones, or highlights of an image—you'll learn which areas of the histogram need to be adjusted to either lighten or darken the image.

figure 2.6

Photographed in the late afternoon, the lower part of the image is in shadow and the upper part is in sunlight. This image has low-, medium-, and high-key areas.

I'm often asked whether there is an ideal histogram shape, and the answer is "No." The image's tonality and character determine the ideal histogram shape. So don't worry if a histogram seems biased to one side or the other; just keep an eye on the histogram as an aid when editing the tonal values.

Note

With color images, the Histogram palette can show RGB or CMYK channel composite, individual R, G, and B or C, M, Y, and K channels, Luminosity, and a Colors display, which overlaps the color channels. The Levels histogram is limited to RGB channel composite or the individual R, G, and B channels. The Histogram palette will also show dual histograms of before and after changes while adjustments are being made.

Assessing Tone with the Measuring Tools

Evaluating the image on a calibrated monitor in a controlled viewing environment is essential when retouching (see Chapter 1, "Photoshop Essentials," for recommendations on setting up a studio). If you are unsure about your monitor or your visual assessment of an image, rely on the Eyedropper and Color Sampler tools and the Info and Histogram palettes when working on a file to evaluate and measure image tone and to track changes as you work. The Eyedropper is a digital densitometer (a fancy word for a measuring tool) that you can move throughout the image to measure tonal and color values. The Color Sampler tool is nested with the Eyedropper tool in the Toolbox and is used to add semi-permanent measuring points as addressed in the next section. Keeping your eye on the Info palette is an essential habit while editing tone, contrast, and color.

Select the Eyedropper tool and set the sample option to 3×3 Average, which also sets the sampling size, in pixels, of the Color Sampler tool. In the Info palette, set the first readout options to reflect the actual image data and the second readout either to suit your own preferences or to reflect your final output. To set readouts in the Info palette, click on the tiny triangle next to the eyedropper and drag to your desired readout. Or from the Info palette menu, select the Palette Options and choose your desired settings. For example, if you are going to use offset printing, your second readout would be CMYK. Photographers who are familiar with the Zone System prefer to use grayscale (K) to read the black tonal-output values.

Tracking Tonal Changes with Color Samplers

Color samplers are lockable probes (up to four) that you can tack onto an image, enabling you to keep your eye on specific areas during the image editing process. The Color Sampler tool is nested under the Eyedropper in the Toolbox and uses the same sample sizes as the Eyedropper. With the

Color Sampler tool active, clicking in your image attaches up to four samplers. Each sampler is numbered and has a corresponding area in the Info palette display. You can move any sampler at any time, as long as the Color Sampler tool is active.

These four color samplers can be used to measure and track shadows, midtones, highlights, and a fourth tone of your choice. In **figure 2.7**, I'm using four samplers to track image highlights, shadows, and midtones, but color samplers can do something even better. While you're actively adjusting tonal values, the color samplers provide a before-and-after readout in the Info palette (see **figure 2.8**)—the number before the slash is the original value, followed by the edited value. As soon as you click OK to any adjustment layer, the before/after readout behavior reverts to the single readout.

Color samplers automatically disappear when you select other tools and reappear when the Eyedropper or Color Sampler tools are activated again.

figure 2.7

Using the Color Sampler tool to track tonal values is a good habit to develop, and each sampler has its own readout on the Info palette.

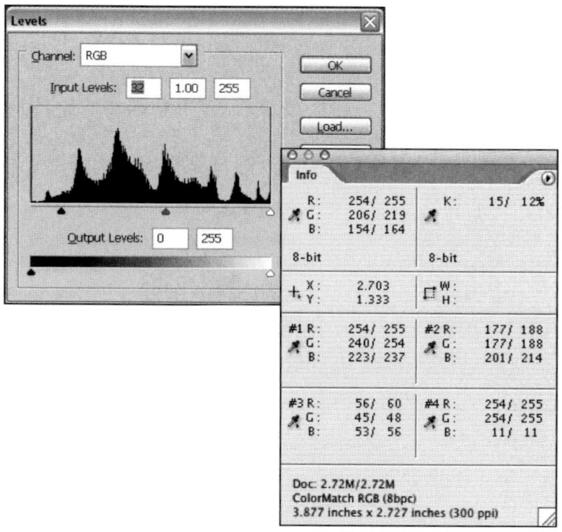

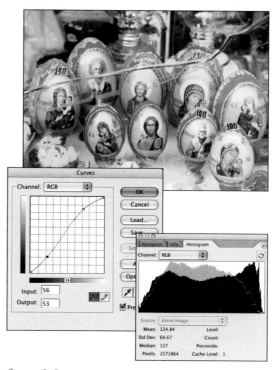

figure 2.8

While making a tonal or color change, the Color Sampler readout shows you the value before a tonal adjustment on the left and the value after the tonal adjustment on the right.

 Note

To remove color samplers, with the Color Sampler tool active, hold down Option/Alt and move the cursor over the sample point; when you see the scissors icon, click and the sample point will be removed. Or Control/right-click while the cursor is over the sample point and select Delete from the context-sensitive menu. Or, click the Clear button in the options bar to remove them all at once.

The Histogram Palette

The Histogram palette was a welcome addition to the Photoshop interface. One of the biggest benefits is the ability to view the histogram while making many types of adjustments, something that was previously only available while using Levels. Additionally, the Histogram palette will show you a live update of before and after while you make adjustments. **Figure 2.9** shows that yes, you can make Curves adjustments and see what is happening to your histogram! Sadly, this only works when working via the Image > Adjustments menu and not when working with adjustment layers.

figure 2.9

While making adjustments the Histogram palette displays before-and-after results with the light gray showing the original data and the black showing the after adjustment data.

Like other palettes, it is customizable to meet your needs and monitor space. It can be very compact or as detailed as showing the individual channels in color. **Figure 2.10** shows a few of the possible customized settings.

Compact View only shows 100 tones and is not accurate enough for critical tonal editing. I recommend you work with the Expanded View, which shows a 256-step scale. Even when working in high-bit files, the Histogram display uses 256 steps, which may sound restrictive. But if the Histogram palette could show true high-bit, the interface would have to be 256 times larger to accommodate the 65,536 levels of brightness. Your monitor would need to be approximately 64 feet wide! For best results, work at and view the Histogram when the image is at Actual Pixels view size. Click the refresh arrows in the upper right corner of the Histogram palette to have Photoshop update the histogram.

Compact View.

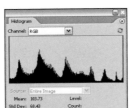

Expanded View showing statistics.

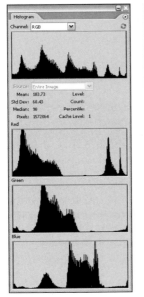

All Channels View

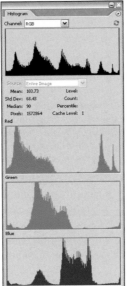

All Channels View in color.

figure 2.10

Some of the Histogram palette options. Use the channel menu to see individual channel, luminosity, and color views.

Using a Stepwedge

To help understand how specific tonalities will look on the print, I use a digital stepwedge that goes from black to white with shades of gray in exact increments, as seen on the left side of **figure 2.11**. Photographers and printers have been using them for years as an objective reference to see and measure how tones are captured, displayed, and reproduced.

The numbers on the couple at the piano in figure 2.11 are the points at which I measured the values in the image. The highlight on the man's face will print at 10 to 12% (a very light gray), the woman's dress will be 25%, a medium light gray, the man's coat in a range from 50 to 70%% (medium to dark

gray), and the piano, at 90%, will be dark gray but not black. By keeping my eye on the Info palette set to grayscale, I can envision how dark or light each area will print.

figure 2.11

Using a 21-step stepwedge to monitor tonal values is helpful to understand the tonality of a print.

ch2_stepwedge.jpg

N o t e

Make your own stepwedge using the Gradient tool. Start with a new 10×1-inch, grayscale, 300ppi image. Select the black to white gradient, and make sure that Dither is unselected in the options bar. Starting on the left edge, hold Shift while drawing the gradient across the entire width of the file. Select Image > Adjustments > Posterize > 21 to create a perfect 21-step stepwedge. Photoshop biases the highlight and shadow information, which is why the black and white steps will be slightly larger, as seen in figure 2.12.

figure 2.12

Make your own stepwedge and use it to monitor how your printer renders tonal information.

THE IMPORTANCE OF ADJUSTMENT LAYERS

Whether you work with Levels or Curves or any of the other supported image-adjustment features, I insist (yes, insist) that you use adjustment layers, one of the very best features in Photoshop. Adjustment layers are layers that enable you to make nondestructive changes to your image. You can change and refine tonal and color adjustments as many times as needed without altering the underlying layer's original data until you choose to apply them by flattening the image. Adjustment layers apply the adjustment math on top of the pixel information, which makes them a fantastic tool to experiment, refine, redo, and learn from tonal and color adjustments.

Use adjustment layers when working with Levels, Curves, Color Balance, Hue/Saturation, Selective Color, Channel Mixer, Photo Filter, Invert, Threshold, and Posterize. I don't recommend using Brightness/Contrast, because working with Levels and Curves offers better control and uses more sophisticated mathematics to apply the tonal changes. The benefits offered by working with adjustment layers include the following:

- They enable you to make tonal corrections without changing or degrading the source image data until you flatten the image.

- Their opacity can be adjusted. By lowering the adjustment layer's opacity, you reduce the strength of the tonal or color correction.

- They support blending modes. Blending modes mathematically change how layers interact with the layer below them. They are a great aid in restoration work as they enable you to improve image tonality quickly.

- They are resolution independent; enabling you to drag and drop them between disparately sized and scaled images.

- They include layer masks with which you can hide and reveal a tonal correction with the use of selections or painting.

- They are especially helpful when making local tonal, contrast, and color adjustments to parts or smaller areas of an image.

- If you don't like an adjustment, just throw the offending adjustment layer into the Layers palette trash and start over.

- They work equally well in 8-bit and 16-bit files.

MASTERING TONALITY WITH LEVELS

Working with Levels enables you to influence three tonal areas of an image: shadows, midtones, and highlights. You can use the sliders and the black-point or white-point eyedroppers to place or reset black or white points (see **figure 2.13**). The gray eyedropper is not available when you are working with black-and-white images; it is used to find neutral points in color images. Often, you can make an image pop right off the page just by setting new white and black points and moving the midtone gamma slider (to the left to lighten or to the right to darken the image).

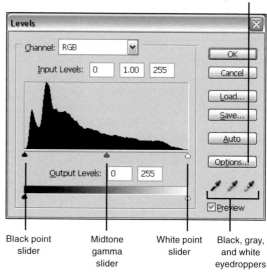

figure 2.13

The Levels dialog box

The most important Levels controls to enhance image tone are these, all of which are addressed in greater detail in this chapter:

- Sliders: Use the highlight and black sliders to determine the black and white points by moving the relevant slider to the area of the histogram where the light or dark information starts.

- Eyedroppers: Use the eyedroppers to set white and black points for both black-and-white and color images and the neutral gray eyedropper to define a neutral tone in color images.

- Auto button: Use the Auto button to prompt Photoshop to apply one of three types of auto corrections as explained in Chapter 4: "Working with Color". You can choose which setting Photoshop uses by clicking the Options button directly underneath Auto

IMPROVING IMAGE TONE WITH LEVELS

In the following exercises, you use Levels to rescue muddy or low-contrast originals and transform them into black-and-white images that are a pleasure to look at because the tones extend across the entire dynamic range from black to white. These exercises use single-channel monochrome (black-and-white) images. You can use the same techniques on color images, but only if you work on the composite channel (the primary histogram) and don't venture into tweaking the individual color channels.

Working with the Black and White Point Sliders

This original image, from 1892, is badly faded, as you can see in **figure 2.14**. The areas that should be white have gotten darker and the shadows are not a rich black, which reduces the contrast and makes the print tonally flat and unattractive. After scanning it on a flatbed scanner, I used the following technique to darken the shadows and brighten up the highlights. The corrected image (**figure 2.15**) has snap to it.

figure 2.14

figure 2.15

⊕▷← **ch2_faded.jpg**

1. Add a Levels adjustment layer by clicking the Add Adjustment Layer icon at the bottom of the Layers palette and selecting Levels (see **figure 2.16**) or select Layer > New Adjustment Layer > Levels and click OK.

figure 2.16

Adding the Levels adjustment layer via the Layers palette.

2. Move the white point slider just to the inside of where the lightest image information begins, as shown on the right side of the histogram (see **figure 2.17**).

3. Move the black point slider until it falls just inside the area of darkest image information, as you see on the left side of the histogram in figure 2.17.

4. Click OK to accept these changes.

When working on your own images, after adjusting the tonal range with Levels, you may want to continue the restoration process as addressed in Chapter 5, "Dust, Mold, and Texture Removal," Chapter 6, "Damage Control and Repair," and Chapter 7, "Rebuilding and Re-creating Images."

figure 2.17

Moving the white and black sliders to improve contrast.

✋ **C a u t i o n**

Dragging the white or black sliders too far into the white or black area of the histogram may clip important information to pure white or pure black. Evaluate the image and the image histogram to see where the image information falls, and take care not to clip it with extreme moves of the Levels sliders.

Working with the Midtone Slider

When working with faded images, using the black and white point sliders to add contrast is a good starting point. If, after using them, the image is too dark, adjust the midtone slider to the left to lighten the image; or if the image is too light, move the midtone slider to the right. The image in **figure 2.18,** taken in 1922, has lost all contrast, while **figure 2.19** shows the improved image which required all three sliders to be adjusted.

© Eckert Family Archives

BEFORE

figure 2.18

AFTER

figure 2.19

ch2_faded2.jpg

1. Add a Levels adjustment layer.

2. Move the highlight slider to the area of lightest image information, as shown on the right side of the histogram in figure 2.20.

3. Move the black point slider to the area of the darkest image information, as you see on the left side of the histogram in figure 2.20.

4. The image is still too dark. Moving the midtone gamma slider to the left lightens the image and makes the entire image more pleasing. The amount you move the midtone gamma slider depends on the original image and how much lighter you want the image to be.

figure 2.20

After adjusting the white and black points, move the midtone gamma slider to the left to lighten the image.

Working with Levels Eyedroppers

When working with historical images or photographs in which you don't have personal knowledge of the tones or color, you can use your visual memory to improve tone. **Figure 2.21** shows a classic photo that lacks the needed contrast. By redefining the white and black points with the Levels eyedroppers, the image is much improved, as shown in **figure 2.22**.

🌐▷⊰ **ch2_very_flat.jpg**

1. Take a moment to look at the image and imagine what could be white and what could black. Take into consideration the subject matter, lighting, and time of day. In this example, I can safely guess that the man's shirt collar is white and that the shadows in the room in the background would be fairly dark.

2. Add a Levels adjustment layer.

figure 2.21

figure 2.22

3. In the Levels dialog box, click the white eye-dropper, and then click an area that needs to be reset to white. In this example, it's the man's shirt collar (see **figure 2.23**). By clicking the area that should be white, Photoshop will remap and redefine the tonal information to change the dingy gray to pure white.

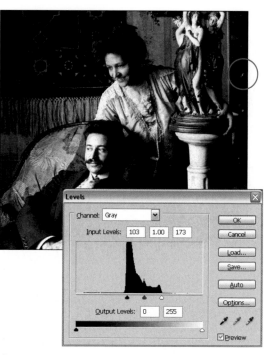

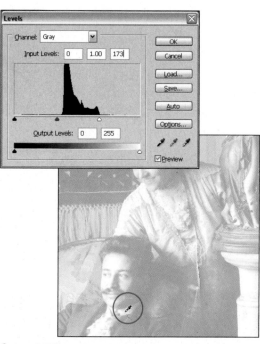

figure 2.23

Use the white eyedropper to identify where the new white point should be.

4. Click the black eyedropper, and then click an area that needs to be reset to black. In **figure 2.24**, I chose the shadow in the room in the background. Just as the white eyedropper remaps white, the black eyedropper defines and remaps the darkest tones. Using the eyedropper approach is both effective and simple—a winning combination.

Note

While in the Levels dialog box, the zoom and hand tool are not accessible but you can zoom in or out by holding down Cmd/Ctrl and pressing "+" or "-". To scroll, use the slider bars along the edge of the image. Other viewing options are available under the View menu.

figure 2.24

Use the black eyedropper to deepen the dark areas of the image.

After using the Levels eyedroppers, you can refine the effects by adjusting the Levels sliders. For example, if setting the black or white point made one image too contrasty, move the highlight slider to the right or the shadow slider to the left.

5. As seen in **figure 2.25**, moving the black point slider from 103 to 97 lightens the shadows. To make quick and subtle adjustments, I prefer to the use the arrows keys versus moving the slider triangles. In this example, I clicked inside the Input Levels shadow box and used the down arrow to change the shadow point to 97.

6. If the image is still too light or too dark, adjust the midtone gamma slider. To lighten an image, move the midtone gamma slider to the left. To darken a light image, move the midtone gamma slider to the right. Again, for minute adjustments, use the arrow keys.

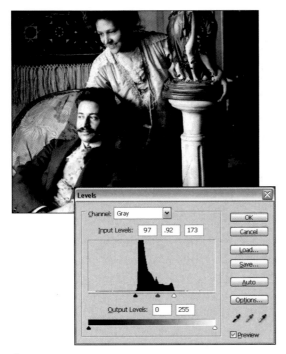

figure 2.25

Using the arrow keys in the Input Levels box enables the subtle adjustment of 103 to 97 producing lighter shadows.

figure 2.26

Note

If you click an area that isn't representative of white in your image, other lighter tones will be forced to white and you could end up losing information that may be important. If you click an area with any Levels or Curves eyedropper and don't like the results, press Option/Alt to change the Cancel button to Reset and click to return the file to its initial state.

Finding the White and Black Points

The image shown in figure 2.26 is so flat and faded that I have no idea what could be a true white or a true black. After finding the black and white points, using the black and white eyedroppers and the midtone gamma slider in Levels, I've added contrast and snap to the image, as you see in figure 2.27.

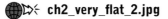 **ch2_very_flat_2.jpg**

figure 2.27

N o t e

There isn't a magic formula when adjusting tonal information. How much lighter or darker you make an image depends on the condition of the original image and your subjective interpretation of how the final image should look. In some cases, a darker image may better reflect the original scene, and in other cases, a tonally lighter approach may be more appropriate.

There are many instances where you might not be sure where the black or white point of an image is. Use a temporary Threshold adjustment layer to find the white and black points and use color samplers to pinpoint those exact spots for reference while adjusting tone.

1. Add a Threshold adjustment layer.

2. The image is now reduced to two tones—black and white—as shown in figure 2.28.

figure 2.28

The Threshold adjustment layer splits the image into black or white.

3. To find the black point, move the slider all the way to the left and then slowly move it back to the right until you see black specks begin to form, as shown in figure 2.29. As soon as the first black specks stop moving the threshold slider. Ignore image frames or edges that might not be part of the actual picture.

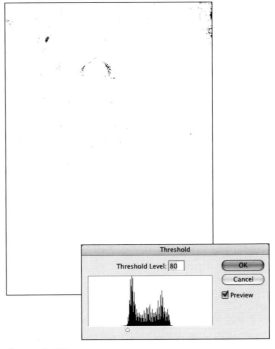

figure 2.29

To find the black point, drag the slider to the left side of the Threshold histogram.

4. Click OK and use the Color Sampler tool (nested under the Eyedropper tool) to tack a marker right on top of the first black specks that appeared.

5. To find the white point, double-click the Threshold adjustment layer icon on the Layers palette to reopen the Threshold dialog box. Then move the slider to the right until you see very small white clumps or specks, as illustrated in figure 2.30. As with the black point location, ignore areas that are not part of the image, such as the edge of the print.

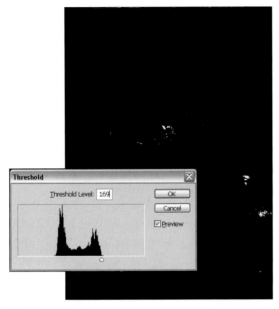

figure 2.30

To find the white point, drag the slider to the right side of the Threshold histogram.

6. Click OK and add a color sampler right on top of the clump of white.

7. Turn off or throw away the Threshold adjustment layer and you'll see that the image hasn't been affected but that the samplers are showing you exactly where the black and white points should be placed, as shown in figure 2.31.

8. Now add a Levels adjustment layer and use the color sampler tacks as reference points in setting the true black and white points. In Levels activate the white eyedropper and click once where the tack is referring to the lightest area of the image and repeat with the black eyedropper to click the black reference tack.

Tip

While working with Levels, you can get an on-the-fly view of where the image detail begins and ends. Press Option/Alt while dragging the white or black output slider to toggle to a temporary threshold view which disappears as you release the mouse button.

figure 2.31

After turning off the Threshold adjustment layer, the color samplers show you exactly where the black and white points should be placed in the image.

Output Levels

A properly adjusted image can print values from rich blacks to clean whites on a printer and paper combination that can handle a wide tonality. If your highlight values are getting blown out to paper white or the shadow information lacks tonal differentiation, you can use the Output Levels in the Levels dialog box to reduce the range of the tones and bring the print within the gamut of your printer. Entering new values under Output Levels, either by moving the sliders or entering numbers in directly, will compress all the tonal values in your image to print within the new high or low values you specify.

For example, the same image printed on different printers or papers can yield different results with regard to brightness. Highlights may hold detail in on a watercolor paper but may lack detail on a glossy paper. When I printed figure 2.32 on one paper stock, the whites were too bright. Look at the highlights on the steeples. Instead of showing detail, it displays pure white or the paper itself. Adding a Levels adjustment layer and reducing the Output Levels highlight to 245, as shown in figure 2.33, brings the file within the gamut of that paper and printer combination.

figure 2.32

The original image has been blown out and the light areas are too white.

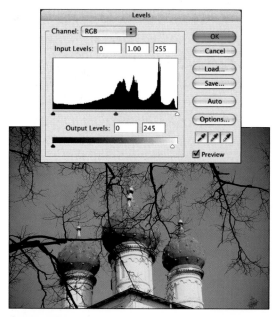

figure 2.33

When the Output Levels highlight is adjusted, the image regains the needed tonality. In this example, I did not need to adjust the Output Levels shadow. Adjusting the shadow will lighten the darkest areas of the image, which may be useful in other situations.

Using the Output feature, a Levels adjustment layer enables you to compensate for a specific printer without permanently changing the image. If you plan to print that same file with a different printer or paper, either turn the Levels adjustment layer off or adjust it to match the gamut of the new printer and paper combination.

CURVES AND CONTRAST

After you're comfortable working with Levels, Curves is the next tool to add to your Photoshop repertoire. The advantage of Curves is that it can give you 16 points to influence the tonal values of an image, whereas Levels allows you just three (highlight, midtone, and shadow points).

The Curves dialog box enables you to work with either 0–100 ink percentages or 0–255 tonal values. Click the small triangles circled in figure 2.34 to toggle between the two. From my experience, people with prepress experience prefer the ink percentage scale, while photographers prefer the tonal value scale—the same values used in Levels. The 0–255 scale places the highlights on the shoulder (upper part) of the curve and the shadows on the toe (lower part) of the curve. This is how a photographer reads film curves and why I prefer to use the 0–255 scale. The 0%–100% values are mapped exactly the opposite, with the highlights at the lower left and the shadows at the upper right.

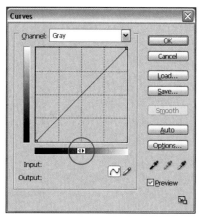

figure 2.34

You can choose to work in dot percentages or tonal values by clicking the small triangles.

Tip

Option/Alt-click in the Curves grid to toggle between a 4×4 quarter tone and 10×10 increment grid. Click the icon at the bottom right of the Curves dialog box to toggle between larger and smaller sizes of the Curves dialog box.

The best aspect of Curves is the control you have over the many points of tonal information. With Curves, you can quickly enhance image contrast by applying a classic S-curve (described in the next section), or you can spend more time with the interface and use bump points to bring out selective tonal details, as we'll do in "Bringing Out Detail with Curves."

Improving Contrast with Curves

Figure 2.35 shows another family heirloom that has aged significantly. The image is flat, as seen in the lack of difference between the highlights in the woman's blouse and the shadow thrown by the horse. I used Curves to deepen the shadows, make the highlights brighter, and enhance the midtone contrast as shown in figure 2.36. When working with such flat originals, start by moving either the highlight or shadow point along the top or bottom of the curve to deepen the shadows or lighten the highlights and then adjust the midtones to refine the contrast.

🌐▷✂ **ch2_curves_ride.jpg**

1. Add a Curves adjustment layer.

2. This example has a lot of dark information, so I started by moving the shadow point along the bottom of the curve to the right. This deepens the shadows nicely, as seen in figure 2.37.

figure 2.35

figure 2.36

figure 2.37

Deepening the shadows to make them look richer

3. Move the white point along the top of the curve to make the dingy grays brighter, as seen in **figure 2.38**. Be careful not force them to pure white.

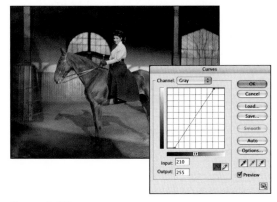

figure 2.38

Brightening the highlights without forcing the whites to pure white

4. To improve the midtone contrast, place the mouse over a light area and Cmd/Ctrl-click to add a control point on the Curves graph. In this example, I clicked the rider's blouse and pressed the left arrow key twice to open up the highlights slightly as shown in **figure 2.39**.

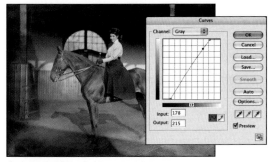

figure 2.39

Subtly opening up the lighter tones

5. Cmd/Ctrl-click a dark area to add a control point on the Curves graph for the dark value. In this example, I used the woman's skirt and pressed the right arrow key twice to deepen the shadows ever so slightly, as shown in figure 2.40.

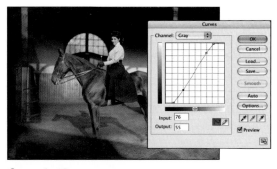

figure 2.40

Subtly darkening the shadow values gives the image the final contrast improvement.

When using Curves, keep an eye on the Info and Histogram palettes as you are adjusting contrast and tonal values. You don't want to force the dark areas so far down that they become pure black. Conversely, you want to keep some details in your highlights, so don't force whites to 0%. The only values that should be completely white are specular highlights, such as reflections on chrome bumpers.

Here are some additional tips for using Curves:

- Be sure to view the Histogram palette when using before opening Curves to see the how the changes affect the histogram.

- Use the mouse to select a control point in the Curve and then use the arrow keys to make fine changes in position. When you use the Shift key, the arrow keys will make larger changes. Use Cmd-Tab/Ctrl-Tab to cycle from point to point on a curve.

- While in the Curves dialog box, shift click to add a Color Sampler to the Info palette.

- To remove a control point, simply click and drag it outside the grid, as if you were using tweezers to pluck the handle off the curve grid.

Caution

When using Curves to increase contrast, there is always a trade-off. Adding contrast in one area takes tonal information away from another. Therefore, making radical adjustments can lead to posterization in the flat areas of the curve.

Bringing Out Detail with Curves

As you can imagine, the original image in figure 2.41 is very important to the family of the man in the picture and even though it is faded, it is still salvageable as seen in figure 2.42. I used Curves to open up the midtones and highlights, deepen the shadows, and fine-tune the blacks and whites.

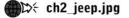 **ch2_jeep.jpg**

© Beckelman Family Archive

BEFORE

figure 2.41

figure 2.43

Mark important tonal areas with the Color Samplers

AFTER

figure 2.42

1. To monitor the tonal changes, add color samplers to the highlight, midtone, and shadow points. In this example, I clicked the white sign in the Jeep window for the highlight, the soldier's helmet and face for the midtone, and the area by the Jeep's wheel well as the shadow point. See figure 2.43.

2. Add a Curves adjustment layer and Cmd/Ctrl-click the highlight point, then use the up arrow key to lighten the image as seen in figure 2.44.

figure 2.44

Making the highlights lighter opens up the entire image.

3. Cmd/Ctrl-click the midpoint point on the man's face. Use the up arrow key to lighten those tones as seen in **figure 2.45**. The helmet midtones need to be darker than the face midtones, so Cmd/Ctrl-click the helmet and use the down arrow key to create the curve seen in **figure 2.46**.

figure 2.45

Lightening the face draws attention to it.

figure 2.46

Darkening the helmet midtones makes the lighter areas appear even brighter.

4. To enrich the shadows and give the image visual depth, Cmd/Ctrl-click the shadow point by the wheel and use the down arrow key to darken the shadow area. To make the shadows even gutsier, on the Curve grab the black point shadow handle and move it slightly to the right as seen in **figure 2.47**.

By identifying the tonal values and enhancing them with Curves the image pops of the page while maintaining the character of a 60-year-old photograph.

figure 2.47

Rich shadows serve as the visual foundation for the image.

WORKING WITH BLENDING MODES

With the exception of the Background layer, every Photoshop layer, including adjustment layers, supports blending modes, which influence how a layer interacts with the layers below it. This happens on a channel-by-channel basis so blending modes can in some instances simultaneously lighten and darken. For retouching work, blending modes simplify and speed up tonal correction, dust clean up, and blemish removal. The blending modes are arranged into functional groups, as labeled in **figure 2.48** and reviewed in **table 2.1**.

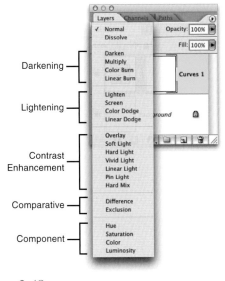

figure 2.48

The blending modes are organized into functional groups.

table 2.1
Blending Modes

Normal	Combines the two sources based on opacity.
Darkening Group	The effect will be progressively stronger as the tones become darker.
Darken	Compares the two sources and replaces light pixel values with dark.
Multiply	Darkens the entire image and is useful to add density to highlights and midtones. It is especially useful for overexposed or very light images.
Color Burn	Results in a darker image with increased contrast.
Linear Burn	Strong combination of Multiply and Color Burn; forces dark values to pure black.
Lightening Group	The effect will be progressively stronger as the tones become lighter.
Lighten	The opposite of Darken, it compares the two sources and replaces the darker pixels with lighter pixels.
Screen	Lightens the entire image. Use it to open up or lighten dark image areas and to bring out tonal information in underexposed images.
Color Dodge	Decreases contrast of areas lighter than 50% gray while preserving black values.
Linear Dodge	Combination of Screen and Color Dodge; forces light areas to pure white.
Contrast Group	Used to boost image contrast.
Overlay	Multiplies dark values and screens light values, which increases contrast but without clipping to pure white or black.
Soft Light	Combination of Dodge, which lightens the light values, and Burn, which darkens the dark values. Adds less contrast than Overlay or Hard Light.
Hard Light	Multiplies the darks and screens the light values and increases contrast dramatically.
Vivid Light	Lightens the values above 50% gray by decreasing the contrast and darkens the values below 50% gray by increasing contrast.

continues

table 2.1   *(continued)*
Blending Modes

Contrast Group	(continued)
Linear Light	*Combines Linear Burn and Linear Dodge; lightens the values above 50% gray by increasing the brightness and darkens the values below 50% gray by decreasing brightness.*
Pin Light	*Combines Darken and Lighten to replace pixel values. Always very contrasty; used for special effects and, less often, to create masks.*
Hard Mix	*Lighter values lighten and darker values darken to the point of threshold and extreme posterization.*
Comparative Group	
Difference	*Reveals identical pixel values as black, similar values as dark and opposite values are inverted.*
Exclusion	*Similar to Difference but with less contrast. Blending with black produces no change and white inverts the compared values to be rendered as gray.*
Image Component Group	Only active in color mode images
Hue	*Combines the luminance and saturation of the underlying layer with the hue of the active layer.*
Saturation	*Combines the luminance and hue of the underlying layer with the saturation of the active layer.*
Color	*Reveals the color of the active layer and maintains the luminance of the underlying layer.*
Luminosity	*Is the opposite of Color and maintains the luminosity information of the active layer in relationship to the color underneath.*

With the following exercises, you'll work with the most important blending modes to solve tonal problems. The best thing about working with blending modes is that they are completely reversible, enabling you to experiment to achieve the desired result. To access the blending modes, use the Blend Mode menu in the Layers palette.

Using Multiply to Build Density

As soon as you see a very light or very faded image, you should be thinking Multiply. The Multiply blending mode works as though you are sandwiching two slides over one another. Imagine that you're standing in front of a window and have a slide in each hand. Now place the two slides over one another and look through the slides—the results will always be darker. By using the Multiply blending mode on a Levels or Curves adjustment layer, you are doubling the tonal density of the image. **Figure 2.49** shows a charming family photo that is fading away. To restore it to the image in **figure 2.50**, we need to build up overall density to strengthen the image.

figure 2.49

figure 2.50

Ch2_boardwalk.jpg

1. Add a Levels adjustment layer and, without changing any settings in Levels, click OK.

2. In the Layers palette, change the blending mode to Multiply. **Figure 2.51** shows how the image becomes darker.

figure 2.51

Setting an adjustment layer to Multiply automatically adds density.

3. In many cases, adding a Multiply Levels adjustment layer is enough to build up enough image density to create a pleasing image. In this example, I wanted to darken the image a bit more—the easiest way to do that is to duplicate the Levels layer and adjust the layer opacity as seen in **figure 2.52**.

Note

Deciding which method to use—duplicating the adjustment layer, finessing the Levels sliders, or, in some cases, duplicating the adjustment layer and changing its blending mode is a matter of experimentation and experience. No one can look at an image and say, "I need to do A, B, and C and use these exact values." Keep in mind that the more you experiment with these techniques, the more experience you will gain and the more skills you'll have to improve images.

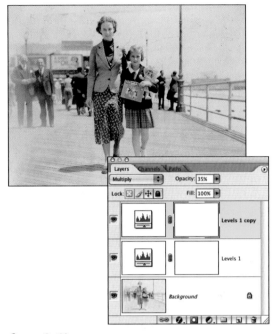

figure 2.52

Duplicating the adjustment layer doubles the effect, which you can refine by reducing the layer opacity.

Adding Contrast with Hard Light

Overlay, Soft Light, and Hard Light are great blending modes to add contrast to an image. In **figure 2.53**, the original image is very badly faded and the boy's face is barely recognizable. Using Levels adjustment layer with the Hard Light blending mode enhances this image quickly and easily (see **figure 2.54**).

 Ch2_ponyride.jpg

1. Add a Levels adjustment layer and click OK when the Levels dialog box comes up.

2. When building contrast try Overlay, then Soft Light, and then Hard Light to see which one add the most contrast and improves the image the best.

3. In this example, Hard Light is a good start and duplicating the Hard Light layer creates a surprisingly good enhancement as **figure 2.55** shows.

BEFORE

figure 2.53

figure 2.55

Two Hard Light Levels layers dramatically improve the image.

4. To bring out the little boy even more, I duplicated the Levels layer again. This made him look great but added too much contrast to the lower part of the image. To protect this area from the contrast enhancement, use a large, black, soft-edged brush to paint over the pony on the Levels layer mask, as seen in figure 2.56.

AFTER

figure 2.54

Of course, if you need to improve the shadow areas of an image, you can still make a luminosity selection and then choose Select > Inverse to make the darker areas the active area. Because the luminosity mask uses a range of selection values, some pixels are affected a great deal by your adjustment while neighboring pixels are affected less, so the adjusted pixels blend smoothly with the ones around them.

Take a look at the shot of St. Sergius Monastery, outside Moscow (**figure 2.57**). Due to the time of year and rainy weather, the sky is rather flat. A more appealing image has depth and richness like **figure 2.58**.

figure 2.56

Painting with black conceals the contrast, and wherever the mask is white, the image is improved.

figure 2.57

figure 2.58

Using Luminosity and Blending Modes to Add Visual Snap

One little-documented feature of Photoshop is the ability to make a selection based on the luminosity of the image. This is called "activating the luminosity mask," and creates a selection based on the luminosity value of each pixel. White areas are selected 100%, black areas are completely unselected, and pixels with intermediate luminosity levels are partially selected. Using the luminosity mask to select the brighter parts of your image lets you apply an adjustment to only those areas, so you can really boost the contrast in the image.

ch2_monastery.jpg

1. To boost the color and contrast of this image, first load a selection of the image's luminosity by Cmd/Ctrl-clicking the RGB icon in the Channels palette to create a selection based on the luminosity of each channel (see **figure 2.59**).

2. Duplicate the selected area by pressing Cmd/Ctrl-J. Note that the layer contents (see **figure 2.60**) are just the bright areas of the image and look transparent.

figure 2.59

Loading the image luminosity.

figure 2.60

The isolated layer showing the areas selected by luminosity.

3. With a little experimentation, I found that changing the layer blending mode to Soft Light blending mode enhanced the bright areas, effectively giving only those areas a contrast boost, as shown in figure 2.61.

figure 2.61

The Soft Light blending mode improves the contrast of the highlights nicely.

4. I duplicated the layer two more times with Ctrl/Cmd + J to get the additional contrast boost shown in the "after" figure, in figure 2.58.

ENHANCING DETAIL WITH SCREEN MODE AND THE CHANNEL MIXER

Think of Screen blending mode as the reverse of Multiply. Instead of darkening everything, Screen lightens everything. Imagine a slide projected onto a screen. Now project another slide on top of it. The image will always be lighter.

This can be used to great advantage with very dark originals, such as the one in figure 2.62. The woman on the right is a Native American princess, so the photograph was very valuable to the owner. The paper base has yellowed and darkened so much it's hard to make out any detail at all. The Screen blending mode brings much of the contrast back to the image, as shown in figure 2.63.

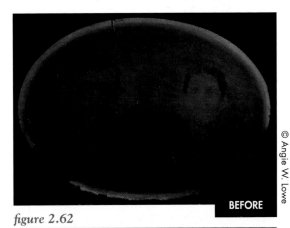

BEFORE

figure 2.62

AFTER

figure 2.63

When I face extreme tone or color problems, I always check the individual color channels to see if I can identify the problem. To see the channels, open the Channels palette and click each channel (red, green, or blue) or use Cmd/Ctrl with 1, 2, or 3 to see the red, green, and blue channels, respectively. Cmd/Ctrl-~) returns you to RGB with all channels displayed. In this example, the blue channel has practically no image information at all, as you can see in **figure 2.64**.

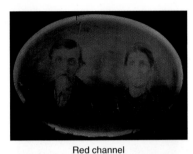

Red channel

Green channel

Blue channel

figure 2.64

Looking at the individual channels can often help identify what is causing extreme problems.

To lighten this detail while maintaining the character of the original, use a Channel Mixer adjustment layer with the Screen blending mode.

1. Keeping in mind that the red and the green channel contain the best image information,

add a Channel Mixer adjustment layer. Channel Mixer uses sliders to blend each of a source image's color channels into a new output channel.

2. The strong color cast in this image is not part of the essential image information, and by checking the Monochrome option in the Channel Mixer, you can quickly remove color problems.

3. Because the red and green channels have the best image information, move those sliders to the right to increase the amount that they are adding to the image. I used 90% red and 60% green, as shown in **figure 2.65**. Click OK.

figure 2.65

Adjusting the Channel Mixer sliders to create an image with the good channel information, while ignoring the severely damaged blue channel.

4. Change the blending mode of the Channel Mixer adjustment layer to Screen, which allows some of the original color character of the image to show through. (For additional information on working with the Channel Mixer, see Chapter 8, "Refining and Polishing the Image.")

ADJUSTMENT LAYERS FOR POWER USERS

You can move and share adjustment layers between documents by using the Move tool to drag them from one open document to another. The files don't have to be the same size or dimension—meaning you can make a tonal correction on one file and just drag the adjustment layer over to another file. Photoshop will apply the same improvement to the second file. Use this drag-and-drop technique when you have a number of similar corrections to make to similar originals.

Sharing Adjustment Layers

Adjustment layers can be dragged and dropped to other files that are in the same color mode to instantly apply the tone or color correction to the target file. On one project, I had to restore more than 100 images that were taken at the same time and stored together; consequently, they all had faded in a similar manner. After scanning in the originals, I opened one representative image and used a Curves adjustment layer to improve the contrast of one. Then I opened the other files and just dragged the initial adjustment layer over to each one, which applied that correction to all the subsequent files. Of course I looked at each image and tweaked the corrections where needed, but by using this technique I was done with the job in no time.

In the following example, the three images were flat and unappealing, as seen in **figure 2.66**. I wanted to quickly boost the contrast on all three to find the best image as shown in **figure 2.67**.

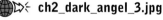 **ch2_dark_angel_1.jpg**

 ch2_dark_angel_2.jpg

 ch2_dark_angel_3.jpg

figure 2.66   *figure 2.67*

1. I opened one representative image and improved the contrast with Curves (see figure 2.68).

2. After clicking OK to the adjustment, I used the Move tool to drag the adjustment layer from the Layers palette onto the next two images one at a time.

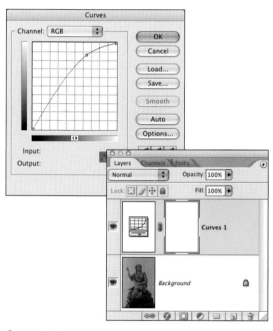

figure 2.69

figure 2.68

Correcting one image.

COMBINING TONAL CORRECTIONS

So far, you've seen numerous examples of correcting tone or contrast problems using one or another type of adjustment layer, but you can expand your Photoshop repertoire by combining numerous types of adjustment layers. Here is an example that illustrates the application of several adjustment layers to restore tone and contrast to a very faded and discolored original (see **figure 2.69**) creating the rich image shown in **figure 2.70**. It also shows the flexibility in using adjustment layers.

figure 2.70

Often an image is so dark and discolored that I simply don't know which problem to take care of first. In this example, even though the image probably had a sepia tone, the passage of time has compressed the tonality of the original and added an unpleasant orange color cast. Try the following technique to clear up both problems with one adjustment.

 Ch2_man_with_vest.jpg

When working with antique images, you may be faced with images that have a strong colorcast and exposure problems. To expand the overall tonality and to remove the strong colorcast, use a Levels adjustment layer and work on the individual color channels to clear up the colorcast in three very easy steps.

1. Create a new Levels adjustment layer.

2. Activate the red channel by using Cmd/Ctrl-1 and move the highlight levels slider to where the majority of the highlight information begins and the shadow slider to where the majority of the shadow information is (see figure 2.71).

3. Select the green channel (Cmd/Ctrl-2) and move the shadow and highlight sliders, as shown in figure 2.72.

4. Select the blue channel Cmd/Ctrl-3 and move the individual highlight and shadow levels sliders to where the majority of the information begins, as shown in figure 2.73 As you can see, both the extreme color cast and the darkness have been removed very well and very easily, returning the image to a sepia tone.

figure 2.72

Adjusting the green channel information.

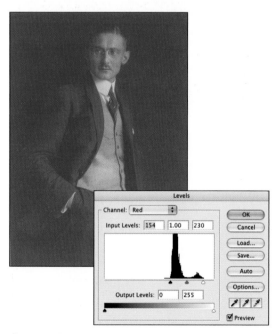

figure 2.71

Adjusting the red channel information.

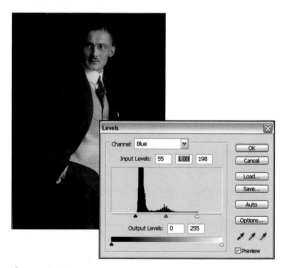

figure 2.73

Adjusting the blue channel information.

5. Several variants of the image were required, including black-and-white, as well as a blue tint, to fit the decoration of the room in which the image would hang. To make the black-and-white variant, add a Channel Mixer adjustment layer, check Monochrome, and use 50% from both the red and green channels, for a lighter rendition of the image, as seen in **figure 2.74**.

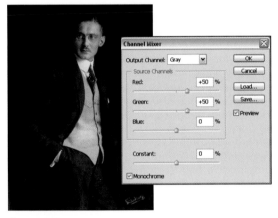

figure 2.74

Using the Channel Mixer to create a black-and-white version of the image.

6. To create the last variant with a cooler blue tone, add a Solid Color adjustment layer and chose a deep blue. To have the blue blend with the image, use the Color blending mode, to allow the grayscale values of the image below to show through. To refine the blue lower the opacity to 60% as seen in **figure 2.75**.

figure 2.75

Using a Color Fill adjustment layer, set to Color Mode to create a color-toned effect.

BASING TONAL CORRECTIONS ON SELECTIONS

We have applied tonal changes to the entire image (global changes), but many times you just want to improve a specific part or area of a file (local changes). That is when you need to start thinking and working selectively. In this section, you use Photoshop's selection and painting tools to control where the changes take place. Selective changes can start with either an active selection or with a global adjustment layer.

If you make a selection before adding an adjustment layer and then add the adjustment layer, Photoshop saves the selection into the adjustment layer mask as illustrated in **figure 2.76**.

figure 2.76

The active selection is transferred to the layer mask. Option/ Alt-click the mask to see it.

The shadow areas in **figure 2.77** are too dark. When I make a selection and then add an adjustment layer, Photoshop knows to change only the actively selected area, as seen in **figure 2.78**. In the layer mask, wherever it is black, the adjustment doesn't take place, while the effect shows through the white areas. The best thing about this approach is that you can use any selection tool you are comfortable with, from the Magic Wand tool to the Color Range command, to create the initial selection.

ch2_cello_cases.jpg

1. Make a selection of the tonal areas that you want to enhance. In this example, I used Select > Color Range set to Shadows, as shown in **figure 2.79**, to create the active selection, and then accepted the selection by clicking OK.

2. Add a Curves adjustment layer. Notice that in **figure 2.80**, Photoshop automatically creates a mask for the adjustment layer using the selection (look at the thumbnail in the Layers palette). Where the mask is black, no tonal correction will take place. Where the mask is white, the tonal adjustments you make will take place.

3. Adjust the curve to open the shadows, as shown in **figure 2.81**. In some situations, you may want to experiment with blending modes to accentuate the adjustments. In this case, Screen is an effective choice.

4. If you notice distinct or abrupt tonal changes like the ones circled in **figure 2.82**, choose Filter > Blur > Gaussian Blur on the layer mask to soften the transition from the black area (no change) to white (change), as shown in **figure 2.83**.

figure 2.77

figure 2.78

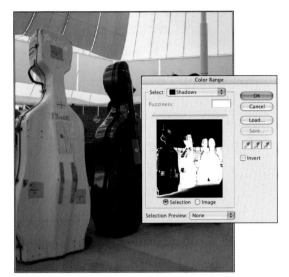

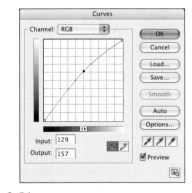

figure 2.79

Using Color Range to select the shadows.

figure 2.81

The edited curve.

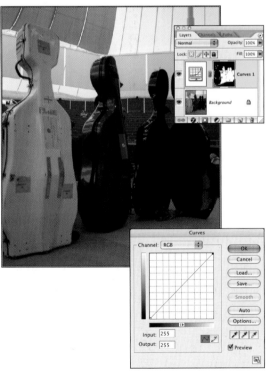

figure 2.80

Adding a Curves adjustment layer when a selection is active creates a mask to control where the tonal adjustments will take place.

figure 2.82

A harsh transition can lead to a tie-dye effect along tonal differences.

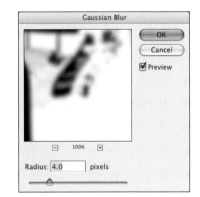

figure 2.83

Softening the layer mask with Gaussian Blur.

Multiple Masked Adjustments

One of the greatest benefits of working with adjustment layers is the ability to use the layer mask to control exactly where the image improvement takes place. Additionally, you can stack up many separate adjustment layers with masks to fine-tune an image with tremendous control and flexibility.

This image is not 85 years old, but the subject is (**figure 2.84**). Pam Herrington took this grab shot at her father-in-law's birthday celebration and caught this interesting array of candle reflections in his glasses. It didn't become the focus of the image until she cropped the image and used masked adjustment layers to make the reflections stand out, as seen in **figure 2.85**.

figure 2.84

The reflection of the candles in the subject's glasses required some masked adjustment layers to reach their maximum impact.

Pam selected the subject and added a Curves adjustment layer, which automatically created a mask. She inverted the mask so the adjustments she made would affect the background instead of the subject. Instead of reselecting the subject again, she simply Cmd/Ctrl-clicked the mask icon, which reloaded the selection again. She did this multiple times for several different adjustment layers to bring out the reflections (as seen in figure 2.85).

figure 2.85

The layer masks control exactly where the tonal changes take place, to darken down the room and bring out the reflections of the 85 candles.

CLOSING THOUGHTS

Even after years of working with Photoshop, it still amazes me to see how improving image tone can turn a so-so image into an absolutely wonderful one. Rely on your visual intuition to access an image and use adjustment layers to bring out tonal detail and information. Working with adjustment layers gives you the opportunity to experiment and learn from the process. You may not get the image just right the very first time you try a technique, but believe me, every time you try something new, you're learning for the next image challenge. So download the exercise files from www.digitalretouch.org, practice with them, and then apply the techniques to your own images. Although some of the specific values may differ, the concepts of working with adjustment layers, blending modes, and selections will hold true.

3

EXPOSURE CORRECTION

Times have changed. Instead of going to the photo store to pick up our photos, many of us now only have to flip our camera over and look at the LCD screen. But whether we use film or shoot digital, we are still disappointed by pictures that are too light, too dark, or just way off because the flash didn't fire correctly. All these problems can be traced back to incorrect exposure. Although modern cameras have sophisticated light meters and exposure controls, strong backlighting or well-intentioned but incorrect camera settings can fool these modern wonders into making the wrong exposure.

Additionally, the ravages of time, displaying the photo in strong sunlight, improper storage conditions, poor chemical processing, and the transient nature of most color photographic substrates can wreak havoc on your fondest memories. When pictures fade, they don't contain any rich blacks or pure whites, and often they suffer odd color shifts.

In this chapter, you'll work with grayscale and color images to

- Brighten dark, underexposed images

- Enhance information in overexposed images

- Work with Smart Objects and Camera Raw

- Fix images with multiple exposure or fading problems

- Master the Shadow/Highlight feature

> When you have the choice between scanning a print or the original film, working with the original film will most often yield better results. Even extremely over- or underexposed film contains more information than a print made from a poor film exposure. Better yet, the negative might produce a print that doesn't need a lot of special attention. Prints are much more likely to shift over time than the original film.

IMPROVING DARK IMAGES

Images that are underexposed are usually dark or dull without a true, rich black or clean white. Shadows that don't have any useful information and white areas, like snow, that look medium gray are also telltale signs that the camera meter was fooled into calculating the wrong exposure. Images that have faded over time also can be symptomatic of underexposure, and these same techniques can be used to rescue them.

Using the Screen Blending Mode

There is nothing worse than trying to rescue a tintype: a non-reflective photograph on a sheet of iron coated with dark enamel. Tintypes were a popular and inexpensive photographic option from 1856 through the early part of the 20th century. **Figure 3.1** shows the original, which is almost too dark to reproduce well at all. To open up—that is, lighten—the image, I used the Screen blending mode on several Curves adjustment layers to create the results seen in **figure 3.2**.

ch3_tintype.jpg

1. When making large tonal or color corrections, it is a good habit to track the important tonal information by adding color samplers as shown in **figure 3.3**. In this example, I added four color samplers to track the highlights on the dress, shadows on the dress, skin tones, and the studio background.

BEFORE

figure 3.1

AFTER

figure 3.2

figure 3.3

Color samplers enable you to measure and track tonal changes.

2. When you are tracking exposure changes, it is often easier to set the Info palette readout to K (black), which uses a 1%–100% scale. To change the Info palette readout, click and hold each eyedropper icon and select Grayscale from the menu.

3. Add a Curves adjustment layer, click OK without changing anything and then change the layer blending mode to Screen.

4. Watching the Info palette is crucial to understanding how blending modes affect the image data. To compare the sampler values before and after the change, double-click the adjustment layer icon. As shown in **figure 3.4**, the first number (before the slash) is the original value of the sample, and the second number (after the slash) shows the value after editing.

   • Sampler 1: The background went from 63% to 37%.

   • Sampler 2: The skin tone went from 65% to 38%.

   • Sampler 3: The dress tone went from 84% to 68%.

   • Sampler 4: In this example the shadow value stayed the same.

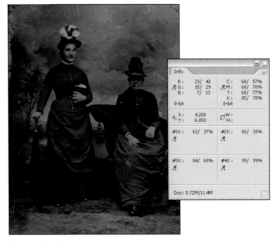

figure 3.4

Using the Screen blending mode will lighten dark images and the Info palette will show the value changes when the adjustment layer is open.

Of course, your numbers will vary, as it would be very difficult to click on the exact same spots I clicked on in this file.

5. To increase the lightening effect, duplicate the Curves adjustment layer by dragging it down onto the New Layer icon or pressing Cmd-J/Ctrl-J.

6. In this example, I duplicated the adjustment layer twice. But the third adjustment layer made the image too light, so I reduced its opacity to create the image shown in **figure 3.5**.

figure 3.5

Duplicating the adjustment layers increases the exposure change, which can be reduced by lowering the opacity of the layer.

Tip

On dark, underexposed images, also try the Linear Dodge blending mode to increase the lightening effect and simultaneously improve image contrast.

Caution

Adding excessive contrast with blending modes or tonal changes may result in image posterization (as illustrated in figure 3.6) that might cause banding when printing. To avoid posterization, be careful how much pushing and pulling (lightening and darkening) of tonal values you do.

figure 3.6

Image posterization can result in banding when printing.

Now that the exposure has been corrected for this image, the damage is quite apparent. Techniques for image repair are addressed in Chapter 6, "Damage Control and Repair."

Transitioning a Tonal Correction

Camera meters can be fooled into giving an incorrect exposure when there is a bright object in the image. In this example, the camera meter was fooled by the sun breaking through the clouds in the light morning sky, underexposing the lower half of the picture, as shown in figure 3.7. As you can see in figure 3.8, the final image is tonally balanced and my memories of that early morning walk have been saved.

figure 3.7

BEFORE

figure 3.8

AFTER

ch3_underexposed_beach.jpg

Because only half the image is underexposed, applying an adjustment layer to the entire image will ruin the half that is correctly exposed. A layer mask enables you to control which part of the image is affected by the adjustment layer—painting black on the mask will protect those areas from the adjustment. When you want an even transition from correctly exposed to poorly exposed, use the Gradient tool. It enables you to draw over the entire surface from black to white with a smooth, gray transition.

1. Add a Curves adjustment layer and click OK. If the problem area is too dark (as in this case), select Screen or Linear Dodge as the layer blending mode. If the problem area is too light, select Multiply or Linear Burn to help darken the image.

2. In this example, I used Linear Dodge, which lightened the image and increased its contrast, as seen in **figure 3.9**, which also makes the sky much too light.

figure 3.9

The Linear Dodge blending mode lightens the entire image a great deal.

3. To control where the change takes place, choose the Gradient tool and click the Linear Gradient button on the options bar. Open

the Gradient picker and choose the black to white preset, which is the third gradient on the upper row (**figure 3.10**).

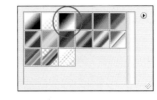

figure 3.10

Selecting the opaque black to white gradient preset.

4. Think of the Gradient tool as a very large paintbrush that paints over the entire image with one fell stroke. Start the gradient where you want to block out the lightening effect (in this example, just under the sun) to where the image adjustment should begin taking effect (in this example, the top of the horizon) (see **figure 3.11**). If you don't draw the gradient perfectly the first time or if you can see a sudden transition, use the Gradient tool to redraw the gradient blend right over the previous one until the transition is to your liking. Wherever the gradient is black, the tonal correction will be hidden, and wherever you leave white, the tonal correction will be revealed.

figure 3.11

Drawing the gradient on the adjustment layer layer mask controls where the effect is applied to the image.

5. To intensify the lightening effect, duplicate the adjustment layer by dragging it down onto the New Layer icon and adjust the layer opacity if necessary as seen in **figure 3.12**. As you can see, duplicating the adjustment layer also duplicates the layer mask.

figure 3.12

Duplicating the adjustment layer with a layer mask increases the effect and maintains the layer mask.

Correcting Light Falloff

In terms of creating shadows and light fall-off, using an off-camera flash often can cause as many problems as it alleviates. **Figure 3.13** shows one type of flash exposure problem in which the flash coverage didn't match the subject size, causing a light fall-off along the bottom of the image. In this instance, you'll use Photoshop to seamlessly blend the poorly lit photo with a lighter version to create the consistently exposed image you see in **figure 3.14**.

 **ch3_unevenflash.jpg**

figure 3.13

figure 3.14

1. To lighten the light fall-off along the bottom and edges of the image, add a Levels adjustment layer, click OK, and set its blending mode to Screen. Invert the layer mask by selecting Image > Adjustments > Invert or press Cmd-I/Ctrl-I, which will turn off the lightening effect. The image will look as though you haven't changed anything at all, as **figure 3.15** illustrates.

2. Select the Gradient tool and make sure that the foreground color is white. On the options bar, select the Foreground to Transparent gradient (see **figure 3.16**). Working with this white to transparent gradient will enable you to combine multiple gradients on one layer mask to build up the lightening effect in more than one area.

figure 3.15

Inverting the layer mask hides the change so you can selectively paint it back in.

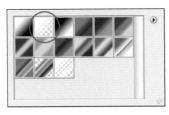

figure 3.16

Selecting the Foreground to Transparent gradient.

3. Tap F to enter full screen mode. Use the Gradient tool and click and drag from the bottom of the image to about the waistband level of the players in the second row. Then draw a gradient from the left outside edge to the shoulder of the left most player and repeat from the outside edge and drag to the shoulder of the player on the right as shown in figure 3.17. To see the layer mask, Option/Alt-click the mask. Use Option/Alt-click to return to the image view.

figure 3.17

Having the gradient option set from Foreground to Transparent allows the combining of multiple gradients on one layer mask.

🔍 **Tip**

It is easier to use the Gradient tool when working in full screen mode, with the image zoomed out enough to see the entire image plus the work area. If needed, you can start the gradient well outside the image and subtly add the gradient blends to lighten or darken an image.

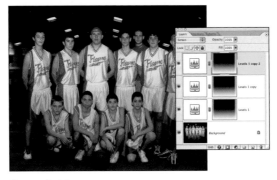

figure 3.18

Duplicating the adjustment layer increases the lightening effect.

4. Duplicate the adjustment layer one or more times to increase the effect, which is shown in figure 3.18.

Painting with Adjustment Layers

Of course, not all image imperfections fall on a straight line or within one tonal area, as they did in the previous examples. When I need to enhance irregular areas, I prefer to use Photoshop's Brush tools and a Wacom pressure-sensitive tablet to paint on the adjustment layer layer masks. In the picture of the boat on an ice-choked Lake Huron (see **figure 3.19**), the camera meter was fooled by the snow. The image is too dark and the beauty of a white boat in the cold emptiness is lost. By lightening the image overall and then selectively lightening the boat and snow in the foreground, the viewer's eye is drawn into the image, as shown in **figure 3.20**.

🌐 ▷✂ **ch3_blueboat.jpg**

1. Add a Levels adjustment layer and as explained in Chapter 2, "Improving Tone and Contrast," move the highlight and shadow sliders inwards to edges of the histogram. While still in Levels, use the Set Gray Point eyedropper and click on the boat to offset the strong blue color cast, as in **figure 3.21**.

2. To lighten the boat, add a Curves adjustment layer and change the blending mode to Screen. **Figure 3.22** shows that the entire image is lightened, which is undesired.

3. To hide the effect of the Curves layer, invert the adjustment layer layer mask (Cmd-I/Ctrl-I).

4. Click the Foreground color box. In the HSB section, use 0, 0, and 50% to select a medium gray (**figure 3.23**). Select a large, soft-edged brush and paint over the boat as seen in **figure 3.24**.

BEFORE

figure 3.19

AFTER

figure 3.20

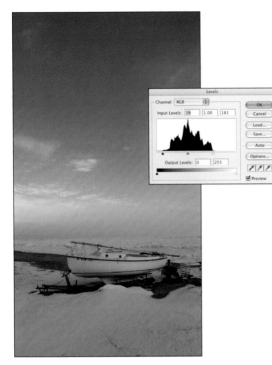

figure 3.21

Improve the overall exposure and remove the color cast with Levels.

figure 3.22

The Screen blending mode lightens the entire file.

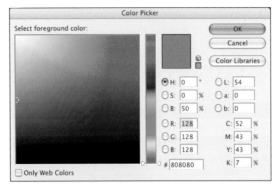

figure 3.23

Use the HSB values of 0, 0 and 50 to choose 50% gray.

figure 3.24

Painting on the Curves adjustment layer layer mask allows you to carefully lighten only the areas that require it.

5. To lighten the boat even further, use this trick that Dave Billman shared with me. Rather than painting with a lighter color on the layer mask, which may create an uneven effect, Dave recommends Cmd/Ctrl-clicking the layer mask to load it as a selection. Dismiss the warning: "No pixels are more than 50% selected. The selection edges will not be visible." All the message really means is that there is an active selection, but there isn't enough difference for Photoshop to draw the selection marquee.

6. Set the foreground color to a gray that is 10–25% lighter (in this case, 0, 0, 75%) and fill the active selection by choosing Edit > Fill and choosing Foreground Color to create the image in progress seen in **figure 3.25**. Repeat as often as desired with lighter values of gray as needed. By filling the selection with gray, Dave avoids lightening the image unevenly.

figure 3.25

Filling the active selection with a lighter gray is more accurate than painting on the layer mask.

7. To lighten the snow, add a new Curves layer and set it to Screen. Invert the layer mask and use a 50% gray, soft-edged brush to paint along the snow in the lower half of the picture as seen in **figure 3.26**. If desired, use Dave's method to lighten the snow to your liking. To fine-tune the lightening effect, adjust the opacity of the adjustment layer.

This technique gives you the ability to decide where and to what extent the tonal changes take place. The soft-edged brush will yield a soft-edged tonal transition that is difficult to detect.

figure 3.26

Using a soft-edged brush along the snow line makes the transition to the lighter areas imperceptible.

Two Are Better than One

The camera raw format enables you to maintain the highest image quality and the greatest processing flexibility. Since each manufacturer has a slightly different raw file format and name, you'll need to check your camera manual to see if your digital camera shoots raw. One strength of shooting in your camera's raw format is the ability to process the same exposure several times in Adobe Camera Raw and then combine them into one ideal image. On a similar note—if you use a tripod while taking a series of bracketed exposures, you can process the image as a HDR (high dynamic range) image to extend the tonal range from image shadow to highlights.

The image shown in the following example was shot hand-held, so I only have one raw capture. I need to process it twice—once for the shadows and once for the highlights. As **figure 3.27** shows, the upper portion of the image is well exposed, while the shadow information is much too dark. By combining two versions of the same raw image, I was able to create the image seen in **figure 3.28**.

🌐 ▷✕ **ch3_grand_canyon.dng**

figure 3.27

figure 3.28

To maintain flexibility when processing the same exposure twice, I highly recommend using the Smart Object feature, which will embed the original camera raw file as a Photoshop layer, allowing you to reprocess the raw files in relationship to the final image to fine-tune the results. All in all, this technique can be broken down into five primary steps—embed two versions of the same camera raw file as Smart Objects, composite the Smart Objects with layer masking, refine the composite with color and tonal corrections, resize, and clean up color and artifacts.

1. Start by ascertaining the smallest and uninterpolated sizes that Camera Raw will open a file to. Open a camera raw file and the Camera Raw dialog box automatically opens. Click and hold the size menu (see **figure 3.29**). In the case of my Canon 20D, the smallest file size is 1024 by 1536 and the native uninterpolated file is 2336 by 3504. Make a note of both file sizes and click cancel.

2. Choose File > New and create an RGB, 16-bit document of the smaller size, as seen in **figure 3.30**.

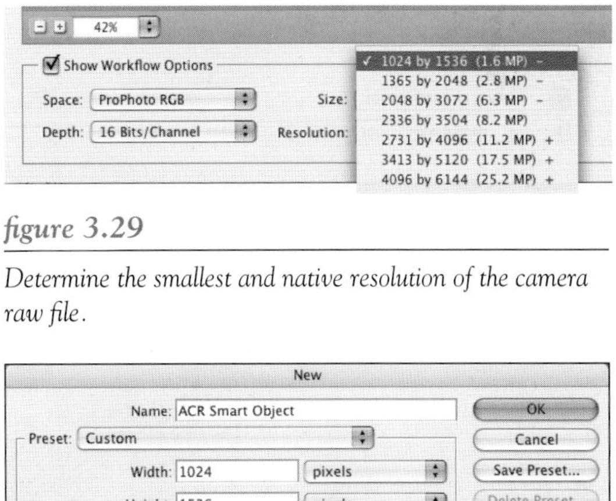

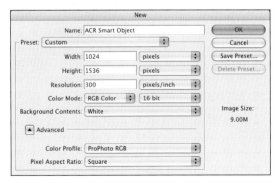

figure 3.29

Determine the smallest and native resolution of the camera raw file.

figure 3.30

Create a new file the size of the smallest camera raw file.

3. Choose File > Place and navigate to the camera raw file. Placing the file embeds the raw file as a Smart Object. Check to make sure that the size, bit depth, and Color Space settings in the Show Workflow Options area match those in the new document you just created.

4. In this first pass of Camera Raw processing, adjust the file so the upper portion of the image that is in sunlight looks good, seen in **figure 3.31**. In this example, I used all of the Auto settings, clicked the Curve tab and choose Strong Contrast from the Tone Curve preset pop-up menu to make the dimension of the Grand Canyon pop a bit more.

5. Click the Open button in the lower right hand corner of the Camera Raw dialog box and Photoshop will place the raw file into the document. Tap the enter key to accept the placement. Name the layer *highlights*.

Warning

To allow for multiple processing of the same Smart Object, two Smart Objects of the same file are required. It is very important to choose Layer > Smart Objects > New Smart Object via Copy. Do not duplicate the Smart Object by dragging it to the New Layer button, as this will not allow you to reprocess each layer separately.

6. With the highlights layer active, choose Layer > Smart Objects > New Smart Object via Copy and name the second layer *shadows*. Double-click the shadows layer thumbnail to open the Camera Raw dialog box again and this time process the file for the shadows. In such an extreme situation, I did not change the Auto settings and find that using the Curve control creates the best results. Click the Curve tab and select Linear from the Tone Curve preset pop-up menu. Pull the shadow point up to lighten the shadows as seen in **figure 3.32**. As you can see I also flattened out the highlights, which will make them all but disappear.

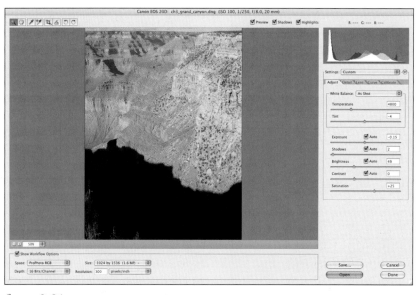

figure 3.31

Process the first version of the camera raw file for the highlights.

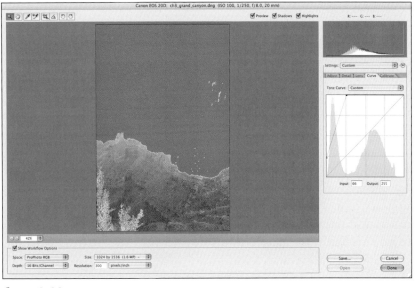

figure 3.32

Using Curves to open up the shadow information in Camera Raw.

7. In the Camera Raw dialog box, click Done and Photoshop will reprocess the file to create the image seen in **figure 3.33**. This completes the first part of the technique.

figure 3.33

After processing the Smart Objects derived from the camera raw file, the preliminary work is done.

8. The next step is to combine the two images, and there are a variety of ways to do this. One straightforward way is to use a layer mask. With the shadows layer active, click the layer mask button at the bottom of the Layers palette. Select a large, soft brush and set black as the foreground color. Paint over the undesired areas—in this case over the white sky. Don't try to be too exact in this initial phase to create the image seen in **figure 3.34**.

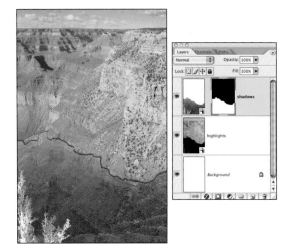

figure 3.34

Painting with black conceals the undesired blown out sky and reveals the desired areas underneath.

9. Zoom in on the edge transitions and use a smaller 50% hardness brush to paint along the edge of the transition. Paint with black to reveal the layer underneath and with white to reveal the active shadow layer. Press X to toggle between black and white as you paint to create the image seen in **figure 3.35**. It's not perfect but well on its way.

figure 3.35

Refining the layer mask with smaller and smaller brushes takes patience but allows tremendous flexibility and control.

10. Chapter 4, "Working with Color," addresses many techniques to correct color, but in this instance using a clipped Color Balance layer will work very well. Choose Layer > New Adjustment Layer > Color Balance and click Use Previous Layer to Create Clipping Mask. Clipping the adjustment layer insures that only the pixels directly underneath the clipped adjustment layer will be affected.

11. Use the Color Balance dialog box to match the color of the lower image area with the upper. In this example, removing all blue and increasing magenta and red in both the shadows and midtones does the job very nicely. Out of pure curiosity I cycled through the layer blending modes and noticed that changing the adjustment layer blending mode to Color maintains more detail as seen in **figure 3.36**.

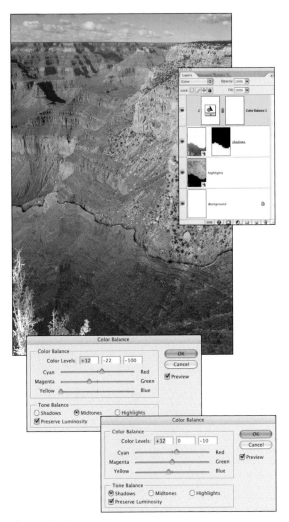

figure 3.36

The clipped Color Balance layer is the first step in matching the color of the two images.

The third phase of this technique is to resize the image to the full camera file resolution, which needs to be done before cleaning up the edges. Smart Objects do not support any painting tools such as cloning and healing, which is required to conceal the seam. In most cases, I try to avoid resizing images; but files with Smart Objects based on camera raw files are much more flexible. The first step is to resize the file, followed by replacing the original camera raw file with the high-resolution version of the same file. In the case of the Canon 20D the full camera raw file size is 2336 by 3504, which are the values to use when resizing the file.

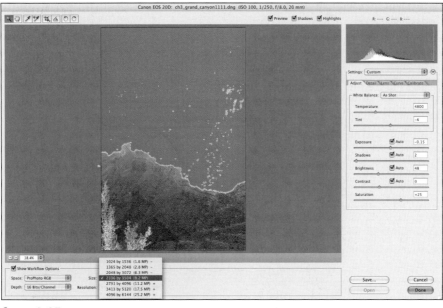

figure 3.37

After upsizing the file, update the Smart Objects with the higher resolution data from the camera raw file.

12. Choose Image > Image Size and type in 2336 by 3504 pixels.

13. To update the Smart Objects to the full resolution, double-click the shadows layer thumbnail and use the size pop-up menu to access the full resolution data as seen in figure 3.37. Click Done and the lower resolution Smart Object will be replaced with the full resolution file. Repeat this step with the highlights layer.

The fourth phase is to refine where the files have come together. In this example the obvious seam needs to be retouched and the color needs some additional refinement.

14. To cover the seam, add a new layer named *clean up* at the top of the stack and use the Clone Stamp set to Sample All Layers with a 50% hardness brush to apply the initial clean up. Sampling from both sides of the seam creates a smoother transition. I also used the Healing Brush also set to Sample All Layers to refine the edges as shown in figure 3.38. For additional information on using the Clone Stamp and Healing Brush please see Chapter 5, "Dust, Mold, and Texture Removal."

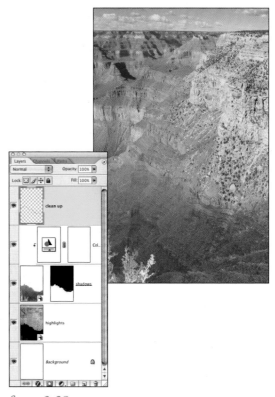

figure 3.38

Cloning and healing on the empty layer to conceal the seam between files.

15. As is often the case, after working on an image for a few hours, I have a change of heart and would like to improve a previous step. In this example, the color still needs refinement, which is easily done by adding a new layer and changing the blending mode to Color.

16. Use the Eyedropper tool to sample a deep orange from the rocks in the upper section of the image and use a large soft-edged brush to paint over the lower image areas to match the colors as seen in **figure 3.39**. For additional information on coloring images please see Chapter 8, "Refining and Polishing the Image."

figure 3.39

Painting with the color of the rocks to blend the images together.

The last refinement step is to apply sharpening, which is discussed in greater detail in Chapter 8. For digital files, I often use the High Pass technique, which is very easy and effective.

17. Use Cmd-Option-Shift-E/Ctrl-Alt-Shift-E to merge all visible layers up to a new layer and change the new layer's blending mode to Overlay.

18. Choose Filter > Other > High Pass and use a setting that brings out the details. Be sure to watch the actual image, not the filter preview. For this image, I used a setting of 3 (**figure 3.40**) to create the final image.

figure 3.40

High Pass sharpening is very effective on digital camera files.

All in all, processing a raw file two, or even three times, allows you to process the image for different tonal requirements. Granted, it takes some effort to composite the files together, but in the end the results are worth it.

SALVAGING OVEREXPOSED IMAGES

Slide positive originals or digital camera files are images that are most likely to be overexposed. Additionally, slide films, such as Kodak Ektachrome and AgfaChrome, and many digital cameras, do not have the exposure latitude that color negative film has, which makes them more sensitive to overexposure. As with underexposure, a severely overexposed image might not give you much (if any) image information to work with. If the overexposed areas are clear, blown-out to white, or if the Info palette reads 255, 255, 255, there is no amount of Photoshop magic that can recreate image information that wasn't captured in the first place. In the following exercises, you work with very light and faded images to learn techniques to bring out subtle information and create images that are saturated and rich.

Using the Multiply Blending Mode

Photos taken on bright, sunny days are frequently prone to overexposure. And days don't get much brighter and sunnier than in the Arizona desert, as you see in the image shown in **figure 3.41**. Luckily, a quick examination using the Eyedropper and Info palette shows we still have highlight detail, so this is a prime candidate for rescue.

Using techniques very similar to those you've already learned, you can expand the limited tonal range of this image without losing detail (see **figure 3.42**).

⊕↘⌇ **ch3_watermelon_woman.jpg**

1. Add a Curves adjustment layer, click OK, and set the blending mode to Multiply. You'll see an instant improvement in the overall density of the image as seen in **figure 3.43**.

BEFORE

figure 3.41

AFTER

figure 3.42

figure 3.43

The Multiply blending mode darkens light images very well.

2. If adding density with Multiply also increases an undesired color shift, as it did in this example, use the Set Gray Point eyedropper (more casually referred to as the gray eyedropper) in the Curves dialog box to neutralize the colorcast. Clicking the back of the white cane chair neutralizes the subtle red cast (see **figure 3.44**).

3. To intensify the effect, duplicate the Curves adjustment layer. Adjust the opacity if the effect is too strong. For this image, two Curves adjustment layers set to Multiply makes the image look muddy. To offset this, I set the blending mode of the topmost layer to Soft Light and adjusted the layer opacity to 35%, as seen in **figure 3.45**.

Often, working with adjustment layer blending modes requires experimentation to find the one blending mode or combination of blending modes that are best for your image. Or as the car advertisements used to say, "your mileage may vary."

figure 3.44

The colorcast is neutralized with the Set Gray Point eyedropper.

figure 3.45

Duplicating Adjustment Layers and combining Blending Modes can be an effective image correction method.

Correcting Overexposed Images from Digital Cameras

Digital cameras don't offer nearly the exposure latitude of traditional film—meaning that if the light is very bright and contrasty or if you over-expose the image, the file will be too light and lack highlight detail. Often the midtone and shadow information will be washed out and gray. The image in **figure 3.46** is overexposed by only about half an *f*stop, but for critical portrait work, that can already be too much to achieve quality results. **Figure 3.47** shows a richer, more attractive skin tone and overall portrait. I learned a great technique from Lee Varis that always impresses me with its ease and effectiveness: using a Channel Mixer adjustment layer to improve channels that are lacking tonal range.

 ch3_overexposedkevin.jpg

1. Inspect the three channels individually by pressing Cmd/Ctrl and 1, 2, and 3 to reveal which one has the greater problems and which one has the best image detail. As shown in **figure 3.48**, the red channel is very light and contains very little useful skin or tonal detail. While both the green and blue channels contain excellent tonal detail, the blue channel is more contrasty, which allows me to conclude that the green channel is the best one. Press Cmd-~/Ctrl-~ to return to the composite view of the file.

© Brent Shirk

BEFORE

figure 3.46

AFTER

figure 3.47

Red   Green

Blue

figure 3.48

Look at the three channels to find the best one.

2. Choose Layer > New Adjustment Layer >
    Channel Mixer and select Luminosity from
    the mode pop-up menu. Make sure the Out-
    put Channel menu is set to Red and set the
    red and blue values to 0% and the green to
    90%, as seen in **figure 3.49**. Click OK.

figure 3.49

*Adding the green channel image information to the weaker
red channel.*

3. The effect has also darkened down the areas
    by the model's camera right eye and shirt too
    much. Applying the changes to only the skin
    would yield a much better result. Select the
    Channel Mixer layer mask and press Cmd-
    I/Ctrl-I to invert it. The darkening effect will
    be concealed. Use soft-edged, white brush and
    paint over his cheek to reveal the toned-down
    facial highlights as shown in **figure 3.50**.

figure 3.50

*The layer mask limits the Channel Mixer adjustment layer
to only the color-sensitive facial area.*

Balancing Exposure and Fading

When working with older images, it may be hard
to say if the problem is one of a poor exposure or of
fading over time. Either way, images that are incon-
sistent, with lighter and darker areas which weren't
part of the original scene, need to be balanced out
before they can be cleaned up and restored. The
original image in **figure 3.51** was originally taken
with strong side lighting, which caused some flare
on the right side of the image. Additionally, over
the years the small print has faded to different
degrees from all edges. The corrected rendition in
figure 3.52 still needs some touch-up work, but
thankfully, the exposure is consistent.

figure 3.51

figure 3.52

⊕▷< **ch3_ursula.jpg**

To correct the multiple exposure and fading artifacts, you'll use two Levels adjustment layers and be introduced to the power of an Overlay-neutral layer to selectively balance tonal exposure.

1. To darken the lower right and upper right image corners, add a Levels adjustment layer and don't make any changes with the sliders. Click OK and change the layer blending mode to Multiply, which darkens the entire image. Invert the layer mask with Cmd-I/Ctrl-I to hide the darkening effect.

2. Tap D to reset the color picker to the default colors and make sure white is the foreground color. Select the Gradient tool and choose the Foreground to Transparent gradient from the Gradient presets, which in this case will be white to transparent.

3. Tap F to enter full screen mode. Start the gradient in the lower right hand corner and pull towards the center of the image, stopping at the woman's knee. Click on the upper right hand corner and drag to the edge of her head to create the image in progress seen in figure 3.53.

figure 3.53

Use gradients on the Level adjustment layer layer mask to lighten the image selectively. Option/Alt-clicking the layer mask displays the mask in the image window.

4. To lighten the dark upper left corner, create another Levels adjustment layer and change the blending mode to Screen. Once again, invert the layer mask (Cmd-I/Ctrl-I) to prevent the layer from affecting the image, use the Gradient tool with the same Foreground to Transparent preset and drag from the upper left to the center of the image to lighten the dark background and create the image in **figure 3.54**.

5. To refine the exposure even further, add a new layer by choosing Layer > New > Layer or Cmd-Shift-N/Ctrl-Shift-N. Select Overlay from the Mode menu. Select Fill with Overlay-neutral color (50% gray) as shown in **figure 3.55**.

figure 3.54

Using the Gradient tool on the layer mask creates a smooth transition.

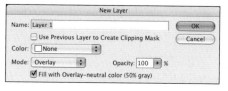

figure 3.55

The Overlay-neutral layer will be the dodging surface to lighten the image selectively.

6. On this new layer, painting with a brush that uses a tone darker than 50% gray will darken (burn in) the image, and painting with a lighter than 50% tone will lighten (dodge) the image. Set a white soft-edged brush to 10% opacity and paint over the dark shadows on the woman's face to draw attention to her expression as seen in **figure 3.56**.

figure 3.56

On a 50% gray layer set to Overlay blending mode, painting with black will darken and painting with white lightens.

The image blending modes are so effective to fix exposure problems that I use them almost every single day to improve images very quickly. The added ability to refine the tone with the Overlay-neutral layer is almost addictive—it's a very simple, yet effective method to lighten or darken images similar to dodging or burning in the traditional wet darkroom.

SHADOW/HIGHLIGHT TO THE RESCUE

The Shadow/Highlight command is a fantastic feature that uses image intelligence analysis to balance exposure. Image intelligence is based on how we see a scene. For example when we look at a person standing in front of a window, our eyes and visual systems balance the brightness so we can see the person. On the other hand a camera can only "see," and therefore capture, a silhouette of the person standing in front of the window. The Shadow/Highlight command does not just lighten or darken an image; it lightens or darkens pixels based on comparing, analyzing, and balancing the neighboring pixels in the image.

Use Shadow/Highlight to lighten shadows in an otherwise well-exposed image, in images that are silhouetted due to strong backlighting, to darken subjects that are washed out because they were too close to the camera flash, and make short order of contrasty images. In **figure 3.57** you see a photograph that I took in silhouette and **figure 3.58** shows how much detail that the Shadow/Highlight brought out.

> **Tip**
>
> The Shadow/Highlight feature is not an adjustment layer and must work on actual pixels. To avoid degrading the file, always duplicate the background layer before accessing the Shadow/Highlight command. This will give you the added flexibility of being able to use layer opacity and layer masking to fine-tune the corrections.

Selecting Image > Adjustments > Shadow/Highlight opens up with a simple interface set to fix images suffering from backlighting problems. Moving the Shadow slider to the right makes the shadows lighter and moving the Highlight slider to the right makes the highlights darker. In practically every image I've worked with, the default setting of 50% shadows is too strong and I usually start with a 20% correction for both shadows and highlights and then I adjust the sliders as needed.

In **figures 3.59** and **3.60** you see how effective a simple 35% shadow adjustment is to add a slight fill flash to the biker.

BEFORE

figure 3.57

AFTER

figure 3.58

figure 3.59

figure 3.60

ch3_Xbiker.jpg

1. Duplicate the Background layer.

2. Choose Image > Adjustments > Shadow/
   Highlight and adjust the shadow slider to
   open up the shadows on the biker's face and
   body. In this example I used a setting of 35%
   for the shadows and 0% for the highlights, as
   seen in figure 3.61.

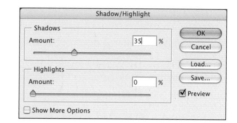

figure 3.61

*Using the Shadow/Highlights adjustment layer to open up
the image.*

Tip

To have Shadow/Highlight open with custom
settings:

1. Type in the desired settings, for example
   Shadows 20% and Highlights 20%.

2. Click Show More Options and in the lower
   left hand corner click Save as Defaults.

3. Click Show More Options to return to the
   smaller interface. Now every time you
   access Shadow/Highlight, 20% will be the
   starting point.

Clicking Show More Options (see figure 3.62)
offers a tremendous amount of control.

- Amount controls the range of tones in the
  shadows or highlights that are modified.
  Larger values include more tonal regions
  (such as adding the midtones). The tonal
  width requirements will vary from image to
  image and using values that are too high will
  add undesired halos around strong dark to
  light edges.

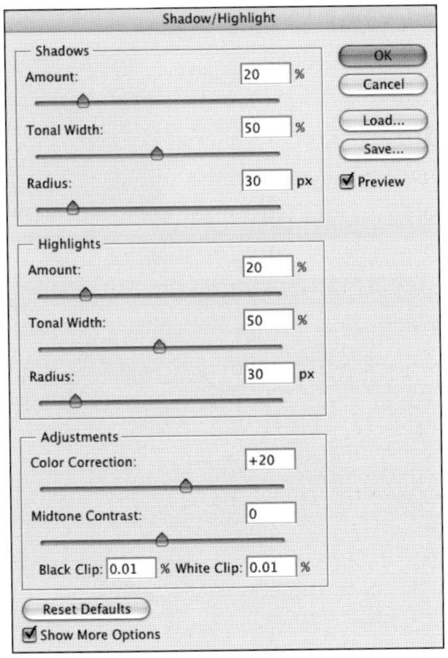

figure 3.62

The additional options allow for precise control and image improvements.

- Radius controls how large an area is taken into consideration when lightening or darkening with lower values, creating a more delicate effect and higher values a broader effect. If the Radius is too large, the adjustment tends to brighten (or darken) the whole image rather than brightening the specific tonal areas.

- Color Correction allows fine-tuning of the colors in regions of the image that have changed. For example, if you increase the Shadows Amount slider, you will bring out colors that were less visible and you may want these colors to be more or less vivid. In general, increasing values tends to produce more saturated colors and decreasing values produces less saturated colors. In a nutshell, I think of the Color Correction slider as being closer to a color saturation slider and by moving the slider to the left the impacted colors become less saturated.

- Brightness is active only when working with grayscale images (and replaces Color Correction in the Adjustments section). Moving the Brightness slider to the left or right darkens or lightens the image, respectively.

- Midtone Contrast adjusts the contrast in the midtones. Move the slider to the left to reduce the contrast and to the right to increase the contrast. Increasing the contrast darkens the shadows and lightens the highlights and vice versa for decreasing contrast.

- Black Clip and White Clip specify how much of the shadows and highlights will be clipped to no detail in the new extreme shadow (level 0) and highlight (level 255). Larger values produce an image with greater contrast. Be careful of setting the clipping values too large, as this will lead to reduced detail in the shadows or highlights as the intensity values get clipped and sent to pure black or white.

Whenever I face an image with a daunting exposure problem—be it extreme under-exposure, high contrast, backlighting, or even a very dark subject—I turn to Shadow/Highlight. A dark subject at night like the one in figure 3.63 is always difficult to photograph. In the following example, we will use the Shadow/Highlight command to separate the dark horse from the dark background that was out of the flash range (see figure 3.64).

🌐▷⊰ **ch3_headlesshorseman.jpg**

1. Remember that the Shadow/Highlight command is not an adjustment layer, so always duplicate the Background layer before starting.

2. Select Image > Adjustments > Shadow/Highlight. Our new default of 20% Shadows and 20% Highlights already reveals an image emerging from the shadows (figure 3.65), but we want to really make the horse and rider stand out from the background.

© Wayne Palmer

BEFORE

figure 3.63

AFTER

figure 3.64

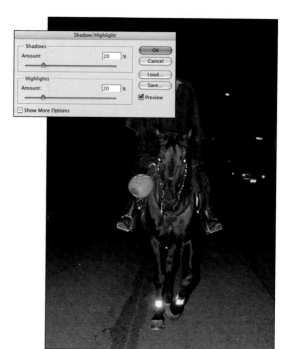

figure 3.65

Lightening the shadows helped separate the dark horse from the even darker background.

3. Click Show More Options to expand the dialog box. By sliding the Shadows Amount to 75% and the Shadows Tonal Width to 65% (see **figure 3.66**) the darker areas are lightening very nicely.

4. Although there aren't very many highlights in this image, moving the Highlights Amount slider all the way to the right makes the pumpkin the rider is carrying less bright.

5. By reducing the Color Correction from the default of +20 to 0, the black horse remains black and a slight increase of the Midtone Contrast adds a hint of sparkle that the late October night held, as seen in **figure 3.67**.

By understanding how to use the additional controls of Shadow/Highlight, we can rescue this digital image that might have otherwise fallen victim to the Delete button.

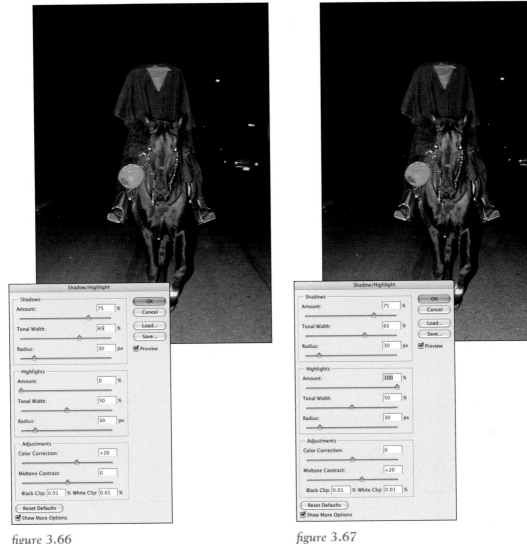

figure 3.66

Increasing the Shadow Amount and Tonal Width improves the image overall.

figure 3.67

Reducing the color correction to 0 allows the horse and the night to be black.

CLOSING THOUGHTS

All in all, it is always better to start with a well-exposed picture. However, for those times when the light meter is fooled, the batteries run out, or the ravages of time wreak havoc on a beloved photo, turn to these Photoshop techniques to do the image justice.

4

WORKING WITH COLOR

We are very sensitive to color, and our eyes are tremendous tools to see and compare an infinite variety of hues. The emotional and subliminal importance of color in our world cannot be denied. For retouchers, being sensitive to color values can make the difference between a so-so print and a print that looks as vibrant as the memories it represents.

The importance of color challenges us to work with our visual memory in combination with the best that Photoshop has to offer: Adjustment layers, the Info and Histogram palettes, painting and selection tools, and blending modes. In this chapter, you work with color images to learn

- Additive and subtractive color correction with image variations and color balance

- Global color correction with Levels and Curves

- Selective color correction and restoring color in historical photographs

- Correcting color temperature problems

- Matching, replacing, and changing color

Many of the tools and techniques discussed in Chapter 2, "Improving Tone and Contrast," and Chapter 3, "Exposure Correction," serve as the foundation for working with color. I highly recommend that you review those two chapters before diving into the wonderful world of color.

COLOR ESSENTIALS

There are two types of color in the world: additive and subtractive. In the additive world, a light source is needed to create color. When the primary colors (red, green, and blue) are combined, they create white, as shown in **figure 4.1**. Your monitor is an example of an additive color device.

In the subtractive world, color is determined by the absorption of light. When the secondary colors—cyan, magenta, and yellow—are combined, they create black-brown, as shown in **figure 4.2**. Printing ink on paper is an example of subtractive color. In creating inks for print, impurities in the pigments result in a muddy black-brown when cyan, magenta, and yellow are combined. To achieve rich shadows and pure blacks, black is added in the printing process, which also cuts down on the amount of the more expensive color inks used.

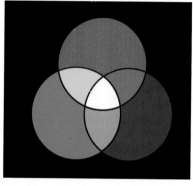

figure 4.1

The additive color space is formed by the red, green, and blue primary colors.

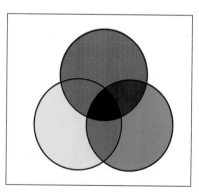

figure 4.2

The subtractive color space is formed by the cyan, yellow, and magenta primary colors.

Combining additive primaries yields the subtractive primaries, and combining the subtractive primaries creates the additive primaries. You can see this change where the circles overlap in each of the examples. For the retoucher, understanding this relationship of opposites can be very useful when identifying and correcting color problems. For example, if an image is too blue, you have two ways to approach the problem: either increase yellow (which is the opposite of blue) or decrease the blue in the image. Both yield the same result: an image with less blue.

In digital imaging, the four most prevalent color modes are RGB, CMYK, Lab, and HSB:

- RGB (for *red*, *green*, and *blue*) is the additive color space that monitors, scanners, and digital cameras use. The advantages to color correcting and retouching in RGB include: smaller file sizes; equal values of red, green, and blue will always result in neutral gray; and a larger RGB color space, like Adobe RGB (1998) or Pro Photo RGB, allows the file to be converted into multiple gamuts and repurposed for multiple final output destinations.

- CMYK (for *cyan*, *magenta*, *yellow*, and *black*) is the subtractive color mode. Many people (especially those with prepress or printing experience) prefer doing color correction and retouching in CMYK because they are more comfortable with CMYK color values, and editing colors that are in the same gamut as your printer can help avoid unhappy surprises after the ink hits the paper.

- Lab is a three-channel color mode in which the black-and-white L (lightness) channel information has been separated from the color information. The lightness (also called luminosity) component is measured from 0 to 100. The a channel carries green to red, the b channel carries blue to yellow information, and each can range from +127 to –128. Lab is a device-independent color space used by color management software and by Photoshop when converting RGB files to CMYK. Color correcting in Lab is a delicate task, because the slightest move on the a or b channels can result in a very strong color shift. On the other hand, Lab is a useful color mode when you are adjusting exposure or cleaning up color artifacts.

- HSB stands for *hue*, *saturation*, and *brightness*. Hue refers to the color, brightness refers to the amount of light in the color, and saturation determines the amount of color. You can take advantage of HSB to emphasize or deemphasize color in portrait retouching.

Each color mode has numerous pros and cons, many of which have been described in detail in *Real World Adobe Photoshop CS2* by David Blatner and Bruce Fraser (Peachpit, 2005) and *Photoshop Lab Color: The Canyon Conundrum and Other Adventures in the Most Powerful Colorspace* by Dan Margulis (Peachpit, 2005). Rather than reworking information that is well explained by these digital maestros, I will focus in this chapter on identifying and correcting color casts in antique and contemporary photographs.

Are All Color Casts Evil?

There are only two types of color casts in the world: those that enhance the image and those that detract. Positive color casts include the golden tones of the early morning or the cool blue cast of a snowy night (see **figure 4.3**), the warm color created by candlelight, and the color tones created when the photographer filters the lens or light to create or accentuate the color atmosphere. Undesired color casts occur if the photographer used the wrong color film or the wrong white balance setting, if the picture has faded over time (**figure 4.4**), or if an undesired color is being reflected into a photograph (as the green carpet is reflecting on the white statue in **figure 4.5**). I'm sure you've seen pictures taken in a stadium or office in which the color temperature of the light doesn't match the color balance of the film or the white balance on a digital camera made the wrong call. The orange, red, or green color casts introduced by using the wrong color film or not compensating for the light temperature with photographic filters are both what I would categorize as undesired.

figure 4.3

The blue cast adds to the cool mood of this image.

figure 4.4

Color prints fade over time.

figure 4.5

The green carpet has cast an undesired green tinge on the white statue.

Color Spaces

Photoshop uses independent Color Spaces, which are containers for your colors similar to imaginary boxes of crayons, which come in many different sizes and styles. The largest box of crayons could represent the total amount of colors visible to the eye, which is a range that cannot be displayed or printed. Different color spaces—smaller boxes of crayons or boxes that may contain a different mix of colors—have been developed to reflect the different environments in which color is visible or printable. Many designers prefer to use a smaller box of crayons like ColorMatch when the image is going to offset press because a CMYK press has a limited color gamut. Many photographers use Adobe RGB which is a larger color space that works well for inkjet printing or ProPhotoRGB which is ideal for working with 16-bit files from camera raw files. For additional information please refer to *Real World Color Management, 2nd edition* by Bruce Fraser, Chris Murphy, and Fred Bunting (Peachpit, 2004) and *Color Management for Photographers* by Andrew Rodney (Focal Press, 2005).

IDENTIFYING A COLOR CAST

The color correction process always starts by identifying the color cast—you have to know what the problem is before you can apply a solution. A color cast, also called a *shade* or *tinge*, is easier to identify in lighter or neutral image areas. For example, a white shirt or a gray sidewalk would be good places to look for a color cast. When evaluating an image for color, find a neutral reference: something that should be white, near-white, or gray. If it looks—for discussion's sake—slightly blue, then you know that the image has a blue cast. Interestingly enough, clearing up the color cast in the lighter and neutral areas usually takes care of most of the required color correction work throughout the entire image.

Tip

Place the Eyedropper over a light area and read the RGB values in the Info palette. Correctly balanced neutral colors have equal values of RGB while images with a color cast do not. Darker neutral areas have lower RGB values and lighter ones have higher RGB values.

The tools used to identify a color cast are your visual memory, the Info palette, the individual image channels, and practice. Color casts that are similar, such as blue and cyan or magenta and red, take a bit of practice to identify correctly. If you have a color cast in your highlights, nine times out of ten you'll have a color cast in the entire image. Just because color casts are harder to see in dark areas doesn't mean they're not there. Once you have identified the color cast, think globally and take care of the general problem first. Fortunately, correcting the big problem usually takes care of many of the smaller problems along the way.

UNDERSTANDING COLOR CORRECTION WITH IMAGE VARIATIONS

If all this talk about identifying color casts is making your head spin, don't worry. Photoshop Variations (Image > Adjustments > Variations) is a useful tool if you're just starting out or need a refresher on color correction. Variations is similar to the color ring-around chart that photographic printers have been using for years to see which way to move color when making a color print. The color-correction part of Variations shows you six pictures, each representing one of the primary colors opposite its counterpart (red to cyan, green to magenta, and blue to yellow), as shown in figure 4.6. For example, if you have an image with a blue color cast, clicking the yellow image would add yellow to remove the blue.

Notice how easy it is to see the color change in the more neutral areas, such as the white-walled tires and white panel on the car, while the saturated red of the car hides the color cast a bit.

Variations conveniently compares your Current Pick in three areas of the menu: against the original, against six possible variations of color change, and against a lighter or darker version.

Next to the OK and Cancel buttons are radio buttons you click to control which image area to affect: Shadows, Midtones, Highlights, or Saturation. When using Variations for color correction, I recommend you start with the midtones and then refine the highlights. The two problems with

Variations are that it does not work on 16-bit images and that it is not an adjustment layer, so your color correction is applied directly to the image pixels. To ensure that you don't alter original image data, always work either on a duplicate file or duplicate the Background layer.

The original image shown in figure 4.7 was taken indoors in with natural light coming from a window with a digital camera that was set to fluorescent light balance, turning the image blue. With a few clicks in Variations, the image is neutral and much more pleasing (see figure 4.8).

ch4_blueamanda.jpg

figure 4.6

Use the Variations dialog box to identify color casts and learn what the opposite color is used to neutralize color casts.

BEFORE

figure 4.7

AFTER

figure 4.8

© Wayne Palmer

1. Use the Eyedropper tool set to 3 by 3 pixels and the Info palette to measure an area in the image that should be neutral. Because you haven't seen this actual scene, how can you know what the real color is? Use your visual memory of a similar scene and it would be a safe guess that the emblem on the shirt or the sheets in the background could be white or at least a very light neutral color. Figure 4.9 shows the readout of 193 red, 214 green, 237 blue.

figure 4.9

Start by sampling an area you believe should be neutral and examining the color readout in the Info palette.

Tip

Variations is a visual perception adjustment tool. The Info palette will not show before/after comparisons while making adjustments, so don't be concerned if the Variations menu covers the entire work area of your monitor, including the Info palette.

The much higher blue readout, in relationship to the other colors, is a dead giveaway of a strong blue color cast, and the low red readout tells you that this image also has a cyan color cast. Properly adjusted, the RGB values will be within a few points of one another.

2. Duplicate the Background layer. This will protect the original pixels while you experiment with Variations.

3. Select Image > Adjustments > Variations and click the Midtones radio button. To see how Variations applies the principle of color opposites, move the strength slider under the Saturation radio button to the right as seen in figure 4.10.

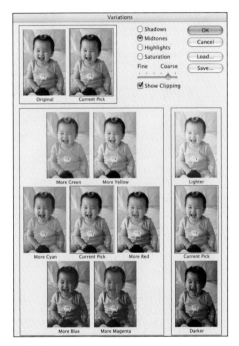

figure 4.10

The slider controls the amount of the Variations change.

4. To work subtly, move the strength slider to the left, one notch away from Fine to reduce the strength of each change. Click More Yellow to reduce the blue. To strengthen the effect, just click the same color image again. In this case, click More Yellow one more time plus click More Red to reduce the Cyan component to produce a favorable result as shown in figure 4.11.

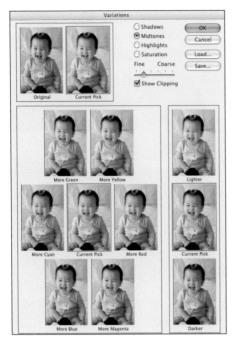

figure 4.11

Start your Variations color corrections with the midtones and work with a finer setting for subtler results.

5. Click OK and check the results with the Info palette as shown in **figure 4.12**, where the RGB readout is now 224, 224, 224, which is completely neutral.

figure 4.12

Check the neutral image areas with the Eyedropper tool and Info palette to double-check that the color cast has been removed.

Tips on Using Variations

- When using Variations, you can undo all changes by clicking the original image in the upper-left corner.

- The changes you make can be saved and reloaded later for other images.

- If you open Variations a second time, the last applied changes will automatically be put into effect upon entering the menu.

- Variations can be used for predictable results such as making a sepia tone, which is as simple as one click red, one click yellow, and one click less saturation.

Variations does not have a keyboard shortcut, so you may want to create one to expedite its use until you learn the power of the other color-corrections tools Photoshop has to offer.

Ron Hirsch, a retired engineer and reader of the first edition of this book, was generous enough to send me an empirical analysis of Image Variations versus Photoshop Color Balance, which explains how Image Variations results can be achieved with Color Balance. You can find this analysis as a PDF in the Chapter 4 section of www.digitalretouch.org.

🌐▷⫶ **ch4_variations.pdf**

MIMICKING THE COLOR DARKROOM WITH COLOR BALANCE

If you've ever done any photographic color printing, using Photoshop's Color Balance adjustment layers will seem familiar to you. Like Variations, it also works on the principle of increasing or decreasing opposite colors to color balance an image.

Figure 4.13 shows a photo of one of my students and me that was taken in the middle of the summer on a very cloudy day. Even though the lighting had a soft, diffused effect, the camera's internal white balance, which was set for tungsten lighting, made us look much too blue.

Figure 4.14 shows the same image after I applied a Color Balance adjustment layer and a Hue/Saturation adjustment layer to remove the undesirable tint, and lastly a little fill flash technique as described in the previous chapter. Our skin tones are now less blue and have more appealing tone. As we work through this example, we will concentrate on the essential—the skin tones—and then tackle the details.

figure 4.13

figure 4.14

⊕▷✕ **ch4_Katrin&friend.jpg**

1. Check the image with the Eyedropper tool and the Info palette. Use the Color Sampler tool to place samplers on the skin tones, my silver blouse, and the concrete on the building in the background. Notice that the sampled points on the concrete and blouse, which should be neutral, have a strong blue cast, as indicated in **figure 4.15**.

2. Add a Color Balance adjustment layer.

3. By default, midtones is active and luminosity is checked—both of which are useful defaults to start the color correction process. To decrease the blue, move the yellow-blue slider to the left to -42 (see **figure 4.16**). A blue color cast can be similar to a cyan color cast, so adding 7 points of red to warm up the skin tones a touch is a good idea. Click OK.

figure 4.15

Two color samplers reveal a strong blue color cast.

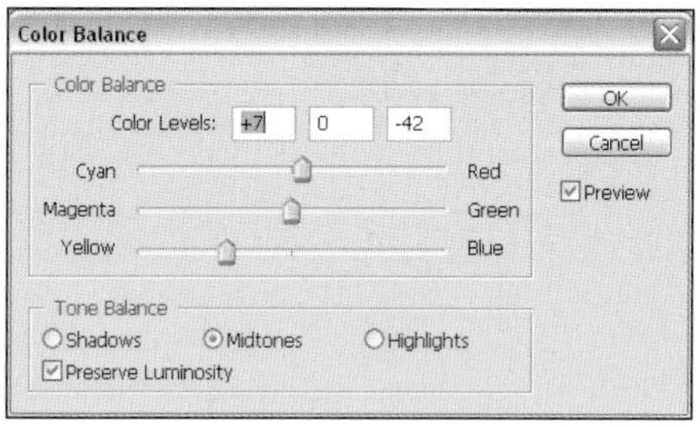

figure 4.16

Work on the image midtones to remove the blue color cast. Often you will need to move more than one of the sliders to make your correction.

> ✒ **N o t e**
>
> Red and magenta color casts can look very similar, as can blue and cyan, and green and yellow, and working on the similar color of the color cast can help clear up color problems. In this example, adding yellow reduced the blue and the addition of red removed the slight traces of cyan.

4. The Color Balance adjustment layer has removed the color cast from the skin tones but the concrete wall that needs to be closer to neutral still has a slight bluish tint. Add a Hue/Saturation adjustment layer. From the Edit drop-down menu, choose Blues. Select the Eyedropper tool and click on the concrete wall. You will see the indicators in the

color spectrum gradient at the bottom of the Hue/Saturation dialog box reflect the color you chose. Holding down the Shift key and dragging across similar colors on the wall will expand the range of your selection.

5. Move the saturation slider all the way to the left and the tint will disappear from the wall. Notice in **figure 4.17** that the readout in the Info palette shows the wall to now be neutral.

figure 4.17

Targeting the blue tinge on the wall and desaturating it by using a Hue/Saturation adjustment layer gets rid of the remaining blue cast.

6. As a final touch, put a little digital fill flash into the image to lighten up the shadows on the faces. Select Layer > New > Layer and choose Overlay from the Mode option and check Fill with Overlay-neutral color (50% gray). Use a soft-edged, white paintbrush with 20% opacity to lighten up the faces by painting over them. If the effect is too strong, lower the layer opacity as shown in **figure 4.18**.

figure 4.18

Painting on an Overlay-neutral layer with white effectively lightens the shadows.

GLOBAL COLOR CORRECTION

As I'm sure you know, Photoshop offers more than one way of reaching the same result. Some people don't like this and believe that their way is the only way. Puh-leeze! Color correction is an art form that relies on your perception, experience, and interpretation of the image. With the following exercises, we'll use Levels and Curves to rescue some pretty sad photos from color-cast fates worse than death. But remember, there is no right or wrong answer when you are correcting color; when working on your own images, experiment to find what works for you.

Using Auto Color Correction

Since version 7, Photoshop has had a much-improved Auto Color Correction function—one that you can control to achieve some remarkable results. I am usually the first one to shy away from anything with the words *auto* or *magic* in its name. However, Auto Color Correction offers a number of controls with which you can get into the color-balance ballpark quickly and easily—especially when working with older faded images and consumer level digital camera files. Once you understand how Auto Color Correction works, it can save you a lot of time.

N o t e

I am not referring to the Auto Levels, Auto Contrast, or Auto Color menu commands in the Image > Adjustments menu. I don't recommend those commands at all because you have no control over the values Photoshop uses to calculate the changes.

Both the Levels and Curves dialog boxes have an Auto button and clicking it will perform the same default corrections, regardless of where you access it. Because the Levels dialog box is smaller, I use this one because I can see more of my image and get identical results. Clicking Options brings up the Auto Color Correction Options interface (see **figure 4.19**). It is here that you can cycle through the types of corrections or influence which values Auto Color references.

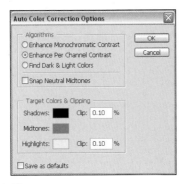

figure 4.19

The Auto Color Correction options can be set from either the Levels or the Curves dialog box.

The Auto Color Correction Options interface has six settings that enable you to control how the color is affected:

- Enhance Monochromatic Contrast: Photoshop clips all color channels at once, using identical values for each, making shadows darker and light areas brighter. This is the same as Image > Adjustments > Auto Contrast, or moving the shadow and highlight slider in Levels to where image information begins on the RGB or CYMK composite histogram.

- Enhance Per Channel Contrast: Photoshop will adjust each channel separately. This is identical to moving the shadow and highlight sliders of the individual image channels to where the image information starts. This is how Image > Adjustments > Auto Levels works.

- Find Dark & Light Colors: Photoshop uses the lightest and darkest pixels in an image for the Shadow and Highlight values. This is the same as Image > Adjustments > Auto Color and may or may not introduce unwanted color casts.

- Snap Neutral Midtones: With this selected, Photoshop looks for a nearly neutral color in your image and then forces it to gray. Image > Adjustments > Auto Color uses this option.

- Target Colors & Clipping: Enter values here to tell Photoshop the percentage of tones to ignore. For example, entering 0.02% for both Shadows and Highlights will skip the brightest and darkest 0.02% pixels before starting calculations. Adobe admits that the default value of 0.1% is too high for the quality being produced by today's cameras and scanners. And Bruce Fraser recommends that you start at 0.00%, stating that "the change for 0 to 0.01% is bigger than you might expect." If you want calculations to be based on non-neutral colors, clicking a color swatch will open the Color Picker, where you can choose any color as the Shadow, Midtone, or Highlight target.

- Save as Defaults: Clicking this tells Photoshop that these are the settings you want to use anytime you click the Auto button in Levels or Curves. If you select this option, the Clipping value you enter will also be the new defaults for the Auto Levels, Auto Contrast, and Auto Color menu commands.

The Beauty is in the Auto Details

Now that Adobe has added the ability to control the Auto Color Correction, I find myself adding a Levels or Curves adjustment layer and clicking through the options to see what is going to happen. Many times the results are very good—if I pay attention to the details.

To get the best results from Auto Color, start by checking Find Dark & Light Colors and Snap Neutral Midtones and making sure that Save as defaults is checked. Don't worry if this ruins your image for now. By setting these as defaults, you're ensuring that Photoshop is starting with Auto Color when you click Auto in either Levels or Curves. Click OK. If making this change ruined your image, just choose Edit > Undo and the change to the image will be reversed, but the settings will be remembered.

To continue controlling how Auto Color works, reopen the interface to adjust the Target Colors & Clipping values, which are both too high at .10% and will result in blocked-up shadows and blown out highlights. Start by reducing the shadow value to 0 and using the up arrow on your keyboard to go up .01% at a time. Keep an eye on the image shadow and highlights; values lower than the default will create pleasant, open shadows with information and printable highlights that aren't pure paper white.

The midtone default of a perfectly neutral gray may or may not be the best choice for your images. In fact, the perfect neutral may be visually too cold. You can adjust the midtone, and best of all, as with the previous changed settings, the change is interactive.

In the image in **figure 4.20**, the dog is a bit dark and the white fur has a distinctive blue/cyan tint to it from an improper white balance. Correcting the midtones colors makes the dog look much more natural (**figure 4.21**).

BEFORE

© Joshua Withers

figure 4.20

AFTER

figure 4.21

figure 4.22

Placing a sample on an area that should be white.

 ch4_bluedog.jpg

1. Place a color sampler on the dog's white hair. Zoom in to whisker level to ensure you pick white, as shown in **figure 4.22**.

Tip

For consistent color results when shooting under a constant light source with a digital camera, manually select the white balance setting to avoid white balance drift from shot to shot.

2. Add a Levels adjustment layer and click Options, which brings up the default settings described previously. The image lightens, making the color cast more noticeable.

3. To reduce the blue/cyan cast, be sure the Snap Neutral Midtones box is selected, and click the midtone color swatch in the Target Colors & Clipping box, which opens the Color Picker. Since the cyan cast is the most obvious, click the C% box of the CMYK readouts. On your keyboard, use the down arrow key to lower the value of the cyan. With each click, you will see the cyan cast being reduced. Stop at 34% and you will notice that the tint has been reduced significantly.

4. Click the B box of the RGB readouts and click the down arrow until you reach 149. With the eyedropper, measure the white area on top of the dog's head. You will get a very neutral reading (**figure 4.23**).

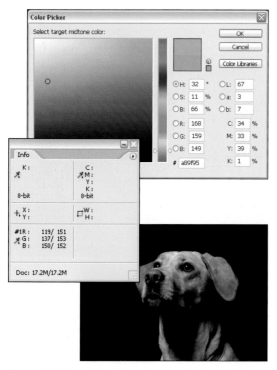

figure 4.23

Lowering the blue and cyan values neutralizes the color cast.

Targeting Auto Color Corrections

Since Auto Color Correction evaluates the entire image it may or not always work as expected. Extraneous white borders or torn edges, like those in **figure 4.24** can undermine its accuracy. To avoid unexpected results either crop the file before using Auto Color or as shown here use a temporary mask to control where Auto Color computes the corrections. Then you'll get great results like **figure 4.25**.

ch4_couchcouple.jpg

1. Use the Marquee tool to select the important area of the image. In this example, it would be the faces of the couple as shown in **figure 4.26**.

2. Add a Levels adjustment layer, which will automatically include a mask.

figure 4.24

figure 4.25

figure 4.26

Select the most important part of the image.

3. Click on the Options button and cycle through the three choices. As seen in figure 4.27 the Enhance Per Channel Contrast with Snap Neutral Midtones creates the best results.

4. To apply the correction to the entire image, either drag the mask to the trash can icon at the bottom of the Layers palette or shift click on the mask to turn it off, as in figure 4.28.

figure 4.27

The mask focuses the correction on essential information.

figure 4.28

Turn off the mask to apply the correction to the whole image.

Color Correction with Levels Eyedroppers

Working with the Levels or Curves eyedroppers to define the neutral areas of white, gray, or black is a very effective method to remove the most color casts. Figure 4.29 shows the typical problems when photographing snow—the bright snow tricked the camera's exposure into recording a darker, bluer scene. With a few clicks in Levels, you can bring back the daylight as seen in figure 4.30.

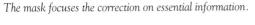 **ch4_bluesnowhouse.jpg**

figure 4.29

figure 4.30

1. The first step is to identify the color cast. If you're working with a well-calibrated monitor and have a good sense for color, you'll see that the snow is too blue. If you're not sure about color or your monitor, use the Info palette. Set your Eyedropper tool to Sample Size 3 × 3 Average on the options bar, and look for something you know should or could be neutral. This image has large expanses of white, but every image will be different. When you position the Eyedropper over a neutral color,

the Info palette will reveal the color cast in the RGB readouts (see **figure 4.31**). In the shadowed foreground the Info palette reports 174 red, 182 green, 206 blue. In this case, that higher blue value where it should be fairly neutral white signifies that the image has a strong blue cast.

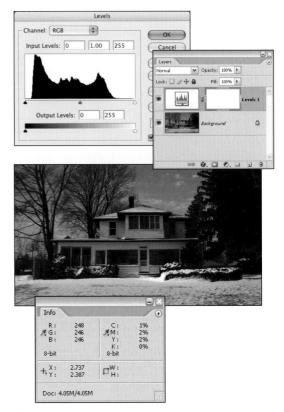

figure 4.31

The RGB values in the Info palette identify the color cast.

2. Add a Levels adjustment layer and select the white target eyedropper. Click the bright area of snow in front of the doorway to define a new white point. In the Info palette, note that the values of red, green, and blue are almost equal, proving that the color cast has been removed, as shown in **figure 4.32**. You should experiment to find the best neutral points and try as many areas as you like. If you don't like a change, use Cmd-Z/Ctrl-Z to undo the last change or return the image to the original state by Option/Alt-clicking the reset button.

Tip

Option/Alt-drag the highlight slider to the left, as you see in **figure 4.33**. Photoshop will reveal where the true highlight is. This technique works for the shadow point as well—just drag the shadow slider to the right.

figure 4.32

Using the Levels white eyedropper to define a new white point improves overall color and contrast.

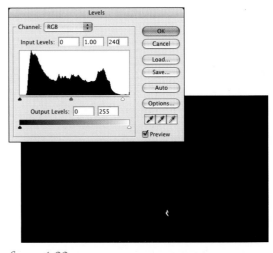

figure 4.33

Finding the highlight point of an image.

3. Even though the majority of the color cast is gone and the image is brightened, it still has a cool appearance. Select the Set Gray Point eyedropper and click the gray fencepost, on the left side of the image, as shown in **figure 4.34**. If your images don't contain such a convenient gray point, a white building in the shade should be gray. In this image, the area around the second floor window is also a good location to find a neutral midpoint.

figure 4.34

Using the Levels gray eyedropper to define a neutral midpoint removes even more of the color cast.

 Tip

Don't forget you can still move around in your image while the Levels dialog box is open. Cmd-"+"/Ctrl-"+" will zoom in and Cmd-"–"/Ctrl-"–" will zoom out. The scroll bars also function when the dialog box is open. If you are working in standard screen mode, Cmd-Option-"+"/Ctrl-Alt-"+" or Cmd-Option-"–"/Ctrl-Alt-"–" will resize the window.

4. On many images, correcting for the white point and midtone may be enough. However, on this image, the histogram shows the black slider to be a little to the left of the darkest information. Sliding the black slider to where the histogram starts improve contrast perfectly (see **figure 4.35**).

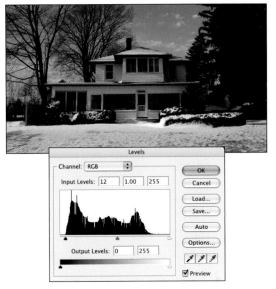

figure 4.35

Moving the shadow point slider to the beginning of the histogram defines a deep rich black, giving the image a strong visual foundation.

5. After defining the white and black points, take a second look at the image. If the image looks too dark or too light, use the midtone slider to lighten (drag to the left) or darken (drag to the right).

The Value of Neutral

The gray point eyedropper in Levels and Curves is a very powerful tool, which I find especially useful when color correcting older images that have faded and color shifted over time as seen in **figure 4.36**. By using the grey eyedropper to remap the neutral areas the image popped into place as seen in **figure 4.37**.

⊕▷〈 **ch4_vacation.jpg**

Only a handful of people actually know what the colors were in this scene, but almost everyone reading this text some sense of what they should be, based on their own memories of scenes similar to this. Take a moment to imagine what could be neutral—the asphalt or silver light pole on the right would be very safe guesses to work with to remove the color cast.

BEFORE

figure 4.36

AFTER

figure 4.37

1. Add a Levels adjustment layer and click the asphalt with the gray point eyedropper (figure 4.38). At this point you can try clicking on other neutral areas, such as the coat the girl is holding or other areas of the asphalt.

2. Move the shadow and highlight sliders to where the primary information edges of the histogram starts as seen in **figure 4.39**. As you can see, neutral remains neutral and moving the sliders yields an image with the correct tonality.

figure 4.38

Using the gray point eyedropper to define a true neutral.

figure 4.39

Remapping the tonality with the shadow and highlight sliders.

I am often asked how I know when to use white, gray, or black eyedroppers when using Levels or Curves. I start with the gray eyedropper when removing stubborn color casts or the white eye-dropper when I know that a specific area should be white. Correcting the lighter areas often makes the darker areas fall into place. Examining and color correcting a lot of images will improve your skills and accelerate the color correction process.

Color Correction with the Photo Filter

There are times a color cast can be so far off you would just like to go as far away as possible from the offending color. Here's a technique to do just that using a Photo Filter adjustment layer and reversing the Lab color readouts. With just a few steps, the faded, off colored image in figure 4.40 was brought back to life in figure 4.41.

1. I added a Photo Filter adjustment layer. By default, the Warming Filter (85) will be displayed. Move the density slider to 100% and be sure the Preserve Luminosity box is checked. The image will temporarily look worse, but follow along to learn this very useful technique (figure 4.42).

2. Click the color swatch in the dialog box to open the Color Picker and sample one of the problem colors in the image. In this example I choose a midtone from the horse's neck (figure 4.43).

© Knoll Family Archive

BEFORE

figure 4.40

AFTER

figure 4.41

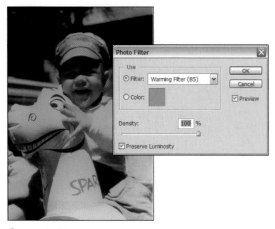

figure 4.42

Using a Photo Filter adjustment layer will temporarily make the image look worse.

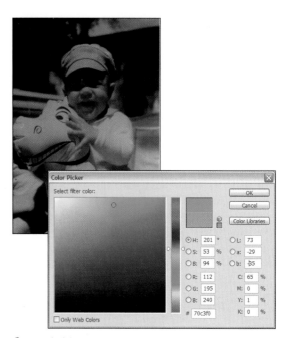

figure 4.44

Inverting the Lab color values reverses the color shift.

figure 4.43

Select the offending color from a light midtone.

3. In the Lab readouts, invert the values for both a and b by adding or deleting minus signs. This will mathematically exchange the offending color for the exact opposite as seen in **figure 4.44**.

4. I added a Levels adjustment layer and adjusted the brightness values to lighten the shadows in the boy's face, as seen in figure **4.45**.

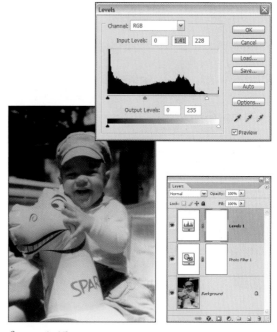

figure 4.45

The Levels adjustment layer lightens the shadows.

Transferring Color Corrections

Often, pictures taken at the same time will share the same problems. Whether it was bad lighting, bad processing, bad storage, or simply bad luck, you can save time and effort by fixing one, then applying that same adjustment to the rest.

The images in figure 4.46 were all taken on the same vacation on a single roll of film, and all suffer from the same amount of fading. By using a Levels adjustment layer on one, then transferring that adjustment layer to the others, I was able to fix all three, as seen in figure 4.47, without three times the work.

🌐▷❊ **ch4_hiking1.jpg**

🌐▷❊ **ch4_hiking2.jpg**

🌐▷❊ **ch4_hiking3.jpg**

figure 4.46

figure 4.47

1. Open all three images and start with the one that contains the broadest range of tones and colors that are in the other images. In this example, I started with the image with the vista that contains snow, sky, and (supposedly) gray rock. Add a Levels adjustment layer and use the gray point eyedropper to click on the rock as seen in **figure 4.48**.

figure 4.48

Defining neutral with the Gray Point eyedropper.

figure 4.49

Adjusting the shadow and highlight point to correct tonal values.

2. Move the shadow and highlight sliders to the start of the histogram (**figure 4.49**) to create a stronger black point and a more accurate highlight. Click OK.

3. Use the Move tool to drag the Levels adjustment layer from the corrected image onto the second and third images (**figure 4.50**).

4. Double click the Levels icon and refine the correction by moving the respective shadow and highlight sliders to the start of the histogram to create the final images.

figure 4.50

Dragging the correction to a new image.

Subtle Color and Exposure Improvement with Curves and Hue/Saturation

Not all images have overwhelming or obvious color casts. In fact, some images require a delicate touch to remove the color cast and adjust exposure. In this example, the photograph is off just a bit—meaning that it is only slightly too dark and red (see **figure 4.51**) In this example, I set new black, white, and gray points and improved the exposure with a Curves adjustment layer, and then fine-tuned the overall saturation with a Hue/Saturation adjustment layer. These changes, shown in **figure**

4.52, enable you to appreciate the beauty of the young woman.

 ch4_flowergirl.jpg

1. Add a Curves adjustment layer. Use the white eyedropper to set the wall just above her flower to white and the gray eyedropper to set the wall in the upper left as neutral gray (see **figure 4.53**).

BEFORE

figure 4.51

© Phil Pool, Omni Photography

AFTER

figure 4.52

figure 4.54

Adjust the curve further to lighten the image.

figure 4.53

Setting new white and gray points using the Curves eyedroppers removes the color cast.

2. The color cast has been reduced, but the image is a bit dark. Boost the shadows and midtones by dragging the center of the curve upward to lighten the image (see **figure 4.54**). Be careful to monitor the highlights on the girl's skin and flower in the Info palette so they are not forced to pure white.

3. Not all portraits require the following step, but in this instance her tanned arms are over-saturated and visually distracting. To reduce the saturation, add a Hue/Saturation adjustment layer and decrease the Master saturation by –25, as seen in **figure 4.55**.

figure 4.55

Decreasing the saturation reduces the visual heaviness.

4. Using the Gradient tool with the preset Black, White, draw a gradient on the Hue/Saturation layer mask to shield the face from the desaturation, as shown in **figure 4.56**.

figure 4.56

Taking advantage of the layer mask to control where the change takes place.

THE NUMBERS DON'T LIE

You're tired, you had a fight with the dog, the kids played with the monitor dials, and you're just not sure what the original image really looked like. Many factors, including your mood, age, gender, and the second drink last night, can influence your color vision. So what are you supposed to do if the files are piling up and you have to finish them before going home tonight? When in doubt, do

your color correction by the numbers to balance images with a mathematician's precision.

Working by the numbers entails monitoring the values in the shadows, midtones, highlights, and skin tones while you adjust individual color channels with Levels or Curves. When the highlight, midtone, and shadow RGB values are equal, your color-cast problems will disappear. Working with skin tones (also called flesh tones) takes a bit more interpretation because people's skin varies with age, race, and sun exposure. (This is addressed in a later section, "Balancing Skin Tones with Curves.")

Tip

Here are some specifics for color correcting by the numbers with RGB files:

- To balance highlights: Use the highest value in the Info palette as the target and match the lower values to the higher.

- To balance midtones: To find neutral, add up the three midtones values and divide by three. Match all three midtones values to the average.

- To balance shadows: Use the lowest value as the target (as read in the Info palette) and match the higher values to the lower.

Balancing Neutral Tones with Levels

Color correction by the numbers always begins by identifying reference points. Look for a highlight, a neutral midtone, and a shadow point to reference. In the following example seen in **figure 4.57**, I used the page of the book for the highlight reference point, a stone in the floor as the midtone reference, and the shirt as a dark reference point. After a color correction, the image looks very natural, as shown in **figure 4.58**.

ch4_templewall.jpg

BEFORE

figure 4.57

AFTER

figure 4.58

1. Add color samplers to the highlight (book page), the midtone (stone floor), and the shadow (shirt), as shown in **figure 4.59**.

2. Add a Levels adjustment layer. To eliminate the color cast in the highlights, the three RGB values should be made equal by matching the two lower values to the highest value. In this example, the 245 readout of the blue channel is the highest value and will be the target number to match.

figure 4.59

The #1 color sampler is measuring the image highlights. The lower red and green values reveal the color cast.

3. In the Levels dialog box, select the channel with the lowest highlight value, the red channel, and lower the highlight value (the field farthest to the right) by pressing the down arrow key until in the Info palette, the red value matches the blue target value of 245 (see **figure 4.60**). This does not change the Input level in the Levels dialog box to 245, (meaning you cannot simply type in 245), but rather adjusts the Input Level until the number for the red channel in the Info palette reads 245.

4. Select the green channel and place the cursor in the highlight field. Tap the down arrow until the green value in the Info palette also matches the target value of 245, as shown in **figure 4.61**. Again, be sure to watch the numbers in the Info palette and match the two lower values to the highest value.

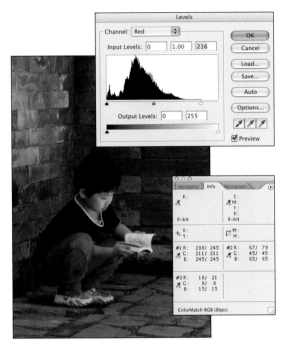

figure 4.60

Decrease the red channel highlight value to balance the highlights.

figure 4.61

Decrease the green channel's highlight value to balance the highlights.

Tip

Tapping the down arrow key changes the color values by one point; press shift to change the values 10 points per arrow tap.

5. When balancing midtones (marked by color sampler #2), use the average of the three values as your target. In this example, 67 + 45 + 65 = 177 divided by 3 determines the target value of 59. Select the red channel and click the Input Levels midtone box (in the center), and use the arrow keys to lower the red midtone to match the target of 59 in the Info palette. Repeat this process on the green and blue channels to match the target of 59 as seen in **figure 4.62**.

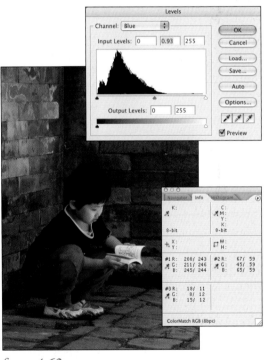

figure 4.62

Neutralizing the midtones also neutralizes the shadows in this example.

After adjusting the highlights and then moving on to the midtones or shadows, you may notice that the highlight values change again. This may happen because Photoshop is referencing the color settings in the Color Preferences and is adjusting the highlight to reflect your color settings. If the highlights are within one or two points of each other, the print will be neutral. When I use this technique, I place more value on the highlights than on the shadows.

You may be wondering why I just didn't use a Levels or Curves adjustment layer and click the page of the book with the white eyedropper. Doing that would have forced the page to a pure white, causing detail loss and a harsh brightness in the child's cheeks.

Balancing Skin Tones with Curves

Most of the recognized color values for reproducing skin tones are based on prepress experience and are therefore expressed in CMYK values. The graphic in **figure 4.63** shows that at one end of the spectrum the skin of a light baby has equal amounts of yellow and magenta without any cyan or black. Moving to the other end, as people mature, the amount of yellow increases in relationship to the magenta. The tanner or darker they are, the higher the amount of cyan ink is. The far end of the spectrum represents people of African descent with the additional black ink needed to accurately represent darker skin.

To the many readers involved with restoration who work in RGB, use photo printers, and do not have contact with the prepress industry: Take heart, you do not have to convert your files to CMYK to take advantage of CMYK readout values. Simply change the second readout of your Info palette to CMYK. Then, while working in RGB, you have a simultaneous readout in CMYK. If you have a color value that is outside the range of CMYK, an exclamation point will appear next to the value.

Here are some specifics for color correcting by the numbers on skin tones in CMYK files:

- In light-skinned babies and young people, yellow and magenta are equal.

- In adults, yellow is one-fifth to one-third greater than magenta.

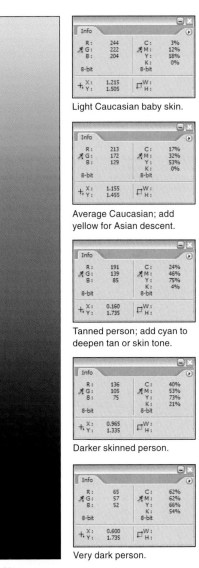

Light Caucasian baby skin.

Average Caucasian; add yellow for Asian descent.

Tanned person; add cyan to deepen tan or skin tone.

Darker skinned person.

Very dark person.

figure 4.63

CMYK *representation of skin tones is shown here.*

- Cyan is around one-fifth to one-third lower than magenta and makes people look darker-complected.

- Only people with very dark skin should have noticeable amounts of black ink in their skin tones.

- Find the cyan value; magenta should be double that and yellow should be around one-fifth to one-third higher than magenta (20c 40m 50y).

As Dan Margulis explained in the online ColorTheory discussion group, "Persons of Hispanic or Asian ancestries tend to share approximately the same range, which is roughly the same as the dark half of the Caucasian population. Persons in these ethnic groups always have significantly more yellow than magenta, normally 10 to 15 points. Cyan plus black tends to be one-quarter to one-third of the magenta value, occasionally higher in the case of unusually dark or very tan skin.

"The ethnicity loosely known as black or African-American has a much wider range of possibilities than any other. Cyan is usually at least one-third of the magenta value but there is no upper limit and there may also be significant black ink. In the case of someone with light ('coffee-colored') skin, the yellow is significantly higher than the magenta. However, unlike other ethnicities, as the skin tone gets darker, the variation between magenta and yellow decreases, so that in the case of a very dark-skinned person, the values would be almost equal."

When color correcting skin tones in RGB, keep the following in mind:

- Red is the opposite of cyan, and it will be the highest color component.

- Green is the opposite of magenta, and it will be one-fifth to one-quarter lower than red.

- Blue is the opposite of yellow, and it will be the lowest value—anywhere from one-third to one-half the value of the red values.

- The lighter-skinned the person is, the closer to equal these RGB values will be, with red being slightly higher.

- The darker-skinned the person is, the higher the blue values will be.

Color correction in RGB depends on the Photoshop color space in which you are working. If you use the wrong working space, the numbers may look awful even though they should be correct. I personally have had fewer problems with skin tones when using ColorMatch RGB because it has a narrower color gamut and is less saturated.

T i p

These tips will help you when working with portrait color correction and retouching:

- When correcting in RGB, set the Info palette's second readout to CMYK and watch the relationships between the two color modes.

- To get an overall feel for the skin tones of a person, measure an average medium value on the person's face. Avoid dark shadows and extreme highlights.

- A woman's makeup can distort the readout. Try to avoid areas that have a lot of makeup, such as cheeks, lips, and eyes.

- Collect patches of various skin tones from the images you work on, or refer to the large selection on the Web. Select a color corrected patch of skin, run the Gaussian Blur on it to destroy any vestige of film grain, copy it, and create a file with various skin tone swatches as seen in **figure 4.64**. Refer to these skin colors when color correcting and during advanced portrait-retouching sessions.

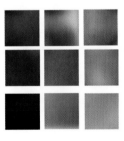

figure 4.64

A collection of blurred skin samples can be used as a reference for color correction.

In **figure 4.65**, the original picture suffers from a color problem, but I'm not even sure what the problem is. In fact, there are many times when I can't seem to identify the problem, which is exactly when I rely on the Info palette and the color correction by the numbers technique to create a pleasing image (see **figure 4.66**).

ch4_fashionwoman.jpg

BEFORE

figure 4.65

AFTER

figure 4.66

1. Start by selecting the Color Sampler tool and adding three color samplers to the image: one on the lighter part of the wall in the upper left corner, and two on the skin (one on the cheek and one on the neck). There is rarely makeup on the neck, which makes it an ideal place to sample a realistic color.

2. Add a Curves adjustment layer and click color sampler #1 with the white target eyedropper to define a neutral value and remove most of the color cast as shown in **figure 4.67**.

figure 4.67

Clicking the background with the white eyedropper in Curves neutralizes the image.

3. Study her skin tones and the Info palette. Her skin contains too much cyan and is too yellow. Red is the opposite of cyan, so activate the red channel in Curves and Cmd/Ctrl-click on her forehead. Use the up arrow key to add red to the curve, which subtracts cyan. As you can see in **figure 4.62**, locking down the midtone by clicking on the grid intersection insures that the color correction does not affect the shadow areas.

figure 4.68

Adjusting the red channel removes cyan.

4. Go to the green channel and lower the green component to balance the magenta and yellow readouts in the Info palette (see **figure 4.69**).

5. As is often the case, removing the color cast shows that the image is still a bit too dark. Return to the composite channel and open the midtones by pulling up slightly as seen in figure 4.70.

figure 4.69

Adjusting the green channel balances the magenta and yellow.

figure 4.70

Improving final exposure.

T i p

While in the Curves dialog box, Cmd/Ctrl-click the area you want to change to add a handle to the curve that you can manipulate with the mouse or the arrow keys. Pressing Ctrl-Tab on both platforms will move from point to point on the curve.

SELECTIVE COLOR CORRECTION

Until now, you've worked on global color correction, but an image can have different problems in different areas. Sometimes one part of the image will be fine and another area is way off color. Differing color casts can occur due to poor storage conditions, mixed lighting when the photo was originally taken, or misprocessing. Always start with the global color correction, and then select the problem areas that remain and apply local color correction.

Targeting the Problem Color

At first glance, I thought this portrait of the bride (**figure 4.71**) would be child's play to color correct; just add either a Curves or Levels adjustment layer, use the gray balance Eyedropper tool to click the neutral background and I'd be done. But I had no such luck and quickly learned that I needed to work selectively to remove the blue to achieve a balanced image, as shown in **figure 4.72**.

 ch4_bluebride.jpg

figure 4.71

figure 4.72

In figure 4.65, the color cast is rather subtle, but the higher blue readout in the Info palette (**figure 4.73**) reveals that the neutral tone of the studio background does have a cast. Another way to see color casts is to look at the individual grayscale channels. Because the studio background is supposed to be a light neutral gray, all three color channels should have the same density. As you can see in **figure 4.74** the red and green channels are almost the same readout with 228 and 224 but the blue channel is brighter at 238. Wherever the channel is lighter, more light has come through, creating a color cast.

figure 4.73

The Info palette reveals a subtle blue color cast.

Red

Green

Blue

figure 4.74

If the background is truly neutral it should look the same in each channel. Seeing a brightness difference in one of the channels would indicate a color cast.

Add a Hue/Saturation adjustment layer. In the Edit list, drop down to the offending color, which in this image is blue. Choose the saturation slider and slide it to the left, which decreases the saturation of the blue as shown in **figure 4.75**.

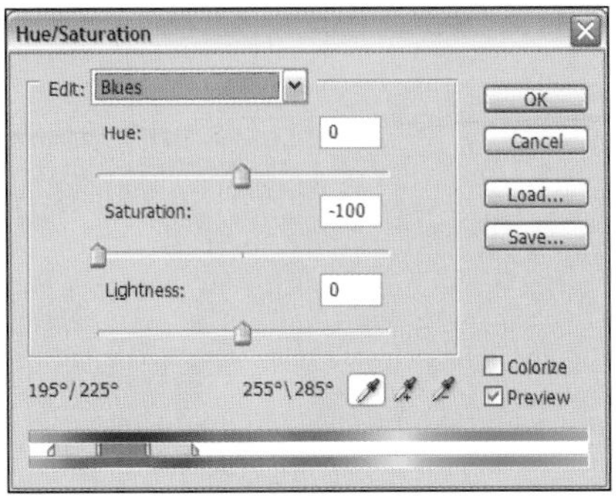

figure 4.75

Move the saturation slider to the left to remove the blue.

Correcting Multiple Color Issues

There are many times when you have to take pictures in mixed lighting situations—such as an office with fluorescent ceiling lights while the windows are letting in daylight or, as shown in **figure 4.76**, a family group shot where the majority of the space is lit with flash but the background is a combination outdoor and tungsten light. The flash was not up to full charge and slightly underexposed the subject while the camera's white balance also gave them a blue cast.

Photographs with mixed lighting are confusing because our eyes naturally neutralize color temperature without us being aware of it. To correct for the mixed lighting, a combination of Photo Filter layers with adjustment masks worked selectively to create the image in **figure 4.77**.

(globe icon) ℣≒ **ch4_mixedlighting.jpg**

1. Add a Levels adjustment layer and use the white eyedropper on the sugar packets in the foreground. The people now look better, but the background lighting is too yellow and even more distracting as shown in **figure 4.78**.

figure 4.76

figure 4.77

figure 4.78

A Levels adjustment layer quickly enhances the family but draws too much attention to the background.

2. Use a soft black brush on the Levels adjustment layer mask to paint out the background as seen in **figure 4.79**. The mask does not have to be very precise as there would be a little bit of natural blending between the light sources.

3. Cmd/Ctrl-click the Levels adjustment layer mask to load the mask as a selection, then press Cmd-Shift-I/Ctrl-Shift-I to inverse the selection (**figure 4.80**).

4. Add a Photo Filter adjustment layer and choose the Cooling Filter (82) from the drop-down list and lower the Density to 15% to neutralize the color cast (see **figure 4.81**).

figure 4.81

The Cooling Filter (82) neutralizes the color cast of the background.

5. To darken the background a bit, Cmd/Ctrl-click the mask of the Photo Filter adjustment layer to load the selection of the background. Add a Levels adjustment layer and move the midtone slider to the right to reduce the brightness of the background to complement the family, as shown in **figure 4.82**.

figure 4.79

Painting on the layer mask returns the background to its original color and exposure.

figure 4.80

Loading the mask as a selection.

figure 4.82

Using the same selection and lowering the background brightness draws more attention to the subjects.

CORRECTING COLOR TEMPERATURE PROBLEMS

As I mentioned earlier, color casts can happen when you use the wrong white balance or color-temperature film for the lighting situation at hand. For example, using daylight film indoors can lead to green or orange pictures. Our eyes don't see color temperature while taking the photograph, because our brain balances light to white no matter how cool or warm the light really is, but these color casts show up on film. Most digital cameras have an auto white balance feature, which can do well but can also drift from image to image. So a series of images taken at the same time can have color shifts due to how the camera evaluates the lighting for each image.

The Photo Filter adjustments have a number of color correction filters similar to what professional photographers use. In the following example, the strong tungsten lighting was not corrected by the digital camera's white balance and the resulting image was overly yellow as seen in figure 4.83.

With a few Photoshop steps, I was able to change the color temperature to a more neutral daylight appearance, as you see in figure 4.84. A variation on the previous technique is a useful method to compensate for the undesired color temperature of the light by filtering the image with the opposite color.

  **ch4_yellowlobby.jpg**

Note

New tools to combat photographic problems are not an excuse for bad photography. It is always better to either set the correct white balance, to use the right color-temperature film, or to filter the lens or your lights to balance the color temperature. As I've said many times, if the picture is taken correctly, there will be less work to do on the computer and a smaller chance of unnatural results. However, this often requires professional equipment, including a color meter, color-correction filters, and colored gels that you might not have on hand.

figure 4.83

figure 4.84

1. Add a Photo Filter adjustment layer.

2. Make no changes in the dialog box and click the color swatch to open the Color Picker. Sample an area of the strong color you want to remove (see figure 4.85).

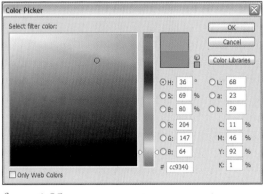

figure 4.85

Select the offending color with the Eyedropper tool.

3. Invert the Lab a and b values by inserting or deleting minuses (see **figure 4.86**).

4. Click OK to close the Color Picker. Use the Photo Filter intensity slider to fine tune the correction as in **figure 4.87**.

figure 4.86

Invert the a and b color values.

figure 4.87

Increasing the percentage on the intensity slider will intensify the effect.

Many times, using this Photo Filter Lab technique is perfectly adequate to remove colorcasts. To add richness to the image, continue with these steps.

1. Duplicate the Photo Filter Layer.

2. Select Layer > Layer Styles > Blending Options or click the Layer Style icon on the bottom of the Layers palette to access the Advanced Blending options (**figure 4.88**).

3. Deselect the green channel in the Advanced Blending options to intensify the correction (see **figure 4.89**).

figure 4.88

Uncheck the green channel in the Advanced Blending options.

figure 4.89

Duplicate the layer and the adjust opacity to intensify the correction.

Thinking Ahead with a Macbeth ColorChecker

If your camera offers image capture in the raw format, I cannot emphasize strongly enough that you should explore it and adopt it as part of your regular photographic workflow. The raw format offers an extended exposure range comparable to film and provides the flexibility to adjust white balance. When you shoot in the raw format, the white balance is not applied to the image but the setting is stored with it. Later in processing you can accept or change the white balance.

Use a Macbeth ColorChecker when working in mixed lighting situations to cut down on a lot of guesswork. The Macbeth target is a known reference in printing and photography, and it is produced to careful specifications. You can purchase it in letter size or in a smaller 2 × 3 inch size from professional camera stores or www.calumetphoto.com.

Figure 4.90 shows a photograph taken in a small chapel near Santa Fe, New Mexico. A mixture of daylight and tungsten light illuminated the scene, which created the strong yellow orange color cast. By photographing a reference image with a Macbeth ColorChecker of the scene and using Adobe Camera Raw I was able to instantly color balance the image as seen in figure 4.91.

Working with the Macbeth ColorChecker and Adobe Camera Raw is very straight forward as described here:

1. Make sure your digital camera supports the raw format.

2. Compose and light the subject and determine the optimal exposure. When working in an uncontrolled lighting situation such as this chapel, compose the shot and determine proper exposure.

3. Place the Macbeth ColorChecker into the picture and take a picture with the same exposure you'll use for the rest of the shoot.

figure 4.90

figure 4.91

4. Remove the Macbeth ColorChecker from the set and shoot the photo as you normally would.

5. Open all the images photographed under similar lighting conditions in Adobe Camera Raw. Click the Select All button and use the White Balance tool to click on the second lightest white square (as circled in figure 4.92) to neutralize all images with one click.

I have done numerous comparisons of processing images with the default color temperature settings or with a known color reference and, in my opinion, the images processed with the ColorChecker yield a much better starting point for additional Photoshop processing. If you don't have a Macbeth ColorChecker, you can use this technique with a Kodak step wedge or Whi-Bal White Balance Reference Cards.

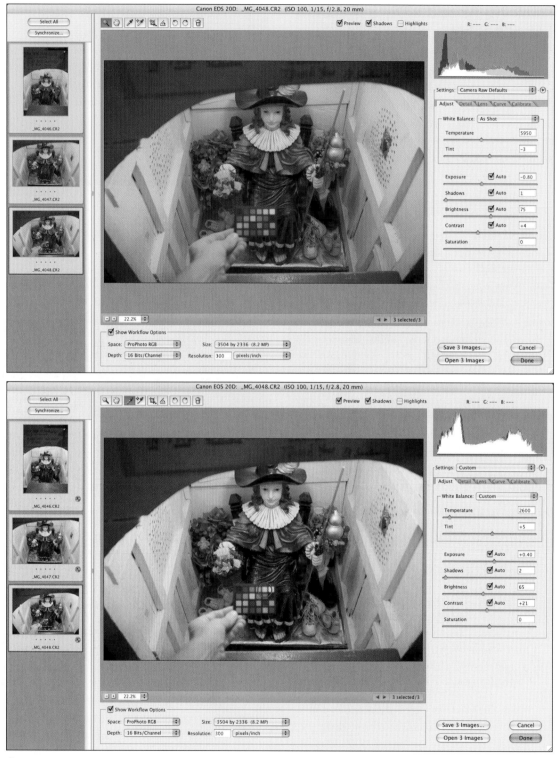

figure 4.92

Open the Macbeth Color Checker image and images photographed under the same lighting conditions into Adobe Camera Raw and use the White Balance tool to neutralize numerous images with one click.

ALLEVIATING EXTREME COLOR PROBLEMS

Color-correction issues can range from subtle to extreme, and sometimes correcting very bad images may seem like a daunting task. In the following section, we'll tackle some of the worst color problems quickly and relatively painlessly.

Extreme Color Correction with Levels

Sometimes an image is so faded, dark, or discolored that you're just not sure what to fix first. Should you tackle the density issue or the heavy color cast first? There is not a single solution that always applies, but in many cases images that are seemingly hopeless can benefit from the following treatment to remove heavy color casts caused by age, poor storage conditions, smoke damage, or underexposed images taken in mixed lighting. The photograph in figure 4.93 is severely faded. Figure 4.94 shows the same image with the undesirable color cast and fading removed.

ch4_honeymoon.jpg

1. Open the problem image and add a Levels adjustment layer.

2. Activate the red channel by pressing Cmd-1/Ctrl-1 and move the sliders to where the majority of the information begins, as shown in figure 4.95.

BEFORE

figure 4.93

AFTER

figure 4.93

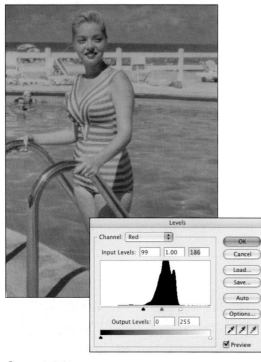

figure 4.95

Moving the red channel sliders.

figure 4.96

Moving the green channel sliders.

3. Select the green channel by pressing Cmd-2/ Ctrl-2 and move the shadow and highlight levels sliders to where the majority of the information begins, as shown in figure 4.96.

4. Pressing Cmd/Ctrl-3 in the Levels histogram to access the blue channel repeat the process (see figure 4.97).

5. If the image requires lightening or darkening, return to the composite histogram by pressing Cmd-~/Ctrl-~ and adjust the midtone slider (to the left to lighten the image or to the right to darken).

 Tip

When you are working with adjustment layers, if you don't like where the color correction is going, sometimes it's just easier to start over. You can get back to the original image by pressing Option/Alt to change the Cancel button to Reset. Select Reset and the image will revert to its original settings.

figure 4.97

Moving the blue channel sliders.

Rebuilding Color Information

Photographic color prints and Father Time rarely make a good partnership, and too often colors fade, shift, or disappear altogether. Take a look at the extremely red saturated family photo in **figure 4.98**. By identifying what is causing the problem and rebuilding the missing color information the image can be saved to share with future generations as seen in **figure 4.99**.

When an image has a blatant color problem like this red image, start by inspecting the individual channels by clicking on the words red, green, and blue in the Channels palette. As shown in **figure 4.100**, the blue and green channels don't have very much useful image information. The Apply Image command enables you to replace and rebuild the weak or damaged channels with percentages of good channels. I included a more detailed explanation of the Apply Image command in my last book, *Photoshop Masking & Compositing*. I've posted the excerpt on this book's Web site as `ch4_image_calculations.pdf`.

🌐▷⊱ **ch4_image_calculations.pdf**

🌐▷⊱ **ch4_redboys.jpg**

© Knoll Family Archives

BEFORE

figure 4.98

Red

Green

Blue

figure 4.100

The blue channel doesn't hold useable image information and needs to be replaced.

AFTER

figure 4.99

1. In the Channels palette, activate the blue channel and turn on the RGB view. Choose Image > Apply Image and set the red channel with Screen blending mode at 25% opacity to lighten the blue channel as seen in **figure 4.101**.

figure 4.101

Blending the red channel information into the weak blue channel.

figure 4.102

Blending the red channel information into the damaged green channel.

2. To improve the green channel, select it and use Image > Apply Image again. This time, use the red channel with Linear Dodge blending mode at 35% opacity. **Figure 4.102** shows the repair thus far.

3. Now the image is well within a Levels correction range. Add a Levels adjustment layer and adjust the individual channels.

4. Activate the red channel by pressing Cmd-1/Ctrl-1 and then move the shadow slider to where the majority of the information begins, as shown in **figure 4.103**.

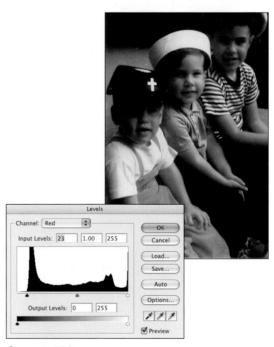

figure 4.103

Moving the red channel sliders.

5. Select the green channel by pressing Cmd-2/ Ctrl-2 and move the shadow slider to where the majority of the information begins, as shown in **figure 4.104**.

6. Select the blue channel by pressing Cmd-3/ Ctrl-3 in the Levels histogram (**figure 4.105**) and move both the highlight and shadow sliders to where the majority of tonal information starts.

7. Return to the composite RGB in Levels and lighten the midtones slightly to add a hint of the summer's day back into the image as shown in **figure 4.106**.

In case you're wondering, two of the little boys in the picture are THE Knoll brothers, Thomas and John, who created Photoshop more than 15 years ago.

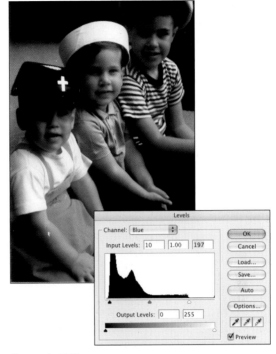

figure 4.105

Moving the blue channel sliders.

figure 4.104

Moving the green channel sliders.

figure 4.106

Lightening the midtones ever so slightly.

Removing Color Fringing

Color fringing, or the milder symptom chromatic aberration, appear on high contrast areas and most often near the edge of the image frame. Both problems look as if there is a false color edge around the subject and it caused by the light rays not focusing on the same spot on the camera CCD or film. In mild cases, the chromatic aberration correction in Adobe Camera Raw or in the Lens Correction filter can resolve the smaller problems. In the extreme cases, such as in figure 4.107, the Lens Correction filter is not powerful enough to reduce the extreme blue fringing. Using the Apply Image command with a bit of restoration work lets the eagles fly proudly as seen in figure 4.108.

 **ch4_blueeagle.jpg**

figure 4.107

BEFORE

figure 4.108

AFTER

1. Inspect the color channels to see which one is causing the problem (figure 4.109). The red and green channels are crisp and well defined while the blue channel has softer edges that are slightly offset in relationship to the rest of the image.

Red

Green

figure 4.110

Add the good red channel information to the weak blue channel.

Blue

figure 4.109

Identify the problem, in this case the weak blue channel, to know what to repair.

2. In the Channels palette, select the blue channel (figure 4.110) and turn on the RGB view. Choose Image > Apply Image and use the red channel as source to add it into the blue channel. Set the Blending to Add, Scale to 1, and Offset to –160. Click OK.

3. With the blue channel still active, select Image > Apply Image and use the green channel as source to add it into the blue channel with blending mode of Add, Scale of 2, and Offset of 20 as seen in figure 4.111.

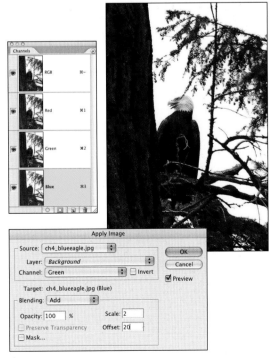

figure 4.111

Add the green channel to the blue channel

4. Click on RGB or Cmd-~/Ctrl-~ and add a new layer. Set it to Color blending mode. Activate a small 50% hardness brush and Option/Alt-sample a good color in the image, such as the pine tree, and paint over any remaining fringing as shown in figure 4.112.

figure 4.112

Refine the repair by coloring over any remaining artifacts.

MATCHING, CHANGING, AND REPLACING COLORS

Whenever I look at color I ask myself, "Do I want to add, subtract, or change the color?" Adding and changing color draws attention to the subject, while subtracting or reducing it lessens visual interest in the subject. You can maintain, add, subtract, or change colors with dozens of methods—from working with dedicated features to applying hand coloring to working in Lab color mode.

Maintaining Color with Luminosity

In most cases, working with Curves is an excellent method for improving image contrast or removing color casts. But as with all good things, sometimes making changes also adds unwanted color shifts or saturation. Too much saturation conceals tonal detail and will cause the image, especially in deep reds and blues, to look splotchy. To avoid the unwanted saturation punch, combine the power of a Curves adjustment layer with the Luminosity blending mode, as illustrated in the before figure 4.113 and after figure 4.114.

figure 4.113

figure 4.114

⊕⫶⫶ ch4_flamingoes.jpg

1. Add a Curves adjustment layer and improve the image contrast with an S curve (see **figure 4.115**) by darkening the shadows and lightening the highlight. The image is improved, but if you look at the red areas you will see they've been exaggerated with false saturation.

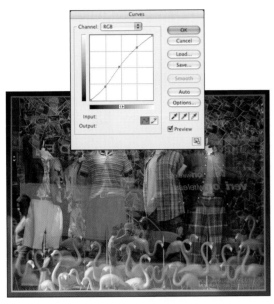

figure 4.115

Using standard settings within Curves creates a pleasing image but the colors are too intense.

2. To confirm which areas are over-saturated or out of gamut, choose View > Gamut Warning (Cmd-Shift-Y/Ctrl-Shift-Y). In your preferences, you can select what color Photoshop will use to indicate out-of-range colors. In this example, I am using 100% blue. The standard clipping values of 0.10% show numerous areas that are out of gamut in **figure 4.116**. If you lowered your clipping values as discussed earlier, the amount is not as great.

3. Change the blending mode of the Curves adjustment layer to Luminosity as seen in **figure 4.117** to offset the unwanted saturation while maintaining the contrast improvement. Toggle the blending mode from Luminosity to Normal to appreciate the difference.

figure 4.116

Choosing View > Gamut Warning will show the colors that are outside the range of color that can be printed.

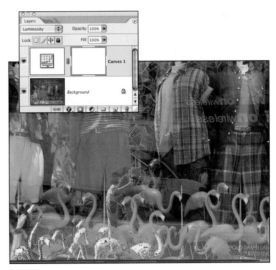

figure 4.117

Changing the adjustment layer blending mode to Luminosity lessens the false saturation.

Matching Colors Across Images

The Match Color command allows you to replace the colors in one image with the colors in another. This can include the entire image, specific layers, and selections within images.

In **figure 4.118**, notice the two images are similar in subject matter but the color is noticeably different, even though they were taken at about the same time. In **figure 4.119**, the magenta color cast has been removed with the Match Color command.

© Wayne Palmer

figure 4.118

figure 4.119

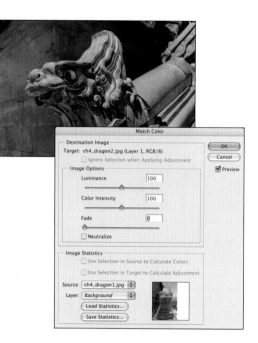

figure 4.120

Select the Source Image

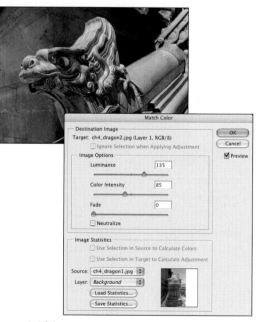

figure 4.121

Adjust Luminosity and Saturation to fine-tune the correction.

🌐▷ **ch4_dragon1.jpg**

🌐▷ **ch4_dragon2.jpg**

1. With both images open, select the one that has the color you want to change and duplicate the Background layer. Select Image > Adjustments > Match Color and start the correction by choosing the Source file you want to match in the Image Statistics section as seen in **figure 4.120**.

2. Use the Luminosity slider to improve overall tonality and the Intensity slider to increase or decrease the color saturation as seen in **figure 4.121**.

Match Color also supports active selections and you can often achieve better color match by selecting a small area in the Source image before entering Match Color.

Replacing Colors

The primary Photoshop features for replacing color are the Replace Color command (found under Image > Adjustment) and the Color Replacement tool (nested with the standard Paint Brush). They perform essentially the same task, but the Replace Color command uses Color Range to select the area to recolor while the Color Replacement tool uses a brush to define and simultaneously recolor an area. Both have their benefits and your choice depends upon how difficult it is to isolate the area you want to recolor. If you choose the Replace Color command and have multiple areas of similar color but don't want to change them all, make a rough selection of the area you do want to change before entering the command

Let's change the color of the car in the image shown in **figure 4.122**. Its current color is close to the color of the sky and changing it to match the woman's jacket, as seen in **figure 4.123**, would be fun.

 ch4_bluecar.jpg

1. Open the file and duplicate the Background layer.

2. The color of the sky is very close to the color of the car. Use the Rectangular Marquee tool to make a rough selection around the car, as in **figure 4.124** to avoid changing the color of the sky.

Note

When I say a "rough" selection, I really mean it. It doesn't matter if other parts of the image are included in your initial selection, as long as they do not have color similar to the area you are changing.

3. Select Image > Adjustments > Replace Color. The dialog box resembles the Color Range dialog box, with the addition of replacement color sliders. Notice in **figure 4.125** that the preview box only shows what was selected with the marquee.

figure 4.122

figure 4.123

figure 4.124

Make a general selection of the area you want to change

figure 4.125

*The Replace Color dialog box contains two sections:
Selection and Replacement.*

4. With the eyedropper, drag over the blue in
   the car image and watch the resulting selection in the dialog box. Hold down the Shift
   key and drag over the entire car to pick up as
   many of the blue shades as possible, without
   picking up the woman's jeans. Use Option/
   Alt, or select the eyedropper with the minus
   sign, to deselect areas. Increase the fuzziness
   to include similar blue colors as shown in
   figure 4.126.

figure 4.126

Use the eyedropper to select the colors to be replaced.

5. Once you have made the color selection,
   use the lower portion of the dialog box to
   change the color. Use either the three slider
   bars to change the Replacement color or
   click the Result color box to open the Color
   Picker. With either option, you will have a
   live update in your image when you choose a
   color. Staying in the main dialog box enables
   you to use the eyedropper to add areas for
   color. Slide the Hue slide over to a nice pur-
   plish color and use the saturation slider to
   tone down the color's intensity, as seen in
   figure 4.127.

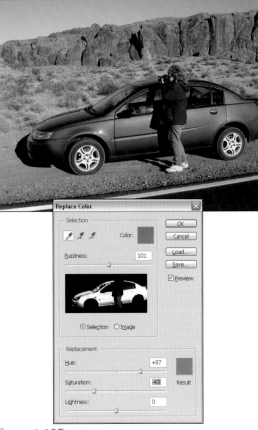

figure 4.127

*Use the hue, saturation, and lightness sliders to control the
color change.*

6. The further you move away from the original color, the more attention you will have to give to the selection. If your selection did pick up some of the other blues in the image, such as in the woman's jeans and the car windshield, add a layer mask and paint with black to protect those areas as seen in figure 4.128.

figure 4.128

Use a layer mask to touch up any areas that were unintentionally changed.

Color Replacement Tool

Use the Color Replacement tool to paint a new color over an existing one. The way it replaces color is similar to Replace Color, but use this tool when the area to be colorized would be too complex a selection for the Color Range tool.

> **T i p**
>
> The effect of the Color Replacement tool or the Replace Color command is directly related to the brightness value of the subject. The closer the brightness is to white or black, the less noticeable the effect. The closer the brightness value is to 128, in RGB mode, the more it will match the color you have chosen to use for replacement.

The tool has several helpful options called Limits to assist color replacement:

- Discontiguous places color anywhere you paint.

- Contiguous places color anywhere you paint, as long as the color you first started to paint on is in the same range.

- Find Edge places color anywhere you paint but senses color changes and does not go into a neighboring color.

Drawing attention to the rose in figure 4.129 by changing its color would make it more interesting, as seen in figure 4.130. Since the rose is very similar in color to the rest of the image, the Replace Color command could not isolate the rose, as seen in my first two attempts in figure 4.131. This is the perfect time to choose the Color Replacement Tool.

ch4_rosecross.jpg

figure 4.129

figure 4.130

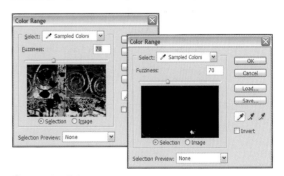

figure 4.131

The Color Replace command cannot separate monochrome image elements very effectively.

1. As you should before working with any tool that will directly affect your Background layer, duplicate the layer (Cmd-J/Ctrl-J) to protect it and zoom in so the rose fills the screen.

2. Choose the Color Replacement tool. In the options bar be sure Mode is set to Color, that Find Edges is selected under Limits, and that Sampling: Once is checked, as seen in **figure 4.132**.

figure 4.132

Use Color mode, Find Edges, and Sampling: Once

3. Choose a red color. I chose a standard one from the Swatches palette. The color you choose will change brilliance depending on the brightness level of the subject you are painting. This is what makes painting with color look believable—the gray value tonalities mix and show through the color.

4. Paint inside the rose. Notice that the brush has a crosshair. With the Find Edges option the color will stay inside the rose if you first click the area you want to paint. The areas outside that point will not be colorized even if the ring of the brush extends outside them, as in **figure 4.133**.

5. If the color is too vibrant, lower the layer's opacity. The layer underneath will slowly reveal the original rose and tone down the color change you made (**figure 4.134**).

figure 4.133

Painting inside the rose.

figure 4.134

Lowering the layer opacity adjusts the color vibrancy.

Changing Color in Lab Color Mode

Editing color in the Lab Color mode has the advantage that the luminosity of the image is not affected. I often turn to this technique when clarity and flexibility are required. In this example, I wanted to change the color of the sign on the truck (figure 4.135) to make it stand out even more (figure 4.136).

🌐⧉✂ **ch4_shrimptruck.jpg**

1. Select Image > Duplicate and convert the image to Lab Color by choosing Image > Mode > Lab Color.

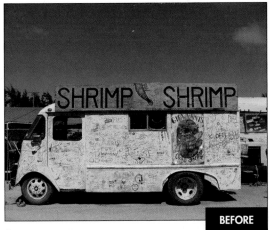

figure 4.135

figure 4.136

2. Use Polygon Lasso tool to select the sign. Add a Curves adjustment layer.

3. Slide the end points of the curve in the a channel to change the color of the sign, as in figure 4.137. Keeping the a and b curve lines straight will change the color and yield more predictable results.

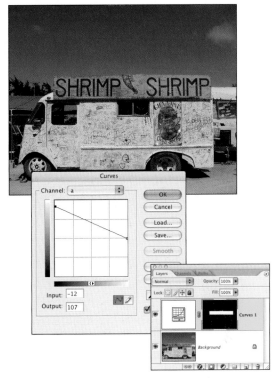

figure 4.137

Use Curves and Lab Color mode to change color while not affecting density.

CLOSING THOUGHTS

The importance of good color—pleasing color—cannot be overestimated. Trying out the techniques in this chapter on your own images will teach you more than any book. So open up some images and learn to really see color, both to remove it, add it, change it, or accentuate it. It's all-important.

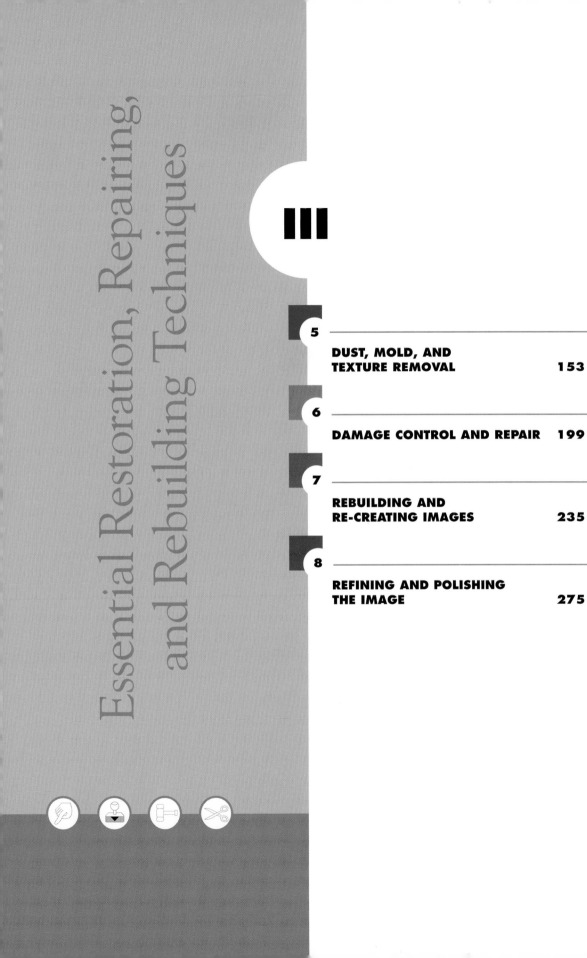

Essential Restoration, Repairing, and Rebuilding Techniques

III

5

DUST, MOLD, AND TEXTURE REMOVAL

Cleanliness is next to godliness, and without start-ing a religious debate, I am sure you agree with me that the bane of all retouchers are issues like dust, mold, moiré patterns, print texture, and film grain. Removing these problems can be a time-consuming, eye-straining, arm-numbing endeavor that can really take the fun out of digital retouching. In this chapter, you face the worst problems and learn the best tech-niques for rescuing your images from the evils that lurk in historical negatives, glass plates, prints, contempo-rary film, and digital images.

The problems tackled in this chapter include

- Removing dust, mold, and scratches

- Minimizing moiré patterns and paper texture

- Reducing digital camera noise

The tools used to conquer these dusty and dirty challenges include

- Layers and blending modes

- The Clone Stamp and Healing Tools

- Creative scanning and digital camera input techniques

- Filters and the Vanishing Point command

So roll up your mousing sleeve, and let's get to work.

Depending on the severity of the problem, you can use numerous Photoshop techniques, many interchangeably or in combination, to clean up dust and mold. My favorite technique is to avoid the problem in the first place by cleaning the negative, print, or scanner before making the scan. By carefully brushing or blowing loose dust off a negative or print, you're removing the source of the problem.

When working with contemporary film such as Kodachrome or Ektachrome, you can carefully remove dust, grease, and tape marks with Rexton Anti-static film cleaner. If the dust is embedded in the emulsion side (duller side) of the film, consider a 10 to 15 minute soak in 72 degree water, with one drop of a mild dish washing liquid per quart, followed by a brief warm water rinse and air drying in a dust-free environment. Do not blow dry film in an attempt to speed up the drying process. Always ask before working on a client's originals and, if possible, test on a less essential area or piece of film. Never rub film, prints, or scanner platens very hard because you can scratch and permanently damage them.

Because there isn't one perfect method to remove dust specks or to reduce mold damage, this chapter includes a variety of methods to tackle these problems. Dust problems are most often seen as very small specks of dark or light pixels, and mold damage looks mottled, patterned, or discolored and affects larger areas. By experimenting with or combining methods, you'll develop techniques to take care of your image's worst problems.

DUSTBUSTING 101

Once an image has been digitized, there is no actual dust. There may have been dust on the image, scanner, or camera sensor, but with a digital file all you really have is lighter or darker pixels in contrast to darker or lighter backgrounds. Taking advantage of this concept can speed up your clean up time, which many photographers refer to as *dustbusting* or *spotting*. In traditional photography, the light specks were caused by dust sitting on the film as the photo paper was being exposed. Although we're working digitally, we face many of the same challenges and use similar language.

Use the Cleanest Channel

Sometimes one of the easiest solutions to dustbusting is to determine whether the specks are primarily located in one channel. If they are, you can either work on the channel with the most problems or, in the case of a black-and-white or sepia image, extract the best channel and save yourself a lot of tedious mouse-time. For this reason, I highly recommend that you scan or photograph all images in color even when working with mono-color images. Frequently, the most noticeable damage to an image is in the blue channel, so by using the information in the red or green channels you may be able to bypass dust or noise altogether.

When working with sepia or yellowed images, with the final goal that includes retaining some of that antique look, it may be better to work with the image in grayscale especially if you have to make a significant brightness change. Maintaining the original color tone through the editing process is difficult, as changes to the brightness and contrast will also shift the original color. It is often more productive to convert the image to grayscale, restore the image, convert the file back to RGB and then put the original tint back as a final step with a Solid Color fill layer set to Color blending mode, as shown later in this chapter.

Figure 5.1 is cracked, yellowed, and very textured and noisy. Figure 5.2 shows the results of extracting the best channel—of course the image still has a crack in it—but the yellowing and texture have disappeared.

⊕▷⋲ ch5_bestchannel.jpg

1. Look through the three channels to see if one channel shows less texture and bothersome noise. Press Cmd/Ctrl and 1, 2, and 3 to cycle through the red, green, and blue channels, as shown in figure 5.3. The red channel shows the least amount of noise and dust. Press Cmd-~/Ctrl-~ to return to RGB.

2. In the Channels palette, select the red channel (as shown in figure 5.4).

BEFORE

figure 5.1

AFTER

figure 5.2

Red

Green

Blue

figure 5.3

Examining the three channels, the red channel reveals the least amount of noise and dust.

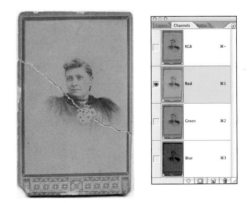

figure 5.4

Extracting the best channel is an effective method to eliminate dust and noise.

3. Select Image > Mode > Grayscale. Click OK to the Photoshop warning dialog box. Better yet, check "Don't show again" and then click OK. The less useful channels are thrown away, and the channel you consider the best becomes the grayscale image.

4. To improve the tonality of the file, add a Levels adjustment layer and move the black and white point sliders inwards and the midtone slider to the left to improve image contrast and lighten the midtones (see **figure 5.5**).

figure 5.5

Improve the overall tonality with a Levels adjustment layer.

Combining Channels with Channel Mixer

If a single channel does not provide enough information to make a good image, often blending two channels together with a Channel Mixer adjustment layer to create a pleasing grayscale image can eradicate spots, dust, and stains as seen in **figures 5.6** and **5.7** as Mark Beckelman did.

⊕▷⊱ **ch5_channel_dust.jpg**

figure 5.6

figure 5.7

1. Press Cmd/Ctrl and 1, 2, and 3 to cycle through the red, green, and blue channels. In this example the red and green channels show less damage than the blue channel as seen in **figure 5.8**. Press Cmd-~/Ctrl-~ to return to RGB.

2. To add the good information and subtract the damaged information, return to the Layers palette, add a Channel Mixer adjustment layer, check Monochrome, increase the red and green components and decrease the blue component as seen in **figure 5.9**. Increasing the "good" channels and subtracting the "bad" channel creates a better initial image much more quickly than using manual labor with the Healing or Cloning tools.

red

green

blue

figure 5.8

The red and green channels are in better shape than the blue.

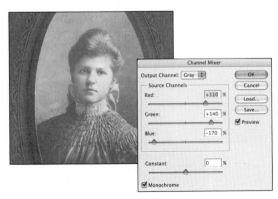

figure 5.9

Increasing the red and green component and subtracting the damaged blue channel information.

3. To improve the overall contrast, add a Levels adjustment layer. Move the shadow point to the right and the highlight point to the left, where the majority of tonal information starts as seen in **figure 5.10**.

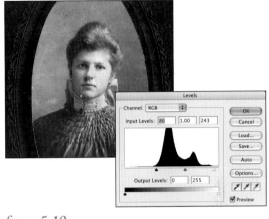

figure 5.10

Adjusting Levels improves the contrast globally.

Mark then continued the restoration with the duplicate-and-move technique as described in the following section. Do a Save As of this file to work along with.

The Duplicate-and-Move Technique

Use the duplicate-and-move technique on unimportant image areas such as skies or backgrounds to quickly disguise dust on large surfaces. Duplicating a troublesome area with a 2- or 3-pixel offset and applying a Lighten blending mode (to remove dark spots) or a Darken blending mode (to remove light specks) is a quick and easy way to remove many flaws. I first heard about this technique from Stephen Johnson (www.sjphoto.com) as he was retouching numerous glass plate negatives for his wonderful book *The Great Central Valley* (University of California, 1998).

Figures **5.11** and **5.12** show before-and-after detail of the identical area that was cleaned up with the duplicate-and-move technique. Notice how the many specks of dust and damage have been minimized. The few remaining larger spots will be removed with the Spot Healing brush.

figure 5.11

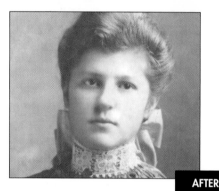

figure 5.12

Tip

To make your dustbusting time as short as possible, squelch the temptation to tediously remove dust spots with the Clone Stamp or the Spot Healing Brush tool. The idea is to spend the least amount of time on unimportant image areas and save your time and visual concentration for the important parts of the image

1. Use Cmd-Option-Shift-E/Ctrl-Alt-Shift-E to merge the work-in-progress layers up, creating a new layer to work on. When using this technique on scans that only have a Background layer, simply duplicate the Background layer and continue as described.

2. Duplicate this new layer once to create a file with two duplicate layers and name the lower one *lighter* and the upper layer *darker*.

3. Hide the darker layer and select the lighter layer. Activate the Move tool and use the arrows keys to nudge the lighter layer down

two pixels (two taps of the down key) and to the right two pixels (two taps of the right key). Change the layer blending mode to Lighten to create a slightly blurry image as seen in **figure 5.13**.

4. Option/Alt-click the Add Layer Mask icon to add a black layer mask to the lighten layer. Use a small, soft-edged white brush at 100% opacity to dab over the dark spots. By painting on the layer mask, the lightened and offset layer information is revealed as seen in **figure 5.14**.

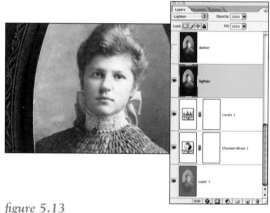

figure 5.13

Slightly moving the copied layer causes the dark spots to disappear.

figure 5.14

Painting on the layer mask reveals the offset lighter information.

5. Make the darker layer visible and repeat steps 3 and 4, except change the blending mode to Darken and paint over the lighter specks and dust flecks, as figure 5.15 illustrates.

figure 5.16

Use the Spot Healing brush to remove remaining specks of dust or damage.

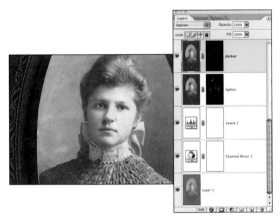

figure 5.15

Slightly moving the copied layer causes the light spots to disappear.

 T i p

If the dust is very fine, use a 1 pixel offset and experiment with moving the darken and lighten layers in opposite directions when offsetting them.

6. Press Cmd-Option-Shift-E/Ctrl-Alt-Shift-E to merge the work-in-progress layers up and use a small Spot Healing Brush tool to remove the remaining specks on the woman's face (figure 5.16).

 T i p

Matching the size of the brush to the size of the dust speck to be removed ensures that you don't overcorrect the image surrounding the dust speck. Use the keyboard shortcuts to control the size of the brushes:

- Left bracket ([) decreases brush size.

- Right bracket (]) increases brush size.

In most cases, using the two duplicate-and-float layers with Lighten and Darken blending modes takes care of the majority of problems. Refining the work with a few taps of the Spot Healing Brush usually takes care of few remaining specks that were larger than the two pixel offset. Ever the professional, Mark Beckelman continued working to soften the texture in the woman's face, clean up the frame, and add a hint of color as described here.

1. Duplicate the spotting layer and use a Gaussian Blur filter setting of 2 to gently soften the face (figure 5.17).

figure 5.17

Softening a merged, repaired layer.

2. Opt/Alt-click on the layer mask icon to add a black layer mask to the blurred layer. Use a soft-edged white brush at 90% opacity to paint over the woman's face and a 50% opacity white brush to paint over the background as seen in **figure 5.18**. By painting on the layer mask, the softer information is revealed.

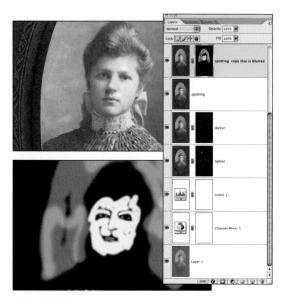

figure 5.18

Painting through a black layer mask reveals the softening.

3. Add a new layer, and use the Clone Stamp tool set to Sample All Layers to refine the edges of the frame. Use a small, hard-edged brush to avoid softening the frame. **Figure 5.19** shows the repaired frame.

4. Finally, to add back a hint of color, add a Solid Color fill layer and choose a warm tone. After selecting the color, change the layer blending mode to Color and adjust the opacity to create the final image seen in **figure 5.20**.

All in all, avoiding a lot of mouse work with the healing or cloning tools gives you more time for the artistic details, such as refining the face and frame.

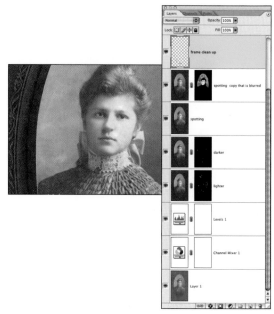

figure 5.19

Use a hard-edged Clone Stamp brush when making fine repairs.

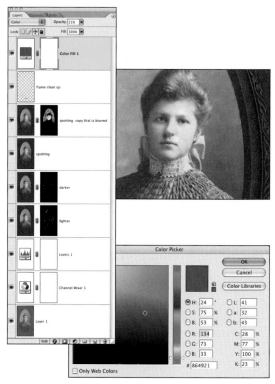

figure 5.20

Adjust the opacity of the Solid Color fill layer to reveal the image.

Dust on Digital Camera Files

With the popularity of high quality digital SLR (single lens reflex) cameras on the rise, so are the inevitable dark spots on the files that are caused by dust on the camera CCD (charged coupled device). No matter how careful you may be to change the lenses quickly and in a dust-free environment, dust has a way of adhering to the CCD. This dust is especially irritating because it is often visible in the exact same place on the every single file. Taking care of it in Photoshop is fairly easy (as described in a moment), when you're working on one or two images. But removing the same dust from dozens and dozens of files can be a daunting and time consuming process.

If you see small soft-edged black blobs on your digital camera files, like those in **figure 5.21**, you have three choices: ignore the dust and remove it in Photoshop, clean your camera CCD, or take the camera to a professional service to be cleaned. Speaking only for myself—I ignore one or two specks but after that I opt for cleaning the CCD myself.

figure 5.21

Dust on camera CCDs is more visible in lighter and even toned areas.

 Caution

I am not condoning that all users open and clean their own cameras, as improper cleaning may damage their camera or low-pass glass that is protecting the CCD and void your warranty. Please visit these Web sites for additional and very useful information.

www.cleaningdigitalcameras.com

www.bythom.com/cleaning.htm

1. To determine if you have dust on your CCD, take a photograph of a clean white surface or the blue sky on a clear day with the lens set to f 16.

2. Bring the image into Photoshop and choose Image > Adjustments > Auto Levels to make the dust stand out.

3. If a lot of black specks are visible, read your camera manual and the afore-mentioned Web sites or take the camera to a service provider for cleaning.

4. **Figure 5.22** shows the results of cleaning the CCD once. Granted, there are a few specks still visible, but upon an additional cleaning with Sensor Brushes by www.visibledust.com my CCD was as clean as a whistle and I could continue taking pictures.

figure 5.22

After physically cleaning the CCD, a few specks remain, which I removed with a second pass of cleaning.

Figure 5.23 shows the whole image and a small sample at 100% for you to see the stubborn dust. This image was photographed with a pinhole (no lens, just a tiny hole in a body cap; www.pinholeformat.com), which is notorious for showing dust. Figure 5.23 shows the same file and crop after digital clean up as described here.

For large dust flakes:

1. Duplicate the Background layer.

2. Use the Patch tool set to Source and circle the offending dust. Move the selection to good image information. Release the mouse to have Photoshop patch the selection.

For small dust specks:

1. Add a new layer.

2. Use the Spot Healing Brush set to Sample All Layers. Select a brush that is slightly larger than the dust and tap the brush on the dust speck.

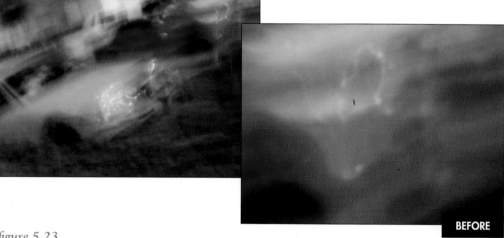

figure 5.23

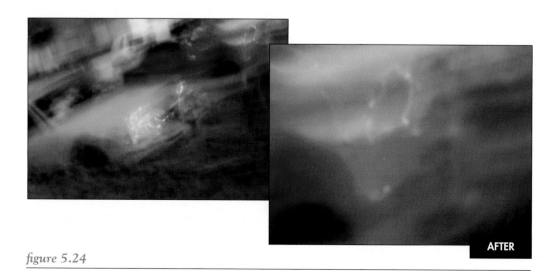
figure 5.24

Removing Fungus and Mold

The best way to avoid mold, fungus, and mildew problems is to store your photographs in a humidity-controlled environment with a relative humidity of 20-50%. According to Henry Wilhelm's book *The Permanence and Care of Color Photographs* (Preservation, 1993), available as a free download at www.wilhem-research.com, the problem lies in the fact that "gelatin, the major component of the emulsion of films and prints, is unfortunately an excellent nutrient for fungi." To make matters worse, insects are attracted to fungus, and they're more than happy to munch on your valuable photographs, too. Film with strong vinegar smell or a white powdery residue is a telltale sign of an image suffering under serious deterioration.

When working with film you may be able to stop the fungus attack by gently cleaning the film with a cotton swab and Kodak Film Cleaner. Then scan in the film and use the Clone Stamp and Healing Brush tools to rid the world of this evil. There is a good chance that fungus has already done its damage and its removal may not reveal any useful information.

On the other hand, removing mold or fungus from a print should be done only by a professional photo conservator because it can grow deeply into the paper fibers. Do not try to wash, clean, or treat original prints unless you can live with the consequences that anything you do to the original print might actually damage the paper more than the mold already has.

To Clone, to Heal, or Spot Heal

Photoshop is truly a professional piece of software that includes a variety of replacement, concealing, and blending brushes—more commonly referred to as the Clone Stamp, Healing Brush, and Spot Healing Brush tools. Sadly, many users seem to think that the Healing Brush and Spot Healing Brush are simply souped-up versions of the Clone Stamp tool—nothing could be further from the truth. In fact, the only true similarity between the Healing Brush and Clone Stamp tool is that both tools enable you to sample from one image area by Option/Alt-clicking then painting to cover up image damage or blemishes. The Spot Healing Brush doesn't even require you to sample good information for it to work its magic.

In general, use the two Healing Brush variants for areas that are not highly detailed and reserve the Clone Stamp tool for precise repair in detailed areas and high contrast areas where preserving critical information is important, such as your subject's eyes and nose. The Spot Healing Brush in Photoshop CS2 is a fantastic tool to remove dust, mold, and damage, and to do quick blemish removal in portraits.

Guidelines for using the Healing and Cloning Tools

- When the Healing Brush samples, it separately analyzes the texture, color, and luminosity attributes of the source area. When you paint, it merges the texture from the sample area into the color and luminosity of the destination area. The Clone Stamp literally duplicates the clone source and paints it over the original information.

- To create a seamless merge between the retouched areas and the original, the Healing Brush adds a 10- to 12-pixel spread to the brush. Due to this built-in spread, use a hard-edged brush just slightly larger than the area you are repairing. The Clone Stamp tool is more effective with a softer and larger brush (in relationship to the problem you're trying to fix).

- Take advantage of the Sample All Layers option on these tools. Work on a dedicated healing or cloning layer, preserving the Background layer. If the performance of your machine really slows when using the Sample All Layers option, duplicate the layer you want to repair and work directly on it.

- With the Healing Brush, using short brush-strokes of 1 to 1½ inches and releasing the mouse allows the healing algorithm time to calculate and will result in better healing than long, sweeping strokes will.

- When you are using the Clone Stamp tool, resample image areas often to avoid the "clone of the clone" patterned look. Resampling from both sides of the damaged area will produce a better blend. Dab with the Clone Stamp; painting can produce an obvious smeared look.

- Avoid the temptation to retouch bad retouching or restoration work. If a Clone or Healing brush stroke doesn't look right, select Edit > Undo and redo the stroke. Cloning or healing over poor work will over-soften image texture or film grain.

- When using the Healing Brush, it is extremely helpful to not continually resample a source, as you would with the Clone Stamp. Sampling good texture area once and painting as long as the sampled texture is effective will yield a better heal. For best results, unlearn the Clone Stamp technique of sampling often. Yes, I know that this is difficult at first, but keep your left hand away from the Option or Alt key, and you'll be a better healer for it.

- When working near image edges, use Select > All to keep the Healing Brush from averaging in white from outside the image.

- When working along an edge of an image with either tool, it is important to sample and brush parallel to the edge you are repairing.

- Both the Healing Brush and Clone Stamp tools can work between multiple open images, meaning you can sample good image information from one image and make repairs with that sample in another.

T i p

Work nondestructively—use techniques that let you undo your changes. The Sample All Layers option is available with the Clone, Healing, and Spot Healing brushes, giving you the ability to work on a separate layer to build up and undo any and all changes.

Spot Healing Brush

The Spot Healing Brush introduced in Photoshop CS2 will probably change your restoration and retouching work habits more than any other brush tool. Like the Healing Brush, it samples tone and texture around the damaged area to then calculate and lay down the blended repair. Unlike the Healing Brush, you do not have to define a source of good image information. This may seem trivial at first glance, but not having to watch where you are sampling from is truly a time saver. But this automation is also the tool's limit, as the area it samples may not give you the result you want.

Spot Healing Brush in Action

Use the Spot Healing Brush on small spots and scratches as seen in **figure 5.25** which I repaired in a few minutes to create the image seen in **figure 5.26**.

ch5_spot_healing.jpg

1. Add a new layer and name it *fixes*. Select the Spot Healing brush and check that Sample All Layers is checked. Choose a hard-edged brush size that is just a bit larger than the specks and spots you want to remove.

2. Start with the easy, more defined spots in the image background. Tap or dab over them. They should disappear as seen in **figure 5.27**.

3. Zoom in on a fine scratch and use the Spot Healing Brush with short strokes. For a few seconds you will see a darker smear, like in **figure 5.28**, but releasing the mouse heals the scratch. If you are unhappy with the results, choose Edit > Undo and try again but use a different brush stroke direction.

figure 5.25

BEFORE

figure 5.27

Dab on the small dust specks.

figure 5.26

AFTER

figure 5.28

While you are still holding the mouse button, the stroke of the Spot Healing brush will be dark.

4. Continue with short strokes to clean up the cracks as seen in **figure 5.29**.

5. Try as I could, I could not get the Spot Healing Brush to repair the damage in the lower left corner (see **figure 5.30**). I had to use a small Clone Stamp tool to build up the initial information. Then, I could use a small Spot Healing brush to refine the details to create the final results.

figure 5.29

Use short brush strokes with the Spot Healing brush.

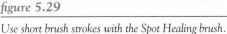

figure 5.30

The Clone Stamp is more effective in rebuilding critical image information.

In most of my projects, I use a variety of tools to get the job done efficiently:

- Use the Spot Healing Brush with short strokes on simple surfaces and backgrounds and with quick dabs remove small spots and blemishes.

- Use the Clone Stamp to rebuild missing information, on areas with high contrast or great color differences, and where precision is required.

- Use the Healing Brush for general work to blend textures and repair restoration artifacts.

- Use the Patch tool to repair wide cracks and rips on simple surfaces.

I'm Seeing Spots

As with any finely tuned piece of equipment, the more you know about the Spot Healing Brush, the better you will be able to control it to perform invisible image restoration and retouching.

An Adobe engineer shared the strategy and thinking behind the Spot Healing Brush with me. "In the real world, the Spot Healing Brush will work well if there is enough good data around the defective area. In other words, if you have a long thin scratch to remove, it will not work very well if you apply one long stroke. You will have better luck if you try to fix the scratch from one end that has more good data around it and paint along the scratch with short strokes. Paint the same area again if you do not like the result."

With the default setting of Proximity Match selected, the Spot Healing Brush tool analyzes the data close to the defective area in all directions, including the average color. When the Create Texture setting is used, the tool works differently in that it mixes the data around the defective area to do a texture synthesis.

- For best results, use a brush that is just slightly larger than the specks, blemishes, or scratches you are trying to remove.

- Use short brush strokes or simply tap the problem away.

- Brushing up, down, left, or right with the Spot Healing Brush can yield very different results. If you don't like the results choose Edit > Undo and try again but pull the brush in a different direction.

- The Spot Healing Brush is best used for simple surfaces and smaller problems.

- You will achieve better results with the Spot Healing Brush when working on higher resolution images—5 Mb or larger are best. On smaller images, the tool may create very odd duplication effects as it samples and replaces information.

- To test drive the Spot Healing Brush, download the file ch5_seeing_spots.jpg that Wayne Palmer created.

🌐⇥ **ch5_seeing_spots.jpg**

Is the Clone Stamp Dead?

No, the Clone Stamp was and is the backbone of photo restoration. You will probably not use it as much as the Healing Brushes, but it is still a great tool for repairing or retouching fine details and rebuilding large areas of missing image information. The results from the Clone Stamp are more predictable than either the Healing or Spot Healing Brushes. Experience and practice will teach you which tool to use.

The corners and edges of **figure 5.31** are missing. Because there were some detailed areas to be fixed in the background, I used the Clone Stamp initially to build up the missing image area and then used the Spot Healing Brush to fine-tune the repair. I switched back and forth between the two as needed to fix the remaining areas as shown in **figure 5.32**.

🌐⇥ **ch5_missing_corner.jpg**

Before working on an image, take a moment to evaluate the image, its format, and the condition of the edges. In this example, the print was scanned crookedly, the top of the deckled edge is missing and the other edges are damaged. You can save a

figure 5.31

figure 5.32

lot of time and effort by straightening out the print when scanning or using Photoshop to straighten it out and by cropping the file as described here.

To straighten and crop the image:

1. Double-click on the Background layer and rename it *original*.

2. Duplicate the original layer.

3. Select the Measure tool, which is nested with the Eyedropper tool. Click at the upper left corner, where the image ends and the border begins. Follow this line between the border and the image down to the lower left corner to show Photoshop the edge that should be vertical, as in **figure 5.33**.

figure 5.34

The amount to rotate has been determined by the Measure tool.

figure 5.33

With the Measure tool, trace down a line that should be straight.

4. Select Image > Rotate Canvas > Arbitrary. Photoshop will calculate the amount of rotation needed as seen in **figure 5.34**.

5. Select the Crop tool and set it to 5×7 inch in the options bar. Leave the resolution box empty and click the Hide button to hide the extra information rather than delete it. In this example, cropping the image to a standard size allows it to fit into a standard frame and as you can see in **figure 5.35** reduces the amount of digital repair.

figure 5.35

Cropping the image to a contemporary frame size.

The Clone Stamp tool is an excellent tool to cover large missing areas in corners. To repair the corner:

1. Add a new layer, set the Clone Stamp tool to Sample All Layers and Option/Alt-click to sample good image information. Paint over the areas where the corner is missing, as shown in **figure 5.36**. Don't worry about perfection yet—after the rips are repaired we'll take the time to refine the restoration.

figure 5.36

Use the Clone Stamp tool to quickly recreate missing image information.

2. To repair the large crack, press Cmd-Option-Shift-E/Ctrl-Alt-Shift-E to merge the work-in-progress layers up. Use the Patch tool set to Source to select about one-third of the large crack as seen in **figure 5.37**.

figure 5.37

Working on smaller sections of a crack creates better results.

3. Use the Patch tool to drag the selection to good image information (**figure 5.38**) and release the mouse.

4. Continue patching the large crack in one-third increments.

figure 5.38

Drag the selection to a relevant image area and release to patch the cracks.

5. Once the initial image information has been restored, add a new layer, and use the Healing brush set to Sample All Layers to cover up any telltale patterns that the cloning or patching may have caused (**figure 5.39**).

figure 5.39

Refine the cloning and patching with the Healing brush.

6. To fix the very fine cracks on the lower areas by the woman's legs use a small, hard-edged Healing Brush and only repair an inch at a time. Making smaller strokes allows the Healing engine to process the restoration and will yield better results.

7. To finish off the restoration, use a small, hard-edged Spot Healing brush and dab over the few remaining specks on her face, hair and background (**figure 5.40**).

figure 5.40

Clean up the tiniest specks with the Spot healing brush.

9. After working with an image, you may notice aspects that need further refinement that you didn't notice earlier. In this example, I felt that the shadows were a bit too dark to do the summer's day image justice. So I merged the layers up with Cmd-Option-Shift-E/Ctrl-Alt-Shift-E and used a mild Shadow/Highlights adjustment (as discussed in Chapter 3 "Exposure Correction") to open up the shadows ever so slightly as seen in **figure 5.41**.

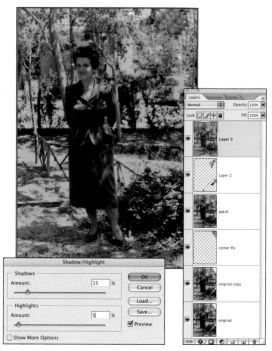

figure 5.41

Lightening the shadows improves the image.

Using the Crop Tool to Restore Images

In the 19th and 20th centuries, many different photographic formats existed—from circular to just about every rectangular dimension imaginable. But often the client wants to frame the restored image in a frame that is standard today. Cropping to the aspect ratio of a contemporary frame can save both time and money, something most clients appreciate. The image seen in **figure 5.42** is a perfect example of a photograph that was shot with a square format film. Rather than rebuilding the image corner, which does not contain useful image information I suggested cropping for a suitable frame size as seen in **figure 5.43**. By cropping the image, I was able to restore the image in a few minutes as described here.

ch5_man_in_suit.jpg

BEFORE

figure 5.42

figure 5.44

Photoshop does an admirable job of automatically straightening an image with clearly defined edges.

2. Select the Crop tool, set the size for 8×10 and leave the resolution box empty. Set the crop as seen in **figure 5.45** and press Enter.

AFTER

figure 5.43

1. To quickly straighten a scan (I use this a lot—more of my scans are crooked than straight!), use the File > Automate > Crop & Straighten function. Photoshop will duplicate the file and do its best to straighten the image, as seen in **figure 5.44**. This feature works better on images with clearly defined edges.

figure 5.45

Set the crop and then use the arrow keys to refine its position.

3. Duplicate the Background layer and use the Clone tool to quickly cover up the distracting pipe and clean up the background with the Healing Brush as seen in **figure 5.46**.

figure 5.46

After cropping, clean up the remaining information with the Clone and Healing tools.

4. Add a blue Solid Color fill layer, change the blending mode to Color and reduce the layer opacity to 26%—the image is ready for printing and framing in no time at all! (See figure 5.47.)

Work smart—consider the Crop tool a powerful restoration tool and you'll save a lot of time, effort, and aggravation.

figure 5.47

Subtle toning enriches the image.

Concentrate on What's Important

Sometimes the solution to restoring a difficult image is to just concentrate on the main focus of the image and creatively hide the worst damage. In figure 5.48, you see a picture of a boy on his homemade tractor; the stain obliterates a third of the image. After removing the stain and cleaning up the other damage, there was nothing to use as a reference in the repair of the tractor. A satisfactory solution, masking out the damage to hide the back end of the tractor as seen in figure 5.49, made the work easier and kept the project within the customer's budget.

© Bonham Family Archive

figure 5.48

The original is badly faded and stained, which seems like a daunting task.

figure 5.49

Sometimes the solution to repairing an image is simply to creatively hide it.

Beg, Borrow, and Steal Information

Another way to fill in a missing area is to use the duplicate-and-mask technique, which, as the name implies, involves copying part of the image—or even information from a similar file—on top of the empty or highly damaged area to fill it in. With a bit of layer masking and blending with the Clone or Healing tools, you can rebuild missing corners and gaps in no time at all.

As illustrated with more dramatic examples in Chapter 7, "Rebuilding and Re-creating Images," it is often easier and faster to use existing images to rebuild a file than it is to using the Clone or Healing tools. **Figure 5.50** is obviously missing a corner and **figure 5.51** has a repaired corner, which took just a couple of minutes to repair as described here.

© Colin Dearing

BEFORE

figure 5.50

AFTER

figure 5.51

1. Select the Lasso tool and set the feather to 2 or 3 to generously select the good corner as seen in **figure 5.52**.

2. Choose Layer > New > Layer via Copy or press Cmd-J/Ctrl-J to duplicate the selected area onto its own layer.

3. Move the new corner into position and choose Edit > Transform > Flip Horizontal as seen in **figure 5.53**.

figure 5.52

Selecting the opposite corner, which has no damage.

figure 5.53

Moving the copied corner into place.

4. Add a layer mask to this layer and use a soft, black brush on the layer mask to build a subtle transition (**figure 5.54**).

5. To refine the new corner, add a new layer and use the Healing Brush set to Sample All Layers and heal away any telltale signs of repair as seen in **figure 5.55**.

figure 5.54

A layer mask helps integrate the copied information into the original.

figure 5.55

A little healing along the edge finishes off the repair.

Caution

If at any time you receive a warning that Photoshop "could not make a new layer from the selection because the selected area is empty" you are trying to copy or duplicate a selected area on a blank layer, which is not possible. (In other words—you cannot copy nothing.) Be sure that the layer you want to copy or duplicate information from is active.

Healing Brush

With the introduction of the Spot Healing Brush, you may find yourself using the original Healing Brush less frequently, but the Healing Brush is still very useful when you need to control where the tool samples from or would like to pull a sample in from another open image. The image in **figure 5.56** is a charming photo with some very obvious problems. The emulsion has been ripped off the center areas but some quick repair creates the image seen in **figure 5.57**.

ch5_girl_with_bow.jpg

1. Create a new blank layer above the Background layer and name it *fixes*.

2. Select the Healing Brush tool and double-check that Sample All Layers is checked in the options bar. Starting on the middle of her stomach, heal away the right side of the brown splotches and some of the yellow specks as seen in **figure 5.58**.

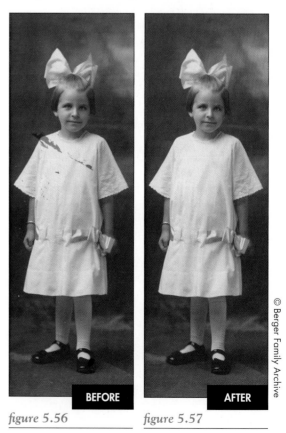

BEFORE

AFTER

figure 5.56

figure 5.57

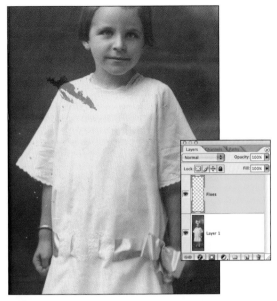

figure 5.58

Healing the damage to the dress.

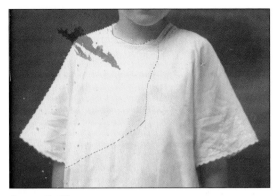

figure 5.60

An active selection limits where the Healing takes place and can be used to avoid the dreaded smudged look.

Tip

If the marching ants are interfering with what you are repairing, you can hide them by pressing Cmd-H/Ctrl-H. Pressing the same sequence a second time will make them visible

3. If you get too close to the edge of the dress, very ugly light and dark smudges will appear where the background is being healed in. (**figure 5.59**). If you see smudges use the History palette to step back until the image is not smudged.

figure 5.59

Getting too close to the edge, where the light dress meets the dark background, creates ugly smudges.

4. Use the Magnetic Lasso tool to select a portion of the dress (**figure 5.60**) and use the Healing Brush well within the selection to build up the good information. Even with the selection, it is advisable to stay well inside the selection to avoid the smudged effect.

5. Invert the selection and clean up the background of the image. Since the contrast is so high, I find it more effective to build up initial information with the Clone tool and refine with the Healing brush. Sadly, the Healing brush doesn't respect selections as well as expected. Ideally it should only heal inside the active selection.

6. Choose Select > Deselect and remove the small specks with the Spot Healing brush.

7. Fixing the hole in her shoe is best done with a hard-edged Clone Stamp tool to build up information from all four directions around the hole to create **figure 5.61**.

figure 5.61

The Clone tool is very effective in rebuilding missing information.

Healing with Pattern

Very often, an image is so mottled and damaged that it is difficult to find enough good information to sample with any of the cloning or healing tools. In most cases you have two choices—to select the background and replace it completely (as is addressed in Chapter 7) or to create a faux reference for the Healing Brush to use as its source.

In **figure 5.62**, you see a charming old photo. The background is stained and mottled and there appears to be very little to sample from to create a good background. The Healing Brush has the option of sampling from a pattern. This pattern could be one you make or one of the presets that Adobe has provided. In this image, one of those presets makes filling in the background a breeze, as shown in **figure 5.63**.

🌐▷ **ch5_dachshund_fan.jpg**

1. To protect your original image, create a new blank layer above the Background layer and name it *Fixes*.

2. Select the Healing Brush tool. Select the Sample All Layers option, select the Pattern option, and click the Pattern thumbnail to open the Pattern pop-up palette. Choose the Grayscale Paper pattern library from the Pattern palette menu, as shown in **figure 5.64**.

3. You will be asked if you wish to replace the current patterns. Select Append, which simply adds the new pattern to the existing ones. To make it easier to find the pattern, use the same small triangle and select Small List (see **figure 5.65**) to see the names of the paper textures; select Kraft Paper.

4. Choose a 60-pixel brush and paint over the background. The tool mixes the pattern with the existing color and tonality, creating a beautiful replacement. When you heal from a pattern, the tool is not pulling in information from the areas of the image around the brush. This means you can paint closer to the subjects without them being smudged, as shown in **figure 5.66**.

BEFORE

figure 5.62

AFTER

figure 5.63

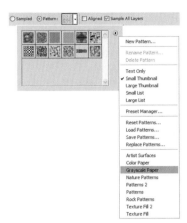

figure 5.64

Select the Grayscale Paper patterns.

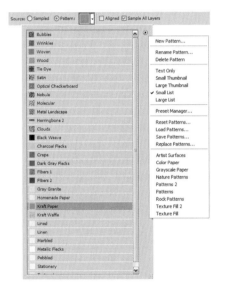

figure 5.65

Kraft Paper is a smooth surfaced paper for a pattern.

figure 5.66

Healing from a pattern allows you to work closer to the edges and simultaneously avoid the smudged look.

Creating Custom Patterns

You may not always be so fortunate to find a preset texture to repair your photographs. That is when you can turn to the Pattern Maker, which generates texture from a small sample in the image (like the one in **figure 5.67**) that you can then save as a custom pattern to use for repairs, to create the results seen in **figure 5.68** and as outlined here.

figure 5.67

© Berger Family Archive

BEFORE

figure 5.68

AFTER

⊕▷⊱ ch5_Mr_Berger.jpg

1. Find an area of the image that has representative texture, select it with the Marquee tool set to 0 feather, and take a few minutes to clean it with the Spot Healing Brush if necessary (figure 5.69). In this example, I used the Spot Healing brush set to Lighten, which cleaned up the darker textured areas very quickly.

2. Copy the cleaned up area to the clipboard by pressing Cmd-C/Ctrl-C followed by Cmd-D/Ctrl-D to deselect. Select Filter > Pattern Maker.

figure 5.69

Clean a small area of the image to use as the pattern.

3. Make sure Use Clipboard as Sample is selected and click Generate. Ignore the fact that your image preview is covered with the selected texture (figure 5.70). Pay attention to the tile in the lower-right corner of the Pattern Maker window; this is the generated pattern you will use to heal. The goal is to create a pattern that shows as few visible artifacts or lines as possible.

4. If need be, click Generate Again, and the Pattern Maker will recalculate the pattern. You can cycle through previously generated pattern tiles by clicking the small left and right triangles in the Tile History section.

5. After deciding which pattern you like, the next two steps are extremely important. Click the small Save icon (looks like the world's smallest floppy disk) under the tile preview in Tile History to save the pattern and name it with a meaningful name—such as including the name of the original file in the pattern name.

6. Then click Cancel to exit the Pattern Maker dialog box without ruining your image.

7. Activate the Healing Brush, click Pattern on the options bar, and the named pattern is now in your pattern library.

8. Use short brushstrokes to avoid repeating artifacts and use a very small Healing Brush to clean up the specks on his face and suit, as seen in figure 5.71. If you do see a visible pattern, a quick pass of the Clone Stamp tool should be all you need to repair this image in no time flat.

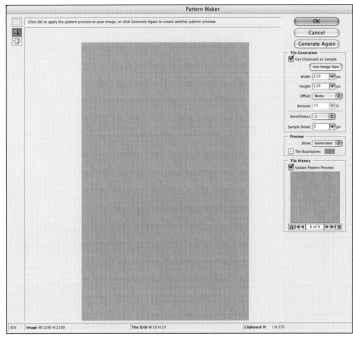

figure 5.70

The Pattern Maker creates new random patterns based upon the copied image information.

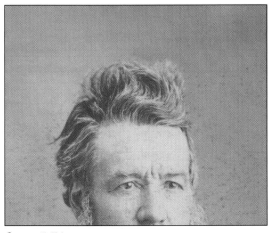

figure 5.71

Use short healing brush strokes to repair the primary areas very quickly.

Working with the Patch Tool

The Patch tool, nested with the Healing Brushes in the Toolbox, lets you repair a selected area with pixels from another area or with a defined pattern. Like the Healing Brush tools, the Patch tool matches the texture with the luminosity and color of the sampled pixels to the source pixels. Similar to the Healing Brush, the Patch tool works best with small initial selections. Of all the restoration tools, the Patch tool is my favorite as it allows me to work very quickly.

In figure 5.72, you see one of the most damaged contemporary images I've ever had to repair. The original medium-format slide had been discarded on a New York street and I found it in a puddle between piles of trash. It took me about eight hours to repair the entire file (figure 5.73).

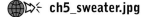 ch5_sweater.jpg

The most important decision to make before using the Patch tool is whether to patch from source, destination, or pattern. You make this choice in the options bar when the Patch tool is active. My personal approach is to use Source when the damaged area is oddly shaped, use Destination when you need to match an image texture or structure, and use Pattern to lay down a fast fix that you can refine with the Healing Brush if need be. Repairing this image made use of all methods:

After using the duplicate-and-move technique (described earlier in this chapter) to minimize the worst of the damage on the unimportant background areas, I had to get down to work and repair the numerous gouges and tears and replace missing image information. I used both of the Healing and Spot Healing Brushes on her face, but I used the Patch tool on the larger areas in the background and her sweater to fix the worst of the image's damage quickly and easily.

figure 5.72

figure 5.73

- **Source:** Requires that you select the damaged image information (**figure 5.74**) and, with the Patch tool, move the selection to a good image area (**figure 5.75**). When you release the mouse, the originally selected area will be healed, as shown in **figure 5.76**. To continue working, either choose Select > Deselect (Cmd-D/Ctrl-D), or simply select a new area outside the existing selection to be patched—all of which will drop the selection around the newly patched area.

figure 5.76

Release the mouse, and the Patch tool heals the original selected area.

- **Destination:** Select good image information (as shown in **figure 5.77**) and use the Patch tool to move the selection over the damaged image area (**figure 5.78**). Before you release the mouse, you can align the good image information with the pattern of the area to be patched.

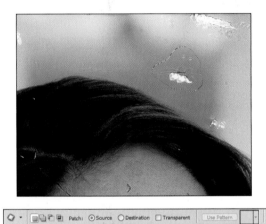

figure 5.74

Roughly select the damaged image area.

figure 5.75

Move the selection to a good image area.

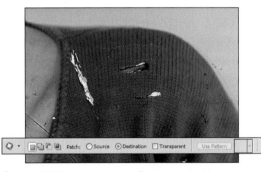

figure 5.77

Selecting good image information with the Patch tool.

figure 5.78

Drag the good image information over the damaged image areas.

- **Pattern:** The Patch tool also can heal with a pattern. After generating an image-specific pattern with the Pattern Maker as explained in the previous section about the Healing Brush, make a selection (figure 5.79), activate the Patch tool, and click the Use Pattern button in the options bar. Patching with a pattern can be a time-saver on large, unimportant image areas such as backdrops or skies, as shown in figure 5.80.

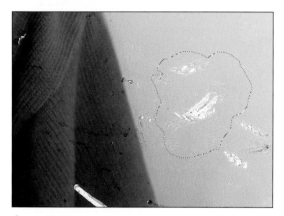

figure 5.79

Select the damaged image area.

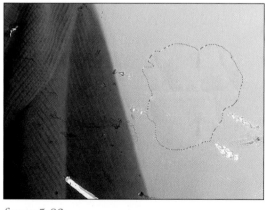

figure 5.80

Patching with a pattern is ideal for large and less important image areas.

To match more complex patterns, use the duplicate-and-patch technique that I learned from Russell Brown at Adobe. This little-documented method enables you to float a temporary patch and transform it into position to match even the most challenging patterns.

1. Select good image information, as shown in figure 5.81, and set the Patch tool to destination.

2. With the Patch tool active, Cmd-Option/Ctrl-Alt-click inside the selection to create a duplicate patch.

figure 5.81

Selecting good image information.

3. Keep the modifier keys depressed and move the selection into position.

4. Still holding the modifier keys, press T to activate the Free Transform command and then release the modifier keys.

5. Use the handles on the bounding box to rotate, scale, or otherwise modify the patch to fit the area, as shown in figure 5.82. Press return/enter to accept the transformation.

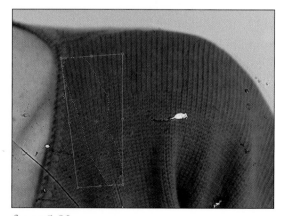

figure 5.82

Narrowing the bottom of the patch allows the sweater ribbing to blend.

6. Now make sure that the Patch tool is active and move the mouse pointer into the active selection. Reposition the patch by one pixel to reactivate the healing engine and press return/enter again to tell Photoshop to heal with the transformed information. The last move with the Patch tool can be as slight as a single pixel move, but you have to do it to reawaken the healing engine and achieve the results shown in **figure 5.83**.

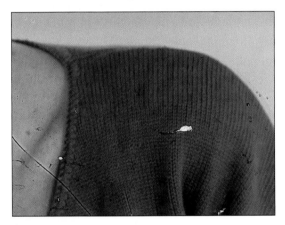

figure 5.83

After reactivating the healing engine, the large gash is practically invisible.

Working with the Patch tool is often even easier and faster than working with the Healing Brush. See Chapter 9, "Portrait Retouching," for a quick technique to hide skin blemishes with the Patch tool.

Healing in Perspective

Repairing patterns or damage on flat surfaces that were photographed straight-on (**figure 5.84**) can be a rather straightforward undertaking. But repairing images in which the subject was photographed in perspective (**figure 5.85**) is more challenging. As the image perspective recedes, the cloning or healing needs to become smaller to match the receding perspective.

figure 5.84

Photographed straight on in one-point perspective.

figure 5.85

Photographed in two-point perspective in which the vanishing lines are receding away from the viewer.

One of the more interesting tools developed for Photoshop CS2 is Vanishing Point. It will be particularly useful to the retoucher when the task at hand is to replace a patterned area that changes perspective. This has always been a difficult problem with healing and patching, as the effect doesn't always blend believably well. As we worked through in the previous example, transforming a patch also works but the Vanishing Point tool combines the best features of the Clone Stamp and Healing Brush tools into one that also can handle changes in perspective.

This image of a historic home reflects some of the grandeur of days gone by (figure 5.86). Unfortunately, the two large patches in the brick street left behind by the utility company mar it. With techniques we have learned with the Healing Brush, we could copy and paste a good section of brick over the bad and, with a little tweaking, also transform that patch to match the existing pattern. However, Vanishing Point is able to do this with so much less effort. So let's save the taxpayers some money and do some Photoshop street repair as seen in figure 5.87.

figure 5.86

figure 5.87

⊕▷⊱ ch5_brickstreet.jpg

1. To protect the original Background layer add a new layer and label it *Street Repair*.

2. Select Filter > Vanishing Point or press Option-Cmd-V/Alt-Ctrl-V to open the Vanishing Point interface.

3. The first step, after entering Vanishing Point, is to establish the proper plane of perspective, so Vanishing Point can correctly shape the new image information. Select the Create Plane tool, which is under the arrow on the left side—it looks like a small piece of mesh.

4. Click where the curb and brick street meet (labeled 1 in figure 5.88), pull the mouse along the curb and click the curb edge well past the to be repaired area (labeled 2), using the rows of the bricks as a guide click (3) and then click the fourth point to complete the plane definition.

Note

If you have done a good job determining the perspective plane, the grid will be blue. If you have a yellow grid, it means you are close but need to make some minor adjustments. If the marquee line is red and does not fill with the grid, then you need to either start over or make some adjustments with the Edit Plane tool. Vanishing Point will work whether the perspective plane is valid or not, but the results will not be satisfactory unless the plane accurately reflects the perspective in the image.

5. With the Create Plane tool, expand the grid with the handles on the sides (not the corners) to take in the entire area from which you might sample. This may cause the grid to run outside the actual image. Use the view options in the lower left hand corner to fit the image to screen to see the entire grid as shown in figure 5.89.

figure 5.88

Create a plane of perspective by clicking points along a visualized perspective view.

figure 5.89

Expand the grid to cover the entire area you may sample from. Zoom out if the grid goes outside the image.

6. The Vanishing Point Clone Stamp tool clones by default, but can be set to heal by selecting On from the Heal drop-down menu. Turn healing on, change the brush size to 150 pixels and make sure that Aligned is checked.

7. As you would with the Clone Stamp or Healing Brush, Option/Alt-click to sample a good area of brick well in front of the asphalt patch. Move your brush over the asphalt and you will see a sampled area lift, move, and resize to match the perspective the existing bricks. Align the lines of the bricks in the brush with the existing bricks and paint. Repeat this step and resample as necessary to cover the rest of the asphalt (see figure 5.90). Click OK.

8. Your changes are now above the Background layer as seen in figure 5.91. If you find that some of the added bricks are not a good match or don't line up with the originals, you can use either a layer mask to blend the edges for a more believable fix or, in this case, apply a bit of standard healing.

figure 5.90

Using the Clone Stamp set to Heal, sample near the undesired sections and clone away the patched street.

figure 5.91

Refine the Vanishing Point healing with a touch up with the healing or cloning tools.

PRINT TEXTURE, MOIRÉ, AND COLOR ARTIFACTS

Many historical photographs were printed on paper with textures, which at the time must have been very beautiful. From the perspective of a restoration artist, these same textures can be among the most difficult issues you'll be confronted with. Maintaining, removing, or concealing textures, patterns, reflections, offset moiré, and digital camera artifacts have caused many a digital retoucher to lose both sleep and hair. By using a combination of Photoshop filters, creative input techniques, layers, and layer masks, you can achieve very good results—as long as you are able to compromise. A retouched image that started with a strong paper texture will never look as smooth or crisp as an original from a negative or from an untextured print.

There are a number of approaches to reducing print texture, including:

- Concentrate on the important image areas and blur the unimportant image areas.

- Minimize the texture in the scanning phase by either overscanning the image as described in the following section or by using the descreen function in the scanning software to minimize the print texture.

- Use a film—or better yet, a digital—camera to make a copy of the negative or file. By using either very soft light or polarized light when photographing original artwork, you can control how much of the pattern is visible.

Reducing Print Texture and Reflections Before Retouching

In the early to mid twentieth century, photographic supply companies offered dozens of black-and-white papers. Many of these were textured, which looked interesting at the time but are a nightmare to scan and retouch today as the texture now becomes part of the image. Experiment with reducing print texture in the input stage with the following techniques. Please note that I used the word *experiment*—each print brings specific challenges in terms of texture, size, warping, how reflective the surface is, and other damage that needs to be deemphasized. The time you use to experiment, make mistakes, and learn how to do copy work or scan a textured print will be well worth it in saved retouching hours.

- Overscan the image by 300 to 400% and downsize the file down via Image > Image Size in two to four increments. The close-up in **figure 5.97** reveals a paper texture throughout the entire image. Stepping the image down by three steps makes it a bit softer but, more importantly, the texture has been softened out of existence (**figure 5.98**).

figure 5.97

The original image with a close-up that reveals distracting image texture.

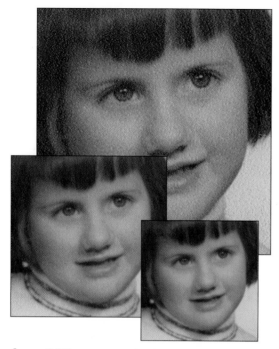

figure 5.98

Stepping the file down in three steps via Image Size reduces the bothersome texture.

- When using a film or digital camera to make digital copies, use polarizing filters on the lights and one on the camera lens and look through the camera viewfinder as you turn the filter to see the effect as the lighter areas of the texture darken and lighten. Or, as shown in **figure 5.99**, tilt the original slightly to help reduce reflections on glass or in the dark silvery areas of an image.

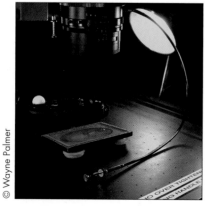

figure 5.99

Tilting the original can reduce reflections.

- Use your digital camera to make a digital copy negative. A 5- to 8-megapixel camera can capture enough information to make most common print sizes. If a copy stand is not part of your restoration equipment, carefully photograph the original on an angle as Mark Beckelman did to avoid having to take the print out of the glass frame (**figure 5.100**), which had become adhered to the print. If you use a flash bounce the light off of a white surface to soften the light. These techniques can also solve problems with digitizing images that will not lie flat or can't be taken out of their frames.

figure 5.100

Photographing the original twice at two different angles provided plenty of information to create the final image.

- Scan images with a flatbed scanner—but scan the print two or three times and rotate the print between scans. Experiment with angles and use the scan in which the light that bounces off of the print makes the texture least visible. This also works very well for images that have silvering and damage problems. Sometimes scans at different rotational angles enhance different parts of the image. Taking the best parts of several scans and putting them together into one image might be the best solution.

Reducing Glare

When a client brought Wayne an image to restore that was heavily silvered, he tried multiple techniques to capture the image while trying get rid of the silvering, but they all seemed to increase the effect, as shown in **figure 5.101**, instead of eliminating it. The blue glare is the metallic silver oxidizing into a colorless silver ion, which then migrates to the surface and reduces back to metallic elemental silver, which is reflective.

🌐▷✦ **ch5_tilted_photo.jpg**

figure 5.101

The image viewed straight on or scanned showed a highly silverized image.

1. Wayne discovered that by tilting the image to an extreme angle while photographing it, he was able to minimize most of the silvering (**figure 5.102**).

2. Converting the image to grayscale eliminated the rest of the silvering (**figure 5.103**).

figure 5.102

When viewed (and subsequently) photographed at a sharp angle, the silvering all but disappeared—but the image appeared distorted.

figure 5.103

Converting the image to grayscale removed the remaining silvering.

3. Photoshop CS2 offers a new option with the Transform tool called Warp, which enables you to freely bend and shape an image (**figure 5.104**). Laying down some guides, he straightened the picture.

4. After some cleanup and a conversion into a sepia tone, the image took on its original appearance as shown in **figure 5.105.**

© Shaw Family Archive

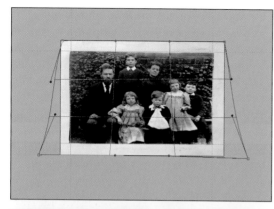

figure 5.104

Using the new Warp feature of the Transform tool enables you to reshape a distorted image.

figure 5.105

The final image straightened and sepia-toned.

Reducing Paper Texture and Print Patterns

The secret to minimizing paper texture and print patterns without giving yourself too many gray hairs is to compromise—let the unimportant image areas blur out and concentrate your efforts on the important image areas. The following technique uses a combination of blurred and masked layers followed by a bit of clean-up to achieve the final results. Because each image is unique and such a large variety of paper textures is available, there are no quick fixes or easy answers to this problem. Photoshop CS2 introduces a new filter called Surface Blur, which can quickly get you on your way to getting rid of paper texture.

Figure 5.106 is a splendid example of a photograph from an earlier time period. The image is in near-perfect condition, but making copies for other family members is a bit troublesome, because the print was made on a textured paper. From a distance, the texture is not noticeable, but looking through a loupe easily displays the problem. After selectively blurring and masking the image the final rendition looks quite good as seen in figure 5.107.

🌐 ▷⊱ **ch5_textureportrait.jpg**

🔍 **Tip**

When clients bring in old prints study them under an 8 x loupe to see if the paper is textured as seen in figure 5.108. Letting the client see the paper texture is helpful to reduce unreasonably high expectations.

1. Duplicate the original layer, rename it *Surface Blur*, and select Filter > Blur > Surface Blur. Choose a radius of 2 and slide the Threshold to 84 (figure 5.109). The highlights of the texture have disappeared but you can still see a pattern to the background.

2. Duplicate the Surface Blur layer and rename it *Gaussian Blur*. Select Filter > Blur > Gaussian Blur. Choose a radius of 3, which eliminates the noticeable pattern left behind in the background (figure 5.110).

BEFORE

figure 5.106

AFTER

figure 5.107

figure 5.108

The original image upon close examination with a loupe reveals the distracting image texture.

figure 5.109

The Surface Blur filter removes most of the pattern, particularly the highlights.

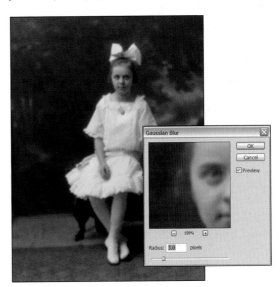

figure 5.110

Running the Gaussian Blur filter removes the rest of the pattern but also make the image very soft.

3. Create a layer mask on the *Gaussian Blur* layer. Choose a soft-edged brush and trace a quick outline of the girl. Be sure to have an enclosed outline when done (**figure 5.111**). Select the Paint Bucket tool and click once inside the outline to fill it with black, completing the layer mask (**figure 5.112**).

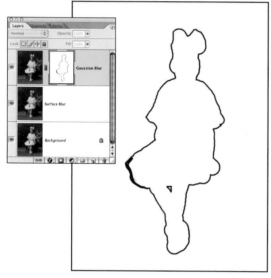

figure 5.111

Painting an outline of the girl with a soft-edged brush and then filling that outline with black completes the mask.

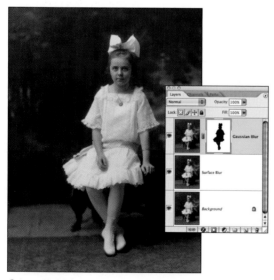

figure 5.112

The final image with the pattern disguised.

Reducing Offset Moiré

Sooner or later, a client will come to you with only a printed image clipped from a newspaper, magazine, or brochure. After scanning it, you may find that the entire image is covered with moiré rosette patterns caused by four-color separation offset printing and often referred to as *screening* (**figure 5.113**).

figure 5.113

A close-up view of a previously printed photo reveals the patterns created in the offset printing process.

Before you start trying to repair the damage, ask the client politely if she might have a photographic original. If not, swallow hard and follow these recommendations to minimize the moiré effect.

With any screened image there is a finite amount of information. Unlike a photograph, magnifying the image will not show any more information than you can see with your eye. Different types of publications use different types of screening rates, with newspapers generally being the lowest. The best time to fix moiré is during scanning. Most scanning software has a descreening function that works at least as well as, and probably much better than, anything you can do later in Photoshop.

To get the best results, determine the image's LPI (lines per inch) with a screen-angle finder like the one by Beta Screen Co. shown in **figure 5.114**. Knowing the LPI will give you better results either in using screening software or in trying to remove it manually. The general LPIs used in the United States are 85 for newspaper, 133 for weekly magazines, 150 for monthly magazines, and 200 or higher for tabletop quality books.

figure 5.114

Screen-angle finders help determine the LPI of a screened image.

The idea behind making a screened image look photographic again is to run the dots together by lowering the image's resolution, so they can no longer be seen, and then resizing the image. The resized image will not reveal any new details and will appear soft. This is the trade-off for getting rid of the dots.

Note

I am not condoning scanning images from magazines, books, or stock catalogs because that would be breaking U.S. copyright law. Rather, I am recognizing that at some point, you or a client may have only a magazine or brochure image of her factory (for example) for you to use. Or in the worst-case scenario, the original negative or film has been lost or damaged and the only image available is a prescreened one.

This image taken from an old brochure shows a computer room from many years ago. Here is a method Wayne uses to reduce moiré patterns when confronted with an image that is screened and scanned.

ch5_computer_room.jpg

1. Enlarge the image view to 100%.

2. Zoom out on the picture by pressing Cmd-"–"/Ctrl-"–". As you zoom out, you will see the moiré pattern change as it interacts with the monitor's resolution.

3. When the pattern is no longer visible, note the % size in the file's title bar. In this example 50% worked well with my monitor.

4. Select Image > Image Size and check Resample Image and Constrain Proportions. In the Pixel Dimensions section use the drop down menu to choose percentage and type in the value from step 3 (see **figure 5.115**). Click OK.

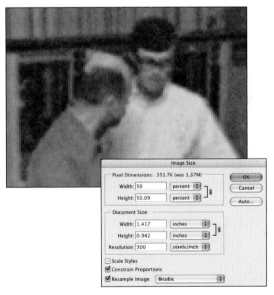

figure 5.115

Reduce the resolution to that percentage shown in the title bar of the original resolution.

5. Reopen the Image Size dialog box and type in the original pixel dimensions (or in my case 200%) and select the Bicubic Smoother option (**figure 5.116**). Click OK. Note you must open and close the dialog box so Photoshop does the calculations.

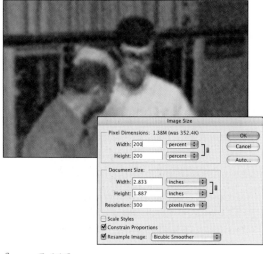

figure 5.116

Resize the image back to its original size.

This should remove most, if not all, of the moiré pattern. If any remains, use the Spot Healing brush to retouch the most important image areas. Remember that this technique requires compromise, but the image will look better than with the dots. As you can imagine, going through all these steps is a last resort technique to remove moiré. It would be best to start by using the original non-screened image.

Reducing Digital Camera Noise and Moiré

Digital camera technology is based on a variety of technologies, including scanning, three-shot, and one-shot cameras. The one-shot cameras work just like your film camera, except that a CCD (charged coupled device) or CMOS chip (complementary metal-oxide semiconductor) with a color mosaic filter replaces the film. The CCD structure, in combination with the filter, can cause color artifacts that look like little twinkles of colored lights

or rainbow-like moiré patterns. They might be visible in areas of high-frequency, fine-detail information, such as eyelashes, flyaway hair strands, specular highlights, small branches of trees, or woven fabrics.

Even if you don't use a digital camera, you might pick up moiré patterns when scanning images with fine fabrics. You can use the following filter to take care of those problems.

CS2 has added a new filter, appropriately named the Reduce Noise filter, to tackle problems equated with images taken at a high ISO or those that are depicting artifacts from being saved as JPEG files.

The filter's adjustments address different types of noise patterns. One is Luminance smoothing, which tackles clusters of noise, and another is Color Noise Reduction, which gets rid of color speckles. The advanced setting button brings up an additional tab that enables you to address the noise by individual channel.

In this image (**figure 5.117**), the model's dark dress shows color noise where there should be solid black. To clean the dress as seen in **figure 5.118**, use the Reduce Noise Filter (see **figure 5.119**.)

After using the Reduce Noise Filter the black looks much cleaner, as seen in figure 5.118.

Caution

The Reduce Noise filter is very memory intensive. Be patient when making adjustments, as you may not see the screen refresh showing your changes as quickly as with other filters. This filter, like any other, changes actual pixels in the image layer (unlike an adjustment layer), so if you want to be able to adjust the effect later, be sure to duplicate the Background layer before starting.

Please note, reducing noise always involves softening the image, which means that details will be lost. If you can take the picture with a low ISO or in the RAW format you will achieve better results from the very start.

© Skyy McKendry

figure 5.117

figure 5.118

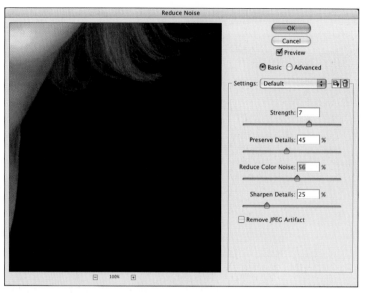

figure 5.119

The Reduce Noise Filter interface.

Maintaining Image Texture

A little bit of good restoration is better than a whole lot of bad restoration. Using brushes with inappropriate (to the image) hardness settings can cause the telltale signs of poor retouching, including cloudiness, ghostly traces, or a loss of original image texture.

When using the Clone Stamp tool, determining the best hardness setting is essential to not leaving obvious traces. In general, I use between 50-80% hardness to blend the edges of the cloning as **figure 5.92** illustrates. Working with a very soft-edged brush leaves traces, particularly if you work over the same area several times, which can create a slight blur. I refer to those traces as *the smudgies*. The original defect is covered, but your eye still identifies that something has been changed.

Despite your best efforts to use the right brush setting or to avoid repeating patterns, you may notice evidence of your work. Generally, it's the missing grain texture of the original image that makes the image editing obvious, like in **figure 5.93**. The soft brush blended in the information tonality, while the grain structure became blurred. Here is a technique to put back the grain (see **figure 5.94**).

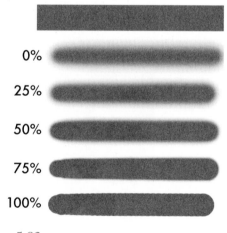

figure 5.92

The brush hardness setting determines the sharpness of the Clone tool edge.

Here is a technique to restore the damaged grain.

1. Select the layer with the over-zealous cloning. Choose Layer > New > Layer and name it *Grain for Fixes*. Change the Mode to Overlay, check Use Previous Layer to Create Clipping Mask and check Fill with Overlay-neutral color (50% gray). The clipping mask limits the steps taken on this layer to affecting only the layer directly underneath. Click OK.

figure 5.93

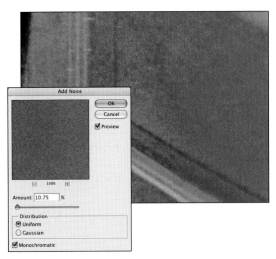

BEFORE

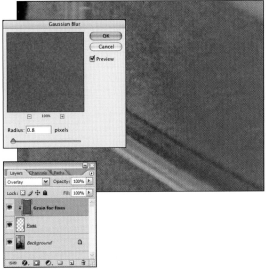

figure 5.95

Generate a noise pattern that is the same size as the grain in the image.

AFTER

figure 5.94

figure 5.96

Use the Gaussian Blur filter to take the sharp edge off the noise.

2. Choose Filter > Noise > Add Noise. Choose a size that matches the granularity of the original; don't be concerned with its sharpness, because we'll take care of that in the next step. Be sure the monochromatic option is selected (**figure 5.95**).

3. Choose Filter > Blur > Gaussian Blur to take the edge off the noise (**figure 5.96**). If you work with older, less sharp originals—try using Filter > Noise > Median to average the digital noise to look more clumpy and authentic.

4. Adjust the layer opacity to blend the noise in.

If need be, return to the Fixes layer and continue cloning or healing. Because of the clipping mask, the new grain texture will be applied to any new restoration as well.

 T i p

You don't have to fix it all. There are times you may notice that as you zoom in further and further on an image, you find more and more to repair. If you have your image sized for output and the view set at 100%, it's a pretty safe bet that if you can't see it on the screen, you won't see it on the print.

CLOSING THOUGHTS

There are some images that will not have any quick fixes. They are fixable but only with a great amount of time. If you are doing this as a family project, it can be a labor of love. If you are doing this as a business, you might be better served by turning down the work if you can't repair the image in a reasonable amount of time or stay within the customer's budget.

In most cases, removing dust and mold while maintaining image structure is all that is needed to bring an image back to life. In the worst-case scenario where time, damage, and missing pieces are plaguing your images, you'll need to use the emergency room techniques discussed in Chapters 6, "Damage Control and Repair," and 7, "Rebuilding and Re-creating Images."

6

DAMAGE CONTROL AND REPAIR

The torture we put our old photographs through—storing them in damp basements or hot attics, carrying them in wallets, folding, tearing, cutting, scribbling on them, and pasting them into albums—all leave telltale marks, cracks, rips, tears, and misshapen corners. So if this is so bad for photographs, why do we put them through the gauntlet of abuse? Because we value, treasure, and cherish them. We like carrying pictures of loved ones in our wallets or purses; we take pleasure in making the family photo album or collage; and sadly, we often don't realize that the basement or attic isn't the best place to store a valuable print.

So rather than relegating the damaged photos to a dark, forgotten basement corner or a hot, dusty attic, let's get them out, scan them in, and learn to:

- Eliminate cracks, tears, and rips

- Make stains, scribbles, and discoloration disappear

- Repair antique documents

- Remove distractions and correct the perspective

Continuing with the techniques addressed in Chapter 5, "Dust, Mold, and Texture Removal," the tools used to tackle these challenges include:

- The Clone Stamp and all the Healing Brush tools

- Layers and Quick Mask

- Warp option of the Transform tool

- The Lens Correction filter

ELIMINATING CRACKS, RIPS, AND TEARS

Prints that have been mishandled or improperly stored often suffer the indignities of cracks, tears, rips, and missing information. Although some of the damaged originals you face may seem daunting, with enough time, care, and realistic expectations you can turn a very poor original into a treasured family heirloom. My restoration strategy is to improve tone and color and then fix the easier problems as I work my way up to the problems that require more care and attention. Working from simpler to more complex repairs allows me to develop a feel for the image and build up confidence before tackling the more challenging aspects.

Patching Good over Bad

We all have that one drawer that is collects all those things we don't know where to put—from rubber bands to single batteries to, as seen in **figure 6.1**, old color prints that somehow end up in the back of the drawer to be cracked and creased as time goes by. When this photo was taken it was a nice snapshot, but now that the young boy is in college and the girl a senior in high school, its sentimental value has increased and it's time to pull it out of the drawer and repair it, as seen in **figure 6.2**.

ch6_cracked_print.jpg

1. Add a Curves adjustment layer and use the Options button to select Enhance per Channel Contrast in the Auto Color Corrections dialog box to quickly and easily color balance the file, as seen in **figure 6.3**.

2. To create a new layer to use the Patch tool on, press Cmd-Option-Shift-E/Ctrl-Alt-Shift-E to merge up the color correction and Background layer. Select the Patch tool (nested with the Healing Brush and Spot Healing Brush tools) and make sure the Source button is selected in the options bar. Use the Patch tool to select a 1- to 2-inch piece of the crack. Drag the selection to good image information and release to repair the crack (**figure 6.4**).

figure 6.1

figure 6.2

figure 6.3

Take advantage of the Auto Color Corrections to quickly and easily improve color and contrast.

figure 6.5

The Patch tool effectively removes the time stamp.

figure 6.4

Select the damaged area with the Patch tool, then drag the selection over good information and release to heal the crack.

3. When you get closer to areas with tonal differences, such as where the sky meets the horizon on the right side of the image, make a more careful selection that does not include any water and drag up into good sky information.

4. Move on to the sand and use the same technique of selecting small sections and dragging the selection to matching areas of sand. Use the Patch tool to select and cover up the time stamp, as seen in figure 6.5. (If the time stamp falls on more complex areas in your own photos, use the Healing Brush and Clone Stamp to conceal it.)

After the sand and sky are repaired, the areas across the people's legs require more careful attention. Due to the high contrast and important detail of these areas, the Patch tool is not the best choice to use to fix them. To maintain the detail, use the Clone Stamp and Healing Brush on a separate layer as described here.

5. Add a new layer and call it *Fine Repair*. Zoom in on the legs, and use the Clone Stamp tool with a small 50% hardness brush with Sample All Layers selected to create the initial repair, as seen in figure 6.6. Admittedly, the first repair may not be perfect, but it is important to lay down initial information that will then be refined with careful use of the healing tools.

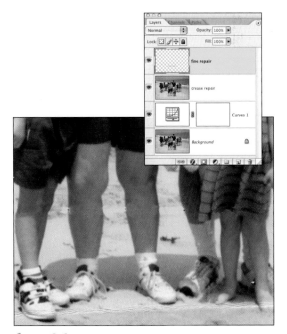

figure 6.6

Use the Clone Stamp tool to build up the initial repair.

6. Use a smaller, hard-edged Healing Brush to refine the cloning. Stay away from areas with strong tonal or color differences to avoid smudging the repair. Follow the Healing Brush with a few dabs of the Spot Healing Brush, also set to Sample All Layers, to clean up any telltale repair artifacts or specks of dust (figure 6.7).

figure 6.7

Refine the cleanup on a separate layer with the Healing and Spot Healing brushes.

7. Finally, cropping the image a bit tighter (figure 6.8) focuses the photograph on the family and creates an image that can be printed and sent to the son's college dorm address as a very nice reminder of a summer vacation on Assateague Island.

figure 6.8

A tighter crop removes distractions.

T i p

When cleaning up dust, if a certain speck does not go away no matter how often you clone, heal, or spot it, make sure that (a) you're on the right layer, (b) you have selected Sample All Layers, (c) the tool's blending mode is set to Normal, and, as silly as it may sound, (d) the dust isn't on the monitor… which has happened to me more often than I care to admit.

Combining the Healing Tools and the Clone Stamp

Improper handling and storage can also create cracks on photos or scratches on negatives. Figure 6.9 shows an original print that was accidentally damaged when the family moved. There are several superficial cracks in the background, as well as more severe cracks on the child's face that go through her eye. Repairing the background can be easily undertaken with the Patch tool. The cracks that fall on important image information such as her arms and dress can be repaired with the Healing Brush and Clone Stamp tools, while repairing the crack over her eye requires more sophisticated skills involving layers, layer masking, and detailed cloning to create the image in figure 6.10.

ch6_cracked_baby.jpg

Before we dive into fixing this image, imagining what the final print will look like can help you to save time and effort. In this example, the client wanted the print to be vignetted with a soft oval falling off to white. This is a common request, and it can be very useful to cover up damage—damage that you do not need to repair. To see how much damage the final vignette will conceal, I add it as the first step and use it as a template to reveal what will be visible in the final image. This keeps me focused on repairing only the areas that will be seen in the final image.

1. Use the Elliptical Marquee tool to draw an oval around the baby as seen in figure 6.11 and inverse the selection via Select > Inverse.

BEFORE

figure 6.9

figure 6.11

Select the subject with the Elliptical Marquee.

2. Add a Solid Color fill layer and choose white from the Color Picker to create a harsh white oval around the infant. To soften the vignette, use Filter > Blur > Gaussian Blur as seen in **figure 6.12**. On a high-resolution file like this one, a filter setting of 75 is not uncommon. Of course your settings will vary depending on file size.

AFTER

figure 6.10

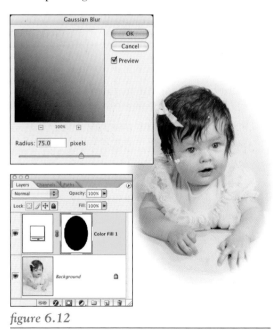

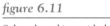

figure 6.12

Blurring the layer mask softens the vignette edge.

3. As the close-up views in **figure 6.13** shows, a lot of damage is covered and so does not need to be repaired. Keep this vignetted layer at the top of your layer stack and turn it on and off to check how much to repair. For safety's sake, I do work past the transparent areas to insure that all required repairs are done.

figure 6.13

Creating the vignette first shows how far you'll have to go with your repairs.

4. To offset the slight fading, add a Levels adjustment layer and move the shadow point to the right to where the tonal information starts and move the highlight slider to the left, as seen in **figure 6.14**.

5. With vignette layer turned off, press Cmd-Option-Shift-E/Ctrl-Alt-Shift-E to merge up the Background and Levels adjustment layer and create a new working surface. Name this new layer *Crack Repair* and activate the Patch tool, making sure that the Patch option is set to Source.

6. Starting with the smaller cracks, circle one section with the Patch tool and move it to good information (**figure 6.15**).

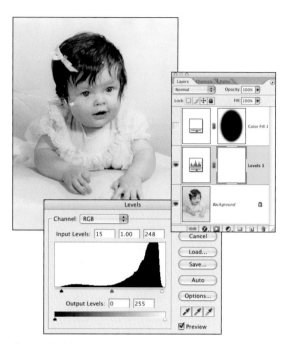

figure 6.14

Improving overall density with Levels.

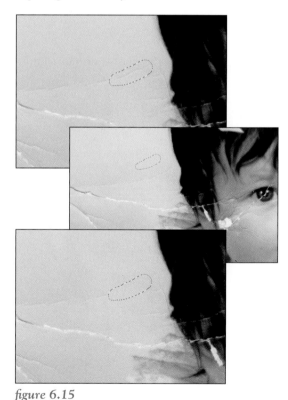

figure 6.15

Repairing smaller areas creates information needed to fix larger problems.

7. Continue fixing the small cracks, as this will create repaired information you can use with the Patch tool to repair the lower, larger crack (**figure 6.16**).

8. Continue patching the monotone areas with no detail on the blanket and her hands, as seen in **figure 6.17**.

figure 6.16

The Patch tool offers the fastest way to repair cracks and damage on even surfaces.

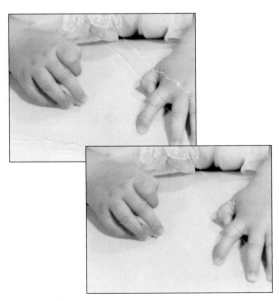

figure 6.17

Avoid high-contrast and highly detailed areas when working quickly with the Patch tool.

After fixing the cracks on the background, it's time to tackle the more delicate areas, such as the damage on her arms and dress, with a combination of healing and cloning. Use the Healing Brush on areas that have only one tonality and the Clone Stamp tool on areas where tones or colors contrast and where there is fine detail.

9. Add a new layer and name it *Fine Repair*. Activate the Healing Brush and make sure its options are Blend Mode: Normal; Source: Sampled; and that both Aligned and Sample All Layers are selected. When Option/Alt-clicking to set the healing source, stay approximately ½ to 1 brush width away from contrasting areas, such as where the little girl's arm meets her dress or on the shadow, to avoid smudging the repair. I like to repair the center of the damage with the Healing Brush and the areas that overlap tonal differences with the Clone Stamp tool (**figure 6.18**).

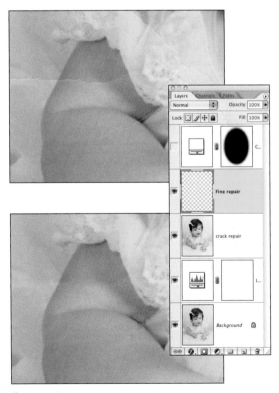

figure 6.18

Combine the Clone Stamp and the Healing Brush to fix contrasting areas.

10. The severe damage on her face requires special care. Repairing areas where entire pieces of print emulsion are missing requires some creative borrowing. Rather than cloning or healing over the large empty surface, use the following technique to rebuild the paper texture quickly. Add a new layer and name it *Face*.

11. Starting from the outside, where the smaller, simpler cracks are, work your way in with the Healing Brush set to Normal and Sample All Layers. By working from outside to inside, as shown in **figure 6.19**, you are building up more and more area to sample from to repair the larger areas.

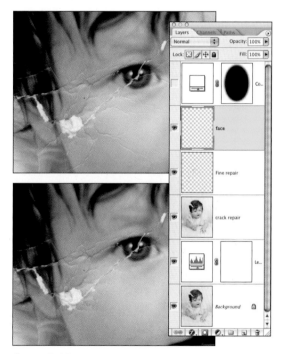

figure 6.19

Working from the easier to the harder areas builds up useful image information.

12. Use a 1- to 2-pixel feathered Lasso tool to generously select good cheek area, as seen in **figure 6.20**.

13. Choose Edit > Copy Merged (Cmd-Shift-C/Ctrl-Shift-C) to copy all the visible layers. Choose Select > Deselect to insure that the copied piece will be pasted without a layer mask. Now choose Edit > Paste.

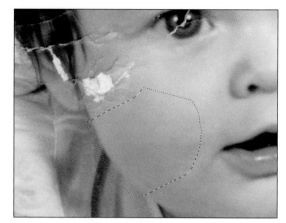

figure 6.20

Select good image information.

14. Move and rotate the pasted piece into position (**figure 6.21**) and press Return/Enter. Then Option/Alt-click the Layer Mask button to add a black layer mask that conceals the new area.

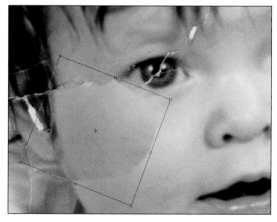

figure 6.21

Rotate the piece into place to cover up as much damage as possible.

15. Use a soft, white Paintbrush on the layer mask to paint back the cheek texture (**figure 6.22**) and to blend in the new area use the Gaussian Blur filter on the layer mask with a setting between 5 and 10 pixels. If necessary, use the Healing Brush to clean up any details on the layer.

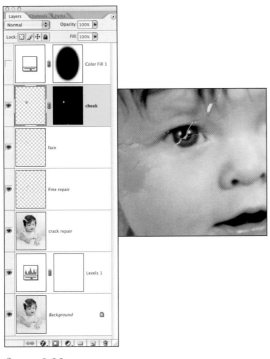

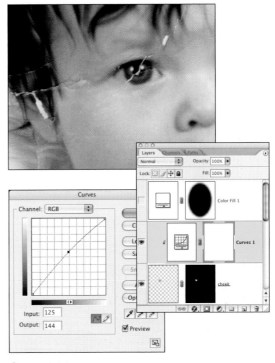

figure 6.22

Paint on the layer mask to conceal the damage.

figure 6.23

Use a clipped Curves layer to match tonality.

16. The patched area is a bit darker than the surrounding area. Option/Alt-click the Create new fill or adjustment layer button, select Curves, and select Group with Previous Layer to Create Clipping Mask to make sure the following tonal adjustment affects only the cheek and not the entire image.

17. Pull the curve up ever so gently to lighten the area and match the rest of the face (**figure 6.23**). I often find it easier to make the clipped area a touch lighter or darker than needed and use the layer opacity to fine-tune the match.

18. Add a new layer and take advantage of the repaired crack to continue healing and cloning her face (**figure 6.24**).

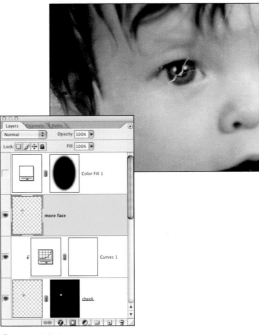

figure 6.24

Working layer by layer and piece by piece rebuilds the face.

19. To repair the delicate eye layer, you could try to use the other eye as a source, similar to repairing the cheek, but we are so sensitive to eyes and how they look that copying, pasting, and flipping eyes seems to make eyes look odd or uncomfortable. I prefer to add a new layer and use a small, hard-edged Clone Stamp tool to build up information, as seen in **figure 6.25**. Most important: If I make a bad stroke, it's easy to immediately undo it and start again. Avoid the temptation to clone over the bad spot—that never works at all.

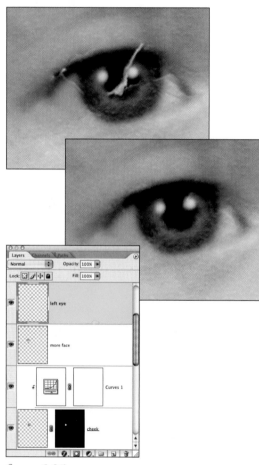

figure **6.25**

Use a small, hard-edged Clone Stamp tool to repair the eye.

20. Use a softer-edged brush when repairing the edges of the iris and catchlight. As you can see in the undamaged eye, these areas are naturally softer and it is best to mimic the natural contours and transitions.

21. Refine the cloned eye repair with a few dabs of the Spot Healing Brush and then continue to fix the remaining cracks. After repairing the cheek and eye, the remaining work will feel very easy.

Putting It All Together

Over the years, the photographs we cherish tend to get folded, cracked, torn, and damaged. If you're lucky, you'll at least have all the pieces to reconstruct the image. If you're not so lucky, you'll have to make up image information to reconstruct missing pieces.

As you can see in **figure 6.26**, the original print had been torn into five pieces. At first this looked like a daunting job, but after scanning the pieces on a flatbed scanner, using a piece of foam core to hold the pieces in place, the challenge morphed into a digital jigsaw puzzle that required piecing the parts together and removing the ragged edges. The image came to life, as you can see in **figure 6.27**.

Tip

When scanning large print pieces or prints that are larger than your flatbed scanner platen, do not overlap pieces or change the print orientation by rotating pieces. That will vary the reflectance of the paper texture, making the pieces difficult to merge.

Many scanners try to auto correct the exposure when you select the area to scan. When working with oversized pieces that you plan to reassemble, either turn off the auto exposure feature or scan the entire bed for each section without doing a new preview to keep the exposures the same.

ch6_sailor.jpg

1. Using the Lasso tool without feather, roughly select the first piece, as shown in **figure 6.28**.

2. Select the Magic Wand and Option/Alt-click the white areas within the selection to subtract the large white areas of the scanner lid (**figure 6.29**). Don't remove the ripped paper edges from the selection; they may contain valuable image details.

figure 6.26

figure 6.28

Roughly select a piece of the image with the Lasso tool.

figure 6.27

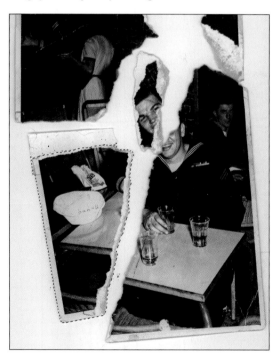

figure 6.29

Use the Magic Wand to quickly subtract the white areas of the scanner bed.

3. Choose Cmd-J/Ctrl-J or Layer > New > Layer via Copy to place the selected print piece onto its own layer. I highly recommend naming the layers, as shown in **figure 6.30**.

figure 6.30

After copying a section to its own layer, it is best to name it.

4. You can make new layers only out of selections with pixel image information. Select the Background layer and repeat steps 1 through 3 for each piece of the image.

5. Because the Background layer is still intact, it could be confusing to see it while you are moving the individual pieces around. To block it from view but maintain the image data, click the Background layer and add a new layer. Fill this with white to conceal the original Background layer.

6. When you have all the pieces on their own layers, the next step is to straighten them out. Select View > Show > Grid to use the grid and guides as a visual aid for alignment. (If the grid doesn't appear, make sure that View > Extras is checked.) Use Edit > Free Transform to position and rotate each piece roughly into place, as shown in **figure 6.31**.

7. With the Move tool set to Auto Select Layer and Show Transform Controls, grab the lower-left corner piece and move it toward the large lower-right corner (**figure 6.32**). These two pieces come together well, but the ripped edge of the right corner print is covering up good image information of the left corner.

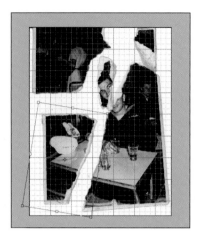

figure 6.31

Use Edit > Free Transform to position and rotate each piece roughly into place.

figure 6.32

Setting Auto Select Layer and Show Transform Controls will allow you to easily grab and move pieces with the Move tool.

8. To control how the pieces come together, you could erase the ripped paper edge, but that approach is risky because it can be difficult to control, and erasing deletes pixels—something that always makes me very nervous. To control what is visible without actually removing it, use a layer mask on the piece of the image that is blocking good image information. In this case, the ripped edge of the large right piece is covering image information of the left piece.

9. Add a layer mask to the lower right corner layer and use a small, hard-edged black brush to paint over the ripped edge. It will look as though you are erasing, but you're not, as you can see in **figure 6.33**. The black brush on the layer mask is concealing the image information, not deleting it.

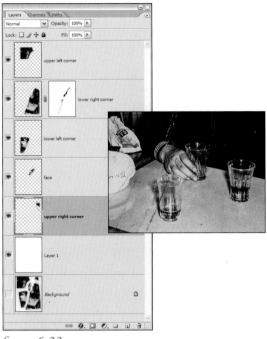

figure 6.33

Adding a layer mask and painting on it with a black brush hides the ripped edges without actually deleting them.

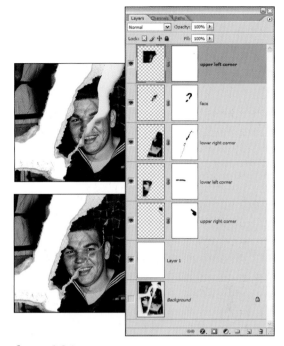

figure 6.34

Continuing to match pieces together while hiding torn areas with layer masks.

10. Continue moving pieces together and adding layer masks wherever the torn paper is blocking good image information, as seen in **figure 6.34**.

11. Once the pieces are together, create a Work in Progress (WIP) layer at the top of the layer stack, as you see in **figure 6.35**. Do this by choosing Select > All, Edit > Copy Merged, and Edit > Paste or use the new CS2 keyboard shortcut Cmd-Option-Shift-E/Ctrl-Alt-Shift-E.

12. Use a combination of cloning and healing as described previously to repair the remaining cracks and to build up image data.

When the pieces first tumbled out of the envelope, the job looked like a hopeless cause. By thinking of them as a puzzle, they can be pieced together seamlessly to create the final image.

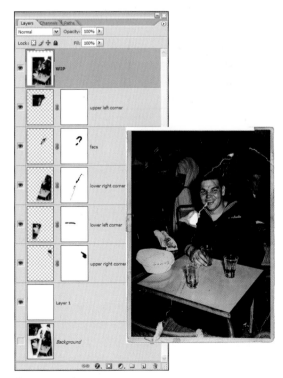

figure 6.35

Refine the restoration on a merged WIP layer with the Clone Stamp and Healing Brush tools.

HIDING CLUTTER AND DISTRACTIONS

In the excitement of taking a picture, we often forget to look at the entire scene. We might not notice distracting clutter, bits of garbage on the sidewalk, or as seen in figure 6.36, the tree perfectly placed behind the bridesmaid, giving her the appearance of a peacock with its feathers open. A second distraction is the tree coming out of one of the groomsmen's shoulders. By removing the clutter and distractions, you focus the viewer's attention on the important aspects of the picture, as in figure 6.37.

figure 6.36

figure 6.37

ch6_wedding_party.jpg

You can't physically take something out of a digital image without leaving a white hole, but you can cover up distractions. You also could take the background out of the image and put in a new one (addressed in Chapter 7, "Rebuilding and Recreating Images"). In the following example, with just a few minutes of borrowing some shrubbery from within the existing picture, you can produce a much better image.

1. When I face a new type of restoration challenge, I prefer to start with the easier parts of the image. In this case, that means removing the tree behind bridesmaid. The tree doesn't need to be completely hidden, just broken up so that its limbs aren't so obvious. Use the Lasso tool with a 5-pixel feather to carefully outline her head and shoulders and then make a generous selection around the lower section of the tree, as shown in figure 6.38.

figure 6.38

Selecting the distracting an area.

2. Choose Select > Feather and use a relatively low setting of 5 pixels.

3. With any selection tool, move the active selection to an area that has uncluttered information to serve as a suitable replacement, as shown in figure 6.39.

figure 6.39

Move the selection marquee to an area with good information.

4. Press Cmd-J/Ctrl-J to create a new layer with the uncluttered shrubbery. Use the Move tool to drag the good information over the bad. Use the arrow keys to nudge the background into place, as in figure 6.40.

figure 6.40

Move the new layer with the good information into place.

5. Add a layer mask by clicking on the Layer Mask button at the bottom of the Layers palette. Use a large, soft-edged black brush to paint in the transition between the new information and the original image, as seen in figure 6.41.

6. Select the Background layer and repeat the process to cover the tree coming out of the groomsman's shoulder.

figure 6.41

Paint with black on the layer mask to blend the bushes into the trees.

7. To refine the effect, add a new blank layer and go over the entire image at high magnification with the Clone Stamp and Healing Brush tools set to Sample All Layers to fix any edges or distractions, as shown in figure 6.42.

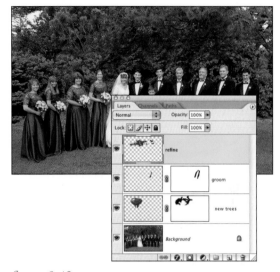

figure 6.42

Refine the details on a separate layer.

What Constitutes a Distraction?

Alan Jones shared this example of his work with me. Many family members liked this candid shot (figure 6.43) taken prior to a family wedding. Knowing of his Photoshop skills, he was asked to remove the "two distracting elements." His first attempt was met with a little dismay, as shown in figure 6.44. With a clarification of what the "distracting elements" were, Alan revisited the image to produce the glorious image seen in figure 6.45.

BEFORE

figure 6.43

figure 6.44

figure 6.45

REMOVING STAINS AND DISCOLORATION

The only dirt you should remove from the physical print original is the type that you can brush or blow off easily. A professionally trained conservator should be the only one to treat stains that are embedded in the film or print emulsion. There are many types of stains and discoloration that can befall an image, ranging from overall yellowing to density changes caused by sun, fire, or water damage to child-inflicted scribbling with pens, markers, or crayons. To hide these indignities, take advantage of channel information to rebuild the image with layers, cloning, and healing; and sometimes you even borrow image information from parts of the image that aren't stained.

Removing the Stain of Age

Photographs change over time. Especially older photographs, which may not have been processed to archival standards, have a tendency to yellow as the paper oxidizes and reacts with the cardboard it is mounted on or the box it is stored in. We can't stop time, but we can stop the staining. In figure 6.46, you see a scan of an original print that has discolored with age. Figure 6.47 shows the image with the staining removed and a slight sepia tone added.

figure 6.46

figure 6.47

The first thing you need to recognize when working with old images from the 19th and early 20th century is that they were not in color and did not have a heavy yellow or sepia tone. They were originally black-and-white images, meaning that the color you see in the yellowed print is not normal and not important. It makes sense to pull the best black-and-white image from the file before doing any restoration work. The easiest (but least effective) method to change a color image to black and white is to use the Image > Mode > Grayscale feature. I highly recommend that you do not use this; I explain why in Chapter 8, "Refining and Polishing the Image." In the meantime, trust me and work along.

ch6_country_car.jpg

1. Before converting a file to grayscale, always inspect the individual image channels either by clicking the words *Red*, *Green*, and *Blue* in the Channels palette or by using the keyboard shortcuts Cmd/Ctrl-1, 2, and 3 to see the quality of each of the three channels (**figure 6.48**). By inspecting the channels, you can see which ones have image information that you either want to preserve or ignore. Notice how the red channel has the most damage while the green and blue channels look fairly similar.

Red

Green

Blue

figure 6.48

Inspecting the individual color channels reveals many differences in detail and apparent damage.

2. Add a Channel Mixer adjustment layer and select Monochrome in the lower-left corner. By adjusting the sliders to mix the green and blue channels and ignore the red (**figure 6.49**), you can create a black-and-white image that has good tonality and detail without including all of the damage that the red channel is carrying.

figure 6.49

Adjust the Channel Mixer sliders to use only the best information from each channel.

3. Make a Work in Progress layer by pressing Cmd-Option-Shift-E/Ctrl-Alt-Shift-E and then label the layer *Dust & Scratches*.

4. To rid the image of the numerous tiny specks, select Filter > Noise > Dust & Scratches. Using the Dust & Scratches filter is always a balancing act of concealing dust and dirt while maintaining image detail and texture. Use a Radius of 1 with the Threshold set at 0, as seen in **figure 6.50**.

5. To emphasize the men and the car, we will sharpen just them and let the less important image background remain soft. Duplicate the *Dust & Scratches* layer and rename it *Overlay Sharpen*.

figure 6.50

Using the Dust & Scratches filter to remove the numerous small specks.

6. Select Filter > Other > High Pass. The image will turn gray and take on an embossed appearance. To better define the edges, use a Radius between 2 and 5; in this example I used 4, as seen in **figure 6.51**.

7. Change the Layer blending mode to Overlay, which makes the gray invisible while revealing the sharpening effect. If you feel that the sharpening effect is too strong, as I do, reduce the layer opacity to 70%.

figure 6.51

Use the High Pass Filter to accentuate the edges in the picture.

8. To sharpen only the men and the car, Option/Alt-click the Layer Mask icon in the Layers palette to add a black layer mask that conceals the entire layer. Use a soft, white Paintbrush and paint over the men and the car, as seen in **figure 6.52**.

8. To clean up any remaining specks or damage, add a New Layer and use the Spot Healing Brush set to Sample All Layers and clean up the spots in the sky (**figure 6.53**) and the edge along the bottom.

figure 6.52

Paint the sharpening back over the men and car.

figure 6.53

The Spot Healing Brush makes quick work of the damage in the sky.

Red

Green

Blue

figure 6.65

Inspect the channels individually to find the best one.

figure 6.66

Using only the blue channel minimizes the blue ink.

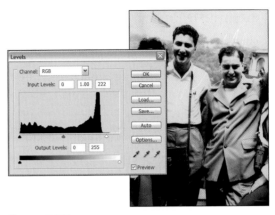

figure 6.67

A Levels adjustment layer brings back the contrast missing in the blue channel.

5. Use the Healing Brush tool set to Sample All Layers and unselect Aligned to repair the less important image areas. One clear advantage to placing your fixes on their own layer is that they are editable. If you don't like the result, erase it and try it again (figure 6.68).

figure 6.68

Use both the Clone Stamp and Healing Brush tools to cover up the vestiges of damage.

Tip

Sometimes the solution is not to fix every scratch but simply to break up the scratch so that the eye does not readily detect it. This has to be balanced against the size of print to be made, with smaller prints being more forgiving than larger ones. If your image is sized for print and the damage is not noticeable at 100% view, then it probably will not be noticeable in the print.

Document Repair

Documents, certificates, and letters are also an important part of family history. And just like photographs, they too can suffer the ravages of time. The techniques to repair them are not all that different from repairing photographs. Repairing a document can be tedious and may require you to work around each and every letter.

George Brinkerhoff shared the family Civil War document seen in **figure 6.69**. It is a handwritten page out of the diary his great-grandfather kept during the conflict. This type of document is particularly difficult to restore because it is handwritten on thin paper and the writing from the other side shows through. Although the strategy for repair is simple, it is anything but quick. To bring this old document back to life, the text needs to be enhanced, the paper needs to be replaced, and any text that shows through needs to be concealed. With a lot of time, patience, and a steady hand, the entire document can look like **figure 6.70**.

🌐⇨✄ **ch6_diary_closeup.jpg**

1. Inspect the three channels and notice how the text is darkest and clearest in the blue channel. Add a Channel Mixer adjustment layer, select the Monochrome option and increase the red and blue components and decrease the green component to make text stand out, as shown in **figure 6.71**.

2. To increase the contrast ever further, create a Levels adjustment layer and slide the midtone slider towards white, which helps separate the text on the back of the page from the text on the front, as shown in **figure 6.72**.

3. To create the new paper-texture background, turn off the visibility of the Channel Mixer and Levels layers. On the Background layer, use the Rectangular Marquee tool to select a good section of the paper. Copy the selected area by pressing Cmd-C/Ctrl-C followed by Cmd-D/Ctrl-D to deselect the rectangle.

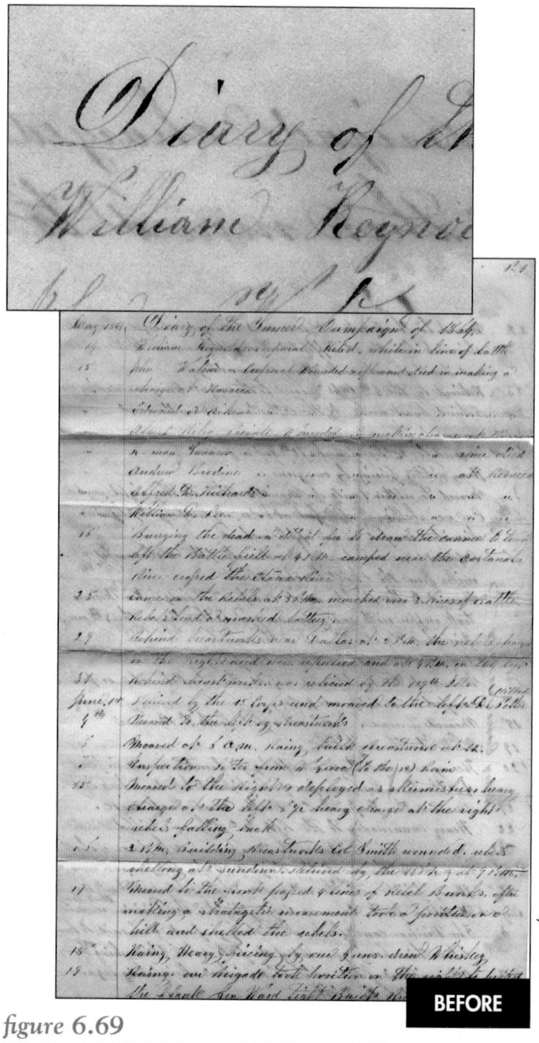

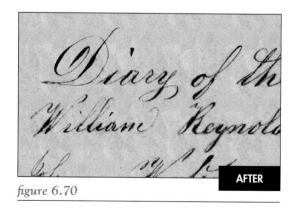

BEFORE

figure 6.69

AFTER

figure 6.70

4. Make the Channel Mixer and Levels layers visible again and click the Levels layer. Create a Work in Progress layer by pressing Cmd-Option-Shift-E/Ctrl-Alt-Shift-E. Name it *WIP*.

5. Add a new layer and select Filter > Pattern Maker and check the Use Clipboard as Sample option and click the Generate button (**figure 6.73**).

figure 6.71

A Channel Mixer adjustment layer enhances the text.

figure 6.72

A Levels adjustment layer further accentuates the contrast and helps to separate the bleed-through of the text from the other side of the page.

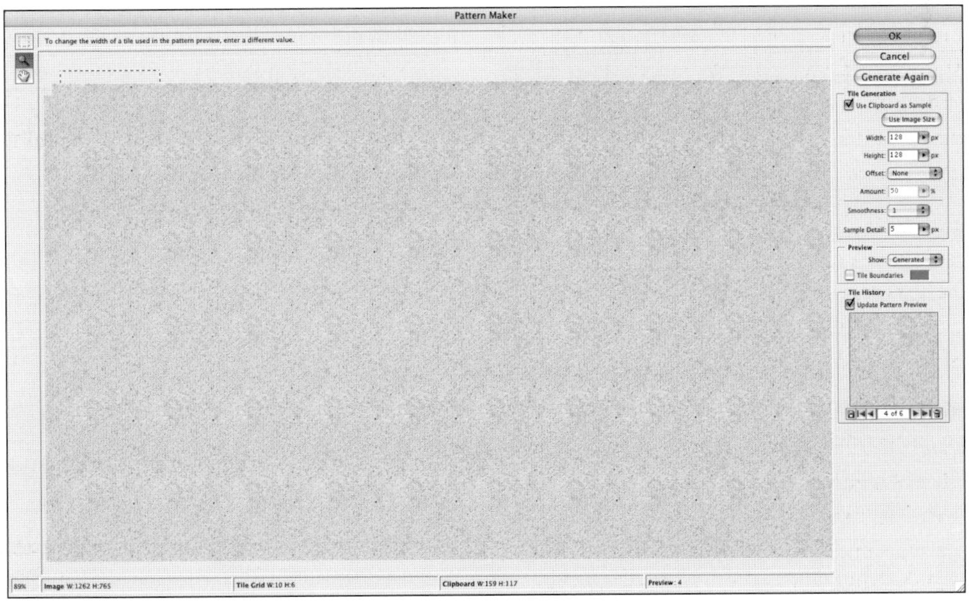

![Pattern Maker dialog]

figure 6.73

The Pattern Maker filter can create a faux paper from a sample of the original document.

5. Repeat clicking the Generate Again button until you get a pattern that looks like paper (**figure 6.74**). As this pattern will be a background for the text, don't be too concerned about pattern repetition. Click OK to exit the filter when satisfied. Name the layer *Paper*.

6. Change the paper layer's blending mode to Multiply to allow the WIP layer text to show through, as shown in **figure 6.75**.

figure 6.74

The faux paper layer.

figure 6.75

Changing the blending mode to Multiply allows the enhanced text to show through the paper layer.

7. The last and most tedious step is removing the bleed-through text. Turn off all layers except the paper and WIP layers. Target the WIP layer and add a layer mask by clicking on the layer mask button. Use small, hard-edged black brush to paint away the bleed-through

text, as seen in **figure 6.76**. You could experiment with different selection techniques to try to isolate the text for easier cleanup. But I have found that, due to the uneven pressures in handwriting, selection tools are not very effective.

figure 6.76

After careful cleaning up to conceal the bleed through.

Here are a few other tips to keep in mind when working on documents:

- Recycle and reuse. Often letters you need for replacement may already be in the document.

- Your font library may contain similar fonts to help fill in missing characters.

- For documents printed on both sides, place a black or blue paper (depending on the color of ink) behind the original to help minimize bleed-through.

- Reflective materials like seals do not reproduce well. Treating the reflective material as a separate image and adding it later to the document might yield better results but printing inks generally do not have reflective properties.

REMOVING CURVATURE, DISTORTION, AND KEYSTONING

The very nature of photography is the flattening of three-dimensional space onto a two-dimensional plane—something that is harder to do well than many people realize. During the flattening process, straight or parallel lines can easily bow, bend, pinch, or become just plain crooked. To control lines and perspective, professional photographers use large-format view cameras that swing, tilt, and pivot to align the film plane, lens board, and subject. This allows architectural and product photographs to be straight—so buildings don't fall backwards and products aren't distorted. No matter how subtle the distortion in your photos may be, correcting it will make your images look professional and polished.

Straightening Pictures with Warp

Photographing an existing image (also called "doing copywork" or "reproduction") is a lot harder to do perfectly than you would think. Even when using a dedicated copystand, a slight misalignment between the camera plane and the original can be quite apparent in the reproduction. To straighten images, use Edit > Transform, which with Photoshop CS2 includes the Warp feature to bend an image into place. This is a tremendous asset when working with images that are either bent, warped, distorted, or simply will not lie flat.

In **figure 6.77** you see a daguerreotype whose hinge would not allow the picture to fully open, which caused the image to become distorted. **Figure 6.78** shows the same image after a careful dose of Warping to straighten it out.

🌐▷✦ **ch6_warp_daguerreotype.jpg**

1. Choose Layer > Smart Objects > Group into New Smart Object.

BEFORE

figure 6.77

AFTER

figure 6.78

2. Turn on the rulers by pressing Cmd-R/Ctrl-R or choose View > Show Rulers. Drag guides from the left and top rulers to frame the four sides of the image and to establish which sides need to be squared. Notice in **figure 6.79** that the image bends slightly inward along the bottom and also along the upper-right corner.

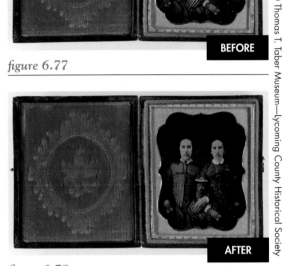

figure 6.79

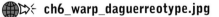
Guides help determine which edges need to be corrected.

3. Select Edit > Transform > Warp. You can move any of the anchor points or click the image itself and drag in any direction. In this example, gently adjust the bottom center of the image to bend it into shape as seen in figure 6.80.

figure 6.80

Pull the bottom edge of the image to align with the guide.

4. Grab the upper-right corner and drag it until it fills in the corner of the upper-right guides, as seen in figure 6.81.

5. Once you are satisfied with the warp correction, press Return/Enter to accept the Warp.

The advantage of using the Smart Object feature is that even after accepting the Warp, if you need to refine the image with additional transformation or Warp you choose Edit > Transform > Warp the original transform bounding box reappears allowing you to continue transforming without degrading the file.

figure 6.81

Pull the upper corner of the image to match the guides.

Working with Lens Correction

Introduced in Photoshop CS2, the Lens Correction filter is an excellent feature to straighten, rotate, remove distortion, and correct vertical or horizontal perspective. Granted, some of these corrections can be accomplished with perspective cropping or Transform, but the ability to apply a variety of corrections while seeing how each one improves the image is the strength of the Lens Correction filter. Although it was developed with architectural images in mind, I use it on a wide variety of images as addressed in the following section.

Working Efficiently with the Lens Correction Filter

- Imagine the feature to be corrected (for example, the building) imposed on a cube—a single face of the cube when the image is in one-point perspective or an angled cube when photographed in two-point perspective. Imagining the subject on a cube makes it easier to see which lines need to be straightened or where distortion needs to be removed.

- Set the grid to a useful size and color. The Default of 16 and gray are usually too small and too subtle to be very helpful.

- During the correction session, use the Move Grid tool to reposition the grid along important lines.

- Start the correction session by straightening the subject with the Straighten tool by dragging along a vertical or horizontal line. If the subject isn't straight, it will be more difficult to use the other correction features.

On the right side of the interface, work from top to bottom:

- Remove Distortion: Corrects bowing or pinching (officially called *barrel distortion*) when the image bows outward and *pincushioning* when the image edges pinch in.

- Chromatic Aberration: Removes color fringing most often found near the edges of images on high-contrast areas. If you work with a digital camera that can capture in the raw format, it is better to remove chromatic aberration with Camera Raw.

- Vignette: Lightens dark corners that were created by large lens shades or zoom lenses. Also use vignette to darken corners for a creative effect.

- Set Lens Default: Useful when using prime lenses (not zoom lenses). After correcting an image, click Set Lens Default to save the corrections for the next time an image is opened that was photographed with that same lens.

- Transform: Corrects perspective to straighten up buildings and boxes and to correct keystoning.

- Edge: As the image is scaled and corrected, transparent areas are created. The options to conceal this are Transparency, Edge Extension (not recommended), and Background Color. I recommend either scaling to increase the image to hide the transparent edges or to ignoring this feature and using the Crop tool afterwards.

Straightening Antique Images

The Kodak Brownie camera popularized photography, which is quite astounding when you consider that the camera was a bulky cardboard box with a viewfinder smaller than half a postage stamp that showed a blurry scene that was very difficult to see in bright sunlight. That difficulty caused a lot of crooked images, such as the one seen in figure 6.82. Thankfully, many decades later, the Photoshop Lens Correction filter can correct the perspective of the image, which was then restored to create the final image as seen in figure 6.83.

🌐▷◁ **ch6_crooked_house.jpg**

1. Duplicate the Background layer. Select Filter > Distort > Lens Correction and unselect Show Grid.

2. Use the Straighten tool (second from the top) to trace a line in the image that should be straight, or (in this sense) aligned vertically or horizontally. In this example, I used the lower edge of the house. The adjusted image is shown in figure 6.84.

BEFORE

figure 6.82

AFTER

figure 6.83

3. Click Show Grid. The default settings (Size: 16 and Color: gray) are not very useful. Increase the grid size to 36 and click on the color picker to select a bright red, as seen in figure 6.85. This grid will serve as a reference to fine-tune the image.

figure 6.84

Start the correction by straightening the image.

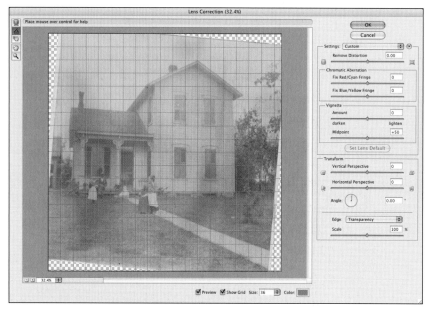

figure 6.85

Use a grid size and color that creates an essential reference.

4. Concentrate on either the vertical or horizontal lines. In this example, straightening the right side of the building by correcting the vertical perspective (**figure 6.86**) straightens the building out very nicely.

5. If you look carefully, you'll see that the front of the house bulges out towards you ever so

slightly. Increase Remove Distortion by +2.00 to push the center of the building back a bit (**figure 6.87**). The Lens Correction filter doesn't allow you to pull individual corners of the image—something Transform does very well. Click OK to accept the correction and continue with the next step.

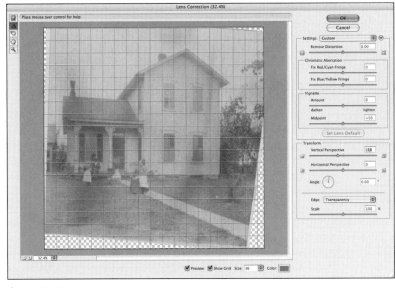

figure 6.86

Tackle one dimension at a time.

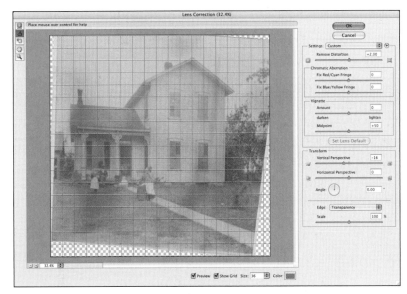

figure 6.87

Correct the bowing with the remove distortion feature.

6. I find it easier to concentrate if I turn off the Background. To pull down the left side of the house, choose Edit > Transform > Skew and pull the center left handle down and the center top handle slightly to the left, as **figure 6.88** shows.

figure 6.88

Continue the correction with the Transform > Skew command

7. To continue the restoration, use the skills presented in Chapter 2, "Improving Tone and Contrast," and Chapter 3, "Exposure Correction," to enhance the tonality with Levels (**figure 6.89**) and Channel Mixer (**figure 6.90**) and clean the image up with techniques presented in Chapter 5.

Although the Lens Correction filter was designed for contemporary digital camera files, it is a wonderful tool to correct images that were photographed in an age when color photography—let alone digital photography—was unimaginable.

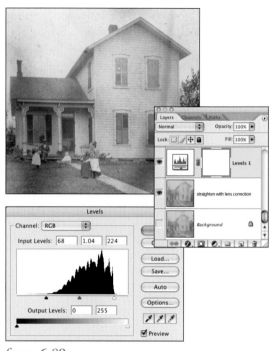

figure 6.89

Improve tonality with Levels.

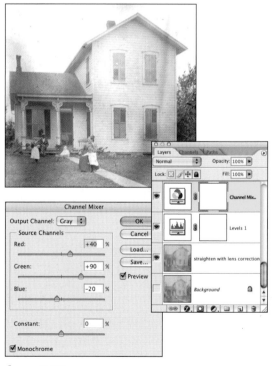

figure 6.90

Converting the image to black and white with a Channel Mixer layer.

Correcting Lens Distortion

When we use different focal length lenses, we often trade off an optical distortion for the ability to get the whole image within our viewfinder. This is very noticeable when a wide-angle lens is used. As the lens takes in a wider view, a noticeable bend is created in straight lines. Lens Correction is the ideal tool to correct distortion problems created by using wide-angle lenses.

This image of a Southwestern service station, taken with a 20mm lens, has visible distortion in figure 6.91. With just a few adjustments inside the Lens Correction filter, the sides are straightened and the bowing is removed, as seen in figure 6.92.

 ch6_service_station.jpg

1. Duplicate the Background layer and turn the original Background layer off.

2. Select Filter > Distort > Lens Correction. Check the Show Grid box for assistance in determining perpendicular lines. Set Remove Distortion to +2.00 to reduce the bowing.

3. Next, use the Transform sliders to correct Vertical and Horizontal Perspective. Slide the Vertical Perspective to –11 to make the building stand up straight. Adjust the Horizontal Perspective to –4 to bring the left side of the building to the foreground ever so slightly, as seen in figure 6.93.

figure 6.91

figure 6.92

figure 6.93

The Lens Correction settings used to bend the image into perfect flatness.

Correcting Architectural Perspective

If you use a 35 mm film or digital SLR camera to photograph a building, you'll notice that the building looks as if it's falling backwards (**figure 6.94**). But when you look at the actual scene, the building isn't tilting at all. Our visual system corrects the perspective just as a photographer who uses the swings and tilts of a large format view camera aligns vertical and horizontal lines to make the building look as straight as it really is (as in **figure 6.95**).

Although it's always better to create the best image in front of the lens and not rely on Photoshop to fix mistakes, I do not use a view camera, which means I rely on the Transform and Lens Correction features to correct images that curve, bend, fall backwards, and generally are out of alignment. You can see in the Lens Correction filter interface shown in **figure 6.96** how I straightened the top of the building, removed distortion, and brought the building up via the Vertical Perspective slider.

⊕⇨ **ch6_lincoln_center.jpg**

figure 6.94

figure 6.95

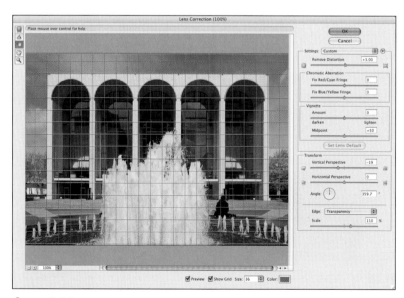

figure 6.96

Removing distortion and improving the vertical perspective makes the building stand straight and tall.

Tip

When photographing a scene with the intent of correcting it with the Lens Correction filter, frame the scene in the viewfinder, and then take a few steps back to allow for space needed to correct and scale the image.

CLOSING THOUGHTS

Although repairing tears or removing clutter sound like mundane endeavors, I hope the techniques shown in this chapter have given you some creative approaches to ridding the world of scratches, distractions, and distortion. Most importantly, always keep in mind the value of the photo that you're working on—the people, the memories, the captured moment might be the only reminder you or your client has of something or someone near and dear to them. By removing those scratches and damage, you're giving them back their memories as clear as the day the picture was taken.

7

REBUILDING AND RE-CREATING IMAGES

The worst images you will face are the ones that are so damaged by mold, fire, water, or neglect that entire portions of the image are either missing or damaged beyond recognition. In these disaster cases, asking the client for the original negative or a better print is futile, because there probably is none. The secret to replacing, rebuilding, and repairing the all-but-beyond-hope images is to beg, borrow, and steal image information from whatever is left of the original image or to find suitable substitutes to re-create missing backgrounds and body parts.

Images without damage can require rebuilding when the person's expression is wrong or the photographer missed the perfect moment. Replacing faces and heads digitally is 100 percent pain free. Get ready to sharpen your digital scalpel and learn to

- Re-create backgrounds
- Rebuild a portrait
- Swap faces and improve group photos
- Tackle light leaks and lens flare issues

The tools and techniques we'll use include

- Texture and sharpening filters
- Clone and Healing tools
- Selections and masking
- Vanishing Point and neutral layers

Note

Many of the techniques used to remove dust and scratches as explained in Chapter 5, "Dust, Mold, and Texture Removal," and Chapter 6, "Damage Control and Repair," will serve as the foundation for repairing the almost hopeless examples used in this chapter.

RE-CREATING BACKGROUNDS

Re-creating or rebuilding backgrounds can be as straightforward as lifting a person off the original image and placing her onto a blank background or as involved as finding suitable replacement background images to create a brand new environment. Backgrounds can come from a variety of sources, including other photographs; CD image stock; digital files you've created in Photoshop or Painter; and even cloth, textures, or objects you've scanned in with a flatbed scanner. Wayne has gone as far as shooting an image from atop a mountain to create an aerial backdrop when asked to put a stationary plane into the air.

When you are replacing or re-creating backgrounds, you can choose from four primary working options:

- Clone the existing background over the damaged area.

- Lift the object or person off the original picture and place it onto a new background.

- Paste the new background into the working file and slip it underneath the subject of the photo.

- Rearrange people or objects to minimize distracting backgrounds.

Your first option of cloning or healing the existing background over damaged areas is self-explanatory, and as long as you work on an empty layer with the Clone Stamp and the Healing Brushes, you can't get into trouble. The additional approaches are explained in the following sections, giving you a great deal of creative flexibility.

Concentrating on the Essential

The power and finesse of the Healing Brushes and Clone Stamp tool are both a blessing and a curse. The ability to invisibly repair and replace damaged image information seems magical. Yet the magic's Siren call can lead you to waste time and effort on image areas that are better cropped away or replaced entirely.

In the example in **figure 7.1**, the photograph is in good condition with the exception of a few dust spots, but the background is very distracting, as the fences, bus, and theater marquee all draw away attention from the man in uniform. The restoration done by Teresa Setterlund in **figure 7.2** is thoughtful and a classily done tribute. Rather than wasting a lot of time covering up the distractions in the background, Teresa honored her grandfather by separating him from the background and creating a digital studio backdrop as described here.

1. Before starting the project, Teresa double-clicked the Quick Mask icon and clicked the radio button for Selected Areas.

2. After duplicating the Background layer, Teresa started the restoration by separating the soldier from the distracting background. She entered Quick Mask by pressing Q. Using a 50% hardness brush with black as the foreground color, Teresa painted over the soldier. Because she is in Quick Mask mode, it looks as though she is painting with a translucent red brush, which signifies that she is painting a mask over the soldier (see **figure 7.3**) that will be used to select him and separate him from the distracting background.

3. To double-check that the entire figure was cleanly selected, Teresa turned off the view column of the RGB channels, as shown in **figure 7.4** to see the Quick Mask in black and white. She then cleaned up the last vestiges of white on the mask by quickly painting over them with a small black brush.

BEFORE

figure 7.1

AFTER

figure 7.2

4. Teresa tapped Q to exit Quick Mask mode, which created an active selection. She then clicked the Add layer mask button at the bottom of the Layers palette. To see how the soldier is separated from the background (also referred to as "dropped out"), Teresa turned off the original Background layer as seen in **figure 7.5**.

figure 7.3

Quick Mask mode shows selected areas in red.

figure 7.4

Viewing the Quick Mask channel in black and white is helpful to see and fix gaps in the mask.

figure 7.5

The isolated soldier.

5. To create the replacement backdrop, Teresa used several Photoshop filters. If you are working along, tap D to reset the Color Picker to the default colors of black and white.

6. She added a new layer underneath the isolated soldier and named it *faux backdrop*. Then she chose Filter > Render > Clouds to generate an abstract mottled pattern like the one in figure 7.6.

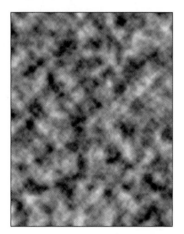

figure 7.6

The cloud filter generates a random pattern that serves as a foundation for additional texture refinement.

7. Next she selected Filter > Blur > Motion Blur. She set the Angle to run diagonally and increased the Distance slider to soften the pattern a great deal as seen in figure 7.7.

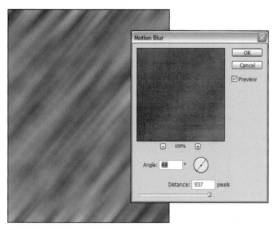

figure 7.7

The Motion Blur filter changes the clouds in soft blurry streaks.

8. Teresa then selected Filter > Blur > Gaussian Blur and moved the Radius slider until the pattern looked like a draped cloth background, similar to one used in a photo studio (see figure 7.8).

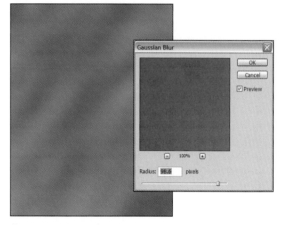

figure 7.8

The Gaussian Blur filter spreads out the lines to resemble folds in a cloth backdrop.

9. When Teresa zoomed in on the image and examined the texture, she saw that the synthetic background was too smooth and did not have any texture in comparison to the texture in the original scan. Working at 100% view, she selected Filter > Noise > Add Noise, checked Monochrome and used a noise amount to mimic the size of the original image's (see figure 7.9). To soften the grain ever so slightly, she used the Gaussian Blur filter with a low setting to smooth out the noise, enabling the computer-generated backdrop to match the original image as seen in figure 7.10.

10. To refine the image edges, Teresa used a small black brush on the soldier layer mask and painted away any remaining edge artifacts.

11. After adding a new layer she cleaned up any remaining dust with the Spot Healing Brush set to Sample All Layers.

figure 7.9

Making the new background look more realistic by adding noise.

figure 7.10

Blurring the noise slightly reduces the obvious results of adding noise.

12. To tone the image, Teresa added a Curves adjustment layer and increased the red curve midtone and decreased the blue and green to create a delicate sepia look as seen in figure 7.11.

13. To vignette the image, she selected the soldier with the Elliptical Marquee tool, then inverted the selection (Cmd-Shift-I/Ctrl-Shift-I). Then she added a Solid Color Fill layer and, using a slight cream color, surround the image with a subtle tone rather than a stark white. To soften the vignette, Teresa used the Gaussian Blur filter on the Color Fill layer mask.

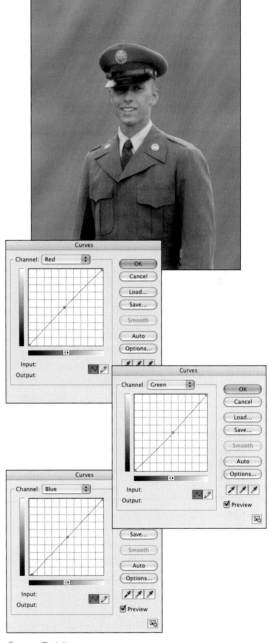

figure 7.11

Gently adjusting the color curves tones the image.

 T i p

Be sure to start the vignette well away from the image edge—otherwise a straight edge will form along the side of the image where the full effect of blurring did not occur.

As you can see in **figures 7.12** and **7.13**, vignetting images is not reserved for older or historical photos. By removing the child and background clutter and retouching the mother, Teresa was able to take a simple snapshot and make it into a wonderful studio portrait.

By not wasting your time, energy, and effort to repair damaged backgrounds or nonessential image information, you are saving your patience, concentration, and time for the most important image areas. Lorie Zirbes did exactly that to bring back the poor image seen in **figure 7.14**, which had suffered decades of neglect. The detailed background was irrelevant and added nothing to the image. Lorie masked out the background, created a new one with the Clouds filter, and concentrated her efforts on the solider. After hours of diligent work with the Clone Stamp tool and the Healing Brushes, Lorie was able to resurrect this image to its original charm as shown in **figure 7.15**.

© Teresa Setterlund

BEFORE

figure 7.12

© Morgan Family Archive

BEFORE

figure 7.14

AFTER

figure 7.13

AFTER

figure 7.15

Lifting the Subject off the Photograph

Many times the reason for retouching or restoring a photograph is that the person in picture has died and the family wants a good photograph to remember the person with. Art Johnson of Memories in Minutes was presented with just such a scenario. The life of the young mother in **figure 7.16** was tragically cut short in a car accident. The family wanted a single image of her for the funeral and only had this recent Christmas card photograph. Art was able to extract her, replace missing pieces, and put her on a new background as shown in **figure 7.17**.

Taking the time to make a good selection is the most important step to creating a realistic composite in which the edges aren't harsh, jagged, or obvious. Believe me, spending a few more minutes at the initial selection stage will save you time as you won't have to tediously retouch poor edges that were caused by an inaccurate selection.

1. Art used the Pen tool to trace the outline of the woman. To turn the Path into an active selection, Art clicked the Load path as a selection icon on the Paths palette.

2. He then clicked the Add layer mask icon on the Layers palette, which concealed the original backdrop and also revealed the areas that need to be replaced, as shown in **figure 7.18**.

Tip

For detailed instruction on the Pen tool and other selection tools and techniques, please see my comprehensive book on making selections, **Photoshop Masking and Compositing**.

BEFORE

figure 7.16

AFTER

figure 7.17

© Art Johnson, Memories in Minutes

figure 7.18

Use a layer mask to conceal what is not wanted in the final image.

figure 7.19

A Hue/Saturation adjustment layer changes the backdrop to a color that harmonizes well with the dress.

2. Art is a photographer by trade and has a supply of backdrops for his studio photography. After photographing a suitable backdrop, he placed it behind the subject and used a Hue/Saturation adjustment layer to create a color that complemented the woman's dress (see figure 7.19).

 Tip

When replacing backgrounds, use a similarly toned or colored background to help make the edges and shadows match.

 Tip

To create a quick and believable studio-like background, select one color from the image and set the background color to black. Use the Gradient tool with either the Linear or Radial options.

3. To build the missing shoulder, Art used the Lasso tool to make a generous selection of the existing shoulder and pressed Cmd-J/Ctrl-J to duplicate it to its own layer. Since this layer would require the identical layer mask as the left shoulder, Art Option/Alt-dragged the original layer mask into the layer containing the new shoulder on the Layers palette.

4. Art chose Edit > Transform > Flip Horizontal to flip the shoulder and slide the new shoulder into the approximate position on the right side of the image as seen in figure 7.20.

figure 7.20

Positioning the duplicate shoulder.

5. The new shoulder needs to be a bit smaller to match the woman's slight tilting. Art used Edit > Free Transform, to rotate and scale the copied shoulder into position as shown in figure 7.21.

figure 7.21

Using Free Transform to position, rotate, and resize the shoulder.

6. To remove the overlap in the center of the figure, Art added a layer mask and painted away the unnecessary information. To fill in the few empty spots on the woman's blouse, Art added a new layer and used the Clone Stamp and Healing Brush to fill the gaps and conceal the baby shoes that remained from the original image (see **figure 7.22**).

7. Finally, to add a hint of texture to the background, Art selected Layer > New > Layer (Cmd-Shift-N/Ctrl-Shift-N), and in the New Layer dialog box, chose Overlay from the Mode menu and checked Fill with Overlay-neutral (50% gray). He used Filter > Noise > Add Noise with the monochrome option checked, followed by a low Gaussian Blur setting to create a soft grain pattern to mimic the structure in the original picture as seen in figure 7.23.

In the greater scheme of things, replacing a backdrop and arm may seem trivial—but more important is that the family had a studio portrait with which to remember and cherish the woman.

figure 7.22

Covering up gaps and repeated information.

figure 7.23

Moving the woman down a bit gives her some needed headroom and the added texture helps tie the image together.

Wayne has told me that many times people come to him to rebuild or create a portrait of a deceased loved one. Sadly, too many times the images he has to work with are damaged or very small. In one extreme case, all he had was a few blurry frames from a videotape to work with. Now both he and I encourage our customers and students to take plenty of pictures of family and friends. Feel free to chastise those people who either make funny faces or cover their faces—as you never know which shot will be their last.

Tip

When doing intensive image repair, take frequent breaks or look away from the monitor every few minutes to clear your visual memory. When you look back you will see remaining problems with a fresh eye.

The Beauty Is in the Details

I love catching continuity mistakes in Hollywood productions—the clock that never changes time; the glass that is full, empty, and then full again; or the shirts that change color from take to take. You can avoid continuity mistakes in your portrait and background retouching by being aware of the following issues:

- Color and contrast: Make sure to match the color and contrast of the pieces you are compositing.

- Film grain and texture: Double-check to see that the grain and texture match.

- Focus and focal plane: Verify that the focus of a newly placed image background matches foreground elements. Use the blur filters to soften backgrounds to visually push them further back.

- Lighting and shadows: Every image has at least one light source. Sometimes it's the sun, other times a studio light, or perhaps even reflected light, illuminating your subjects. Study how the light falls in an image and use that information when creating shadows. Look for colors that might be reflected into your image from surrounding areas, such as brightly colored walls or trees.

- Edges and transitions: Mimic the softness or hardness of the edges in the original image to create seamless edges between retouched areas.

- Size relationships: Match the size of dropped-in objects with the people and objects in the original scene.

- Reflections: If someone has glasses on or there are windows in a scene, double-check that the reflections in these surfaces actually reflect the environment in the picture.

- Hollow areas: If someone is standing with his hands on his hips or with his legs spread apart, make sure to mask out the hollow triangle so that the new image background can show through.

When reconstructing images and backgrounds, keep these details in mind to create seamless and invisible retouching.

REBUILDING PEOPLE, PLACES, AND THINGS

Many times the background doesn't need replacing—it needs a complete overhaul. Images are torn, tattered, and ripped apart and you only have scraps to work with. In those instances you can photograph suitable replacements, create abstract backgrounds, or carefully use whatever remnants remain, as the following examples show.

Sometimes fixing an image requires more than a new background or a bit of healing to bring it back to life. In figure 7.24, you see the sad scrap that a client handed to Art Johnson of Memories in Minutes with the request that he make the image suitable for framing. As Art explained, "I was stymied with this job, as I had done it a year earlier and the client didn't like it. On that first attempt, I used flowers to fill in the missing corner, which just didn't look right. But this time, the client also gave me another photo of the same person for me to see the woman's hair" (see figure 7.25). With this additional reference, Art was able to create a finished image the client loved, as seen in figure 7.26.

BEFORE

figure 7.24

AFTER

© Art Johnson, Memories in Minutes

figure 7.26

figure 7.25

The client provided an additional reference of what the woman's hair looked like.

1. As Art explains, "While I was working on this, I decided to try something new. One of my employees was wearing a spaghetti-strap blouse one day, so I took her into the photo studio, wrapped her in cloth and tulle, and did several shots with and without flowers (**figures 7.27** and **7.28**). While I was taking the pictures, I tried to position her like the original."

N o t e

Matching the focus or sharpness of image elements is a challenge. I prefer to soften the sharper image to match the softer image. Sharpening an out-of-focus image is usually a futile undertaking.

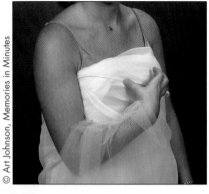

figure 7.27

Art took several photos of a model posed like the woman in the photo.

figure 7.28

Art's modern-day replacement model holding flowers.

2. Art started the restoration process by repairing the damage with the Clone Stamp and Healing Brush (see **figure 7.29**). Then he added the new photographs and used both the image with and without the roses, which enabled him to position them as needed (see **figures 7.30** and **7.31**).

Art concludes, "The customer loved this new version, and I've used this 'photograph to fix' technique on several orders now. I'm also busy building a stock file of body parts and clothes from both contemporary and antique photographs for me to use as a library."

figure 7.29

Art first repaired the damaged original.

figure 7.30

The repaired image combined with the modern model.

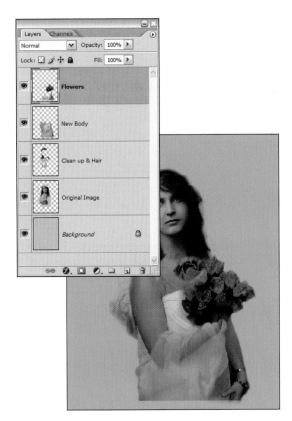

figure 7.31

Compositing the model holding the roses separately gave Art greater freedom in positioning.

Tip

Family photos are often stored haphazardly and in a variety of boxes and containers, which may be harmful to the photographs. As Ken Allen from Image Conservator explains, "Storing old photographs in archival sleeves and boxes, until you have the time to scan or photograph them, ensures that they won't suffer more damage than they may already have. For small photos (up to 5 × 7"), I like using 6 × 8½ × 12" True core FlipTop boxes with either interleaving lignon-free paper or polyester or polypropylene fold lock transparent sleeves. Adding identification tabs by subject or year helps you find a print easily. This sure beats digging through a stack of photos. If your photo collection includes larger prints use thin flat print boxes with clear print sleeves, which is how the George Eastman House in Rochester, NY handles their collection."

Reader Robert Malarz took a similar approach to rebuild a background in figure 7.32, which he shared with me. He painstakingly re-created the background through extensive reuse of what remained in the original image as well as by photographing part of his own bathtub to use for materials to rebuild the tub and the tiles. Twenty-eight layers later, he had an image he was rightly pleased with, as seen in figure 7.33.

BEFORE

figure 7.32

AFTER

figure 7.33

© Robert Malarz

Beg, Borrow, and Steal Image Information

If you don't have access to a photo studio to re-create body parts or a time machine to rephotograph a scene, follow the lead of Alan, who rebuilt the image in **figure 7.34** to create the wonderful version seen in **figure 7.35**.

figure 7.34

figure 7.35

Alan broke the restoration into five general steps:

- Correct overall tonality: A Levels adjustment layer removes the fading and color corrects the brown tones (**figure 7.36**).

- Repair asphalt by adding a new layer and cloning over the damage, which he then roughened up by adding monochrome noise as seen in **figure 7.37**.

figure 7.36

The first step is to always correct tone and color.

figure 7.37

Rebuilding the parking lot with cloning and a noise layer.

- Repair building by selecting, duplicating, moving, and transforming existing pieces to cover up the damaged window and siding. To rebuild the gutter, Alan used the Polygon Lasso tool to select the old gutter, which he filled with two shades of blue to create dimension as seen in **figure 7.38**.

- Replace sky: After selecting the sky area, Alan used the Clouds filter to add fake clouds, which he refined with a subtle gradient to darken down the corners ever so slightly and effectively (**figure 7.39**).

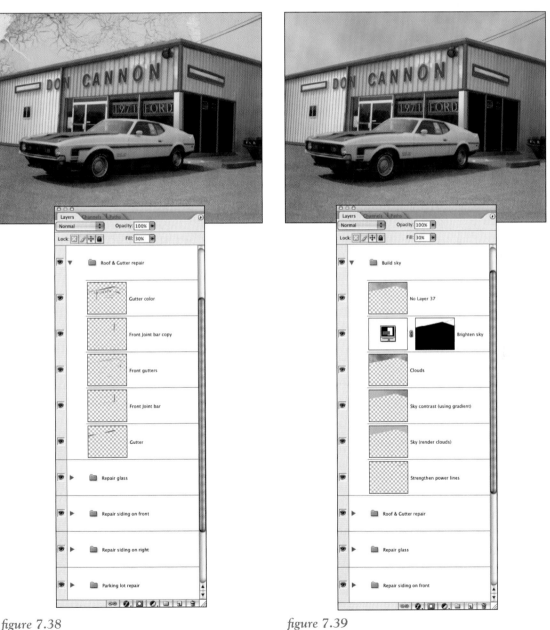

figure 7.38

Selecting and duplicating every scrap of available information.

figure 7.39

Replacing the sky yields better results than repairing it.

- Detail car: Being an auto aficionado, Alan took special care detailing the car to accentuate the engine, stripes, and tires. He even cleaned up, repaired, and colored the car at the right edge of the image frame, which shows the care and attention that Alan puts into his restoration work (figure 7.40).

Different Photoshop artists approach image problems with a variety of strategies. Alan used the smart strategy of carefully building up image information and saving all selections as channels to work with as he repaired the image. In the end, the results are what matter.

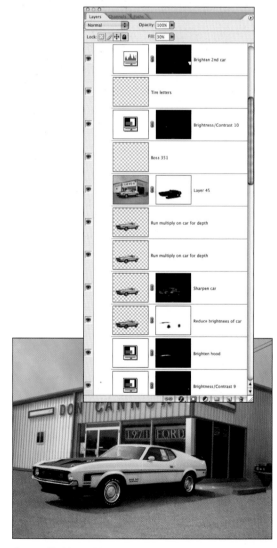

figure 7.40

When you do what you love—it shows.

Flattening Your Image

When a retouch or restoration is made up of numerous layers, it can be more manageable and less confusing to work on a flattened version—a Work in Progress or WIP—while maintaining the working layers. Working on one layer simplifies the process of making selections, applying color correction, and cloning information. To create a WIP layer or file:

- In Photoshop CS2, click the topmost layer and use Cmd-Option-Shift-E/Ctrl-Opt-Shift-E to merge all visible layers up into a new layer.

- To create a WIP layer with previous versions of Photoshop, click the top layer, add a new layer, and hold Option/Alt while selecting Layer > Merge Visible. When working with large files, make sure to keep the Option/Alt key depressed until the new layer is complete. Or use Cmd-Option-Shift-N/Ctrl-Alt-Shift-N followed by Cmd-Option-Shift-E/Ctrl-Alt-Shift-E.

- To merge the layers in a layer group into a new layer, leaving the group intact, highlight the group to be merged and press Option/Alt and from the Layers palette menu choose Merge Group (Cmd-Option-E/Ctrl-Alt-E).

- To create a separate flattened file, choose Image > Duplicate and check Duplicate Merged Layers Only. Save and close the original layered file and save this new untitled file and continue working.

Bringing People Closer Together

If you've ever seen a professional photographer take pictures, you know that he or she takes a lot of exposures. But even then the perfect moment may be missed, as the photographer changes the roll of film or media card or has to wait for the flash to recycle. For example, a wedding photographer has to anticipate every moment he or she wants to capture and sometimes the right moments are missed by a fraction of a second as expressions change, people blink, or poses become awkward. The following section addresses how to re-create the perfect moment by moving, nudging, and swapping people and body parts to create the perfect moment—or, as Henri Cartier-Bresson coined, the decisive moment—when light, gesture, and frame were perfectly aligned.

In this image of the bride and groom kissing (figure 7.41), a split second difference would have made this a more interesting shot, as the groom's lips would be closer to the bride's, evoking a more intimate moment. Fortunately, with a quick copy of the groom to his own layer and a "digital push" closer, that moment has been created as seen in figure 7.42.

Ch7_kiss_closer.jpg

figure 7.41

figure 7.42

1. Use the Lasso tool to draw a selection line between the bride and groom to encircle the groom (figure 7.43). Use Cmd-J/Ctrl-J to duplicate him onto a new layer.

2. Activate the Move tool and use the left arrow key to nudge him closer to the bride.

3. Add a layer mask and use a small 50% hardness black brush to create the transition where the bride and groom meet as shown in figure 7.44.

figure 7.43

Selecting the groom.

figure 7.44

Use a layer mask to refine the intimate moment between bride and groom.

4. To make the image richer, add a Levels adjustment layer and move the shadow and highlight sliders to the edges of the histogram. So the bride's dress doesn't lose detail or be forced to pure, paper-base white, reduce the white output level to 245 as seen in **figure 7.45**.

figure 7.46

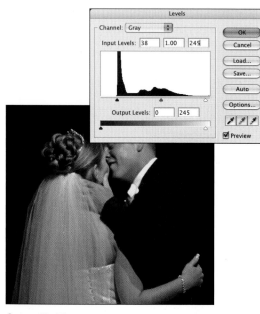

figure 7.45

The addition of a Levels adjustment layer adds contrast and controls the highlights.

Refining the Casual Reception Photo

During a wedding, many images are recorded. Some are posed, some are candid—and, of course, some are more successful than others. As happens at many weddings, the most relaxed and enjoyable photos are caught during the reception (**figure 7.46**). In this example, the bride and groom had many wonderful images but really liked the casual look and expressions of this image. They requested that Grandma and the distracting background be removed (as seen in **figure 7.47**) to create a more intimate portrait.

figure 7.47

1. I started by lightening the image and removing the red-yellow color cast with a Curves adjustment layer as seen in **figure 7.48**.

2. With the Marquee tool, I selected the groom and used Edit > Copy Merged to copy him with the color correction, followed by Edit > Paste to place him on his own layer. I repeated this for the bride. After naming the layers, I pushed them into the approximate position. As you can see in **figure 7.49**, turning off the Background layer cuts down the visual distractions, which lets me concentrate on bringing the couple togther.

figure 7.49

The bridge and groom copied to their own layers are placed into a closer position.

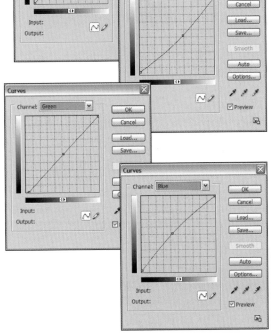

figure 7.48

Lightening and color correcting the image with Curves.

3. I created a Layer Mask for the groom's layer and painted away the information behind his head and camera right shoulder. I repeated the process for the bride's layer to conceal the background that covered the groom. Nudging the bride in a little closer created the results seen in **figure 7.50.**

figure 7.50

Conceal the unwanted elements of the image with layer masks on both the bride and groom layers.

4. Turning Grandmother's blue sleeve black with a Solid Color fill layer maintained the natural gesture of the bride's hand on what was her grandmother's arm, which became her husband's arm (**figure 7.51**).

figure 7.51

A *Color Fill adjustment layer turned Grandmother's sleeve black and helped it become the groom's arm.*

5. Whenever you do work like this, pay special attention to the details. In this example, I carefully cloned out the bride's camera right hand, filled in the neckline of her dress, and rebuilt the wall in the background (see **figure 7.52**).

6. To rebuild the window in the background, I turned off all the production layers and turned on the original Background and Curves adjustment layer. I selected the section of the window that did not contain the bride's reflection and chose Edit > Copy Merged and Edit > Paste, naming it *window fill* (**figure 7.53**). After turning on all the upper production layers, I slid the window section into position behind the groom's head.

7. I realized that the reflection of the back of the grandmother's head was still in the picture. I removed it and cleaned up the last artifacts on a new layer on which I cloned in any missing pieces and refined the edges around the couple.

figure 7.52

Careful cloning on a new layer removed the last of the unwanted elements.

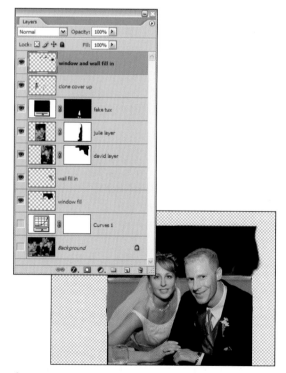

figure 7.53

Borrowing information from the Background layer provided most of the window that needed to be filled in.

8. The picture was nearing completion and I needed to preview the final crop to make sure I hadn't missed anything. Using the Marquee tool, I selected the image, used Select > Inverse and added a Solid Color fill layer with black (figure 7.54).

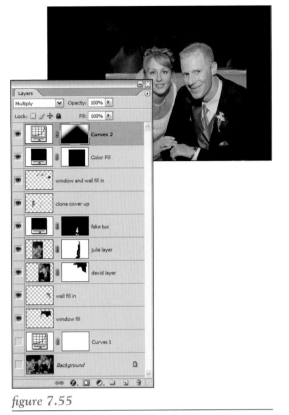

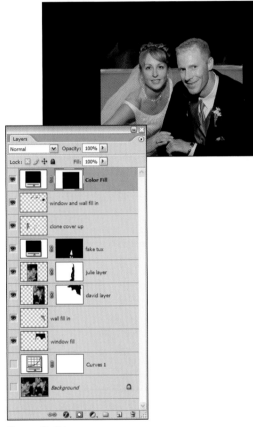

figure 7.55

A Curves adjustment layer darkens the background to draw attention to the couple.

10. After saving the file, I Cmd/Ctrl-clicked the icon of the Solid Color fill layer to activate the selection and then inverted it. I chose Image > Crop to trim the picture for the final print as seen in figure 7.56.

figure 7.54

A Color Fill adjustment layer is used to preview the final image area.

9. To tone down the background, I added a Curves adjustment layer set to Multiply. To control where the darkening took place, I changed the foreground color to white and activated the Gradient tool. Selecting the foreground to transparent preset, I drew in a gradient from each upper corner, as seen in figure 7.55, darkening down the corners and drawing more attention to the bride and groom.

figure 7.56

The final image.

Head Swapping and Zipper Necking

If you think photographing one person is challenging, just consider how challenging it can be to photograph groups or families, in which everyone is blinking and focusing on the camera at a different moment. Professional photographers know to shoot multiple images because some pictures will be unusable due to blinks, odd expressions, or reflections in glasses. Finally, as the number of people in the picture increases so does the chance of having this type of problem. I first heard the term *zipper necking* from Lee Varis, a Los Angeles-based photographer who is often hired to photograph body doubles for movie posters, onto which he places the movie stars' heads.

Rebuilding a Face

In the original picture of this wedding couple, both the bride and groom's expressions are very nice (**figure 7.57**) except that the wind blew her veil across his face. Rebuilding the groom's face (see **figure 7.58**) earned the portrait a prized location in the wedding album.

1. To rebuild his face, I started by selecting the unobstructed side of his face with a 1-pixel feathered Lasso (see **figure 7.59**) and duplicated it onto a new layer.

2. After flipping the head and adding a layer mask, I used a small soft-edged brush to paint in a transition between the new and old face.

3. To match and balance tones, I held Option/Alt while selecting the Curves Adjustment layer and checked Use Previous Layer to Create Clipping Mask. By clipping both the Curves and Hue/Saturation adjustment layers, the corrections only affect the non-transparent pixels on the base layer, which I used to refine the color and saturation of the skin as seen in **figure 7.60**.

BEFORE

figure 7.57

© Alyssa Duncan

AFTER

figure 7.58

figure 7.59

A generous selection insures enough image information to work with.

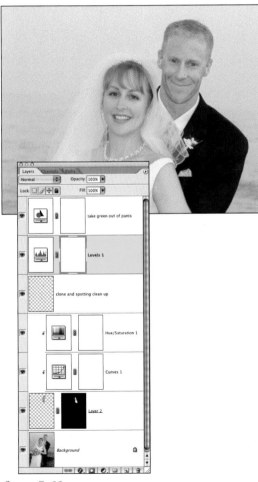

figure 7.60

Adjustment layers in clipping groups only affect the non-transparent pixels in the base layer.

4. To finish the image, I added a new layer and used the Spot Healing Brush and Clone Stamp tool to clean up any telltale artifacts, and applied a final pass of color correction as seen in **figure 7.61**.

figure 7.61

Final cleanup and color correction create the perfect moment.

Replacing a Face

Figure 7.62 shows another photograph from the same wedding, in which the bride and groom never seemed to have good expressions in the same frame. The challenge in this example is that the bride's best expression is in color and the groom's is in black and white (**figure 7.63**). Making the color image into a black and white would have been child's play, but the bride requested that the final composite be in color. Here's how I created the results seen in **figure 7.64**.

BEFORE

figure 7.62

BEFORE

figure 7.63

AFTER

figure 7.64

1. After generously selecting the groom's head in the black-and-white image, I brought it into the color image as seen in **figure 7.65**. I find it easier to select more image information than needed and then conceal it with a layer mask rather than spending a lot of time trying to select the perfect amount of image needed. Changing the layer Blend Mode to Luminosity reveals the color of the underlying image so I could use the Transform command to position and scale his head in relationship to the bride.

figure 7.65

Refining size and position of the groom's head.

2. I added a layer mask and used a 75% hardness black brush to paint away the extra image information (**figure 7.66**).

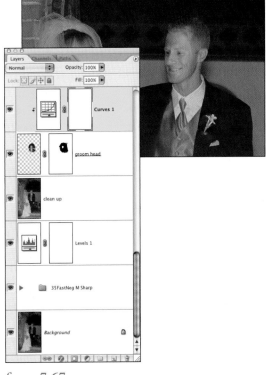

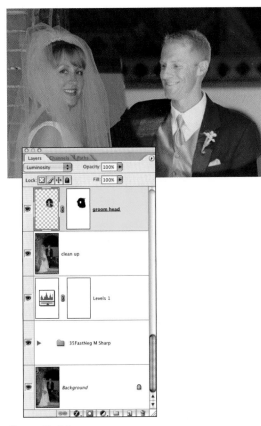

figure 7.66

Concealing unneeded information with a layer mask.

figure 7.67

The clipped adjustment layer enables me to match color and tone.

3. To darken his face, I added a clipped Curves adjustment layer as seen in **figure 7.67**. On separate layers, I lightened his teeth and cleaned up any telltale artifacts with the Spot Healing Brush to complete the new face (**figure 7.68**).

4. To refine the image further, I lightened the bride's dress, added a hint of contrast, and softened the image overall to create the final image.

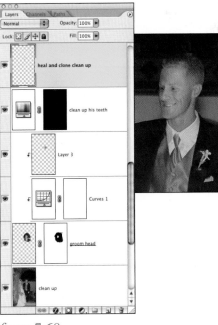

figure 7.68

A final pass with the Spot Healing Brush cleans up the file.

Working with Group Portraits

Photographing people in a studio gives you more control over lighting and composition, but you still need to shoot plenty of frames to guarantee the best expressions on the most people. As Art Johnson explains, "I always overshoot. That way, if I don't have the perfect pose or expression (**figure 7.69**), I can mix and match from the other shots to create the best image possible (**figure 7.70**)."

figure 7.69

Adding to a Group Portrait

In addition to changing faces, clients may ask you to add people or, as seen in this example, to add the family dog. As Art said, "During the portrait session the kids were distracted by the family dog, so I took her out of the shot. Once I was satisfied that I had the family (**figure 7.71**) I could concentrate on the photographing the dog (**figure 7.72**), knowing I could put her back in sans leash later with Photoshop (**figure 7.73**)."

figures 7.71 and 7.72

figure 7.70

figure 7.73

Tip

When replacing faces or heads, duplicate the new face, reduce the layer opacity to 50%, and align the eyes. Select Edit > Transform and move the transform center point in-between the eyes so that all rotating and scaling pivots from the eyes.

REDUCING REFLECTIONS, LENS FLARE, AND LIGHT LEAKS

Light is the very foundation of photography yet it can also be one of photography's biggest problems when too much, too little, or wrong placement creates unique and challenging problems.

Reducing Reflections

Taking pictures of or through windows is challenging. To reduce reflections while taking the picture, use a polarizing filter. But sometimes the moment calls out for the shot to be taken regardless of the outcome. Such is the case of this couple, who saw the camera and struck a quick pose (figure 7.74). Unfortunately, the reflection in the window is distracting and reshooting it would have ruined the spontaneity. The reflection was removed with adjustment layers and Lens Correction was used to straighten out the image to create figure 7.75.

figure 7.74

BEFORE

figure 7.75

AFTER

 Ch7_happycouple.jpg

1. To darken down the reflection, start by selecting the interior of the window with the Polygonal Lasso tool. Switch to the standard Lasso tool and hold Option/Alt while outlining the couple to subtract them from the active selection as seen in figure 7.76.

figure 7.76

Starting the selection with the Polygonal Lasso and finishing it with the standard Lasso tool.

2. Add a Levels adjustment layer and move the black slider to the right until the window reflection just about disappears, as in figure 7.77. Leaving a hint of the reflection visible maintains environmental context and interest.

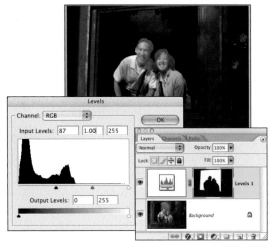

figure 7.77

After selecting the window and creating an adjustment layer, increasing the black levels reduces most of the glare.

3. If the edge of your selection is too harsh, use Filter > Blur > Gaussian Blur with a setting of 3 on the Levels layer mask to soften the transition (**figure 7.78**).

figure 7.78

Soften the edges of the layer mask with the Gaussian Blur filter.

4. To darken down the couple select them with the Elliptical Marquee (**figure 7.79**), add a Curves adjustment layer, and darken down the shadows as seen in **figure 7.80**. Use the Gaussian Blur filter with a setting of 5 to soften the transition.

5. Add a new layer and use the Spot Healing Brush set to Sample All Layers and remove any remaining specks to clean up the window.

6. Use Cmd-Option-Shift-E/Ctrl-Alt-Shift-E to merge all of the production layers up, then select Filter > Distort > Lens Correction.

7. As explained in Chapter 6, start by straightening the image with the Straighten tool by dragging along the horizontal bottom edge of the window. Use the Lens Distortion slider to remove the barrel distortion and correct the Vertical Perspective to straighten the image as seen in the Lens Correction interface in **figure 7.81**.

figure 7.79

Selecting just the couple.

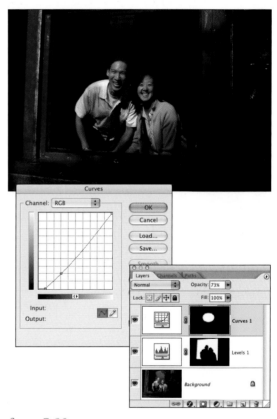

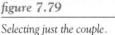

figure 7.80

Darkening the couple and softening the transition removes a lot of the glare.

figure 7.81

Use the Lens Correction filter to straighten and correct perspective.

Of course it is better to compose the best picture in front of the lens, but sometimes speed and spontaneity are more important than formal compositional rules, which is where Photoshop comes into play—to help create the better image.

Correcting Lens Flare

Lens flare is caused by the light bouncing off and around the inside of the lens barrel and can, in most cases, be avoided by shielding the lens from getting hit directly by the sun or using large lens shades. Sometimes lens flare can be considered an artistic addition to an image, but many times it is distracting.

I hear from readers all around the world (it's one of my favorite things about writing books) and Jose Basbus from Argentina contacted me about this beautiful photograph taken in Patagonia (figure 7.82). Although Jose was trying to create an artistic effect with the sun, the lens flare in the foreground detracts from the image. Rather than relying on the standard cloning or healing techniques to cover up the flare, I suggested he use good channel information to replace the poorer channel areas to create the final image in figure 7.83.

🌐 ▷ϟ **ch7_patagonia.jpg**

1. Zoom in on the flare and use Cmd/Ctrl with 1, 2, and 3 to view the channels. As you can see in figure 7.84, more damage is visible in the red and the green channels but not the blue channel.

2. Return to the RGB composite channel (Cmd-~/Ctrl-~) and use a 3-pixel feathered Lasso tool to select the flare spot (figure 7.85).

3. In the Channels palette, activate the blue channel (Cmd-3/Ctrl-3) and select Edit > Copy. Activate the red channel (Cmd-1/Ctrl-1) and select Edit > Paste Into or Cmd-Shift-V/Ctrl-Shift-V to paste the good blue information into the damaged red channel.

© Jose A. Basbus

BEFORE

figure 7.82

AFTER

figure 7.83

Red

Green

Blue

figure 7.84

The blue channel was least affected by the lens flare.

figure 7.85

Select the damaged area with a feathered Lasso.

4. Activate the green channel (Cmd-2/Ctrl-2 and select Edit > Paste Into or Cmd-Shift-V/ Ctrl-Shift-V to paste the good blue information into the damaged green channel. Press Cmd-~/Ctrl-~ to return to the composite channel. As you can see in **figure 7.86**, the flare is gone, but the since all channels have equal values there is also no color.

figure 7.86

Pasting the selected area of the blue channel into both the red and green channel conceals the flare but also removes all color.

5. Return to the Layers palette and add a new layer. Change the blend mode to Color. With the Clone Stamp tool, sample similarly colored areas and clone over the black-and-white area (**figure 7.87**).

figure 7.87

Sampling from similarly colored areas, use the Clone Stamp set to Color blend mode to re-create color.

Channel replacement may not work for all types of flare, but it's always a good idea to see if undamaged information exists that you can take advantage of.

Repairing Extreme Lens Flare

When the flare was so extreme that every channel is damaged (**figure 7.88**), then reworking image density, duplicating information, cloning, and healing image information are required to turn the ruined photo into the final image (**figure 7.89**).

ch7_flare2.jpg

figure 7.88

figure 7.89

1. Flare always reduces contrast, and improving the contrast is the first step in rebuilding the image. Add a Curves adjustment layer and click the Options button to open the Auto Color Correction Options dialog box. Click the Enhance per Channel Contrast button and check Snap Neutral Midtones, then click OK twice to exit Curves.

2. Select the large flared-out area with a 10-pixel feathered Lasso tool and add a Curves adjustment layer to darken down the area, as seen in **figure** 7.90. Refine the transition by painting on the layer mask.

3. Use a 5-pixel feathered Lasso to select an area that is not damaged and would be a suitable substitute, as seen in **figure** 7.91.

figure 7.91

Finding and selecting undamaged information.

4. Choose Edit > Copy Merged followed by Select > Deselect and Edit > Paste. Now move the area into position as seen in **figure** 7.92.

5. Repeat steps 2 and 3 to copy and paste more mountains into place as seen in **figure** 7.93, which also shows how I used a layer mask to refine the transition between the new and damaged areas.

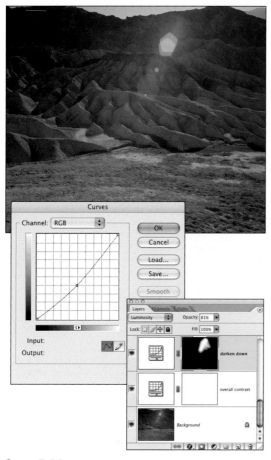

figure 7.90

Improving the overall contrast.

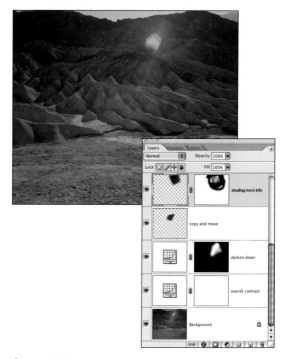

figure 7.92

Positioning the replacement information.

figure 7.93

Continue copying and pasting information to conceal the flare.

6. Add a new layer and use the Clone Stamp and Healing Brush, both set to Sample All Layers, to refine the edges of the flare fix.

7. To match the landscape density, select Layer > New Layer; change the blending mode to Soft Light and check Fill with Soft Light-neutral color (50% gray). Use a small, soft-edged 25% opacity white brush to lighten areas and tap X to switch to black to darken the contours as seen in **figure 7.94**.

8. To color balance the upper and lower portions of the image, add a Photo Filter adjustment layer and choose Cooling Filter (LBB) from the Filter menu to neutralize the yellow. Use the black-to-white linear Gradient tool on the layer mask to transition the color correction as seen in **figure 7.95**.

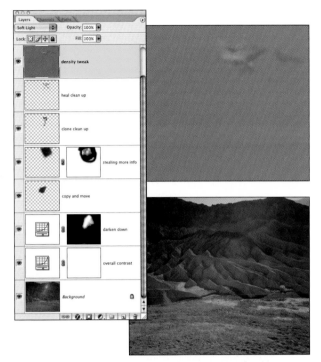

figure 7.94

Refining the density with a Soft light-neutral layer.

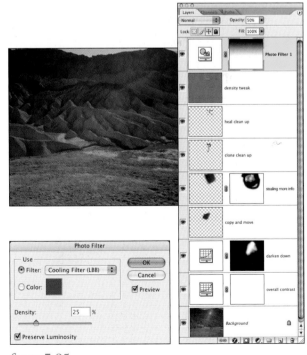

figure 7.95

Fine-tuning the image with a subtle color improvement using Photo Filter.

Removing Flare in Perspective

Photographing into the sun always poses a challenge, as seen in **figure 7.96**. I used Vanishing Point and refined the density to create the image seen in **figure 7.97**. For more information on the Vanishing Point command, revisit the section "Healing in Perspective" in Chapter 5, "Dust, Mold, and Texture Removal."

ch7_flare3.jpg

1. Choose Filter > Vanishing Point and use the Create Plane tool to determine the perspective of the walkway (**figure 7.98**).

2. Use the Vanishing Point Stamp with Heal turned on as seen in **figure 7.99** to conceal the flare. For better results, Option/Alt-click and sample good information as far as possible from the flare problem you are trying to conceal.

figure 7.96

figure 7.97

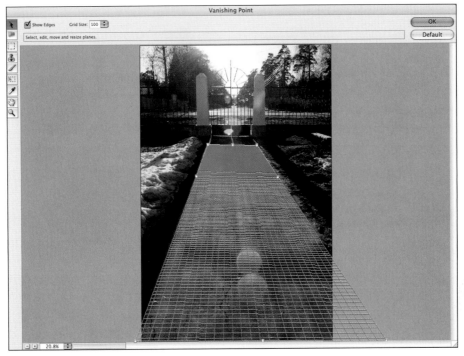

figure 7.98

Finding the correct perspective.

figure 7.99

Cloning and healing in perspective.

3. After exiting the Vanishing Point interface, Cmd-Option-Shift-E/Ctrl-Alt-Shift-E to merge all of the production layers up, then fine-tune the repairs with the Spot Healing Brush (figure 7.100).

figure 7.100

Refining the repair on a merged WIP layer.

4. To refine the density, add a Curves adjustment layer set to Multiply blending mode. Invert the layer mask (Cmd-I/Ctrl-I) and paint back the darkening effect as needed and seen in figure 7.101.

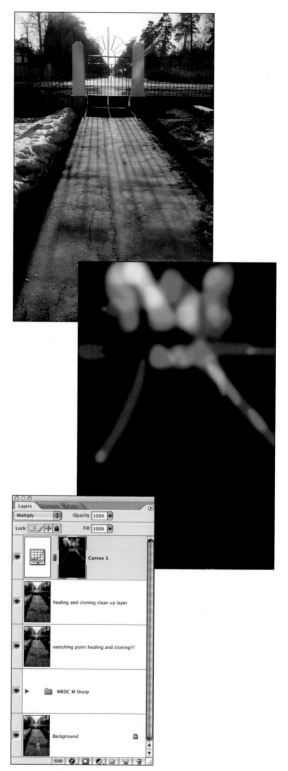

figure 7.101

Refining the density with a Curves layer.

Repairing Light Leaks

Correcting overall color casts as described in Chapter 4, "Working with Color," can alleviate many problems, but often the actual color information of the file is extremely damaged by light leaks, chemical staining, or dye coupler failure, causing severe color splotches or radical color shifts.

The damage seen in **figure 7.102** could have been caused by opening the camera before the film was entirely rewound or by light leaks in the camera or on the film roll. Using the best channel information, dodge and burn layers, as well as multiple Color Fill layers, the charm of the moment in time has been brought back to life (**figure 7.103**). Of course, a repaired image will never be as perfect as one that wasn't damaged to begin with.

🌐▷✂ **Ch7_lightleak.jpg**

figure 7.102

figure 7.103

1. The scan shows the rough edges and rounded corners of the slide mount, both of which can be cropped out to make a rectangular print and save a lot of needless restoration work.

2. Inspect each color channel (Cmd/Ctrl with 1, 2, and 3) to ascertain where the most damage is. Notice that the blue channel contains useful information (**figure 7.104**). Due to the extreme damage, I decided to convert it to a black-and-white image and then recolor it rather than trying to resurrect the color.

Red

Green

Blue

figure 7.104

The blue channel shows the best information.

© Ehrman Family Archive

3. Add a Channel Mixer adjustment layer, check Monochrome, and move the blue slider to 100% while setting the red and green sliders to 0. This reduces the streaks a great deal (figure 7.105).

figure 7.105

A Channel Mixer adjustment layer set to Monochrome view conceals most of the damage.

4. To improve the density, choose Layer > New > Layer, change the Mode to Overlay, and check Fill with Overlay-neural color (50% gray). Use a soft, low-opacity black brush to darken down the remaining lighter streaks (figure 7.106). If your own images have darker streaks, simply paint with white to lighten them appropriately.

figure 7.106

Painting on an Overlay neutral layer to balance density.

5. Create a Work in Progress (WIP) layer by pressing Cmd-Option-Shift-E/Ctrl-Alt-Shift-E, then use the Spot Healing Brush and Clone Stamp tool to remove the most distracting dust on the children and in the foreground.

6. To remove the dust in the sky, select the sky with a 3-pixel feathered Lasso and select Filter > Noise > Dust & Scratches. Set Radius and Threshold both to 2. After deselecting, use the Healing Brush to repair any remaining streaks in the clouds (figure 7.107).

figure 7.107

Dust spots and the clouds were repaired on a Work in Progress layer.

To color the image while maintaining flexibility, use solid Color Fill layers as described here and addressed in greater detail in Chapter 8, "Refining and Polishing the Image."

7. Starting with the sky, add a solid Color Fill layer, chose a light blue color and click OK. Change the blending mode to Color and use Cmd-I/Ctrl-I to invert the layer mask. Use a soft-edged white brush and paint over the sky. If the blue is too strong, reduce the layer opacity. To change the blue, double-click the Color Fill icon and choose a new blue.

8. Create separate layers for the grass, skin tones, clothes, hair, boots, and dirt. For added realism, sample colors from the original Background layer to use when coloring the image (figure 7.108).

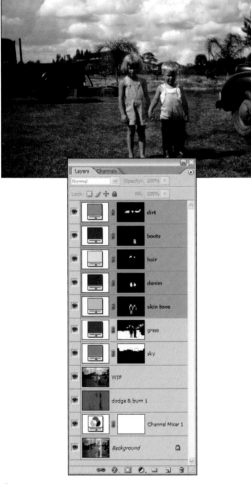

figure 7.108

Seven Color Fill layers later, the image looks similar to its initial color.

 Note

When mouse coloring, have the least important areas lower in the layer stack as the top color takes precedence.

9. After working with this image for a few minutes, I noticed that the car on the right side still maintained some of the original color. To add a heightened sense of realism, duplicate the Background layer and place it on the very top of the layer stack. Option/Alt-click the layer mask button to add a black layer mask and use a soft-edged white brush to paint back the original car as seen in figure 7.109.

figure 7.109

Reusing part of the original image.

10. To hide the last vestiges of the light leaks, choose Layer > New > Layer, set the blending mode to Overlay, and check Fill with Overlay-neutral color (50% gray). Use a soft, low-opacity black brush to darken down the remaining lighter streaks and a white brush to lighten darker streaks as shown in **figure 7.110**.

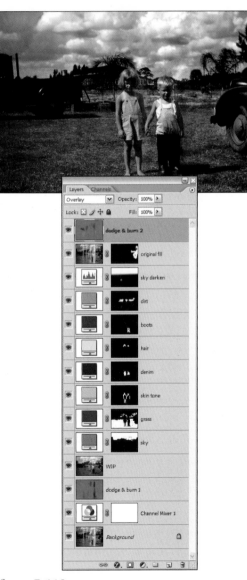

figure 7.110

A final dodge and burn layer removes the last of the light leaks.

CLOSING THOUGHTS

Replacing, rebuilding, and re-creating missing image elements requires creative problem-solving skills, the willingness to dig around in a file to look for useful material, and the ability to appropriate suitable pieces from other photographs and scenes. The search will result in new images that are much more pleasing and meaningful to display and cherish.

8

REFINING AND POLISHING THE IMAGE

After perfecting an image's color and contrast and repairing the ravages of time, it's time to apply the final polish, the frosting, the cherry on top. Finishing an image can be as simple as converting a so-so color image into a snappy black-and-white photograph or colorizing a black-and-white photo. You can make the difference between "Ho-hum" and "Wow!" by adding just the right amount of sharpening or a subtle color effect or by experimenting with creative painterly and edge techniques to accentuate the image.

All in all, this chapter is about experimenting, dabbling, exploring, and adding a touch of pizzazz to retouched images or forgotten snapshots to make them stand out. Here you learn how to do the following:

- Convert color images to black-and-white

- Add color to black-and-white images

- Apply painterly effects and creative edges

- Sharpen images to add snap

CONVERTING COLOR TO BLACK AND WHITE

Recently, the Eastman Kodak Company announced that it would no longer produce black-and-white paper for the wet darkroom, yet demand for beautiful black-and-white prints is increasing. Creating rich black-and-white images from color scans or digital camera files can be especially fulfilling and I find myself exploring and experimenting with variations on the color to black-and-white translations, tweaking files late into the night to see how tonal interpretations influence the expression of the image.

As with many techniques in Photoshop, there are numerous methods of converting an RGB file from color to grayscale, ranging from a one-click solution with no control, to multi-step techniques with infinite control, to processing camera raw files.

Of course, I'd like you to avoid the one-click method because it removes important image information. However, please don't jump to the most involved method because you think it must be the best. It may not be the best for the images you're working with, and why spend all that time if you can achieve the desired results with less effort?

 Note

All of the techniques I describe here work with both RGB and CMYK images. Your numeric values will vary depending on your color and separation setup.

Converting to Grayscale Mode

The fastest (but worst) way to convert a color file to grayscale is to select Image > Mode > Grayscale, which discards color information without any input for you. As benign as this process seems, the behind-the-scenes math is rather complicated. Photoshop references your color and ink settings and then takes approximately 30% red, 59% green, and 11% blue to make the single-channel grayscale file. The worst part of this conversion process is that there's no preview and you have no control over the actual percentages applied or the final outcome.

To simplify this, Photoshop takes all three channels and smashes them down into a single channel. If one channel is damaged or excessively noisy, those flaws go into the grayscale file as well. Additionally, if an image relies on strong color, like figure 8.1, the standard grayscale conversion will most likely not yield pleasing results, as seen in figure 8.2.

figure 8.1

The original image.

figure 8.2

Converting saturated color images with Mode > Grayscale rarely produces pleasing results.

Although this method is fast and easy, I cannot recommend it for either RGB or CMYK files because you can achieve better results with the following methods.

Using a Color Channel

A second way to convert from color to grayscale gives you a chance to choose the best channel before discarding the color information. Inspect the quality and characteristics of each channel and decide which one has the best tonal information. Press Cmd/Ctrl with 1, 2, and 3 to view channels individually.

In most cases, the green channel will be best, but for some pictures, such as creative portraits, the red channel may offer a pleasingly glowing alternative. In figure 8.3, the blue channel offers the grittiest rendition of the scene. When converting to grayscale, make the best channel active (as shown in figure 8.4), and select Image > Mode > Grayscale. The less-useful channels are thrown away, and the channel you consider the best becomes the grayscale image. Many newspaper productions use this technique to convert a color image to grayscale quickly.

 ch8_batteries.jpg

Using the Lightness Channel

A third method to convert a color image to grayscale starts by converting it from RGB or CMYK to Lab Color (choose Image > Mode > Lab Color), as shown in figure 8.5. Then, make the L channel (lightness) active and select Image > Mode > Grayscale. As in the previous example, the other channels are discarded and the Lightness channel becomes the grayscale image. This method maintains the luminance value of the image more closely than using a single channel from an RGB or CMYK file and often produces a noise-free and pleasing rendition.

figure 8.3

The original image.

figure 8.4

Converting to grayscale with the best channel active will delete the weaker or less desirable channels.

figure 8.5

Converting a color image to Lab Color separates the tonal information from the color information.

Using the Channel Mixer

The Channel Mixer enables you to add and subtract varying amounts of each color channel to build grayscale files with a wide tonal and interpretive range. This method balances ease of use and quality of results when converting RGB or CMYK images to grayscale. It is especially useful when more than one channel has tonal attributes you would like to maintain.

 ch8_yellow_poppy.jpg

1. In the Channels palette, inspect the quality and characteristics of each channel, by pressing Cmd/Ctrl with 1, 2, and 3 to identify the most pleasing channels. As seen in **figure 8.6**, each channel of this image has useful tonal information.

2. Add a Channel Mixer adjustment layer and make sure the monochrome (another word for grayscale or single channel) check box is selected.

Composite   Red

Green   Blue

figure 8.6

Assess the quality of each channel individually.

3. Adjust the color sliders to create a grayscale image that uses tonal attributes from the desired channels. To maintain tonality when converting, the total of the numeric values should not exceed 100. However, if your goal is to create the best grayscale image possible, experiment with the sliders until you're satisfied with the results (see **figure 8.7**). I rarely use the Constant slider because it applies a linear lightening and darkening effect like Brightness/Contrast. I'd rather use Levels or Curves to finesse the final tonality of the image after conversion.

4. Keep an eye on the Info palette, and don't let the highlights go over 248, 248, 248, which would blow them out to pure white. Click OK to close the Channel Mixer dialog box.

figure 8.7

Using a Channel Mixer adjustment layer to create quality black-and-white images from a color file gives you tremendous control.

Tip

You can open and close the Info palette by pressing the F8 key. This works even while you're in the Channel Mixer dialog box (or any adjustment layer dialog box).

Tip

When using the Channel Mixer, you can start with the 100% green channel rather than the default 100% red channel by pressing Cmd-2/ Ctrl-2 before checking the Monochrome box.

The Channel Mixer enables you to interpret and influence how the color values are translated into black and white. In figures 8.9, 8.10, and 8.11, I've created three interpretations of the color image shown in figure 8.8 from subtle to dramatic.

ch8_exit.jpg

figure 8.8

The original image.

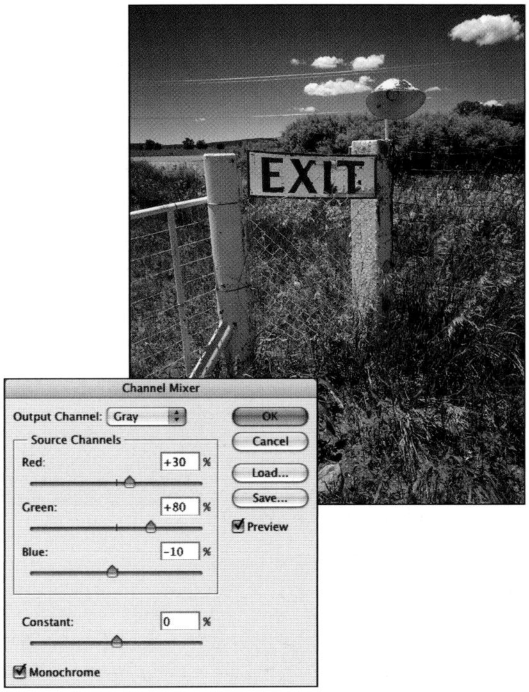

figure 8.9

The Channel Mixer can be used to create a classic black-and-white image…

figure 8.10

…or something a little more dramatic…

figure 8.11

...or something quite eerie in the day-for-night genre.

Mimicking Photographic Film and Filters

I learned the following technique from Russell Brown (www.russellbrown.com), the ultimate Photoshop evangelist. It uses two Hue/Saturation image adjustment layers—the first acts as the color to black-and-white conversion filter on the lens, and the second is the black-and-white film surface. By combining these layers with blending modes, you can mimic how black-and-white photographers use color filters and black and white film types to influence scene rendition.

 ch8_cupids_chapel.jpg

1. Choose Layer > Smart Objects > Group into New Smart Object.

2. To create the photographic filter layer, add a Hue/Saturation adjustment layer and simply click OK without changing anything in the dialog box. Change the blending mode to Color, as seen in figure 8.12.

figure 8.12

The filter layer starts as an unadjusted Hue/Saturation layer set to Color blending mode.

3. To create the film layer, add a second Hue/Saturation adjustment layer and set the saturation to –100, as shown in figure 8.13. To reduce possible confusion, you may want to name the top layer *film* and the lower layer *filter*.

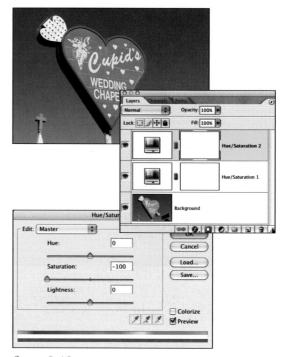

figure 8.13

The film layer is another Hue/Saturation layer, this time set to –100 saturation.

4. After you've added these two layers, the fun and creativity can begin. Double-click the filter layer thumbnail and adjust the Hue slider. Notice how the color values are translated into black and white. **Figure 8.14** shows a variation in which I emphasized the sky, and **figure 8.15** places more importance on the sign.

figure 8.14

Adjusting the Hue slider on the filter layer to emphasize the sky.

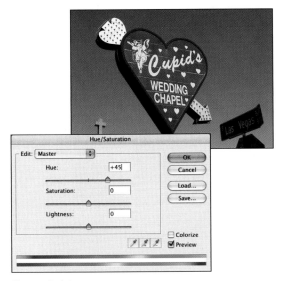

figure 8.15

Changing the Hue setting for a brighter version to bring out the sign.

5. You also can adjust the saturation, which emphasizes the area of the color wheel corresponding to the Hue slider setting even more (see **figures 8.16** and **8.17**).

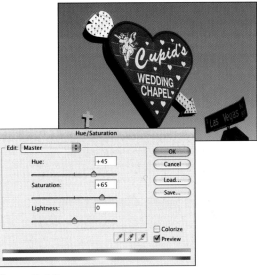

figure 8.16

Adjusting the Saturation slider allows the sign to remain the same, while reducing the importance of the sky.

figure 8.17

Adjusting the Saturation slider creates an almost day-for-night feeling.

6. For additional control, you can choose a color range from the Edit menu in the filter layer's Hue/Saturation dialog box and make further adjustments on specific colors.

This technique avoids a common pitfall of the simpler Channel Mixer technique in that it is nearly impossible to over-influence the image and force the highlights to pure white.

Tip

To speed up production when converting similar color files to grayscale, place the adjustment layers into a layer group and drag the layer group to other files to convert them.

Be Smart with Grayscale

Smart Objects are a Photoshop CS2 feature, which allows for great flexibility, as the original file information is embedded into the file—think of it as a container of data that you can access, change, and edit without ruining the file. In the case of interpreting color images into grayscale convert the file to a Smart Object before changing the file mode from RGB or CMYK to grayscale, as described here.

1. In the Layers palette, select the adjustment layers and Background layer as seen in figure 8.18. Choose Layer > Smart Objects > Group into New Smart Object.

figure 8.18

Shift-click each layer to select them.

2. Choose Image > Mode > Grayscale.

3. To maintain the flexibility of the Smart Object, click Don't Rasterize in the ensuing dialog box, after which a new warning pops up, asking whether if it's OK to discard color information, to which you should click OK. This creates the image seen in figure 8.19.

4. Save the file as a format that supports Smart Objects including (in my preference order) .TIF, .PSD, .PSB, or .PDF. Do not uncheck Layers in the Save dialog box, as the Smart Object is a layer that needs to be maintained.

5. Now you can close the file and, when you reopen it, if you choose Image > Mode > RGB and check Don't Rasterize, Photoshop will recall the original Smart Object in full color as shown in figure 8.20.

figure 8.19

The grayscale Smart Object

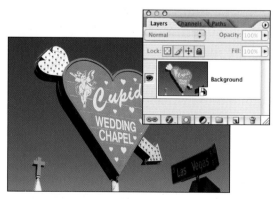

figure 8.20

Converting a color Smart Object into grayscale does not discard the color information.

6. Double-click the Smart Object icon in the Layers palette, click OK to the saving explanation, and note, as **figure 8.21** shows, the original layered file with the color information intact.

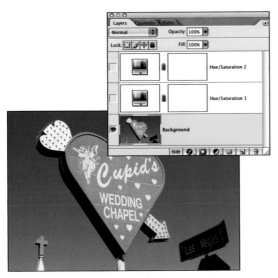

figure 8.22

figure 8.21

As long as the file is still a Smart Object, the color information has been saved with the file.

Blending Channels

Black-and-white photography has such a rich history that it comes as no surprise that there are numerous methods to convert beautiful color images like **figure 8.22** into beautiful digital black-and-white images like **figure 8.23**. This method takes advantage of layer blending modes, layer masks, and selective sharpening to create an image using the best parts of an image's channels. Before beginning this technique, I cannot emphasize enough that you need to work on a duplicate or a backup of your color file. OK, you've been warned—let's get started.

 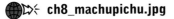 **ch8_machupichu.jpg**

figure 8.23

Caution

Before splitting the color channels into individual files, you should flatten the color image, delete all alpha channels, and duplicate the image.

© John McIntosh

1. Open a color image and select Image > Duplicate and then select Image > Duplicate again so that you have three identical color files.

2. Click either of the duplicated files and choose Image > Mode > Lab Color. In the Channels palette, click the Lightness channel then choose Select > All and Edit > Copy as seen in figure 8.24.

figure 8.24

Convert one file to Lab and copy the L channel.

3. Click the original color file and choose Edit > Paste to paste the lightness channel onto the color file (see figure 8.25). Save the layered file as a Photoshop file and give it a new name. I used ch8_machupichu_BW.psd.

figure 8.25

Paste the L channel onto the color image.

4. Return to the Lab file and close it without saving it. On the remaining duplicate file, in the Channels palette, select Split Channels from the palette menu. This will separate the three image channels into individual files (see figure 8.26) that are named after the channels from which they originated.

figure 8.26

Selecting Split Channels creates three separate grayscale files.

5. Take a look at the three files to determine which ones contain valuable tonal and detail information. In this example, the blue channel has the best rocks and the red channel has the most dramatic sky. Of course, in your own files you may prefer other channels or all three channels. With the Move tool, drag the blue channel file onto the layered file. To ensure perfect registration, hold down the Shift key while dragging one file to another. Repeat with the red channel file and name the layers to reflect their origins, as shown in figure 8.27. Save this file and close the separate red, green, and blue channel files without saving them.

figure 8.27

Holding the Shift key while using the Move tool to drag one file onto another will add it as a perfectly registered layer.

figure 8.28

Using the Multiply blending mode quickly makes the sky more dramatic.

6. Phew—the tedious production work is done and now the creative, fun part begins. To accentuate the billowing clouds, change the blending mode of the sky to Multiply as seen in figure 8.28.

7. This makes the entire file darker. To block the darkening effect from affecting the rocks, choose Layer > Layer Mask > Reveal All or click on the layer mask button on the bottom of the Layers palette. Use a large, soft-edged black brush to paint over the rocks on the layer mask, as seen in figure 8.29.

figure 8.29

Use a large black brush to conceal areas you do not want affected.

8. To increase the impact of the clouds, duplicate the sky layer. I liked the effect so much I duplicated the sky layer again (figure 8.30). If this makes the image too dramatic, you can always adjust the effect by reducing the layer opacity.

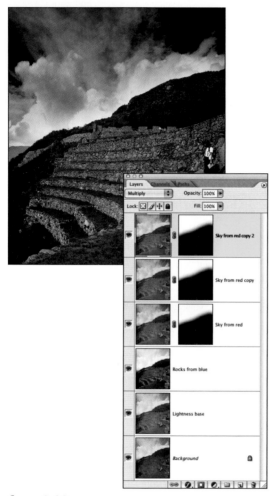

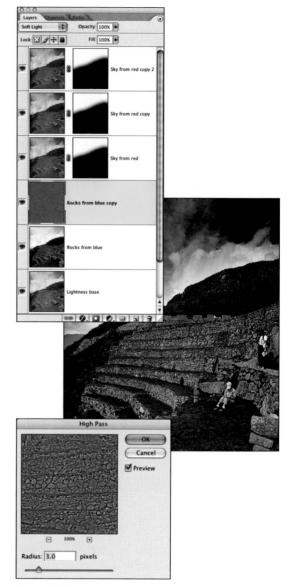

figure 8.30

Duplicating a layer with a blending mode is a fast way to increase the effect.

9. The best attribute of the rocks is the texture, which can be sharpened to make the rocks more tangible. Duplicate the rocks layer and change the layer blending mode of the duplicate layer to Soft Light. Select Filter > Other > High Pass. Use a setting between 2 and 4; in this example I used a 3 as seen in figure 8.31.

figure 8.31

Sharpening just the rocks to bring out the texture.

 Note

Remember that you can increase and decrease intensity by duplicating layers and experimenting with blending modes. If one layer isn't dramatic but two layers is too much, lower the opacity of the second layer to fine-tune the effect.

10. If desired, click the topmost layer and use a Curves adjustment layer to refine the final contrast as seen in figure 8.32.

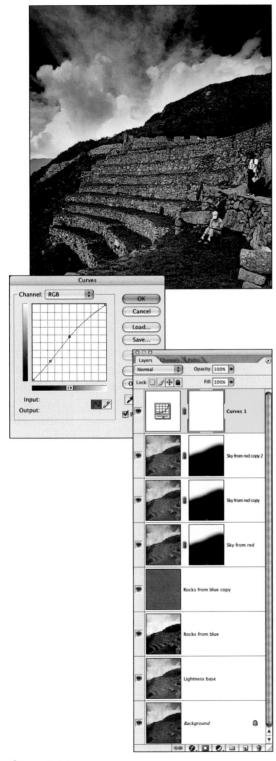

figure 8.32

Consider adding a Curves layer to add the final tone and contrast effect.

If you're wondering why we didn't use the L channel in this particular conversion—I often just have it there as a black-and-white buffer between the interpreted file and the original color file. It would have been especially useful if I decided to reduce the opacity of the rocks layer. Of course all of these changes are purely subjective, and your interpretation of a file may vary greatly from mine. Experimenting with blending modes and layer position can create wonderful tonal juxtapositions that are sure to surprise and intrigue the viewer.

Raw Color to Black and White

Many prosumer and professional digital cameras produce camera raw files, which is the native data as captured by the camera CCD. There are numerous advantages to camera raw files including high bit depth, lack of compression artifacts, and flexibility in image processing. Please check your camera documentation to see if it will shoot raw. Due to its smooth integration with Photoshop CS2 and Bridge, I work with Adobe's Camera Raw plug-in to process all of my camera raw files into both color and black-and-white images.

To use Camera Raw to create beautiful black-and-white images as seen in the example in figure 8.33 and 8.34, follow along with these steps, but feel free to make adjustments to suit your taste and images anytime in the process.

 ch8_monument_valley.CR2

1. Double-click the raw file to open it in the Camera Raw dialog box. Working in the Adjust tab, move the Saturation slider all the way to the left to remove all vestiges of color (figure 8.35).

figure 8.33

BEFORE

figure 8.34

AFTER

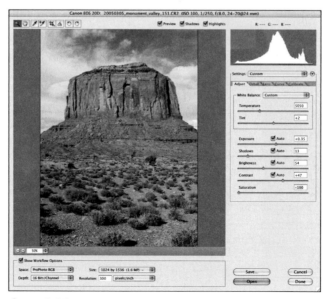

figure 8.35

Remove all Saturation to create the initial grayscale image.

2. Select the Lens tab and, if desired, adjust the Vignetting slider to the left to darken the corners as seen in figure 8.36.

3. Click on the Curve tab and adjust the contrast of the image as seen in figure 8.37.

figure 8.36

Add a darkening burned-corner effect.

figure 8.37

Anytime in the process, use the curves to refine the tonal range of the image.

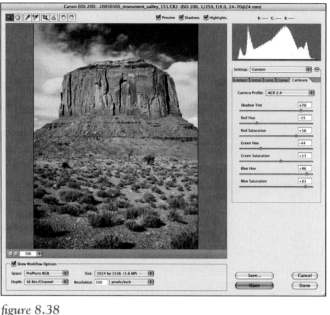

figure 8.38

Adjusting the Hue and Saturation sliders allows for endless interpretations.

4. To adjust the conversion, click on the Calibrate tab and adjust the Hue and Saturation sliders (figure 8.38). To be quite honest, knowing how these sliders work is less important than creating attractive images—meaning I move the sliders around until I'm happy, rather than getting caught up in the background mathematics of the sliders.

5. Click Open and admire your final image.

All in all, I've shown you seven different ways to convert a color file to grayscale, and I hope that you take the time to experiment to see which one gives you the most pleasing results.

TONING IMAGES WITH COLOR

Photographers tone their prints for a number of reasons. Selenium toners add warmth to a print and make it last longer. Ferric oxide toners add a beautiful blue tone, and gold toners add richness that is hard to resist. But toning prints in a traditional darkroom can also pose both health and environmental hazards. Unless you have proper ventilation and chemical disposal options, traditional darkroom toning is not recommended. With Photoshop, you can tone images to your heart's content without having to clean up messy sinks and smelly trays or dispose of noxious chemicals.

Toning with Variations

The Variations dialog box is the easiest way to experiment with image toning options. The original image is shown, along with a collection of variations (hence the name) created by strengthening or weakening the colors in the image. It doesn't require a great deal of guesswork on your part because Variations gives you a preview of the finished image. For more details on the Variations dialog box, see "Understanding Color Correction with Image Variations" in Chapter 4, "Working with Color."

Figure 8.39 shows the original image, and figure 8.40 shows the toned version. To me, the sepia version is much warmer, more attractive, and fitting to the subject.

ch8_little_girl.jpg

1. Duplicate the Background layer by dragging it to the New Layer button on the bottom of the Layers palette. Select Image > Adjustments > Variations.

BEFORE

figure 8.39

AFTER

figure 8.40

2. The ring of six color options (see figure 8.41) enables you to experiment by clicking the color you want to add to the image. I recommend reducing the strength of the effect by moving the Fine to Coarse slider to the left.

3. You can click a color more than once to strengthen the effect, or click the opposite color to subtract the first color.

 Tip

When working with Variations, you can zero out the effect by clicking the original thumbnail in the upper left of the Variations interface.

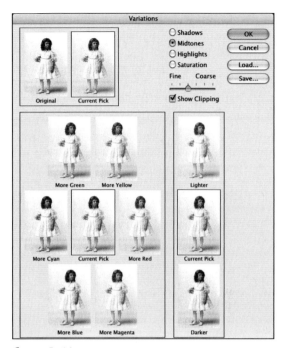

figure 8.41

The visual feedback you get from Variations is often a good place to start when toning a black-and-white image.

Caution

For any black-and-white image to be colorized or toned, the file must be in either RGB, CMYK, or Lab Color mode. Before you begin, convert the file from grayscale to a color mode, preferably RGB or CMYK.

Monocolor Toning

Variations is very easy to use, but that simplicity comes with a price because your changes aren't applied to a separate layer or added as an adjustment layer. In other words, you're changing the actual image data and not working on a separate layer. To maintain control and flexibility, I prefer to work with separate layers and do my toning with the tools described here and in the next section, "Multicolor Toning." Monocolor toning is a straightforward method of adding one color to an image (as shown in figures 8.42 and 8.43) and can be used to tie a group of images together visually or to add an interpretive mood to an image.

 **ch8_rose.jpg**

1. Select Layer > New Fill Layer > Solid Color. In the New Layer dialog box, give the layer a name if you wish, then click OK. Select a color from the Color Picker and click OK.

2. Change the layer's blending mode to create the effects shown in figures 8.44, 8.45, and 8.46.

3. The advantages to using the Color Fill layer, as shown in figure 8.47, are that you can work with the opacity and blending modes to reduce the effect; use layer masks to control where the effect takes place; and, by double-clicking the Solid Color layer, select new colors. If you don't like the results, you can just throw away the entire layer and start over again.

figure 8.42   **BEFORE**

figure 8.43

figure 8.44

The Color Burn blending mode at 50% opacity.

figure 8.45

The Color Dodge blending mode at 100% opacity.

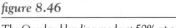

figure 8.46

The Overlay blending mode at 50% opacity.

figure 8.47

Placing the color on a separate layer enables you to fine-tune the effect with opacity and blending mode settings.

Multicolor Toning

The world is your Photoshop oyster when you work with adjustment layers. The Color Balance tool enables you to tone and color highlights, midtones, or shadows separately, just as a fine art photographer would in a traditional darkroom.

The original car wreck photo used in this example is a black-and-white RGB file, as shown in figure 8.48. Figure 8.49 shows how adding complementary colors into the highlights and shadows make the image more dimensional and attractive. By working in opposites—cooling the shadows with blues and cyans and warming the highlights with yellows and reds—visual tension is added to the image.

figure 8.48

figure 8.49

⊕▷ᘛ ch8_rusty_car.jpg

1. To add subtle colors to the shadows, mid-tones, and highlights, add a Color Balance adjustment layer and click shadow, midtone, or highlight, depending on the area you want to tone.

2. Adjust each area so that it complements and offsets the others. Often, I tone the shadows and highlights and don't alter the midtones. This adds color tension to an image.

3. As shown in figure 8.50, I toned the shadows blue-cyan. In figure 8.51, I chose to contrast the cool tones with warm tones in the highlights.

The only correct setting for any of these techniques is what looks good to you. So have fun, experiment, and bring those black-and-white images to life.

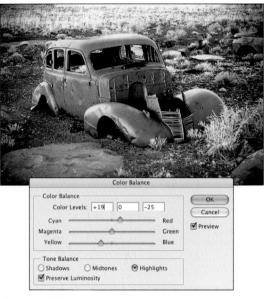

figure 8.51

Adding red and yellow to the highlights.

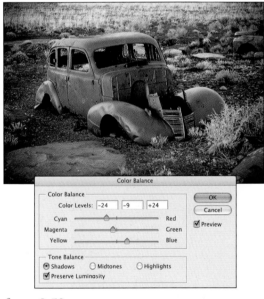

figure 8.50

Adding cyan and blue to the shadows.

HAND-COLORING A BLACK-AND-WHITE IMAGE

Since the advent of photography, photographers and artists have hand-colored photographs to add realism. Even in today's era of computers and Photoshop, there are many professional retouchers and photo enthusiasts who still enjoy working with Marshall Oils to add a handcrafted look to their photos. I've never been very good at hand-coloring traditional darkroom prints, which is why I especially like doing it on the computer.

The most straightforward method of hand-coloring an image entails adding an empty layer that has been set to the Color blending mode and using any painting tool to color it, as shown in figure 8.52.

In the examples in figures 8.53, 8.54, and 8.55, you see the original image, the restored image, and the final hand-colored version as restored and colored by Alan of PhotoRescuer, who explained, "Instead of trying to rescue the washed-out and faded colors in the original print, I decided it would be easier to restore a grayscale version and then hand-color it." After restoring the image, Alan used individual empty layers set to Color blending mode to add the color. For additional information as to how Alan restored and colored the file please download the ch8 _ restore _ and _ color.pdf posted in the Chapter 8 section of the book's Web site.

⊕⇨ ch8_restore_and_color.pdf

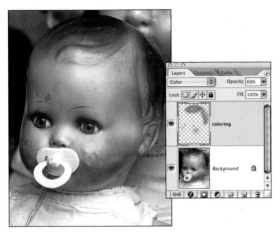

figure 8.52

By painting on an empty layer set to the Color blending mode, you can hand-paint details onto the doll.

figure 8.54

After restoration.

figure 8.53

BEFORE

figure 8.55

After hand-coloring.

You can hand-color an image by making selections and using Color Fill adjustment layers, as illustrated by the black-and-white image shown in **figure 8.56**, which Frank Eirund, a Munich-based computer specialist and Photoshop enthusiast, has hand-colored (well, mouse-colored) beautifully, as shown in **figure 8.57**. This coloring method requires a bit more patience, but the flexibility of working with Color Fill adjustment layers is well worth the effort.

After scanning in RGB color mode in the original photograph of his parents' wedding photo from August 1963, Frank decided to turn the black-and-white photo into a color one as a gift for their 40th wedding anniversary celebration. Frank took a moment to decide which colors he would use. Of course, the flower bouquet needed to be red and green and he decided to make the background blue to frame the couple wonderfully.

1. Frank started by selecting the roses with the Lasso tool, as shown in **figure 8.58** and adding a Solid Color adjustment layer.

2. He selected a red for the roses, which automatically filled the Fill layer with the color (see **figure 8.59**). Setting the layer's blending mode to Color to let details from the original image show through.

figure 8.56

figure 8.57

figure 8.58

The roses are the first element selected for coloring.

figure 8.59

The image after the selection has been filled with color and the layer's blending mode has been changed to Color.

3. Frank selected the green leaves of the bouquet, added a new Color Fill layer with green, and set the blending mode to Color. Of course, the entire flower bouquet shouldn't all be an identical shade of green, so he made another selection and filled this with a darker shade of green (see **figure 8.60**).

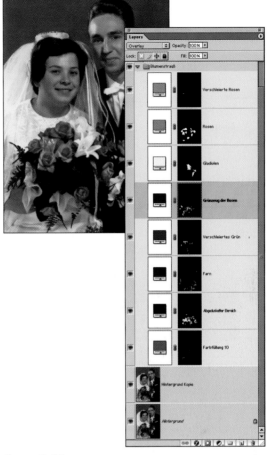

figure 8.60

Using different shades of red and green makes the bouquet more realistic.

4. With the patience of a saint, Frank continued selecting his way up the image, using individual layers for elements as small as individual flowers and his parents' eyes for a total of 24 Color Fill layers to create the final image.

5. When a color was too strong, Frank double-clicked the adjustment layer icon and selected a new color with the Color Picker or reduced the opacity of the layer.

Because the Color Fill layers are based on selections and have masks with them, you can refine where the coloring takes place by painting with a black or white brush on the Color Fill's layer mask.

Hand-Coloring Tips

Hand-coloring can be both tedious and rewarding. Here are a few tips to help you work a little faster and make your results more realistic:

- As Wayne explains, "When you mix color with white, you only get white. When you mix color with black, you only get black. For the best results, you need shades of gray that the color can interact with." As shown in figure 8.61, where the red strip is over the darkest or lightest areas of the gradient, you cannot see the red, which also illustrates that using different types of adjustment layers creates a variety of coloring effects.

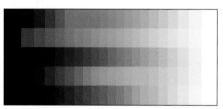

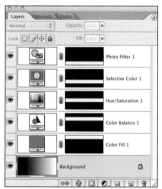

figure 8.61

When using a Color Fill layer, the very dark and very light areas aren't visibly affected.

- To speed up hand-coloring work, press Option/Alt while adding a new Solid Color layer from the Layers palette. This brings up the New Layer window where you can change the blending mode to Color before selecting the color.

- Use reference photographs from CD stock collections or from your own photos to collect, record, and select colors. This is especially useful when hand-coloring skin tones. Save your colors into your color swatches and use the Preset Manager to name them.

- To simplify choosing colors from reference files, select Filter > Pixelate > Mosaic to create tiles of color, which I find easier to work with.

- Due to the many, many layers that a good colorization requires, it is imperative that you name your layers.

- When coloring skin tones, vary the shades of colors to make the hand-coloring look more realistic. Figure 8.62 shows a close-up of the beautiful colorization that Lorie Zirbes did. As you can see, the woman's face, cheeks, and lips are of a similar color palette, yet they offer enough visual distinction to be effective.

© Mary Holmes

figure 8.62

Vary the shades of skin tones to make your hand-coloring look more lifelike.

- Finally, as Wayne so aptly says, "Colorization is very subjective. Even though your customer has told you which colors to put into a picture, it is common for them to change their minds according to their recollection. For this reason, I always use Color Fill adjustment layers, which give me the ability to easily change colors."

From Traditional to Digital

Lorie Zirbes is a traditionally trained restoration artist with more than 25 years of experience. A traditional retoucher or restoration artist would work directly on a film negative or paper print with dyes and chemicals to enhance an image. As you can imagine, the realm of the traditional retoucher is shrinking, and Lorie is now working with Photoshop. I find it interesting that she approaches a hand-coloring job differently than I would.

Figure 8.63 shows the original image and figure 8.64 shows the hand-colored image. Now take a look at the Layers palette and the isolated layer (see figure 8.65). Rather than working with selections and Color Fill adjustment layers, Lorie has developed a technique in which she duplicates the layers and isolates the essential image information with layer masks. She then paints directly on the image information with a soft-edged brush set to Color blending mode.

Once again, I am surprised as to how many ways there are to accomplish similar results with Photoshop. In the end, whatever achieves the best results for you is what works the best.

figure 8.64

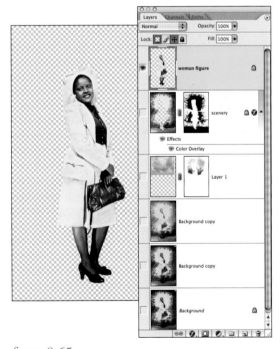

figure 8.65

Lorie paints directly on the image with a soft brush set to Color.

figure 8.63

ADDING PAINTERLY EFFECTS

Transforming a photograph into a sketch or painting can be as straightforward as experimenting with the Photoshop filters or as involved as applying colors and textured brushstrokes to create a work of art. In all cases, it does take time and experimentation to create a personal look. Or as Janee Aronoff, an Adobe Certified Instructor and artist, says, "No one else has your vision. No one else can do your art."

Watercolor Effects

Adding watercolor or sketchy effects to an image works best on files with strong graphical elements. In most cases, you want to avoid images with a lot of fine detail, as the multiple passes with the Photoshop filters will average out and destroy detail. Use bold, colorful images as seen in **figure 8.66**, which Janee turned into the watercolor-type image seen in **figure 8.67**.

⊕⊃⊱ **ch8_tulips.jpg**

1. Duplicate the Background layer three times. Hide the top two layers and make sure that layer above the Background layer is active (**figure 8.68**).

2. For the first duplicated layer, choose Filter > Artistic > Cutout and use settings 4, 4, 2. Click OK and change the layer blending mode to Luminosity (**figure 8.69**). Notice how Janee names her layers—using the name of the filter, the settings used, and the blending mode. This lets her keep track of her progress and will help her create similar effects on other images.

3. On the second duplicated layer, use Filter > Artistic > Dry Brush with settings of 10, 10, 3. Change the layer blending mode to Screen (**figure 8.70**).

4. On the third layer, use Filter > Noise > Median with a radius of 12 and change the layer blending mode to Soft Light (**figure 8.71**).

figure 8.66

figure 8.67

figure 8.68

Duplicate the layer three times.

figure 8.69

Use the Cutout filter to simplify the image.

figure 8.70

Use the Dry Brush filter to add texture.

figure 8.71

The Median filter averages the image without blurring it.

5. Finish this with a deckled edge layer. Add a white Solid Color fill layer and choose Image > Adjustments > Invert to invert the layer mask from white to black as the Layers palette in figure 8.72 shows.

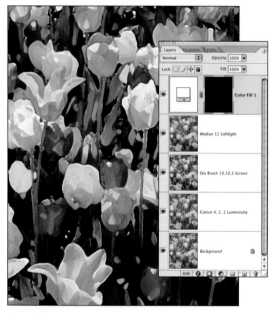

figure 8.72

Use a Color fill layer to create the edge effect.

6. Select the Brush tool and, using either the Brush Preset picker menu or the Brushes palette menu, choose Dry Media Brushes. Click Append to add the new brushes to the Brushes palette (figure 8.73).

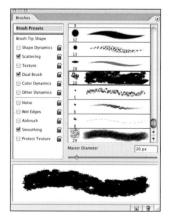

figure 8.73

Add the Dry Media brushes to the Brushes palette.

7. Use a large rough brush and paint with white along the edges of the Color Fill mask to create an edge as seen in figure 8.74. Paint with black to take away or refine the edges.

figure 8.74

Paint on the layer mask to create the roughened edges.

Sketched Texture Effects

Shan Canfield turned a photo (figure 8.75) into a watercolor sketch using multiple painted and filter layers to create the textured image seen in figure 8.76. As Shan so wisely says, "Watercolor painting, whether traditional or digital, requires patience." The process takes the image through three primary changes—sketch, color, texture—to create the final effect. Shan has shared the whole process in a step-by-step tutorial you can download from the book's Web site.

🌐▷€ **ch8_BabyWatercolor.pdf**

🌐▷€ **ch8_babyoriginal.jpg**

🔍 **Tip**

For excellent digital painting tutorials please visit www.helenyancystudio.com.

© Shan Canfield

BEFORE

figure 8.75

CREATIVE EDGES

Of all the image-making processes, digital image creation is the most precise. The computer lets us change a single pixel or make radical global changes to the entire image. But the power and precision of the computer can give many images a machine-made feel. Simply put, the perfection of the image-making process eliminates any sense of the human craft—those interesting imperfections and unique qualities that come with handwork. Using creative edges can be an effective way to give computer-generated images a handmade appearance.

Adding Creative Edges

One of my favorite techniques to add painterly edges was used in the previous section to add a roughened border to the tulip image by Janee Aronoff. Phil Pool takes that idea one step further, by using numerous brushstrokes to add creative edge to the covers of the proof books that the students and family receive as seen in **figure 8.77**.

AFTER

figure 8.76

© Phil Pool, Omni Photography

figure 8.77

Going the extra mile to make the high school proof books unique distinguishes an innovative studio from an average one.

⊕⊅← ch8_flute_player.jpg

To experiment with creative edges all you need is a blank document and some time to doodle.

1. Before you can make creative edges, you need to find the brushstrokes that appeal to you. Choose Reset Brushes from the Brushes palette menu. I personally prefer to work with the small thumbnail view (see **figure 8.78**) because it's easier to navigate.

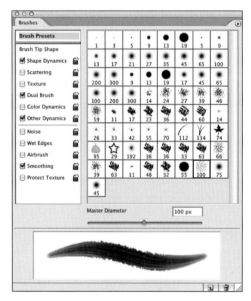

figure 8.78

The small thumbnail view provides enough information and is easier to navigate than the other brush views.

2. Choose File > New. Choose 8 by 10 inches from the preset and use 300 ppi to make a surface to doodle on.

3. Using 50% gray as your foreground color, choose a creative brush from the brush picker and make one stroke. When you find a brush you like, make a note of its name or click on the first empty area at the end of the Brushes palette to add a new brush. Use a name that will help remind you what the edge looks like (**figure 8.79**).

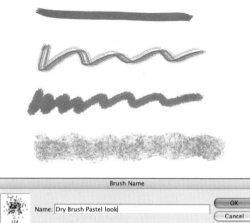

figure 8.79

Name the brushes you like so you will be able to find them again.

4. Load additional artistic media brush libraries as described previously and keep doodling strokes to find edges that appeal to you.

5. Once you've identified a few strokes that you like, make a new 8 by 10 inch 300 ppi file to serve as your template.

6. Add a new layer and make a rectangular selection with the Marquee tool feathered by 25 pixels. Fill this selection with 50% gray as seen in **figure 8.80**. Choose Select > Deselect.

figure 8.80

Make a soft-edged rectangle filled with gray to serve as the image placeholder.

7. Use an artistic brush to paint around the edge of the rectangle. In this example I used the Rough Round Bristle as a 175-pixel brush to create the template edge seen in **figure 8.81**.

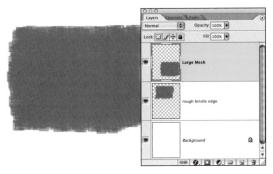

figure 8.81

Paint along the edges with an artistic brush.

8. Add a new layer containing another gray rectangle and continue experimenting with brushes. To create the geometric look that Phil used, load the Faux Finish brushes and use the Large Mesh preset to create the effect seen in figure 8.82.

figure 8.82

The Large Mesh brush creates a techno-looking edge.

9. To add images to the file, Cmd/Ctrl-click the Large Mesh layer thumbnail to create an active selection as seen in figure 8.83.

10. Open an image (I am using one of Phil's portraits) and choose Select > All followed by Edit > Copy.

figure 8.83

Load the layer transparency to create an active selection.

11. Return to the template file and select Edit > Paste Into to paste the file into the shape you created. As you can see in figure 8.84, the portrait is a bit smaller than the shape and the edges have not been applied.

12. To fit the portrait to the creative shape, turn off the visibility of the painted edge layer and click the portrait's layer mask, choose Edit > Free Transform or Cmd-T/Ctrl-T and scale the layer mask as seen in figure 8.85.

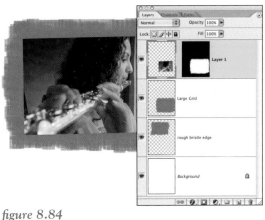

figure 8.84

Paste the image into the selection

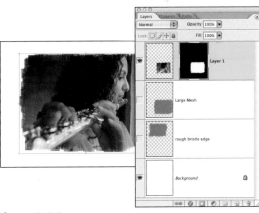

figure 8.85

Scaling the layer mask applies the creative edge to the portrait.

All in all, you can add as many new layers as you like and continue experimenting with the many brushes that come with Photoshop. I've heard that there are more than 10,000 possible brush combinations to work with, which should give you plenty of edges to personalize your own images with.

SHARPENING IMAGES

Although Photoshop comes with five sharpening filters, all in the Filter > Sharpen menu, the Smart Sharpen and the Unsharp Mask filter (also referred to as USM) are the most powerful and professional. Introduced with Photoshop CS2, the Smart Sharpen filter produces better results than USM and I find myself using USM less and less often. Since the Unsharp Mask filter is so well established and has been extensively documented, I will focus on the new Smart Sharpen filter which offers a tremendous amount of control. I've found that it works especially well on high quality digital camera files.

Note

All images will benefit from multiple passes of sharpening and the folks at Pixelgenius have developed a three-step approach for sharpening that takes into account the origin of the image (film format, type of digital camera, and subject matter), creative sharpening effects, and type of output (inkjet, monitor, offset press, and continuous tone). Applying image sharpening with the complete workflow in mind results in better images and Pixelgenius PhotoKit Sharpener is an excellent product.

Smart Sharpen Filter

All sharpening methods are edge-detection processes, and wherever an edge is found, it is exaggerated by making the dark areas of the edge darker and the light areas lighter. The Smart Sharpen filter enables you to set which sharpening algorithm is used and to control the amount of sharpening in the shadow and highlight areas. Plus, by clicking on the small floppy disk-like button you can save successful settings for reuse, which will speed up your image workflow.

Basic Mode:

- Amount: Sets the amount of sharpening. A higher value increases the contrast between edge pixels, giving the appearance of greater sharpness.

- Radius: Determines the number of pixels surrounding the edge pixels affected by the sharpening. The greater the radius value, the wider the edge effects and the more obvious the sharpening—meaning the more visible the light/dark halo will be, which is something you want to avoid.

- Remove: Sets the sharpening algorithm used to sharpen the image from the following three options:

  - Gaussian Blur is the method used by the Unsharp Mask filter and is the fastest.

  - Lens Blur detects the edges and detail in an image, and provides finer sharpening of detail and reduced sharpening halos. In my opinion, Lens Blur produces the best results.

  - Motion Blur attempts to reduce the effects of blur due to camera or subject movement. If you plan on using the Motion Blur option, measure the angle of blur with the Measure tool before entering the Smart Sharpen interface and enter the measured angle in the Angle control.

- More Accurate: Processes the file twice for a better removal of blurring. Although this can double processing time, I always have this option checked—as more accurate is more better.

Advanced Mode uses all of the basic mode settings and enables you to control the sharpening applied to shadow and highlight areas.

- Fade Amount: Adjusts the amount of sharpening in the highlights or shadows—100% fade conceals the sharpening and decreasing the fade reveals the sharpening amount.

- Tonal Width: Controls the range of tones in the shadows or highlights that are modified. Lower values restrict the adjustments to the darker areas for shadows and only the lighter regions for highlight correction. Think of this as the spread—how far out do you want the sharpening to take place? Lower settings are more delicate.

- Radius: Controls the size of the area around each pixel that is used to determine whether a pixel is in the shadows or highlights. Moving the slider to the left specifies a smaller area, and moving it to the right specifies a larger area.

The true challenge in working with the Smart Sharpen filter is to find the right balance between the Amount and the Radius settings. For digital camera files or scans with minimal grain, use Amount setting between 75 and 200 and low Radius settings between .3 and 1.5 (figure 8.86). Granted this may look too crispy on screen, but you have to print the file to see the results that really matter. For images with noticeable grain, use lower Amount settings of 10–40 and higher Radius

settings 10–20 to help avoid exacerbating noise or grain. When I use the Smart Sharpen, I view the filter interface at 100% view in order to refine the settings, but I keep the actual file at 50% as seen in figure 8.86 as a 50% view better mimics the line screen of a print.

 T i p

Always reduce file noise as explained in Chapter 5, "Dust, Mold, and Texture Removal," before sharpening a file.

Smart Sharpen in Action

In figure 8.87, you see a 6 by 7 cm Ektachrome slide, scanned on an Imacon Precision 3 film scanner. In this case, I wanted to sharpen the highlights slightly more than the shadows to accentuate the dimension and texture of the sign as seen in figure 8.88.

ch8_exit_sharpen.jpg

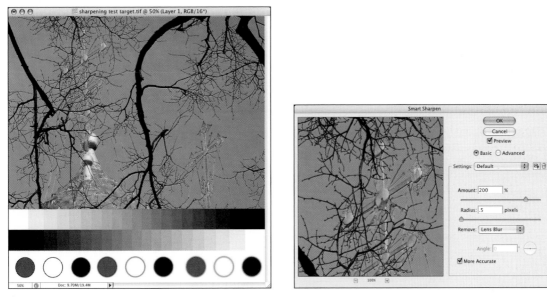

figure 8.86

Use a low Radius setting on fine-grained and high quality digital camera files.

figure 8.87

figure 8.88

1. Choose Filter > Sharpen > Smart Sharpen, click the Advanced button, and start with the Sharpen settings of 200 and .8 with Remove Lens Blur and More Accurate as seen in figure 8.89.

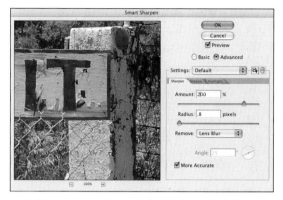

figure 8.89

Start with good overall sharpening.

2. Click on the Shadow tab and use a high Fade and low Tonal Width to not sharpen the shadows very much as seen in figure 8.90.

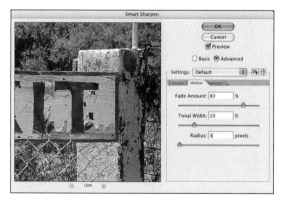

figure 8.90

A high Fade and low Tonal Width makes sure that the shadows are not sharpened very much.

3. On the Highlight tab, I decreased the Fade Amount to let the filter affect the highlights more as seen in figure 8.91.

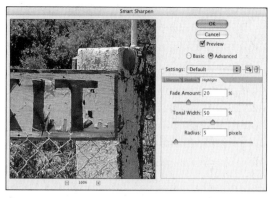

figure 8.91

The low Fade amount insures that the highlights receive a higher dose of sharpening.

Sharpening Tips

- Images that are uniformly sharp seem unnatural; blurring parts of an image will draw the eye to the sharper image areas.

- Experiment with selective sharpening by masking out image areas that don't need to be sharp.

- Print your sharpening tests with the printer and paper that you'll use for the final document.

- Avoid resizing or retouching a sharpened file.

- When you send files to a service bureau, tell them whether you've already applied sharpening or you want them to do it. Too much sharpening can be just as bad as no sharpening.

- Sharpen on a duplicate layer and control the intensity with layer opacity and blending modes. In most cases, changing the layer blending mode to Luminosity will help avoid aggravating color artifacts.

- To speed up the Smart Sharpen preview, before entering the Smart Sharpen dialogue, select a section of the image with the Marquee tool. Upon determining the correct sharpen settings, click OK to accept them, immediately followed by Edit > Undo (Cmd-Z/Ctrl-Z), Select > Deselect (Cmd-D/Ctrl-D), and use Cmd-F/Ctrl-F to apply the Smart Sharpen to the entire image.

Contrast Sharpening

On images with fine detail and a wide tonal range, you can use the Smart Sharpen filter to enhance the contrast to make the image look sharper and simultaneously improve contrast. In many of my full resolution digital camera files, especially in my landscape and architectural work, I often apply a contrast sharpening to punch the image up as seen in the before and after images in **figures 8.92** and **8.93**. My process is very simple: I duplicate the Background layer, change the layer blending mode to Luminosity, and choose Filter > Sharpen > Smart Sharpen and use a 20 Amount with a 50 Radius setting as seen in **figure 8.94**.

figure 8.92

figure 8.93

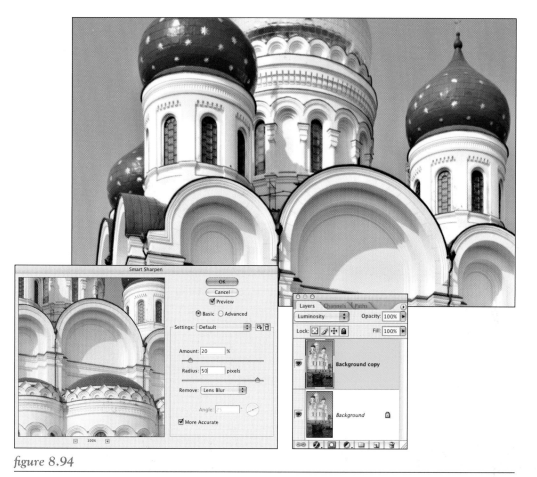

figure 8.94

The low Amount and high Radius enhances dynamic contrast.

Neutral Sharpening

The technique of sharpening on a neutral layer with the High Pass filter is a very popular and successful technique. In fact, I still use it to bring out detail as seen in this chapter on the convert to black-and-white example with the Machu Pichu photograph and to sharpen eyes and details in portraits as shown in both chapters of Part IV, "Putting the Best Face Forward."

The High Pass filter turns all non-edge areas to neutral gray but leaves image edges intact. This,

combined with Soft Light, Overlay, and Hard Light blending modes, yields a sharpening effect that is especially effective on digital camera files and images with a shallow depth of field as seen in **figure 8.95** in which I shot the cross with a wide-open aperture to throw the background out of focus. I used the High Pass technique to sharpen the rusty details while not affecting the background as seen in **figure 8.96**.

ch8_rust_sharpen.jpg

figure 8.95

figure 8.96

1. To apply neutral sharpening after retouching or restoring a file, select the topmost layer and use Cmd-Option-Shift-E/Ctrl-Alt-Shift-E to merge all visible layers up onto a new layer. If your file is flat, simply use Cmd-J/Ctrl-J to duplicate the layer.

2. Use Cmd-Option-0 (zero)/Ctrl-Alt-0 (zero) to view the actual pixels of the file, then change the layer blending mode to Overlay, and select Filter > Other > High Pass.

3. Use the Radius slider to bring out the image edges. A very high Radius setting is less effective than a lower setting. Start with a setting between 2 and 5 and experiment with the Radius slider to increase or decrease the edge enhancement effect, as shown in **figure 8.97**.

4. After clicking OK, change the filtered layer's blending mode to Soft Light or Hard Light. Using the Overlay blending mode adds a bit more contrast to the image than Soft Light does and Hard Light creates the most aggressive results.

5. If the image is too sharp, decrease the filtered layer's opacity to achieve just the right amount of sharpening.

CLOSING THOUGHTS

All in all, digital tools and techniques give you tremendous control and creative possibilities. The most important thing to do is to duplicate your Background layer and then go to town with these techniques to interpret your images to your creative heart's content. Listen to your heart and create compelling and meaningful images.

figure 8.97

Changing the blending mode to Overlay, Soft Light, or Hard Light before entering the High Pass filter enables you to see the effect on the image.

Putting the Best Face Forward

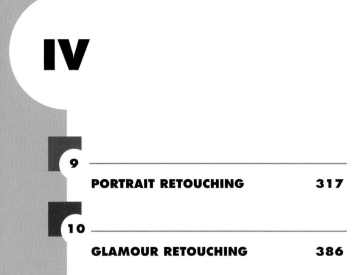

IV

9

PORTRAIT RETOUCHING

Good retouching requires a careful eye, an empathetic heart, and a patient mouse. The best retouching is never done when you're pressed for time, tired, or distracted—and, believe me, a little bit of careful retouching is always better than a lot of poor retouching. My personal goal when doing portrait retouching is to make the person look positive and refreshed, as if he or she had just returned from a relaxing two-week vacation. So before you grab the Clone Stamp tool or run the Gaussian Blur filter, take a moment to recognize that each portrait you work with represents a unique person to be handled with care and respect.

As a retoucher, it's your job to bring out the best in each person. In this chapter, you'll learn to work with contrast, color, and detail to make people look their best. The areas we'll concentrate on in this chapter are

- Developing a portrait retouch strategy

- Removing distractions and improving contours

- Improving skin texture and facial features

- Applying creative and painterly effects

Your role as a portrait retoucher is to accentuate the person's natural features while minimizing the distractions and blemishes that can detract from a pleasing portrait. Most importantly, you want to maintain the individuality of the person. Not every person will have a Hollywood ingénue's flawless skin or a lion's head of hair.

Caution

If, by chance, you jumped to this chapter first, please understand that the very first step to working with any digital image is to apply global exposure and color correction, as explained in earlier chapters. When those problems are solved, you can move on to correcting and enhancing portraits as described in this chapter.

STAGES OF RETOUCHING

Retouching a person's face can be a sensitive undertaking. You don't want to take away important characteristics or accentuate less-than-flattering features. Additionally, you don't want to put time and effort into a portrait retouch that the client isn't willing to pay for. Before you begin any retouching, it is imperative that you discuss with your clients exactly what they want done.

Clients may have a hard time envisioning the possibilities of retouching. To avoid any confusion or miscommunication, create a sample portfolio of your retouching services. As clients page through the portfolio or view examples displayed in your studio, explain that you can remove blemishes and wrinkles for X number of dollars; if they would like additional retouching as seen in your more advanced examples, it will cost them X additional dollars. Not all clients will want the full treatment, and knowing this before you begin will save you time, effort, and money.

I recommend that you develop a retouching scale, as shown in figure 9.1 (the original) through figure 9.5:

A four-level approach enables you to develop a plan as to the amount of retouching you will do, which in the end determines how much you will charge the client. A Level 1, straightforward blemish removal or subtle wrinkle reduction can be accomplished very quickly, whereas applying Levels 3 or 4 of retouching requires more time and an artist's touch—which both add much more to the final

bill. Communicating with your clients and knowing what their wishes are and what your final outcome will be before reaching for a mouse will help you work confidently, economically, and efficiently.

Level 1

Removes obvious blemishes, wrinkles, and distractions with a process similar to applying a little makeup. If you are the photographer, color correction and quick cleanup should be included in the initial capture fee and no portrait should leave the studio without this basic cleanup applied. This basic improvement should take 3 to 10 minutes per portrait.

Level 2

Continues where Level 1 stops, to perfect the facial characteristics including smoothing skin, removing multiple catchlights in the eyes, and reducing glare on skin. Level 2 improvements should take an additional 10 to 20 minutes.

figure 9.1

The original image.

figure 9.2

Level 1.

figure 9.3

Level 2.

figure 9.4

Level 3.

figure 9.5

Level 4.

Level 3

Finely sculpts the face with contrast, color, and detail to accentuate the eyes, lips, and facial contours just as a classic painter would use light and shadow to define important details. Eyes are enhanced, lips are refined, and hair is given a final polish. These enhancements require care and, depending upon experience, should take 45 to 60 minutes per portrait.

Level 4

Adds creative interpretation, such as working in black and white, toning the image, accentuating lighting and focus, or adding a creative frame or painterly effects. This level enables you to add personal interpretation to an image and although you will not apply it to every portrait, it can be the most enjoyable as you explore unique effects, which set your portraits apart. The time involved depends entirely upon how much experimentation you enjoy and varies from image to image, as you learn that what works on one portrait isn't appropriate for the next person. I prefer not to estimate the time on this level—as I am guilty of doodling away the hours without even noticing the time of day.

> ### Tip
>
> Retouching is more than a skill; it is an art form. Don't rush through any job, and try to avoid working when you're overtired. Remember that you're working with a person's face and identity—something that requires your full concentration and empathy.

DEVELOPING A PORTRAIT RETOUCH STRATEGY

Start each portrait retouch by looking at the entire image—too often I've seen people dive into a retouch by randomly removing blemishes or whitening teeth without first understanding the overall image. Mapping out a portrait retouch strategy will make your retouching time more efficient and effective. Before beginning to work on a portrait, use the following five steps to plan out and complete a successful retouch:

- **Assess the person** and determine which facial features you can accentuate or minimize to help that person shine through the picture. Imagine that you had to retouch three portraits: a high school athlete, a corporate executive, and a successful judge. Each of these people has different personalities and characteristics you need to recognize and enhance. The teenager's skin might need to be cleaned up, whereas the executive's focus and alertness needs to be emphasized—no matter how tired he or she was from traveling the day the portrait was taken. In the senior judge's portrait, you wouldn't want to take out every wrinkle or gray hair because lines in the face and gray hair represent wisdom and experience. Before you reach for the mouse, take a moment to look at the portrait and assess and recognize what type of person you're working with.

- **Identify and remove distractions** that draw the viewer's eye away from the portrait. To find them, look at the portrait while squinting or defocusing your eyes and notice what your eyes register. Distractions include irrelevant background elements, light areas by the image edges, and unattractive folds of clothing.

  Squint your eyes and take a look at **figure 9.6**. Do you notice any distractions? The car behind the man is screaming, "Look at me!" Now take a look at **figure 9.7**—and notice how your eye stays on his face.

figure 9.6

The cluttered background distracts from the subject.

figure 9.7

Replacing the car with trees transforms the snapshot into a portrait.

- **Refine contours** of the body, hair, face, and neck to be smooth and flattering. Bulges caused by awkward posing, body position, weight, or age should be carefully reduced or smoothed out. Let your eye follow the contours of the person to find anything that breaks up the smooth flow. Primary items to watch for are flyaway hair, uncomfortable arm or shoulder angles, unsightly bulges in clothing, wide heads, unflattering body contours, double chins, and the folds of skin in an older person's neck.

Art Johnson was asked to photograph the three women seen in **figure 9.8**, Upon client review, the center woman requested that her hips be slimmed down a touch to remove the bulges caused by the pose. Rather than reshooting the group, Art cloned the white seamless backdrop over her hips to create a more flattering silhouette, as seen in **figure 9.9**.

figure 9.8

The pose created wide hips on the woman in the center.

figure 9.9

Contouring her hips created a perfect photograph of the group.

- **Enhance facial features** including the eyes, lips, teeth, nose, and skin. The eyes are the most important facial attribute to emphasize, followed by the mouth, as shown in **figures 9.10** and **9.11**. Refine the skin, but don't smooth it so much that it looks like plastic wrap. The goal is to reduce wrinkles, remove blemishes, and smooth the skin to make the person look like a well-rested and well-lit version of him- or herself.

- **Refine lighting and focus** to draw the viewer's eye to the person's face. In the example shown in **figures 9.12** and **9.13**, darkening down the background emphasized the little girl very effectively. This simple yet essential step should be applied subtly so as not to be obvious, but rather mimic what a photographer would do with studio lighting or soft-focus filters.

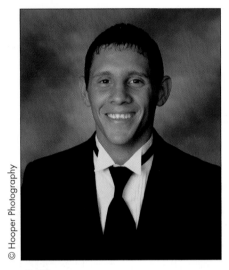

© Hooper Photography

figure 9.10

The eyes and mouth can disproportionately affect our memories of a person's appearance.

© Phil Pool Omni Photography

figure 9.12

The portrait after all retouching is very sweet.

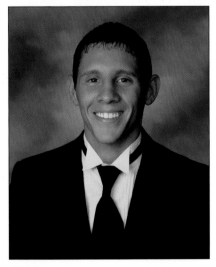

figure 9.11

Reducing the wrinkles and brightening the athlete's teeth lets his personality shine through.

figure 9.13

Darkening the background emphasizes the little girl.

- **Evaluate the results**, which is best done after taking a break from the image or by getting a second opinion. After spending an hour with a file or when working under a tight deadline it is easy to overlook details or colorcasts to which you've grown accustomed. Asking someone you trust for a second opinion can be a lifesaver. If you're working by yourself, make a work print, study it, and mark it up. Often the print reveals details you overlooked when the image was on screen.

I approach each retouch with this five-step strategy of "assess, remove distractions, flatter contours, enhance facial features, and evaluate." All in all, my final goal when doing portrait retouching is to make people look as though they have just come back from a relaxing vacation. They should look well rested, alert, and positive. By removing the distractions, flattering the contours, cleaning up the skin, and accentuating the eyes and mouth, you help your clients look their very best.

Note

Due to copyright and privacy issues, a number of the featured images in this chapter are not available for download.

REMOVING DISTRACTIONS

In the 1950s and '60s, Kodak included photo tips in its film packaging. One I remember very clearly recommended avoiding distracting objects in the background. The example showed a tree coming out of a person's head. Back in those pre-digital days, the suggestion was to either reposition the camera or the person. Nowadays it would still be better to take the picture correctly, but sometimes the cluttered picture turns out to be the best portrait. The primary methods to reduce background distractions are judicious cropping, cloning good information over bad, blurring and darkening, or replacing the background completely.

Cropping and Framing

The next time you are in a museum or looking at a good photography book, relax your eyes and notice how they move through the image. Good composition enables your eye to move, while bringing you back to the subject. Light areas attract the viewer's eye and it is better not to have distracting light areas near the edges of the image frame, as they will draw the viewer's eye away from the primary subject. Cropping an image is an often-overlooked yet very effective tool to improve image composition. Basic image cropping can be done in two primary ways, in which pixels are either deleted or hidden.

Tip

Our visual system relies on tonality, color, and detail, as our eyes go from dark to light areas, soft to sharper areas, and less color to more colorful. In other words, you need to emphasize or downplay these three image attributes to keep the viewer's eyes on the portrait.

In the following example, the large white light floating above the people's heads draws your eye away from the group (**figure 9.14**). By cropping the light away, the image is much more harmonious and focused (**figure 9.15**).

 ch9_crop_the_light.jpg

Cropping an image can be very destructive if you use the standard Crop tool approach of setting the crop and accepting it, as you are throwing pixels away; after you've saved the file, those pixels are gone forever. Instead, use the following technique to practice safe cropping:

1. Change the Background layer to a standard layer by double-clicking on it in the Layers palette. Click OK in the Layer name dialog box.

BEFORE

figure 9.14

AFTER

figure 9.15

2. Frame the crop and click the Hide radio button in the options bar, as circled in **figure 9.16**.

3. Continue retouching or enhancing the image as desired. To see the image area that is hidden, select Image > Reveal All or when working in Full Screen mode use the Move tool to pull the image back and forth to see what has been cropped out or to reposition the image within the crop frame.

figure 9.16

Use the Hide option to crop or reframe in image.

Inspect the Edges

Scan the edges of the image. If there are distracting white splotches, either reduce them or remove them altogether, as illustrated in **figures 9.17** and **9.18**. In this example, using the Crop tool to remove the light distraction would have cropped the woman and changed the image composition. Since the composition relies on the off-center position of the woman, that's not a good option. Therefore, it makes more sense to cover up the distraction as described here.

© Shan Canfield

BEFORE

figure 9.17

AFTER

figure 9.18

⊕⯈✂ **ch9_splotch.jpg**

1. Duplicate the Background layer. Use the Patch tool set to Source and generously circle the light splotch (**figure 9.19**). Use the Patch tool to move the selection up or down to a selection of darker image information (**figure 9.20**).

2. Before you click outside the selected area, which would deselect the patched area, compare the image density of the patch to the rest of the image. If it doesn't match, add a Curves adjustment layer and adjust density by darkening down the selected area as shown in **figure 9.21**.

figure 9.19

Use the Patch tool to select the light area.

figure 9.20

Dragging the active area to a darker area helps to tone down the light splotch.

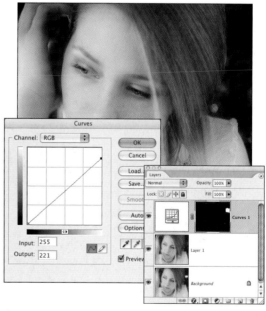

figure 9.21

Darken the patched area to match image density.

3. Use Filter > Blur > Gaussian Blur with a setting of 5–15 pixels to blur the selection edges of the Curves layer mask to soften the transition between the original and the darkened areas.

FLATTERING THE CONTOURS

How we see a person in real life or in a video or movie is very different from how we perceive them in a still photograph. In real life or in a movie, the sound, motion, and interaction often conceals undesired attributes, which are glaringly apparent when a person is frozen in a still photograph. An odd lick of hair, a double chin, an unflattering pose, or a lumpy piece of clothing is much more apparent in a photo than when you're talking with a person in a real-life scenario. Removing the distracting flyaway hair, smoothing out bulges in clothing or contours, and adjusting uncomfortable poses are essential steps in the retouch process. So listen to your mother—stand up straight the next time your picture is taken and you'll have less retouching to do.

◯ T i p

Apply body contouring before feature retouching, as changes in the contours may make some retouching unnecessary.

The Digital Seamstress

Photographing a person can often cause odd folds in clothing or unsightly lumps to become noticeable. In **figure 9.22**, you see stock portrait of a young businesswoman. Tailoring her jacket and covering up the white blouse below her folded arms makes her look much more professional and moves the visual emphasis to her face, as seen in **figure 9.23.**

🌐▷⋲ ch9_tailor.jpg

The simplest method to tailor a person's clothing is to clone background information over the bothersome bulges, but this may cover up important aspects of the clothing. In the following example, you will narrow her waistline while maintaining the integrity of the pockets of the suit jacket:

1. Use the Pen tool in Paths mode to draw in the desired body contour for the left side of the waistline and then create a separate path for the right side, as shown in the Paths palette in **figure 9.24**. If you are not comfortable

BEFORE

figure 9.22

AFTER

figure 9.23

with the Pen tool, you can also use the Lasso tool to outline the desired contours. If working with the Lasso tool, select the left side and continue with step 3.

2. Turn the left path into a selection by dragging it down to the Load Path as Selection icon on the Paths palette. Choose Select > Feather > 1 to soften the edges slightly.

figure 9.24

The Pen tool makes a smooth selection for the new contour.

3. Choose Layer > New > Layer via Copy and move the new layer to the right to define the new waistline, as shown in **figure 9.25**.

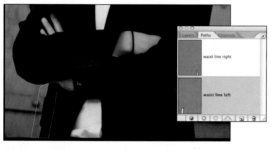

figure 9.25

Moving the duplicated section inward forms the foundation for the new waist contour.

4. Click on the background layer and repeat steps 2 and 3 for the path on the right side, as shown in **figure 9.26**.

5. To clean up any telltale signs of repetition on the jacket and in the background, use the Clone Stamp set to Sample All Layers on the high-contrast areas, such as where the dark jacket touches the lighter background.

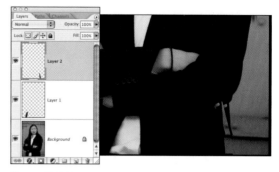

figure 9.26

Copying and moving pieces of the body contours inwards is the foundation for the new body contours.

6. Use the Healing Brush set to Sample All Layers to refine the cleanup on areas with low tonal or contrast differences.

7. The white blouse by the model's stomach is very close to the edge of the frame and draws a lot of attention away from her face. To close the jacket, add a new layer and start with the Clone Stamp tool to build up initial jacket information (**figure 9.27**). Then touch up the cloning with the Healing Brush.

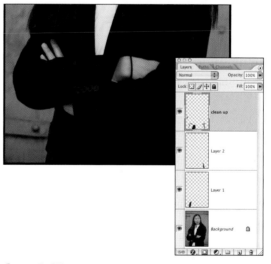

figure 9.27

Use the Clone Stamp tool to create initial image information and the Healing Brush to refine the details.

Keep the digital seamstress handy to clean up wrinkles in suits, straighten crooked collars, or repair uneven seams.

The Digital Workout

Photoshop can't replace going to the gym, but it can help slim those troublesome areas that no amount of sit-ups or leg extensions seem to take care of. The primary tools for body slimming are: Cloning, the Pinch filter, Transform, and Liquify—some of which are addressed here—with additional body sculpting techniques addressed in Chapter 10.

Work Those Abs

Blame the extra weight on the camera or the second visit to the dessert buffet—either way, Photoshop's Pinch filter, Transform command, and careful use of the Liquify filter melted away a few extra pounds as seen in the **figures 9.28** and **9.29**.

🌐 ⇥ **ch9_beach_boy.jpg**

1. Duplicate the Background layer and generously select the abdomen area. Apply a very high feather of at least 50 to add a very subtle transition (**figure 9.30**); on high-resolution files use 75- to 100-pixel feather settings. If you're following along with the file from the book's Web site, use a feather of 25 because the file is smaller.

2. Choose Filter > Distort > Pinch and use a 15–20 setting to narrow his stomach as shown in **figure 9.31**. Don't overdo it, as you can run the filter again on a smaller feathered selection to refine the effect.

3. To further push in his stomach, repeat the select, feather, and pinch with lower settings on a smaller area as seen in **figure 9.32**. In many cases, the Pinch technique is enough. To make him even slimmer two additional steps are required: an overall stretch and slightly pushing in his love handles.

figure 9.28

figure 9.29

figure 9.30

Make a generous selection that includes background information. A high feather amount provides the required transition.

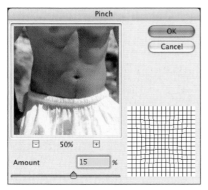

figure 9.31

Use a positive Pinch filter setting to push the abdomen inwards.

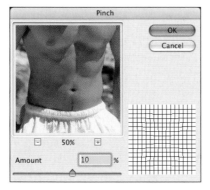

figure 9.32

Repeating the select, feather, and Pinch on smaller areas refines the end results.

4. To stretch him, start by increasing the canvas size on the bottom of the image by 10%. Select Edit > Transform > Scale and use the lower center handle to stretch the figure down (**figure 9.33**) to 105% at the most.

figure 9.33

Stretching a photograph is a classic technique to make a person appear slimmer.

5. His head is noticeably distorted by the stretch, so add a layer mask to the stretched layer and use a black-to-white linear Gradient tool on the layer mask over the neck and shoulder area to draw in a transition, as seen in **figure 9.34**.

figure 9.34

Blending the stretched image with the unstretched image conceals undesired distortion.

6. Refine the transition by painting on the layer mask with black to conceal stretched areas (figure 9.35).

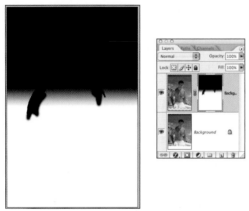

figure 9.35

Paint with black on the layer mask to improve the blending of the two layers.

7. Use Cmd-Option-Shift-E/Ctrl-Alt-Shift-E to merge the two improved layers, creating a new layer in progress to work on.

8. The Liquify filter is ideal to push and tighten contours. Before entering the Liquify interface, select the general area with the Marquee tool (figure 9.36) and then select Filter > Liquify.

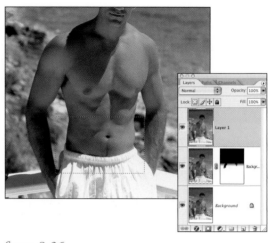

figure 9.36

Selecting the area before entering Liquify will speed up the loading, previewing, and applying of the Liquify filter.

9. To avoid changing the grain structure of the file, use the Forward Warp tool with a large brush and low density and strength settings and gently push in on the person's skin from the inside edge of the waistline toward the center of the stomach (figure 9.37).

9. Clicking Show Backdrop (as circled in figure 9.38) shows you that a little bit of Liquify goes along way. For additional information on Liquify, please see Chapter 10, "Glamour Retouching."

Flattering Necklines

Gravity has a way of sneaking up on us. All of a sudden, we have a double chin or jowls that we just don't like to see in the mirror—or in a photograph. Some people may turn to plastic surgery, but I prefer to turn to Photoshop because it has less uncomfortable side effects. In most cases, the goal is to reduce the contrast of the shadows of the wrinkles and to form a more flattering neckline. In figure 9.39 you see the original portrait and in figure 9.40 the retouched version. This is an excellent example of how Joshua Withers applied minimal retouching, light modulation, and color correction to refine the portrait very naturally.

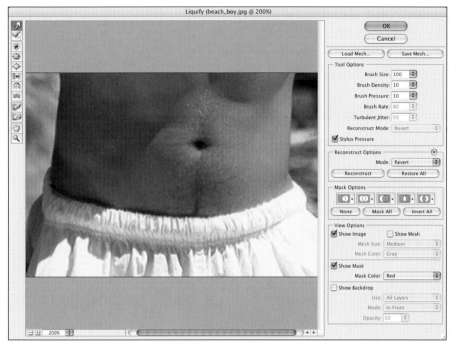

figure 9.37

Using a large brush with a low density helps to maintain film grain.

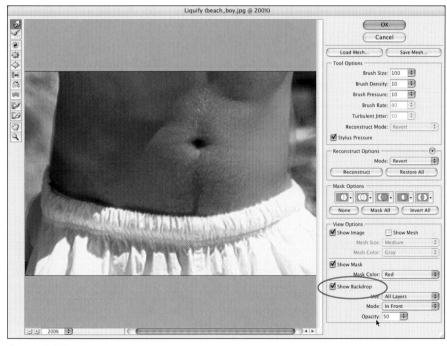

figure 9.38

Comparing the Liquify results with the original to evaluate and refine the results.

BEFORE

figure 9.39

AFTER

figure 9.40

1. Josh added a new layer and used the Healing Brush tool to hide the wrinkle in the man's neck, reduce the spottiness of the skin, and remove distracting specks of light and dark in the background environment (**figure 9.41**).

figure 9.41

Working on a separate layer to remove wrinkles and distractions.

2. He then generously selected the man's chin area with the Marquee tool (**figure 9.42**) and chose Edit > Copy Merged to copy all visible layers, in this case the original Background layer and the retouching layer. He then chose Edit > Paste to create a separate layer of just the head and neck area.

figure 9.42

Working with partial layers keeps the file size manageable.

3. Before entering Liquify, always select the area you want to work on. Josh Cmd/Ctrl-clicked on the icon of the chin layer to load the transparency as a selection and then he selected Filter > Liquify and carefully pushed the neck in and up with a large, low-pressure Forward Warp Brush (figure 9.43).

4. Josh added a new layer and used the Clone Stamp and Healing Brush to refine the neckline as seen in figure 9.44.

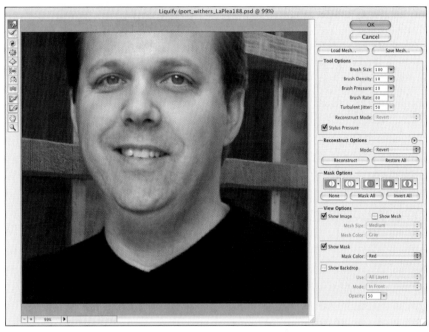

figure 9.43

Use a large, low-density, low-pressure brush to gently reform the neckline.

figure 9.44

Liquify often leaves artifacts that need to be concealed with cloning and healing.

Tip

When working with the Clone Stamp tool, use brushes with 50–80% hardness to avoid the ghostly edges that soft-edged Clone brushes cause. Because the Healing Brush has a built-in spread, use very hard brushes.

5. To further reduce the visual interest of the neck, Josh darkened it with a Curves layer by adding a curve, pulling it down a touch, inverting the layer mask (Cmd-I/Ctrl-I) and using a soft white brush on the Curves layer mask to gently darken the area under the chin (figure 9.45).

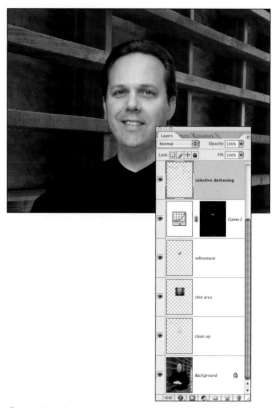

figure 9.46

Darkening the background causes it to recede.

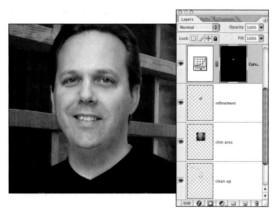

figure 9.45

Darkening the area under the chin creates the illusion of a neckline.

6. To bring more attention to the man versus the background, Josh added a new layer and used a very low opacity (10–15%) black, soft-edged brush to gently paint over the brighter shelves in the background, as seen in figure 9.46.

7. The final refinement is to warm up the man's skin tones and refine the color of the background. By working with Photo Filter adjustment layers and large, soft-edged brushes Josh subtly adjusted the final color. To warm the man, Josh added a Photo Filter adjustment layer and used the 85A-warming filter as seen in figure 9.47. He then used a very large black brush to paint away warming from the environment. Making the man visually warmer draws our eyes toward the man.

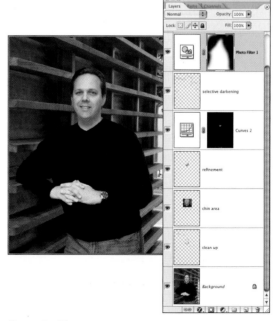

figure 9.47

Warming the figure increases his visual interest.

8. The final color tweak of adding blue removes the hint of yellow in the wood and makes the entire scene more inviting (**figure 9.48**).

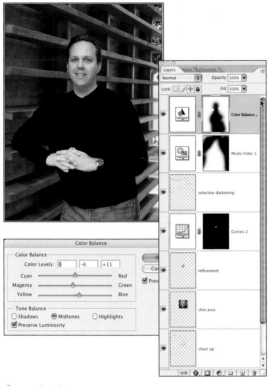

figure 9.49

figure 9.48

A final color-correction pass balances the image perfectly.

This retouch is an excellent example of how applying a little bit of good retouching by modifying the tonality and color is much better than overpowering an image with a lot of rushed retouching.

How Tall Are You?

Height is one physical attribute that is very difficult to change. Making someone taller gives him or her more stature and presence in an image. In the original in **figure 9.49** although the woman is wearing high heels she still seems out of proportion to the men. In **figure 9.50**, I stretched her to balance the image composition.

ch9_standing_woman.jpg

figure 9.50

To add a bit of stature, use these steps:

1. Use the Magnetic Lasso or Pen tool to outline the woman (**figure 9.51**) and select Layer > New > Layer via Copy (Cmd-J/Ctrl-J) to duplicate the selected area onto its own layer named *woman*.

figure 9.51

Selecting and duplicating the woman onto her own layer.

Tip

When using the Magnetic Lasso tool, always turn on caps lock to see the size of the area that the Magnetic Lasso is using to calculate the selection.

2. Choose Edit > Transform > Scale and use the center top handle to stretch the woman up to the desired height (**figure 9.52**).

3. Remnants of the original woman are still visible. Add a new layer named *conceal edges* underneath *woman*. Hide the *woman* layer, and use the Clone Stamp and Healing Brush tools set to Sample All Layers to conceal her original outside edges (see **figure 9.53**).

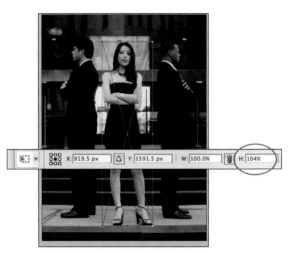

figure 9.52

Use Transform > Scale to make her taller.

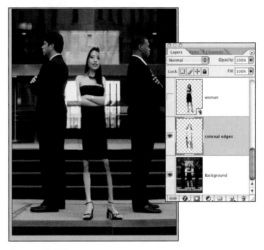

figure 9.53

Conceal remnants of the original image with cloning and healing.

4. Use Cmd-Option-Shift-E/Ctrl-Alt-Shift-E to merge all layers. Use the Clone Stamp, Healing Brush, and Liquify tools to smooth out her contours and remove the distracting light spots in the image background, as seen in **figure 9.54**.

Note

Not everyone needs to wear a size 6 dress or fit into 28-inch-waist blue jeans, but with careful slimming and stretching you can help clients look their very best.

figure 9.54

Refine her contours to create the final image.

THE IMPORTANCE OF SKIN

Retouching skin requires a balance between concealing blemishes, balancing skin tones, and reducing wrinkles while not making the skin look as if it were made out of plastic. A person's skin should be appropriate to his or her age—the younger the person the smoother the skin should be, and the older the person the more appropriate it is to let some of the signifiers of experience (wrinkles) remain.

Many people are self-conscious about their skin. Perhaps we suffered through the teenage years of acne, we're older and can already see the first crow's feet, or we didn't get enough sleep and look puffy and pale. It's a wonder we even get out of bed at all! Improving the appearance of skin in a portrait can be as simple as covering a few blemishes or as global as softening the entire portrait and then using a layer mask to paint back areas of selective focus.

Note

Please see Chapter 10, "Glamour Retouching" for additional skin refinement techniques.

Skin Blemishes ... the Teenage Years

Why is it that blemishes seem to pop up when you're about to have your picture taken, need to go for a job interview, or are about to have a first date? Photoshop can't help you with the job interview or the date, but removing blemishes in a photograph is a snap.

This first method of removing blemishes is similar to removing dust or mold from an old photograph (and there were plenty of examples of those problems in Chapter 5, "Dust, Mold, and Texture Removal"). By working on a duplicate layer with the Spot Healing Brush and Patch tools, you can quickly remove blemishes while maintaining skin texture, as shown in **figures 9.55** and **9.56**. The standard method of using the Spot Healing Brush is to use it with a normal blending mode, which has certainly been shown in enough books and tutorials. I prefer to take advantage of the Spot Healing Brush blending modes for additional control of the effectiveness of the brush.

ch9_blemish1.jpg

1. Duplicate the Background layer and name it *Blemish Removal*.

2. Set the Spot Healing Brush blending mode to Lighten (as circled in **figure 9.57**) and select a brush size that is slightly larger than the blemish to be concealed. Using the Lighten blending mode tells Photoshop to change only those pixels that are darker than the source area; this makes the spot healing even less visible than when working in the Normal blending mode. Starting with the small ones, tap the dark blemishes 1 to 3 times to make them disappear.

BEFORE

figure 9.55

AFTER

figure 9.56

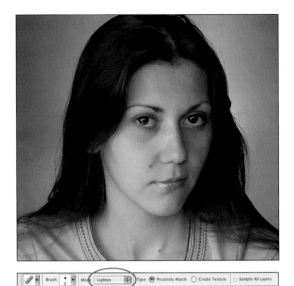

figure 9.57

Use Lighten blending mode to cover up dark blemishes.

3. Change the Spot Healing brush blending mode to Darken and tap over small light blemishes.

Tip

With the Spot Healing Brush active use Shift-"+" or Shift-"-" to quickly change blending modes from Lighten to Darken.

4. If you slip or the blemish removal is too obvious, step back via the History palette and then redo the Spot Healing.

Use the Patch tool to quickly and effectively cover up larger skin blemishes or moles, as described here.

1. Select the Patch tool. In the options bar, make sure that Source is selected.

2. Zoom in on the blemish or mark to be removed and circle it with the Patch tool, as shown in **figure 9.58**.

3. Drag the selected area to good skin information and release the mouse, as shown in **figure 9.59**. Repeat this process for each blemish.

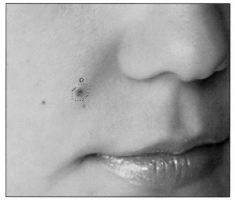

figure 9.58

Set the Patch tool to Source and circle the blemish.

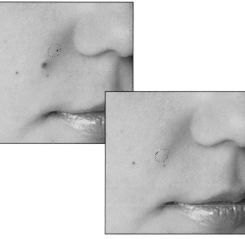

figure 9.59

Drag to good skin and release to make the blemish disappear.

4. Zoom in and fine-tune with the Healing Brush set to Normal blending mode.

Tip

If the Healing Brush or Spot Healing Brush is not working as expected, double check the tool's blending mode in the options bar. Often, I use Lighten or Darken for a retouching project and forget that I've changed the blending mode when I return to work the next day.

Patch Tool Tips

- You do not need to deselect between patching one blemish and another, so you can work very quickly. Using the Patch tool to remove larger blemishes is much more efficient than using the Healing Brush or Spot Healing Brush.

- When making a new patch selection, start the selection of the new patch outside the current selection.

- If a black smudge appears inside your patch, then you overlapped your current patch with the last area you patched.

- If a white smudge appears, the tool is averaging from outside the image.

- If you can see the edges of the Patch, use the Lasso tool with a 2-pixel feather to make the selection. Activate the Patch tool and drag it to the good skin.

Barbie Doll Skin

Until now I've emphasized that making people look too plasticky is not desired, but sometimes a person's skin is so full of blemishes that it seems impossible to find good skin to clone, heal, or patch with, such as in **figure 9.60**. In those instances, it's time to resort to extreme measures—creating perfect skin by using the Healing Brush with an artificial pattern that represents ideal skin, as seen in **figure 9.61**.

ch9_blemish2.jpg

This technique is incredibly easy and effective, so the next time you're faced with a teenage acne nightmare—turn to Barbie for help:

1. Duplicate the Background layer.

2. Choose File > New and create a custom file that is in RGB and 64×64 pixels large. Then select Edit > Fill and use 50% gray.

3. Select Filter > Artistic > Film Grain and use a grain setting of 1 and an intensity of 5. On your own images, the grain filter settings will vary depending on the existing film grain or image structure and the file resolution. Use higher settings for grainier images.

© Wagner Portrait Group

BEFORE

figure 9.60

AFTER

figure 9.61

4. Select all and choose Edit > Define Pattern and use a name that will mean something to you in a few days, weeks, or months (**figure 9.62**).

5. Activate the Healing Brush and set the source to Pattern, choose the Screen Blending Mode, and select the film grain pattern you just created, as seen in **figure 9.63**.

figure 9.62

Making and naming the pattern just takes a few seconds but can save you time when you are looking for it later.

figure 9.63

Use the pattern as the Healing source.

6. Use a large brush and paint over all the skin areas—go ahead and overdo it. Reduce layer opacity to approximately 75% to bring back some of the original skin texture (**figure 9.64**).

figure 9.64

Make the face very smooth and use the layer opacity to reveal some of the original texture.

7. Duplicate the retouched layer, change the Healing Brush to the Multiply Blending Mode, and use the same pattern to refine the face, as seen in **figure 9.65**.

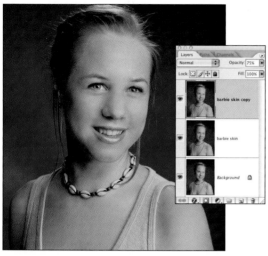

figure **9.65**

Working on multiple layers gives you great control.

This is a very easy and effective method to smooth out skin. Build a pattern library with patches that have more or less film grain to use on a variety of originals.

Evening and Softening Skin

Similar to applying a hint of concealer to lighten darker areas, evening out the skin tones can have a remarkable effect without changing skin texture. Darker tones on a portrait appear near eyes, next to noses, and under mouths—if left in the picture, the person may look bruised. To effectively remove darkness without changing image structure, as seen in **figures 9.66** and **9.67,** use the following method.

⊕⇥ **ch9_smooth_skin.jpg**

1. Use a 10-pixel feathered Lasso to select a darker area (**figure 9.68**).

2. Add a Curves adjustment layer and Cmd/Ctrl-click the dark spot to add a handle to the curve. Use the up arrow key to gently nudge the tonal values up and balance the darker area with the rest of the face (**figure 9.69**).

figure **9.66**

BEFORE

figure **9.67**

AFTER

figure 9.68

Select a representative dark tone.

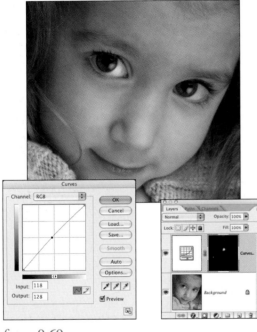

figure 9.69

Gently nudge the tonal value up to match the face.

3. If you see a defined edge between the lightened area and the rest of the skin, run the Gaussian Blur filter with a setting between 3–8 pixels to soften the transitions.

4. Use a large, soft white brush at 50% opacity to paint over other dark areas with repeated brushing, adding additional lightness, as seen in figure 9.70.

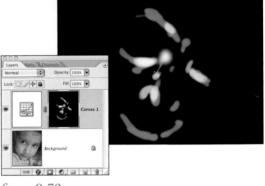
figure 9.70

Painting with a soft white brush lightens darker values without changing skin texture.

5. To add additional refinement, add a new layer and use the Healing Brush with Sample All Layers selected in the options bar, to refine the transitions and textures as seen in **figure 9.71**.

figure 9.71

Working on an empty layer allows for greater flexibility.

6. Photoshop has a large number of Blur filters, you can experiment with to create soft-focus effects—but to smooth and soften skin try out the Reduce Noise filter to add a beautiful, soft, smooth sheen to skin. Press Cmd-Option-Shift-E/Ctrl-Alt-Shift-E to merge the layers and select Filter > Noise > Reduce Noise. Using a high strength setting and low value for preserve details setting softens the skin while the eyes, eyebrows, lips, and hair remain crisp, as shown in figure 9.72.

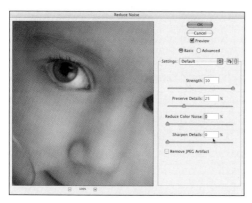

figure 9.72

Use the Noise Reduction filter to soften skin beautifully.

7. To refine the softening effect, adjust the layer opacity or add a layer mask and paint with a soft black brush on the layer mask to conceal areas that were unnecessarily softened.

 Tip

To increase the skin-softening effect, rerun the Reduce Noise filter two to five more times. If a noticeable color shift occurs (usually in the highlights), change the filtered layer blending mode to Luminosity to maintain the softening effect while negating the color shift.

Dealing with 5 O'Clock Shadow

On a rugged, outdoorsy photograph, beard stubble can be quite attractive. On a formal portrait of a U.S. Navy rear admiral (see figure 9.73), the Five o'clock shadow has a tendency to make a man look unrested. By using the Healing Brush and the Dust & Scratches filter, you can give even the toughest beard a quick trim, as shown in figure 9.74.

figure 9.73

figure 9.74

🌐➤ **ch9_beard.jpg**

1. Duplicate the Background layer.

2. Select Filter > Noise > Dust & Scratches and use a radius setting high enough to obliterate the beard, as shown in figure 9.75.

3. Choose Edit > Define Pattern and name the new pattern.

4. Select Edit > Undo to undo the Dust & Scratches filter.

5. Set the Healing Brush to Pattern and Aligned, and make sure that the correct pattern is selected, as circled in figure 9.76. Reduce the duplicated layer's opacity to 50% and then brush over the man's beard, as shown in figure 9.77.

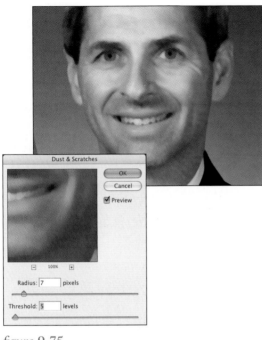

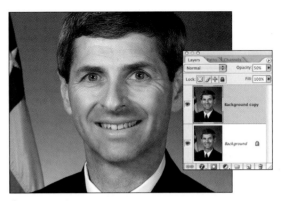

figure 9.77

When using a pattern source, simply brush in your corrections with the Healing Brush.

figure 9.75

The Dust & Scratches filter removes the stubble.

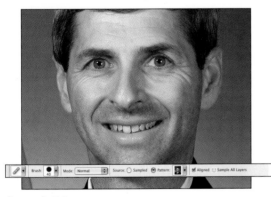

figure 9.76

Set the Healing Brush source to the saved pattern.

Tip

Experiment with this Dust & Scratches method and pattern to soften away wrinkles, blemishes, or deep furrows.

Caution

Delete unneeded patterns to reduce the size of the pattern preference file. Select Edit > Preset Manager > Pattern to delete unnecessary patterns.

Reducing Irritation and Rosacea

People can be very self-conscious about their skin and redness that insinuates irritation should be reduced or concealed. Whenever I face skin irritation, I do my best to avoid the temptation of grabbing the Clone Stamp or Healing Brush, as that would be a very tedious approach, requiring a lot of handwork. Rather I try to accomplish general improvements with filters and color correction and save the Clone and Healing effort for the final refinement.

Reducing Hives

In this first example, the bride suffered from hives caused by anxiety and they are very visible on her arm (figure 9.78). With a bit of Photoshop skin care, the image is ready for framing and proud display (figure 9.79).

ch9_bride_arm.jpg

1. Use the Lasso or Magnetic lasso tool to select the bride's arm, as seen in figure 9.80, and then Select > Feather and use a low setting of 2 to soften the edge transition.

2. Choose Layer > New > Layer via Copy (Cmd-J/Ctrl-J) to copy the arm onto its own layer. To insure that the arm stays in exactly the right place, click the Lock Position button on the top of the Layers palette, as circled in figure 9.81.

figure 9.80

Selecting the arm with the Magnetic Lasso tool

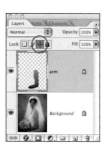

figure 9.81

Locking the isolated arm in place insures perfect registration.

3. To smooth out the texture, select Filter > Noise > Dust & Scratches and use the Radius setting to reduce the hives then use the Threshold setting to bring back original image structure as seen in **figure 9.82**.

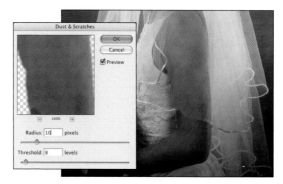

figure 9.82

The Radius eradicates differences and the Threshold determines the visibility of image structure.

figure 9.78

BEFORE

figure 9.79

AFTER

4. Add a layer mask and use a small brush and paint with black to restore the texture of the veil back into the image, as shown in **figure 9.83**.

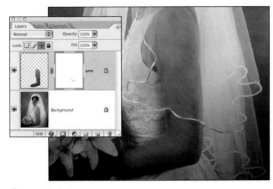

figure 9.83

Painting with black along the seam of the veil reveals the original image.

5. Option/Alt-click the Add Image Adjustment icon, select Hue/Saturation, and select the Group with Previous Layer to Create Clipping Mask option to make sure that the following color adjustment only affects the arm and not the entire image.

6. In the Edit menu, select Red and reduce the Saturation to –15, as seen in **figure 9.84**.

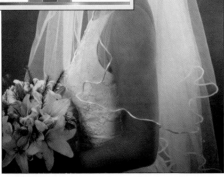

figure 9.84

Reducing the redness makes the arm look less irritated.

7. Click the arm layer and use the Healing Brush to smooth any existing texture.

Using the Dust & Scratches filter resolves most of the problem much more quickly than clone or healing alone could do.

Reducing Rosacea

According to www.rosacea.org, "14 million people have rosacea, a reddening of the skin that primarily affects the cheeks, chin, nose, or central forehead." From a retoucher's perspective, reducing the redness and texture requires a combination of color correction and texture smoothing, as seen in **figure 9.85** and **9.86**.

BEFORE

figure 9.85

AFTER

figure 9.86

ch9_rosacea.jpg

1. When I face a challenging file, I start by inspecting the channels to find channels that show more or less damage. As you can see in **figure 9.87**, the red channel shows the least damage and the green and blue carry a lot of texture. You can take advantage of this information when using a Channel Mixer layer to emphasize the good and conceal the bad.

red

green

blue

figure 9.87

Inspect the image channels to see which one contains the least damage.

2. Choose Layer > New Adjustment Layer > Channel Mixer and immediately change the blending mode to Lighten, which will help lighten the dark pigmentation. Leave the red channel alone. Select the green channel and add red. Select the blue channel to add blue to offset the strong yellow cast as seen in **figure 9.88**. Of course, these settings will vary on your own files but the concept remains the same: Inspect the channels and resolve the color issue separately from the texture issue.

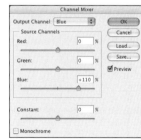

figure 9.88

The Channel Mixer can be effective to correct extreme color issues.

3. Add a Hue/Saturation adjustment layer and reduce the saturation to –20. Add a Curves adjustment layer to improve the overall tonality (**figure 9.89**).

figure 9.89

Use a Curves layer to lighten the face a bit.

4. To simplify the Layers palette, Shift-click each adjustment layer and choose New Group from Layers from the Layers palette menu.

5. Use Cmd-Option-Shift-E/Ctrl-Alt-Shift-E to merge all the production layers and to create a working surface for further refinement. Use the Healing Brush or Spot Healing Brush to touch up any remaining blemishes or traces of rosacea.

6. Apply a final correction tweak. In this instance I added a Photo Filter adjustment layer and added red at 10%, as seen in **figure 9.90,** to warm up his face just a bit.

figure 9.90

The red Photo Filter adjustment layer offsets the pasty look.

To learn how to remove the distortion caused by the wide-angle lens, please see "Removing Optical Distortion" later in this chapter.

Improving a Person's Health

We all know that when you're ill you just don't photograph very well. In **figure 9.91** you see a snapshot taken after a long illness and in **figure 9.92** you see some Photoshop health care, in which I prescribed color and contrast correction, teeth and eye enhancement, and a hint of hair color to make the man look healthier.

ch9_health.jpg

1. The first thing that needs to be corrected is the man's skin tone, which is much too red. To control where correction takes place choose Select > Color Range and use the dropdown menu to select Reds (see **figure 9.93**) and click OK. Click OK in the warning dialog box that pops up—it's just Photoshop telling you that it cannot show you the selection marquee.

figure **9.91**

BEFORE

figure **9.93**

In Color Range use the red preset to quickly select the overall redness of the skin.

2. Add a Selective Color adjustment layer and aggressively remove red in the reds and neutrals. You can use high settings, as seen in **figure 9.94**, as the adjustment layer mask is protecting the rest of the image and you are only working on the red tones his face.

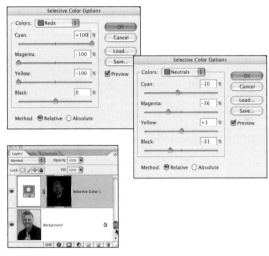

figure **9.94**

Only the red areas will be affected.

figure **9.92**

AFTER

3. When working with problematic skin tones, a colorcast problem is often a combination of color and saturation issues and working with a Hue/Saturation layer to adjust saturation can be very effective. Add a Hue/Saturation layer and click OK before adjusting the sliders.

4. To transfer the layer mask from the Selective Color adjustment layer to the Hue/Saturation layer, Option/ Alt-drag the Selective Color adjustment layer mask into the slot of the Hue/Saturation adjustment layer. Now double-click the Hue/Saturation layer and reduce the Saturation on the Master channel and in the Reds, as seen in **figure 9.95**.

figure 9.95

Reduce the overall and red saturation makes the skin less pasty looking.

5. To improve image contrast, add a Curves adjustment layer and adjust the contrast with a slight 'S' curve, as seen in **figure 9.96**.

figure 9.96

Increasing contrast adds snap.

6. To simplify the Layers palette, Shift-click and select the three initial adjustment layers and select New Group From Layers.

After doing the global corrections, it is time to concentrate on the details. The four features that require attention are his teeth, eyes, skin, and hair.

1. As addressed later in the chapter, lightening teeth is a fairly easy thing to do—but when the teeth are stained you need to use a bit more finesse. Use the Lasso tool with a 1-pixel feather to select the teeth. Add a Hue/Saturation layer and drop shown to the yellows to reduce the yellow saturation and make the teeth lighter, as shown in **figure 9.97**.

2. Use the Lasso tool with a 1-pixel feather to select the eye whites and add Hue/Saturation adjustment layer. Edit the reds to desaturate them and lighten his eyes (**figure 9.98**).

figure 9.99

The Photo Filter adjustment layer allows the natural texture and tonality to show through the new color.

4. Use Cmd-Option-Shift-E/Ctrl-Alt-Shift-E to merge all of the layers. Then use the Spot Healing Brush to even out the skin, on his nose, forehead, and cheeks.

5. Select the Sponge tool and make sure that the Options are set to Desaturate. Use a low Flow of 15–20% and gently brush away any additional redness along his chin and cheeks (**figure 9.100**).

figure 9.97

Desaturating yellow makes the teeth appear less stained.

figure 9.98

Desaturating the reds by –100% makes the eyes look less bloodshot.

3. Use the Lasso tool with a 1-pixel feather to select the irises. Add Photo Filter adjustment layer and chose the Cooling Filter (80) to beautifully enhance his eyes (**figure 9.99**).

figure 9.100

Desaturating redness with the Sponge tool works well on smaller areas.

6. To enhance the hair color, add a new layer and change its blending mode to Color. Sample the hair color from the highlight tips and use a soft-edged brush to paint in a bit more color, as shown in **figure 9.101**.

figure 9.101

Covering up a bit of gray with a color layer.

Taking the time to make people look their very best is especially appreciated when the person isn't feeling their best.

Reducing the Marks of Time

As people get older, gravity, sun exposure, and changes in skin structure cause wrinkles. Not every wrinkle is created equal, and rather than removing all of them, I suggest you remove only the most distracting ones. Horizontal lines, such as the lines on our foreheads when we raise our eyebrows in surprise, are friendly and require the least amount of work. Vertical lines are caused by age and worry; if they are dark or deep, they should be reduced. Diagonal lines make a person look tense and anxious, and these are the wrinkles you should reduce the most.

As people age, their wrinkles become longer and deeper. By shortening the length of the wrinkle, you can "take off" a few years without making people look as though they had plastic surgery. To reduce the length of the wrinkle, start at the

youngest (the narrowest) end, not its origin (see **figure 9.102**), and use the techniques described in the following section to turn back the clock.

In a photograph, a wrinkle is not a wrinkle; it's actually a dark area against a lighter area. By lightening the wrinkle, you are reducing the contrast of that part of the face and thereby reducing the visual impact. There are a great number of wrinkle reduction techniques and I usually use a combination of the ones presented here to refine a portrait. Try them all out to see which fit your photography the best.

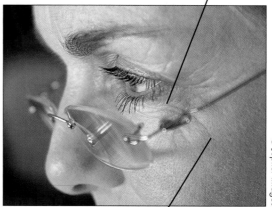

Oldest part of the wrinkle

Youngest part of the wrinkle

figure 9.102

For effective wrinkle reduction, retouch wrinkles from the youngest part in toward the older part of the wrinkle.

Working on a Duplicate Layer

The following technique uses the Dodge tool to lighten the dark creases, which emphasizes the wrinkles to create the mild effect illustrated in **figures 9.103** and **9.104**.

1. Duplicate the Background layer (or the layer with the person's face) and change the Background copy's blending mode to Lighten.

2. Set the Dodge tool to 5–15% Exposure and the Range to Midtones.

3. Set the brush size to match the width of wrinkle to be removed.

© JupiterImages

BEFORE

figure 9.103

AFTER

figure 9.104

4. Zoom in on the wrinkle, and, starting at its youngest end, dodge inward toward the origin of the wrinkle. Concentrate on the darkest areas. As you can see in **figure 9.105**, the doctor is looking less imposing.

figure 9.105

Using the Dodge tool on the youngest part of the wrinkle makes it appear shallower and softer.

Working on a Soft Light Neutral Layer

Working with a Soft Light neutral layer has three advantages. Wrinkles are often caused by dark areas adjacent to light areas, both of which can be corrected easily. Paint with a low-opacity white brush to lighten dark areas and paint with a low-opacity black brush to darken the light areas. If you overwork an area, you can paint those areas with 50% gray at 100% opacity and then rework that area.

Another benefit to this method is that adding a neutral layer does not double the file size as duplicating the Background layer in the first method does.

1. Option/Alt-click the New Layer icon on the Layers palette.

2. Select Soft Light from the Mode menu and click Fill with Soft Light neutral color (50% gray).

3. Set the foreground color to white, the Brush tool to 5–10% opacity, and the brush size to match the width of the wrinkle to be reduced.

4. To lighten the dark areas of the wrinkles, paint with white on the Soft Light neutral layer with the Brush tool (see **figure 9.106**). To darken the light areas of the wrinkles, paint with black on the Soft Light neutral layer. Always start the wrinkle-removal process with the youngest part of the wrinkle.

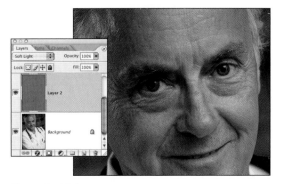

figure 9.106

Use the Brush tool with white paint and a soft brush on the Soft Light neutral layer to reduce the darkness and contrast of the wrinkles.

Better than Botox

To reduce the signs of aging, work on a duplicate layer and use the Patch tool in conjunction with the Fade command to quickly decrease wrinkles and furrows. **Figure 9.107** shows a friendly man; after a bit of patching (**figure 9.108**) he retains his warmth without looking artificial.

figure 9.107

figure 9.108

🌐⧓ **ch9_matureman.jpg**

1. Duplicate the Background layer.

2. Set the Patch tool to Source and circle the wrinkle, as shown in **figure 9.109**. Move the selection to a good skin area—in this case, I moved the patch selection to the man's cheek. At 100% layer opacity, the patch is too apparent, as shown in **figure 9.110**.

figure 9.109

On a duplicate layer, select the wrinkle with the Patch tool.

figure 9.110

The Patch tool completely removes the wrinkle, leaving an unnatural look.

3. Immediately after using the Patch tool, choose Edit > Fade (Cmd-Shift-F/Ctrl-Shift-F) and adjust the Opacity (see **figure 9.111**); the original image information blends with the patch layer. This makes the wrinkle removal blend in and also helps you to avoid the over-retouched look that would not be appropriate for a mature man.

4. Continue selecting and patching his furrows and wrinkles.

5. In most cases, you will need to refine the details with the Healing Brush. Add a new layer and make sure that Sample All Layers is selected in the options bar. Carefully refine the details, as shown in **figure 9.112**.

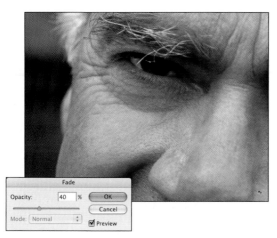

figure 9.111

Reducing the Fade opacity blends the original and patched versions.

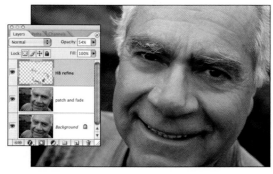

figure 9.112

Use an empty layer to refine the details with the Healing Brush.

I prefer the Patch tool over the Healing Brush to reduce wrinkles because it is faster and easier to use.

 W a r n i n g

When using the Clone or Healing tools on a dedicated retouch layer with the Sample All Layers option checked, it is very important to place the retouch layer above all adjustment layers to avoid adjusting the cloned and healed pixels twice. If it is imperative that the dedicated retouch layer be below adjustment layers, turn the adjustment layers off before cloning or healing.

ENHANCING THE FACE

After you've removed distractions, shaped contours, and improved a person's skin texture, it's time to get into the nitty-gritty details of portrait retouching. In most cases, this involves working on a person's eyes, mouth, and hair.

Eyeball Fundamentals

We look into people's eyes to see their soul, to see whether they are speaking the truth, and to make one-on-one contact. The eyes are the most important aspect of most portraits and require special care. Accentuating a person's eyes can make the portrait more intriguing, and by increasing contrast, color, and detail in a person's eyes, you also draw the viewer's eye away from less interesting aspects of the portrait. I use a variety of methods to retouch a person's eyes. In the following examples, we'll work with layers, the Dodge and Burn tools, and the painting tools to bring out the very best in a person's eyes.

Our eyes are spheres, and you should avoid overworking them with overzealous cloning or lightening of the whites or darkening of the iris. Being heavy-handed in the eyes will flatten them out and make them appear lifeless. Before you retouch a person's eyes, take a moment to study the light origin so that you can work with the light and not against it. To keep the eyes lively and interesting, it is essential to maintain moisture and highlights and to keep the red tones in the corners by the tear ducts (see **figure 9.113**).

The lightest areas of the irises are opposite the main light.

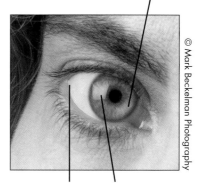

Make sure to keep moisture and highlights in the eye.

figure 9.113

Our eyes are round and translucent, and light plays off and through them.

Reducing Red Eye (or Becoming a Digital Exorcist)

Removing red eye is one of the most common retouching jobs. Red eye occurs when the flash bounces off the back of the eyeball and makes people and pets look as though they are possessed by Linda Blair demons. Red eye has a higher chance of occurring if the flash is on the camera or very close to the lens. This is the case with most consumer point-and-shoot or low-end digital cameras. Red eye is also more likely to be a problem if the subject is in a dark room and the pupils are wide open.

To prevent red eye, use any or all of the following photographic techniques:

- Move the flash off the camera using a sync cable or radio slave.

- Increase the ambient light or move the subject into a better-lit position. This will cause the pupils to shrink, reducing the likelihood of red eye, and you might not need to use flash at all.

- Some cameras offer a red eye reduction mode that fires a preflash before the main flash to trick the iris into closing. Personally, I'm not a huge fan of this preflash method because people think that you've taken the picture when the preflash fires, and they have a tendency to look away.

As every Photoshop user knows, a number of different ways are often available to accomplish the same task. The following text outlines two techniques for removing red eye—using the Red Eye tool and another slightly more involved—but very effective—method.

The Red Eye Tool

Nested with the Healing Brush and Spot Healing Brush, the Red Eye tool is an excellent and tremendously easy tool to use—even on the most dramatic red eye problems, like those in **figure 9.114**. With just one or two clicks on each eye, you can reduce red eye, as seen in **figure 9.115**.

figure 9.114

figure 9.115

⊕▷ ch9_redeye1.jpg

1. Duplicate the Background layer.

2. Activate the Red Eye tool and click the red pupil. There is no need to drag—just click and the red eye will disappear.

3. If the pupils are very large, increase the Pupil Size slider before using the brush. Increasing the Darken amount darkens the pupils more.

Adobe claims that this tool also works on the white and green eye that animals can get. I haven't tried that yet, but if you have good examples of it, I'd love to share them on the book's Web site.

Select and Substitute

The following method maintains both pupil texture and catchlights and can be used in earlier versions of Photoshop (before CS2). **Figure 9.116** shows an infant with very bad red eye, and **figure 9.117** shows the results of some crafty retouching.

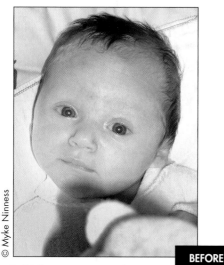

figure 9.116

2. Use the Elliptical Marquee tool to select one of the pupils. Hold down Shift to select the second pupil, as shown in **figure 9.118.**

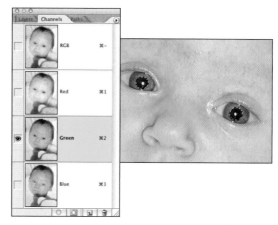

figure 9.118

Find the channel with the best information and select both pupils.

3. Choose Select > Feather and use a setting of 1 to slightly soften the edge of the selection.

4. Copy the selected pupils. With the selection active, click the red channel and choose Edit > Paste Into. This will paste the good green pupil into the bad red pupil.

5. Make the blue channel active and repeat the Paste Into command, as shown in **figure 9.119.**

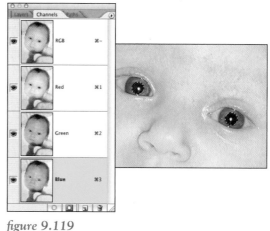

figure 9.119

Repeat the Paste Into in the blue channel.

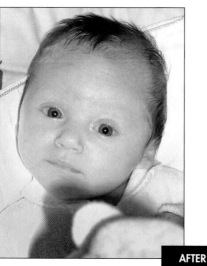

figure 9.117

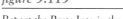 **ch9_redeye2.jpg**

1. Open the Channels palette and select the channel with the best (darkest) pupil. It will most likely be the green channel—it will definitely not be the red channel.

Retouching and Enhancing Eyes

There are numerous methods to enhance a person's eyes—from working with the Dodge and Burn tools, Clone Stamp, and Brushes, to working with Levels and Curves (as described in Chapter 10). The basic steps are: Remove bloodshot veins, brighten eye whites, deepen pupils, simplify catchlights, enhance iris color, and refine eyelashes. In addition to accentuating the natural beauty in a person's eyes, you may be asked to remove red eye or apply dramatic lighting effects and makeup, as addressed later in this section.

Making Eyes Brighter and Refining Color

Since our subjects' eyes are recessed in the eye sockets, they often seem darker in a photograph than we remember. By lightening them and adding a bit more color, the eyes gain visual emphasis, as illustrated in **figures 9.120**, **9.121**, and **9.122**.

figure 9.121

After lightening the entire eye.

figure 9.120

The original image.

figure 9.122

After enhancing the color.

ch9_eyes1.jpg

1. Use a 2- to 3-pixel feathered Lasso to select one eye and then hold the Shift key while selecting the second eye (**figure 9.123**).

figure 9.123

Selecting both eyes with a feathered Lasso tool.

2. Add a Levels adjustment layer and move the midtone slider gently to the left. In some examples, such as this one, moving the white point slider slightly to the left improves the lightening effect (**figure 9.124**). In this example, the eyes have an overall bluish colorcast, which you can remove by using the Levels gray point eyedropper and clicking on her pupil.

figure 9.124

Moving the midtone and highlight sliders gently to the left to lightens the entire eye.

3. Use a 2- to 3-pixel feathered Lasso to select one iris, and then hold Shift while selecting the second iris.

4. Add a Curves adjustment layer, select the blue channel curve and pull it up slightly, as seen in **figure 9.125**.

For more dramatic effects, rather than using Curves, use a Hue/Saturation adjustment layer, click Colorize, and adjust the Master Hue slider to make the eyes whatever possibly bizarre color you desire.

figure 9.125

Increasing the blue component in the iris.

Painterly Accentuation

The painterly approach emphasizes the play of lights, shadows, and colors in the eyes. The best aspect of this technique is that all of the enhancements are built up on separate layers, giving you tremendous control over the intensity of the retouch. As you can see in **figure 9.126**, the original eyes are attractive, but the enhanced ones in **figure 9.127** have a romantic, painterly quality to them. In the following technique, you will darken the eyelashes, lighten the eye whites, enhance the irises, fine-tune the catchlights, and warm the eyes.

 ch9_painterly_eyes.jpg

1. Zoom in to 200% and generously select the eyes, as seen in **figure 9.128**.

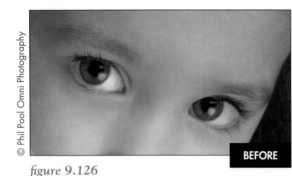

BEFORE

figure 9.126

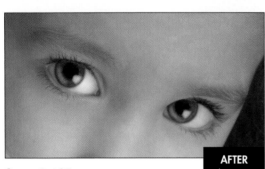

AFTER

figure 9.127

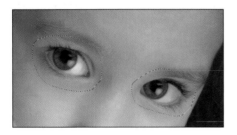

figure 9.128

Select more eye information than needed.

2. Use Cmd-J/Ctrl-J to duplicate the selected area onto a new layer. Change the blending mode to Multiply and select Layer > Layer Mask > Hide All (**figure 9.129**).

figure 9.129

The Multiply blending mode will dramatically darken the areas to be painted back through the layer mask.

3. Select a small hard-edged brush with 10–20% opacity and make sure that the foreground color is set to white. The brush should be just as large as the individual eyelashes. Trace the actual eyelashes on the layer mask and feel free to add additional eyelashes to create a fuller look, as seen in **figure 9.130**.

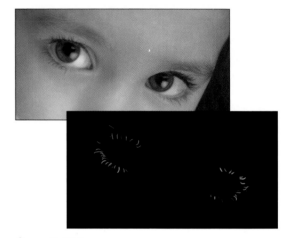

figure 9.130

Painting eyelashes through the layer mask to reveal the darker multiplied layer information.

🔍 **Tip**

When using a Wacom tablet to enhance eyelashes, press harder near the eye and lighten pressure as you move away from the eye to create a slightly tapered look.

4. If needed, add a new layer and clean up any obvious veins with the Clone Stamp tool set to Sample All Layers.

5. To lighten the eye whites, add a new layer and select a large, soft, 10% opacity white brush and dab a hint of white onto the eye whites to the left and right of the iris. Don't worry about staying "inside the lines" because you can use the Eraser tool to clean up any color spill to create the effect seen in **figure 9.131**.

✒ **Note**

The eye closest to the main light should be slightly brighter and the side of the iris on both eyes farther from the main light should be slightly dimmer.

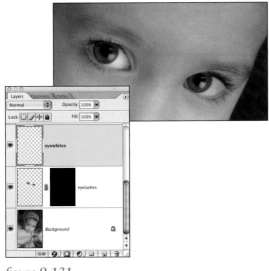

figure 9.131

Daubing in a soft white to lighten the eyes' whites.

4. Add a new layer. Use the Clone Stamp tool set to Sample All Layers to remove the distracting catchlights in the left side of her iris.

5. Cmd-Option-Shift-E/Ctrl-Alt-Shift-E merges all of the production layers to create a working surface required for further refinement. Use a very small Dodge tool set to Midtones and 20% exposure set to add a hint of the highlight to the iris opposite the catchlight, as seen in **figure 9.132**.

 N o t e

Eyes are translucent spheres, and light travels through them. Adding a touch of white on the opposite side of the primary light source accentuates the roundness and liveliness of the eye.

T i p

Get a second opinion. After working on a portrait, you become very familiar with it and might not even notice problems or areas that are overworked or don't look right. Ask someone else to take a look at the portrait and tell you what he or she notices or thinks about the image.

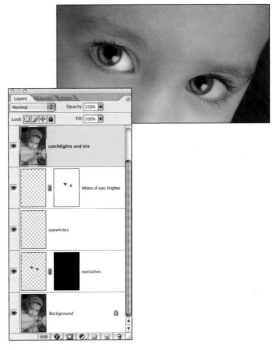

figure 9.132

Opposite the main catchlight, dodge in hints of light on the irises.

Creating Bette Davis Eyes

For a more dramatic approach to eye enhancement I turn to the talented Shan Canfield—fondly referred to as the Photoshop Mama—and thank her for sharing her techniques to transform pretty eyes into dramatic eyes, as seen in **figures 9.133** and **9.134**.

ch9_bettedavis_eyes.jpg

1. Add a Curves adjustment layer and click OK—do not make any adjustments to the curve. Change the blending mode to Linear Dodge and reduce the layer's opacity to 70%.

2. Invert the layer mask (Cmd-I/Ctrl-I) and use a small, hard, round, 9-pixel brush to etch scratches on the mask around the inside of the irises with white (**figure 9.135**). Select Filter > Blur > Gaussian Blur to soften the lightening in the iris (**figure 9.136**).

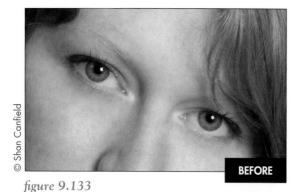

© Shan Canfield

figure 9.133

figure 9.134

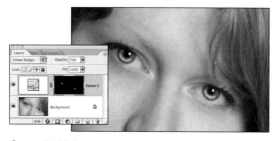

figure 9.135

Etching in highlights.

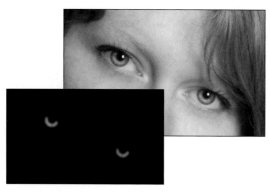

figure 9.136

Softening the lighter striations by blurring the Curves layer mask.

3. Add another Curves adjustment layer and click OK—do not make any adjustments to the curve. Change the blending mode to Linear Burn and reduce the opacity to 70%. Invert the layer mask (Cmd-I/Ctrl-I) and use a small, hard, round, 9-pixel brush to ring the iris with white which will darken the perimeter of the iris (**figure 9.137**). Repeat the Filter > Blur > Gaussian Blur to soften the dark ring around the iris.

figure 9.137

Ringing the iris adds dimension.

4. To accentuate the eyebrows, on the same Linear Burn layer trace the eyebrows with a small, hard, white brush to add depth (see **figure 9.138**).

figure 9.138

Painting with a small, hard white brush on the Linear Dodge layer adds dimension and definition to the eyebrows.

5. Add another Curves adjustment layer and click OK—do not make any adjustments to the curve. Change the blending mode to Multiply. Invert the layer mask (Cmd-I/Ctrl-I).

6. To build a custom tapered brush for the eyelashes, click the Brush tool and choose a small soft-edged brush. For this example, make it a size 8. In your own work, the brush size may vary depending on the file resolution. Make the brush just a tad larger than a natural eyelash. Select Window > Brushes and click Shape Dynamics, set the Size Jitter Control window to Fade (100); and the Minimum Diameter to 15% (**figure 9.139**). If you are using a Wacom tablet, click Other Dynamics and set the Opacity to Pen Pressure.

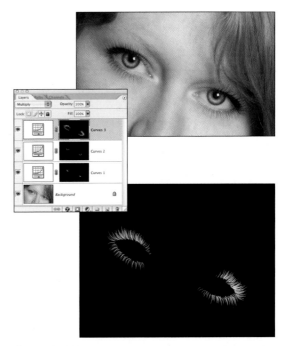

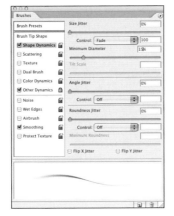

figure 9.139

Building a custom brush.

figure 9.140

Painting in fantastic eyelashes.

7. With white as the foreground color, begin painting wisps of lashes on the layer mask starting near the nose and brush away from the lid to follow the natural growth direction of the eyelash. Paint each eyelash in one solid complete stroke to achieve the taper of the custom brush (**figure 9.140**). When using a Wacom tablet, start the stroke by pressing hard and then ease up on the pressure as you end the stroke.

8. To emphasize lashes more and create the illusion that they existed when the image was photographed, add a subtle drop shadow. Click the Add Layer Style icon at the bottom of the Layers palette and choose Drop Shadow. Use these settings: Blending Mode: Multiply, Opacity: 30%, Distance: 12px, Spread: 10%, Size: 3px (**figure 9.141**). In your own images, use the drop shadow to mimic the direction of the existing light source.

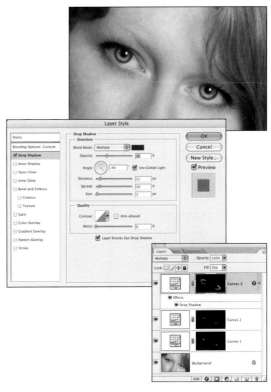

figure 9.141

Adding a drop shadow will make the eyelashes richer.

9. Click the black color swatch in the Drop Shadow dialog box; change the color to #3E0505 (a burnt sienna color) in the Hexadecimal field of the Color Picker. On the Layers palette, reduce the Fill to 70%, which will reduce the strength of the eyelashes while maintaining the shadow effect.

10. To add eye shadow, add a new Curves adjustment layer and move it underneath the eyelash layer. To select dark, smoky tones drag the RGB midtone down. Change the channel to red and drag that curve down to emphasize cyan tones (figure 9.142).

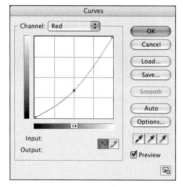

figure 9.142

Use Curves to darken and color-enhance the eye shadow.

11. Invert the layer mask (Cmd-I/Ctrl-I). With white as the foreground color, use a large soft brush to paint shadow over and under the eyes. Lower this adjustment layer's Opacity to around 80% and admire your work, as seen in figure 9.143.

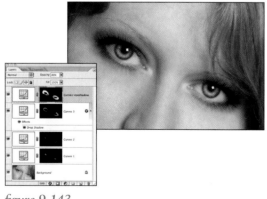

figure 9.143

Paint in the eye shadow with a large, soft-edged brush.

Digital Dentistry

Lightening teeth, reducing discoloration or staining, and—if needed—closing gaps or removing braces is much more pleasant with Photoshop than in the dentist's chair, as you see in figures 9.144 and 9.145. Keep in mind that a 20-year-old's teeth will be brighter than a senior citizen's, and it is appropriate to maintain some tone and color in the teeth and not make them so bright that they just shout, "Look at us—we're fake!"

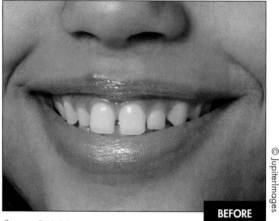

figure 9.144

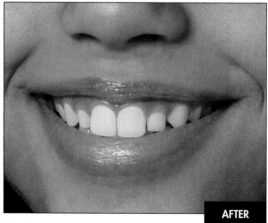

figure 9.145

🌐 ▷ **ch9_teeth.jpg**

1. Select the teeth with a 1-pixel feathered lasso, as shown in figure 9.146.

2. Add a Levels adjustment layer and move the midtone slider to the left (see figure 9.147) to lighten the teeth.

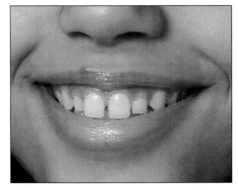

figure 9.146

Use the Lasso tool to select the teeth.

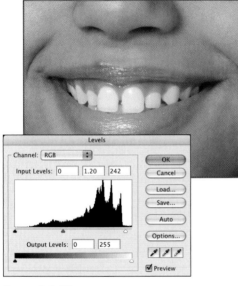

figure 9.147

Use Levels to whiten the teeth (but not too much).

3. To remove the red colorcast, select the red channel in the Levels dialog box and move the red midtone to the right, as seen in figure 9.148.

4. To close the gap in her smile, use the Lasso tool with a 1-pixel feather to select the right tooth and select Edit > Copy Merged followed by Edit > Paste.

5. Move the new right tooth slightly to the left and repeat the select and copy procedure with the left tooth (figure 9.149).

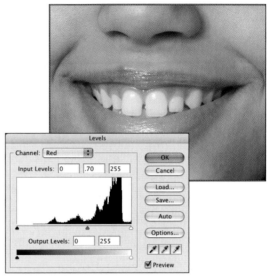

figure 9.148

Adjust the red channel to decrease the red color cast.

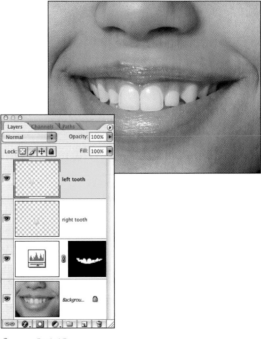

figure 9.149

Copy, paste, and position each tooth separately.

6. Add a new layer and use the Clone Stamp and Healing Brush set to Sample All Layers to clean up any artifacts like the edges seen in figure 9.162. Figure 9.150 shows a much improved smile.

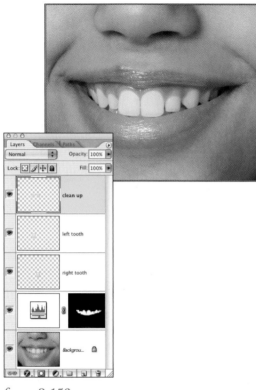

figure 9.151

BEFORE

figure 9.150

Refine the teeth on a new layer to clean up any telltale artifacts.

Teeth naturally have a wide variety of colors, and the teeth of smokers or coffee and red wine drinkers can be unpleasantly discolored. In these cases, it is necessary both to reduce the color staining and brighten the teeth, as shown earlier in this chapter in the "Improving a Person's Health" tutorial.

A Photoshop Nose Job

Our noses and ears never stop growing and as we age they can become disproportionately larger compared to the rest of the face. OK, that sounds like a rationalization when you look at the Before photograph of yours truly seen in figure 9.151. With a slightly smaller nose, as seen in figure 9.152, I feel that the portrait is about my eyes rather than my nose … really, I don't have a problem with it.

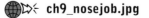 **ch9_nosejob.jpg**

AFTER

figure 9.152

How you reduce the size of the nose or refine the shape of the nose depends upon how the portrait was photographed. A frontal or three-quarter shot (as featured here) can be reworked with the Warp transformation or Liquify. A profile shot requires both Liquify and cloning to reform the nose.

To transform a nose:

1. Use a highly feathered Lasso or Elliptical Marquee tool to generously select the nose area. In this example, I feathered the Elliptical Marquee tool by 20 pixels to create the selection seen in **figure 9.153**.

figure 9.153

Select more nose information than needed.

2. Use Cmd-J/Ctrl-J to copy the selection to a new layer. Choose Edit > Transform > Warp and gently use the mesh points to push the nose in and make it a bit longer, as seen in **figure 9.154**.

3. Change the nose layer's blending mode to Difference and add a layer mask. The Difference blending mode enables you to see what is extraneous on the nose layer (**figure 9.155**). Use a soft-edge black brush on the layer mask to paint away unneeded skin and create subtle transitions.

4. Change the blending mode back to Normal, add a new layer, and use the Healing Brush set to Sample All Layers to refine the transitions between old face and new nose (**figure 9.156**).

figure 9.154

Use the Warp Transform to squeeze in and lengthen my nose.

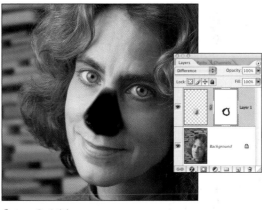

figure 9.155

The Difference blending mode makes it easy to see where there is too much skin.

figure 9.156

Refine the transition between the original and the new nose.

Removing Optical Distortion

Use Filter > Distort> Lens Correction to offset the exaggeration caused by photographing with a wide-angle lens, as seen in **figures 9.157** and **9.158**.

1. Duplicate the Background layer and select Filter > Distort > Lens Correction.

2. Use the Lens Correction Remove Distortion slider to offset the exaggerated bowing caused by the wide-angle lens.

3. Scale the Edge Transparency up to increase the image size and conceal the empty edges as shown in **figure 9.159**.

BEFORE

figure **9.157**

AFTER

figure **9.158**

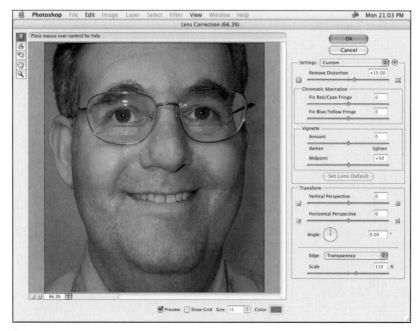

figure **9.159**

Remove lens distortion and scale the image up to flatten the portrait to be optically correct.

Only Your Hairdresser Knows

Consider the hair the frame around the person's face. It should frame the subject, not become the subject of the image. The most popular hair improvements include filling in gaps in hair, removing flyaway hair, recoloring hair and roots, and finely polishing the hair to add a hint of sparkle.

Enhancing Hair Color

 T i p

For best results when enriching hair color, sample actual hair color from reference photos or use the file I created from the L'Oreal Web site that you can download from the book's Web site (see figure 9.160).

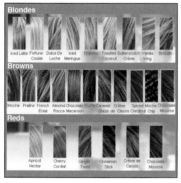

figure 9.160

A reference hair-color sample chart.

 ch9_haircolor_chart.jpg

In the following example, we will enrich the natural color of the hair to take it from a dark blonde (figure 9.161) to a warmer strawberry blonde replete with tonal and color shading as seen in figure 9.162.

 ch9_haircolor.jpg

1. Add a new layer and change the blending mode to Soft Light. Use the Eyedropper tool to sample the new color. In this example I started with Almond Rocca. Paint over the hair in the direction it naturally falls (figure 9.163).

figure 9.161

BEFORE

figure 9.162

AFTER

figure 9.163

Working on a Soft Light layer allows the hair detail to shimmer through.

2. To make the coloring more realistic, choose a darker or lighter color for some additional streaks. I used Toasted Coconut to paint in the contrasting color and give the hair greater dimension.

3. Use a high Gaussian Blur to soften any brushstrokes and adjust the layer opacity to taste (**figure 9.164**).

figure 9.164

Blurring the brushstrokes avoids the streaky look.

Recoloring Roots

As dyed or colored hair grows out, the person's original hair color is revealed, as in **figure 9.165**. Using Photoshop to recolor the roots can make a person feel much better about a portrait instead of dwelling on the missed hairdresser appointment (see **figure 9.166**).

 ch9_hair_roots.jpg

1. Make a rough selection with a 3-pixel feathered Lasso tool around the dark root areas of the hair (see **figure 9.167**). Avoid selecting any forehead skin.

2. Use the Eyedropper tool (set to 3×3 sample) to sample a lighter shade in the person's hair.

3. With the selection still active, select the Create new fill or adjustment layer icon at the bottom of the Layers palette. Choose Solid Color. The sampled color will automatically be used (**figure 9.168**).

figure 9.165

figure 9.166

figure 9.167

Roughly select the roots and as little skin as possible.

figure 9.168

Use a Solid Color adjustment layer.

4. Change the Color Fill layer's blending mode to Soft Light. Refine the transition of the colored area using a soft, white brush. Use white as the foreground color to reveal the lighter shade; use black as the foreground color to conceal the lighter shade (**figure 9.169**).

figure 9.169

Refine the blending of new color by painting on the layer mask.

5. Use a high Gaussian Blur to soften the edges. If you do not like the color, double click the Solid Color icon in the Layers palette and use the eyedropper to select a new shade from the existing hair (**figure 9.170**).

6. If additional lightening or color is needed, duplicate the Solid Color fill layer and adjust opacity.

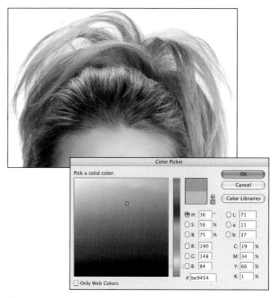

figure 9.170

Once the mask is refined, it's easy to choose a new color as needed.

Shaping the Hair with Light

After retouching a subject's face, take a few minutes to shape the hair by adding highlights and shadow to the natural form of the hair. **Figure 9.171** is yours truly before visiting the Photoshop salon, and **figure 9.172** shows my hair with sparkle and life added to it. Enhancing highlights and shadows adds dimension and liveliness to hair. This technique is called *wedging*, and you can use it to add tonal depth to hair or a person's clothing. It only takes a few seconds, but it makes the final portrait look richer.

ch9_hairshaping.jpg

1. To accentuate highlights, add a Color Dodge neutral layer by Option/Alt-clicking the New Layer icon on the Layers palette. Select the Color Dodge Blending Mode and select Fill with Color-Dodge-neutral color (black).

2. Because you want to work subtly and build up the contouring, use a large, soft, white brush set to 2–5% opacity to trace the contours of the natural hair highlights, as shown in **figure 9.173**.

© Mark Beckelman Photography

BEFORE

figure 9.171

figure 9.173

Painting on a neutral Color Dodge layer with a large, soft brush emphasizes the highlights.

3. To accentuate shadows, add a Color Burn neutral layer by Option/Alt-clicking the New Layer icon on the Layers palette. Select the Color Burn Mode and select Fill with Color-Burn-neutral color (white).

4. Use a large, soft, black brush set to 2–5% opacity to accentuate the contours of the shadows, as shown in **figure 9.174**.

AFTER

figure 9.172

figure 9.174

Painting on a Color Burn neutral layer with a large, soft brush emphasizes the shadows.

5. To finish up, I treated my roots as presented in the previous example (don't tell anyone) and as seen in **figure 9.175**.

With Photoshop, there are no more reasons to have a bad hair day!

figure 9.175

Using a Color Fill layer set to Color Burn improved the roots.

REFINING LIGHTING AND FOCUS

The fourth stage of portrait retouching is to enhance the lighting and focus of the image. Since our eyes are attracted to the lighter and sharper areas in the image, darkening or softening areas that are less important makes them visually less interesting. To learn about lighting, study classical painting by Rembrandt or Caravaggio or take a studio lighting class at a local community college or photography workshop. In essence, this stage concentrates on focusing the viewer's attention to the essential aspects of the portrait without overwhelming the image.

Vignetting Backgrounds

In a portrait the emphasis should, of course, be on the person in the picture. On darker, low-key portraits, darkening the background makes the face more prominent (**figures 9.176** and **9.177**), and on high-key portraits lightening the background removes visual interest from the edges of the image (**figures 9.178** and **9.179**).

BEFORE

figure 9.176

AFTER

figure 9.177

© Phil Pool Omni Photography

BEFORE

figure 9.178

AFTER

figure 9.179

 ch9_dark_vignette.jpg

 ch9_light_vignette.jpg

To darken a background:

1. Use the Elliptical Marquee tool to generously select the subject.

2. Choose Select > Inverse. Add a Color Fill adjustment layer and choose black from the color picker (**figure 9.180**).

figure 9.180

Use black to darken low-key portraits.

3. Reduce layer opacity to approximately 35% and use a high Gaussian Blur filter to soften the mask edge (**figure 9.181**). Smaller files require less blur than larger ones.

figure 9.181

Running the Gaussian Blur filter is identical to feathering the selection.

4. As Phil Pool explained to me, after the vignette he adds a Curves adjustment layer underneath the vignette and pops the contrast ever so slightly, as seen in figure 9.182. This enables him to refine the lighting contrast in relationship to the dark vignette.

figure 9.182

Adding a subtle contrast tweak makes this image shine.

Deemphasizing the Distractions

By darkening or blurring the background you deemphasize the less important, which automatically draws more attention to the more important subject, while maintaining the photographic integrity of the image. In the original image seen in figure 9.183, the picture of the brother and sister is fine, but by defocusing the background Mark Beckelman has gracefully decreased the importance of the living room background, which focuses your attention on the people (figure 9.184).

BEFORE

figure 9.183

AFTER

figure 9.184

After retouching the two people, Mark created a new working layer by duplicating this layer using Cmd-Opt-Shift-E/Ctrl-Alt-Shift-E. He blurred the first merged layer with the Gaussian Blur filter, activated the second merged layered and created a mask around the siblings, which protected the people and revealed the softened background as seen in figure 9.185. He then added a Curves adjustment layer and darkened the image ever so slightly. By Opt/Alt-dragging the mask for the softening layer to the Curves layer, only the living room background was darkened (see figure 9.186).

figure 9.185

Softening the background reduces its visual importance.

figure 9.186

Darkening the background emphasizes the foreground, in this case, the people.

ADDING CREATIVE INTERPRETATION

Removing distractions, improving contours, cleaning up the skin, and accentuating the eyes and mouth is primary retouching and all that most clients want. Adding creative effects is what can make your retouching stand apart from anyone else's. Creative effects can include converting the portrait to black and white and adding painterly effects (see Chapter 8), adding a new background (see my other book, "Photoshop Masking and Compositing"), or creating a stylized illustration as described here. Please note: I don't add these effects to all my portrait or image work—that would look rather silly on the rear admiral featured previously in this chapter—but experimenting with these ideas and effects can lead to unique images that are fun to work on and exciting to view.

Photographic Effects

Soft-focus effects can be used to soften a portrait or to add a romantic atmospheric effect to an image. Photographers use many types of materials to create soft-focus effects, from stretching nylon stockings or applying Vaseline to a filter on the enlarger lens to taking the picture through a window screen.

Softening a portrait also minimizes skin imperfections and adds a glow to the person's skin. **Figure 9.187** shows the original portrait for this example, which is rather contrasty. Softening the portrait makes the new version more romantic (see **figure 9.188**).

ch9_soft_focus.jpg

1. Duplicate the Background layer and set the blending mode to Screen. Although the image will look too light, this will let you see the true effect of the next step.

2. Select Filter > Blur > Gaussian Blur and use a high setting of at least 10. Without the Screen blending mode, the blur would soften the image into oblivion.

© JupiterImages

BEFORE

figure 9.187

AFTER

figure 9.188

3. Adjust the blurred layer's opacity between 40% and 60% to blend the two images.

4. Duplicate the blurred layer and set its blending mode to Multiply, as shown in **figure 9.189**. The combination of lightening and darkening layers mimics an optical blur better than one layer alone can.

figure 9.189

Duplicate blurred layers set to Screen and Multiply mimic an optical blur.

5. To bring the eyes back into focus, Shift-click the light and dark blur layers in the Layers palette and, from the Layers palette fly-out menu, select New Group From Layers. Add a layer mask to the new group and use a 50% black brush to paint back the eyes and lips (**figure 9.190**).

figure 9.190

Paint the eyes and lips back into focus.

6. The last step is to add image grain back into the image. When you use a soft-focus filter on a camera lens, the image grain will still be sharp even though the photograph is soft.

7. Select Layer > New > Layer and change the blending mode to Soft Light and select Fill with Soft Light-neutral color (50% gray). Select Filter > Artistic > Film Grain and adjust the film grain to your taste. In this example, I used 5 Grain, 0 Highlight, and 10 Intensity to create the image seen in figure 9.191.

figure 9.192

figure 9.191

The film grain layer creates essential visual structure.

High-Key Effects

Increasing contrast and adding a hint of texture is very popular and works especially well on portraits where the face and its surfaces are dominant, like figure 9.192. By using the separate image channels as layers, you can build a seemingly endless array of effects, such as the one in figure 9.193. The following technique shows you the tip of the iceberg.

 ch9_texture.jpg

figure 9.193

BEFORE

AFTER

© JupiterImages

1. Inspect the channels and notice which ones carry useful information. In this example the red channel has nice contrast, while the eyes in the blue channel are stunning (**figure 9.194**). We'll use these channels as new layers to add some extra interest to this image.

Red

Green

Blue

figure 9.194

Inspect the three channels to find the best image information.

2. Activate the red channel by clicking on it in the channels palette, choose Select > All and Edit > Copy, then return to the RGB channel. Select the Layers palette and paste the copied channel, which adds it as a new layer.

3. Hide the new layer and select the Background layer. Activate the blue channel, choose Select > All and Edit > Copy, then return to the RGB channel. Select the Layers palette and paste in the copied channel. Move the new layer (blue channel) to the top of the layer stack (**figure 9.195**) and hide it.

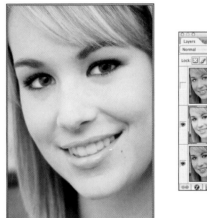

figure 9.195

After pasting the red and blue image channels as layers.

4. Now the fun begins! Add a texture to the red layer with Filter > Brush Strokes > Sprayed Strokes and use very high settings, as seen in **figure 9.196**. Change the Layer blending mode to Hard Light and continue experimenting with filters. In this example I ran the Sprayed Strokes again but changed the stroke direction from right to left.

5. To increase the textured effect even more, use the Filter > Sharpen > Unsharp Mask to increase the contrast of the texture (**figure 9.197**).

figure 9.196

Experiment with the Artistic Filters.

figure 9.197

Use high Unsharp Mask settings to emphasize the texture.

figure 9.198

Reveal the eyes back into the image.

6. Activate the eyes layer and select Layer > Add Layer Mask > Hide All. Use a soft, white brush on the layer mask to paint the eyes back in. Change the Layer blending mode to Hard Light and adjust opacity to create the final effect (**figure 9.198**).

All in all, you can spend endless hours experimenting with effects and ideas—all of which will serve to make your images stand out from the ordinary.

Saturday Night Live Effect

The opening credits on Saturday Night Live featured the high key and saturated portraits of the guest hosts and inspired Shan Canfield to experiment in Photoshop to create the following tutorial. After the release of the first edition of this book, Shan sent me this before-and-after example (**figures 9.199** and **9.200**) and I posted it on the book's Web site. The effect was so popular that Shan has received numerous emails about it. So she wrote up the steps and I am lucky enough to be able to share them here with you.

figure 9.199

figure 9.200

🌐 ▷÷ **ch9_SaturdayNightLive.jpg**

1. The image has some digital noise that will be used to an advantage as texture in the background, hair, and clothing and will be eliminated in the facial area with this quick digital makeup technique. Duplicate the Background layer and select Filter > Blur > Gaussian Blur and use a high setting of 10–20 pixels. Name the layer Digital Make up.

2. Choose Layer > Add Layer Mask > Hide All to add a black layer mask. Click the Mask thumbnail of the digital makeup layer to activate the mask. Chose a large, soft white brush set to 65% opacity and paint over her skin to create a base of blurry powder on the skin areas. Avoid brushing over the eyes, nostrils, mouth, and hair, as shown in **figure 9.201**.

figure 9.201

The layer mask reveals the softened layer underneath.

3. To add painted contouring, add a Curves adjustment layer and darken the image. Press Cmd-I/Ctrl-I to invert the layer mask to black. Paint in selective areas with a soft, white brush set to 35% to reveal a darker shade of some blush and lipstick and then use a smaller brush to accentuate the eyes by painting over the lashes, eyebrows, and eyelids (**figure 9.202**).

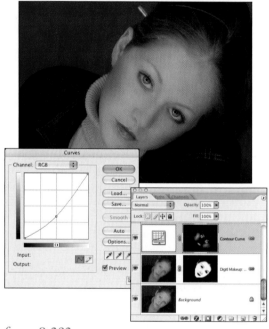

figure 9.202

Contouring the face with soft darker values.

4. To add highlights, add a Curves adjustment layer and lighten the image, as seen in **figure 9.203**.

You could stop here, and have an attractive finished portrait but for the SNL glow effect there's more to do to exaggerate colors and features.

5. At this point you need to make a selection for the glow effect. Turn off all layers except the Background layer and use the Magic Wand with a tolerance of 22 to select the red background, press Shift to add the left and top corners to create the selection seen in **figure 9.204**. Choose Select > Modify > Smooth and use a setting of 4. Select > Inverse so that the Model is selected, then Select > Save Selection. Name the new channel *Outline*.

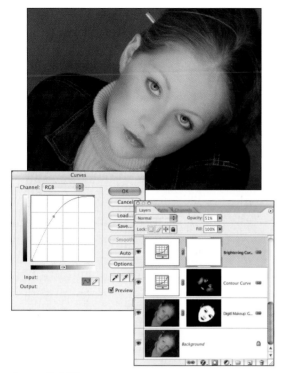

figure 9.203

Improving the overall image tonality.

figure 9.204

Selecting the red background that will be used to create the final glow.

6. Turn on all layers and activate the top layer. Add a Curves adjustment layer and select the red channel in the Curves dialog box. Click a point in the middle of the line; type 225 for Input and 126 for Output, as shown in **figure 9.205**.

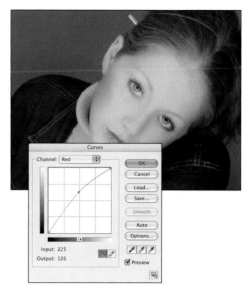

figure 9.205

Enhancing the background and red tones in the hair.

7. Choose Select > Load Selection and choose Outline from the Channel tab. Choose Edit > Fill with black and then Select > Deselect. Use a large, soft white brush with at least 75% opacity and paint in the hair to exaggerate the red color (**figure 9.206**).

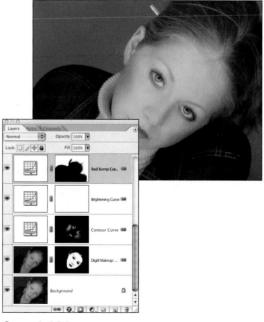

figure 9.206

Using the layer mask to control the increased red effect.

8. To exaggerate the blue jacket, add a Selective Color adjustment layer. In the Selective Color dialog box, set the Colors to Blacks. Input the following settings here: cyan +18, magenta +16, yellow (-27), black (-18), Method: Relative to exaggerate the blues of the jacket. In your own images, consider pushing the colors to a surreal realm by exaggerating the color. Click OK.

9. Change the adjustment layer's blending mode to Screen. Invert the Selective Color layer mask (Cmd-I/Ctrl-I). Paint with white to reveal the jacket, some soft highlights in the sweater and add a few light strokes in the irises of the eyes (**figure 9.207**).

figure 9.207

Making the blue jacket pop.

9. To intensify the blue jacket, duplicate the Selective Color layer and fill the mask with black. Change the blending mode to Overlay and lower the opacity to 70%. Paint solid white in the jacket area of the mask, as shown in **figure 9.208**.

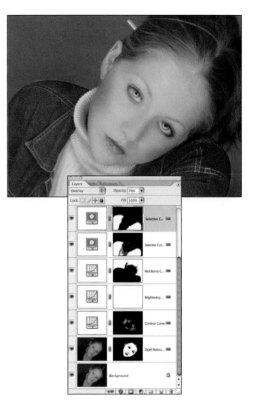

figure 9.208

Adding creative effects that veer away from reality.

10. To change the sweater to a chartreuse green, add another Curves adjustment layer. In the green channel of the Curves dialog box, click any point on the diagonal line, then type in 126 for Input; 181 for Output. Select the RGB channel in the same Curves dialog box. Click any point on the diagonal line and type in 156 for Input; 26 for Output. Click OK.

11. Use Cmd-I/Ctrl-I to invert the mask and paint with a white brush in the sweater area to reveal the new funky color, as shown in **figure 9.209**.

12. Use Cmd-Option-Shift-E/Ctrl-Alt-Shift-E to merge all of the production layers up. Select > Load Selection and choose Outline. Click the Add Layer Mask icon at the bottom of the Layers palette. This will create a mask thumbnail on the layer, where the white area of the mask silhouettes the Model. The image will not look any different at this point.

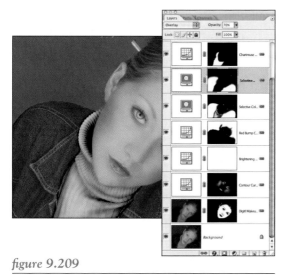

figure 9.209

Changing the turtleneck from cream to chartreuse in no time at all.

13. Click the Add Layer Styles/Effects icon at the bottom of the Layers palette and choose Outer Glow. Click the square color box for the glow and choose an orange shade or type *ED883D* in the hexadecimal field in the Color Picker. The settings are as follows: Blending Mode: Screen, Opacity: 100%, Technique: Softer, Spread: 25%, Size: 128 px, Range: 100, Jitter: 0 as shown in **figure 9.210**.

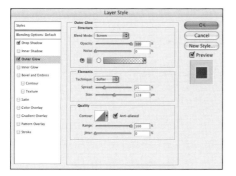

figure 9.210

Using Layer Styles to add a backlit glow.

14. Before exiting the Layer Styles box, turn on Drop Shadow in the left side of the panel. Change the shadow color swatch to white. The other settings are as follows: Blend Mode: Screen, Opacity: 75%, Distance: 0, Spread: 2%, Size: 62 px. Click OK to exit the Layer Styles box (**figure 9.211**).

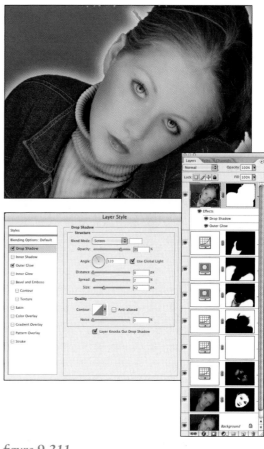

figure 9.211

Adding a Drop Shadow creates dimension.

15. Tighten and soften the layer mask edge by highlighting the Glow layer mask thumbnail on the layer. Select Filter > Other > Minimum 3 pixels followed by Filter > Blur > Gaussian Blur of 2 to create the final effect.

CLOSING THOUGHTS

Retouching a portrait is the most challenging type of retouching you can do. Remember to work with the contrast, color, and detail of the image. Before we move on to Chapter 10, I'd like to give you one last hint: When you are retouching a person's face, keep his or her mother in mind. Try to see the retouching as she would. If the changes were too obvious, she would notice it and, most likely, not like it. If Mom can see the retouching, then she can't see her child; and if her child isn't in the picture, then you've overworked the portrait.

10

GLAMOUR RETOUCHING

We've all seen pictures of supermodels, actors, and the so-called beautiful people and been astounded by their blemish-free skin, sparkling eyes, perfectly balanced faces, and cellulite-free thighs. I've always wondered: Don't those people ever eat anything, have a bad hair day, or get a pimple?

The glamour, fashion, advertising, and publishing industries create an illusion of perfection. It is an ideal that is unachievable without rare genetic good fortune, and a bevy of makeup artists, professional photographers, and highly skilled digital retouchers. These industries rely on Photoshop to remove the slightest imperfections in makeup, to straighten professionally coifed hair, and to make an already beautiful face perfectly symmetrical.

This chapter shows the techniques used to make the beautiful perfect, and the less-than-perfect beautiful. It is important to me to show you that, without extensive help, the ideal is unattainable and shouldn't be chased after by anyone—especially teenage girls and boys. Am I against digital retouching? Of course not, but we do need to learn to recognize, cherish, and appreciate the natural beauty of each individual.

In this chapter, you learn how to

- Develop a retouch strategy

- Perfect skin, eyes, and hair

- Shape faces and bodies

- Add glamour lighting

TYPES OF GLAMOUR RETOUCHING

The three general types of glamour retouching are: standard beauty, rescue and rebuild, and creative. Standard beauty is what you see in advertisements every single day—people with perfect skin and bodies that make the products they represent look fabulous (figure 10.1). Rescue and rebuild is used on the shots where the film is damaged (figures 10.2 and 10.3) or body parts are distorted due to posing or using too wide a lens. Rebuilding includes swapping body parts, extending backgrounds (figures 10.4 and 10.5), or changing clothing. In creative retouching, your imagination and time are the only limits and you may be asked to composite a model into a new scene (figures 10.6 and 10.7), enhance extreme makeup, or create surreal illustrations (figure 10.8).

© Katrin Eismann and Wayne Palmer

figure 10.1

From Moscow to Beijing to New York City—glamour retouching is everywhere you look.

© Andrew Matusik

figure 10.2

A badly damaged original.

figure 10.3

After restoring and retouching the image was stylized with faux film grain.

© Andrew Matusik

figure 10.4

Photographed on location, the shot lacks mystery and light.

figure 10.5

Adding woods, a pathway, and light creates a moody story.

figure 10.6

The Guggenheim Museum in Bilbao, Spain.

figure 10.7

The model was photographed in the studio and digitally transported to Bilbao.

figure 10.8

Classical art and surrealism are the themes of this complex composition.

DEVISING A WORKING STRATEGY

Before you move the mouse to retouch a glamour or fashion photograph, devise a retouching plan with the client to save hours of unnecessary work, haggling, and redos. To be able to talk knowledgeably with the client, research the person or product in the picture before your first meeting. For example, a portrait of a gritty blues musician requires a completely different approach than a picture of the latest teenage pop star. By knowing the person or product, you can emphasize the important, positive aspects while minimizing the less-important or less-flattering aspects. Research helps you communicate with the client and, in the end, deliver the best results.

The Big Picture

The first time you look at a picture, sweep around the image with your eyes. Don't focus on the details, but rather follow the line of the image and notice any distractions that break the smooth flow of your eye, such as lumps in clothing, gaps in hair, or distortion caused by awkward posing or wide-angle lenses.

Questions to keep in mind and issues to consider are

- Is the overall image tone correct and color balanced?

- Are the clothing and body contours smooth?

- Are body parts balanced and shapely or distorted and out of proportion?

- Is the environment helping or distracting?

- Are the subject and environment correctly in or out of focus?

- Is the lighting working?

The closer the retoucher works with the photographer, the more these big-picture issues can be addressed during the initial photo shoot. As Andrew Matusik so clearly said, "As the photographer, I am always thinking about post-production—from finding the location to planning the lighting to casting the models. Ideally, 80% of a beauty shot should be achieved photographically with 20% of post-production used to polish and perfect the image." However, as you can imagine, during a location fashion shoot, some details may slip by the wayside while the photographer concentrates on the perfect facial expression and doesn't notice a bathing suit strap that slipped.

The Details

Next, look at the details. Zoom in to 100% or 200% view and note all the details that require your attention.

- Does the image need dust removal?

- Is the skin texture appealing?

- What blemishes, wrinkles, or shadows need to be removed?

- Is the makeup applied evenly?

- Do the eyes need cleaning up?

- Are the lips full, round, and attractive?

- Are creative effects requested?

The longer you retouch and the more images you examine, the faster this process becomes. The goal is for the viewer to be able to get the image's message as quickly as possible. After you remove the distractions and perfect the model, the viewers will get the message as quickly as they can turn the pages of the latest fashion magazines.

Tip

Study contemporary fashion and design magazines to learn the latest trends in makeup, lighting, and styling.

Working with Clients

After researching and evaluating an image, make sure that you establish what the client needs. More importantly, make sure that the client agrees with your retouching plan before you start. Do not put any work into a file until you have a signed work order or a reliable agreement. If it sounds as if I'm speaking from experience, you're right. I had one job in which the photographer requested I rebuild a woman's legs, which took me two hours per leg. The next day, the art director told me the image was going to be cropped. I lost four hours and learned the lesson very quickly that you need to know who has final approval of a job.

I've worked with clients whose entire instruction set was, "Make her beautiful." I've also had clients who provide extremely precise directions that address every possible detail. The very best ones provide a guide print that is marked up with clear directions, such as the one in **figure 10.9**. But the great majority of clients provide some guidance and I often review the goals of the retouch via phone conversations. During those calls I'll point out details that I've noticed and ask if they would like the additional work done. Clients will come to rely on your careful eye to help them look their very best.

Use a combination of Photoshop layers and a work-order form to create a retouch to-do list. **Figure 10.10** shows a file that I marked up while on the phone with the photographer. The "notes" are scribbled on an empty layer that I named *Notes*. From top to bottom, they remind me to: close gaps in hair; smooth out skin; remove distracting highlight on background; rework shape of shoulders, waist, and thigh; refine underwire in bikini top; remove wrinkles by her arms and waist; remove fingers under left leg; clean up feet and knees; and close the gaps on the stone seat. As you can see in **figure 10.11**, I also color-corrected the file to render her the classic California golden girl.

figure 10.9

Extensive notes that address every aspect of the job.

figure 10.10

Make notes directly on the file to record what needs to be improved or changed.

© 2005 Douglas Dubler 3

figure 10.11

The final retouched file.

T i p

When talking with clients, make sure that you are both using the same directions: "Is right, right?" or "is right, camera right?" The first definition is from the model's perspective and the second is from the photographer's. The photographer's point of view is also the viewer's point of view and it is the one more commonly used.

You also can add written or voice annotations to a file with the Notes tool. This is incredibly useful when emailing files back and forth; instead of trying to describe something over the phone, a client can just add an annotation right on the file that needs the work. Quite honestly, the Notes tool is used much more than the Voice Annotation tool.

With each file, you should include a work order or job ticket. This form should list what needs to be done, how and when the final file should be delivered, and include an area for client's initialed approval for

when the job is complete. As you can see in **figure 10.12**, the form starts with the usual job-tracking information and then addresses the retouching requirements—from global to specific, from color and contrast to blemishes and wrinkles. I've posted a generic order form on www.digitalretouch.org. Use it as a reference when developing your own work orders.

🌐▷⌖ **ch10_orderform.pdf**

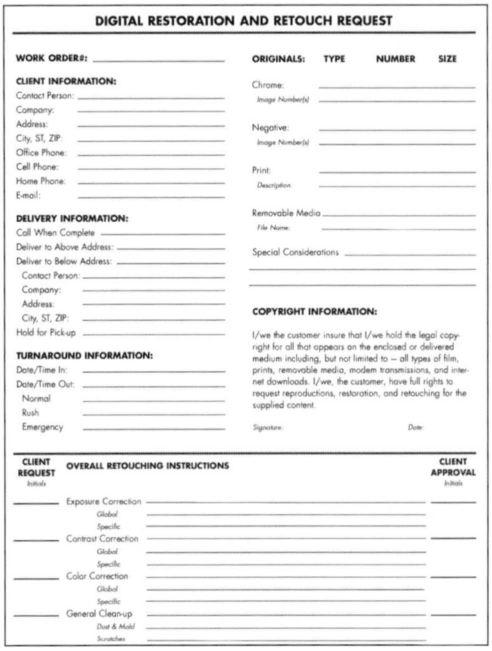

DIGITAL RESTORATION AND RETOUCH REQUEST

figure 10.12

A generic order form used to track retouching tasks.

THE BEAUTY WORKFLOW

The techniques discussed in Chapter 9, "Portrait Retouching," form the foundation for many of the following glamour retouching techniques. Key techniques for retouching include working on empty layers, using neutral layers to lighten or darken areas, and (of course) never changing the Background layer because it is as valuable as your original file. Also always make a backup copy of the original scan and store it in a safe place. For additional information on workflow and file organization, please see Chapter 1, "Photoshop Essentials."

The fundamental glamour (also called beauty) workflow is

1. Apply overall color correction

2. Perform general cleanup and distraction removal

3. Balance facial symmetry

4. Reshape or rebuild body

5. Refine clothing; perfect skin

6. Enhance eyes, lips, and hair

7. Apply selective color correction

8. Improve lighting, focus, and sharpness

9. Size, convert, sharpen, and deliver file

Of course, the exact order you apply these changes will vary as you gain experience and "get to know" the file as you work, but in general start with contrast and color, move on to shape and form, and then refine skin and features.

I had a long talk about beauty retouching with Andrew Matusik from DigitalRetouch.net and he said, "Anyone can learn how to use the Photoshop tools and there are usually at least three ways of applying a tool, but it is very important to look at the image and take the route that is based on maximum efficiency. How I approach a retouch depends on the file and the amount of work required. Each file represents a unique challenge and finding the best approach is a skill developed over many years of working with critical clients."

 Tip

Glamour retouching requires many small steps. To insure the ability to take advantage of the Photoshop History feature, increase the number of History steps in Edit > Preferences > General to at least 100, if not higher. In the History Options choose Allow Non-linear History. By recording states in a non-linear way, you can select a state and make a change to the image, which enables you to try out more than one approach.

Color Modes

Each color mode has its strengths and weaknesses, and which mode you work in is an essential decision often dictated by the output device the file will be printed with. I prefer to work in RGB because the color gamut is larger, the files are one-third smaller, and all filters function. While retouching I check the file with View > Proof Setup > Working CMYK and, if time allows, I have proofs made, as the print will reveal subtle color casts or retouching flaws that you do not see on the monitor. After doing the retouch, if the client needs a CMYK file I apply a conversion based on prepress information they have provided. After the conversion, a subtle color correction is often required as the mode conversion may cause colors to shift.

Other very successful retouchers convert the file to CMYK as the first step of the workflow, which can counter the possibility of enhancing colors and saturation that are simply out of printing range. CMYK is the classic reference color mode when doing skin color correction, as explained in Chapter 4, and the ability to work on the black channel to open up skin density is a plus.

The Lab color mode is ideal for specialized situations to adjust file density, open up shadows, or change color.

One thing all retouchers can agree on: Do not convert and reconvert the file between color modes without a very good reason. Even if you feel more comfortable working in RGB and a client provides you with a CMYK file, do not convert it to RGB, work on it, and then convert it back to CMYK. Mode conversions are destructive and should be used only as a final step to target the file for a specific output device.

For additional information please refer to "Real World Photoshop CS2" by David Blatner and Bruce Fraser.

Color Correction

Chapter 4, "Working with Color", is a comprehensive overview of color correction strategies and techniques to which I would like to add one specifically used in the glamour business. Most high-end glamour files I've either worked on or had the pleasure to poke around in start with a layer group with three adjustment layers: from bottom to top—Curves for tonality and contrast, Curves for color correction, and either a Hue/Saturation layer to tweak saturation, or a Selective Color layer to fine tune the color component as shown in **figures 10.13 and 10.14.**

⊕▷⌿ ch10_color_correct.jpg

1. In the Layers palette, click the Create a new group icon—it looks like a small folder—and name it CC, for *color correction*.

2. Add a Curves adjustment layer and increase the overall exposure and adjust the contrast as seen in **figure 10.15.**

3. Add a second Curves adjustment layer and increase the blue curve to offset the strong yellow in the image (**figure 10.16**).

4. Add a Selective Color adjustment layer and use it to offset the heaviness of the file. Taking yellow out of the reds and slightly reducing ink in the neutrals opens up the file and lets the woman shine (**figure 10.17**).

This first group is often named CC or *Overalls* and either remains on top of the retouching layer stack to color correct all layers underneath it or can be moved lower in the layer stack if selective color or tone correction needs to be done (**figure 10.18**). When working with the Clone Stamp or Healing tools on empty layers that are **above** the color correction layers, make sure to select Sample All Layers in the options bar so the color correction is also applied to the retouched areas. When working with the Clone Stamp or Healing tools on empty layers that are **below** the color correction layers, turn off the adjustment layers when cloning or healing so that the color correction is not applied twice to the retouched areas.

BEFORE

figure 10.13

AFTER

figure 10.14

figure 10.15

The initial curve corrects exposure.

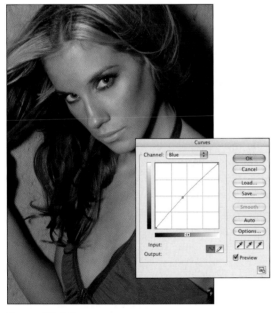

figure 10.16

The second curve corrects overall color.

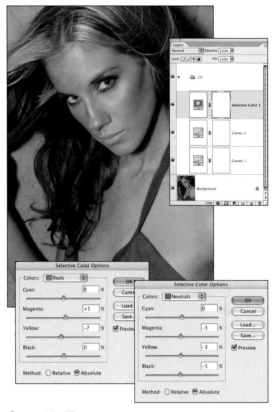

figure 10.17

The Selective Color adjustment layer fine-tunes the color components.

figure 10.18

Selective changes need to be above overall adjustments.

The second pass of color correction targets specific areas, such as the skin (usually called *flesh*) and hair, and requires masking to control where the change takes place as seen in figure 10.19. This pass is often applied after retouching to fine-tune the color for a specific look or feel.

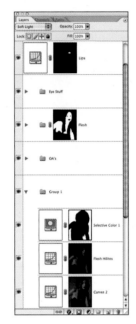

figure 10.19

Take advantage of layer masking to refine color and density.

SYMMETRY AND SHAPE

Perfect symmetry, balance, and shape are essential attributes in a glamour model, but nature has a way of adding her own quirks: eyes that are not aligned, ears that protrude too much, waistlines that need a nip or tuck, asymmetrical jawlines, shoulders that are too strong, muscle tone that needs a Photoshop workout, breasts that need to be a bit fuller, the list goes on and on.

The primary tools to perfect symmetry and shape are the Clone Stamp tool, Warp transform, and Liquify. The problem with all these tools is that when used improperly they cause skin and film

grain structure to change, which needs to be avoided as much as possible. To maintain image structure, with the Clone Stamp use 70–85% brush hardness and with Liquify use large, low-density, low-pressure, and low-rate brushes.

In the examples seen in figure 10.20 you see a very lovely model who obviously takes great care of herself…but in today's publishing world even she needs a bit of refinement to narrow her nose, lessen her jawline, smooth her shoulders, flatter her waistline, and slim her thighs, as seen in the final file in figure 10.21.

In this example, the required reshaping is so subtle that a gentle use of the Liquify tool and a bit of Cloning to narrow the inside of her arms will suffice.

1. I add an empty Notes layer and quickly mark up what needs to be addressed—starting with her face (narrow nose and refine jawline) and moving down her body to refine her shoulders, arms, waistline, and thighs.

2. By duplicating the Background layer, I create a working surface and the ability to check the progress by turning the layer on and off to compare it with the original.

3. To speed up the Liquify command, I select her head with the Elliptical Marquee tool and select Filter > Liquify. To narrow her nose, I use a large brush with a very low density and pressure and gently push her nose inward. I use a larger brush to reduce the strength of her jawline ever so slightly, as seen in figure 10.22.

Tip

If the Liquify tool is destroying image texture, use lower pressure and density brushes and, rather than trying to achieve all reshaping at once, use the Liquify command in smaller passes, between which you can clone or heal texture back in.

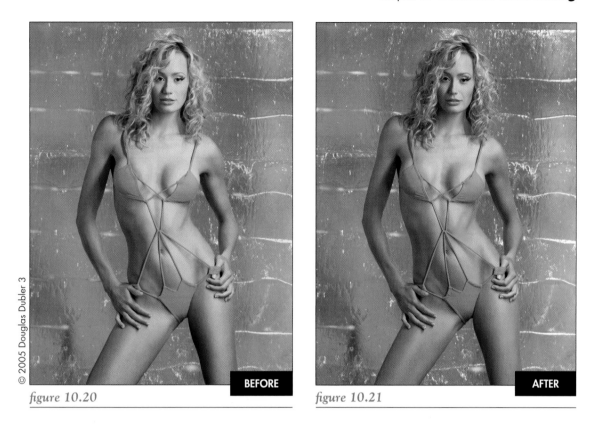

figure 10.20 — BEFORE

figure 10.21 — AFTER

figure 10.22

The slightest correction is the best correction.

4. I then select her camera-right shoulder with the Rectangular Marquee tool and enter Liquify again to smooth the shape of her shoulder. To check my progress, I select Show Backdrop and choose Background layer, as circled in **figure 10.23**, to see how well a little bit of reshaping is working.

5. In tighter areas, such as between her under-arm and breast, cloning a new shape is more effective than Liquify, as the Liquify could noticeably distort the small background area.

I start by adding an empty layer and outlining the new arm shape with the Pen tool, as in **figure 10.24**.

6. After activating the Path into a selection, I used a small, hard-edged Clone Stamp set to Sample All Layers to refine the contour of her arm, as seen in **figure 10.25**. Please note: Cloning background over skin to create a new contour should only be used in less important image areas.

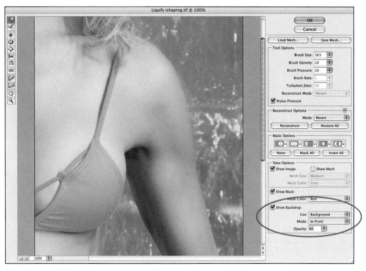

figure 10.23

Monitor progress with the Show Backdrop option to reference original or notes layers.

figure 10.24

Selecting the area of the arm to trim.

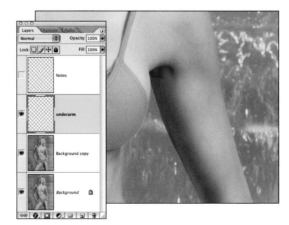

figure 10.25

Cloning the background over the arm.

7. Turning the Notes layer on to check my progress is a great reminder of what needs to be done next. In this case, I need to narrow her camera-left thigh a bit. I start by selecting her thigh generously with the Lasso tool and feathering the selection by 45 pixels, then use Layer > New > Layer via Copy to place the thigh onto a separate layer. I then choose Edit > Transform > Warp and gently push the grid lines inward as seen in **figure 10.26**.

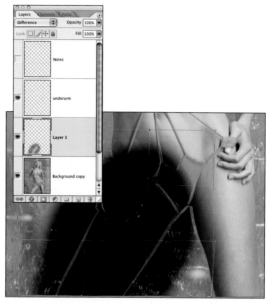

figure 10.27

While in Warp, changing the blending mode to Difference shows the progress.

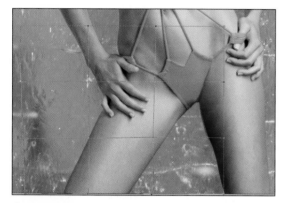

figure 10.26

Narrowing her thigh with Warp Transform.

8. Before clicking OK, I like to check how much warp I've applied. Changing the blending mode to Difference while still in the Warp dialog box Photoshop shows me the difference of the two layers as seen in **figure 10.27**.

9. After clicking OK and changing the blend mode back to Normal, I add a layer mask and paint away areas such as her hand, which had been unnecessarily warped (**figure 10.28**).

In images that require more aggressive reshaping, use the techniques as described the "Flattering the Contours" section in Chapter 9 or as Shawn Gibson did in the before-and-after images seen in **figures 10.29** and **10.30**. Shawn narrowed the model by lengthening her body with cloning to make her lower body longer, followed by judicious use of Liquify and additional cloning to flatter the model's figure perfectly.

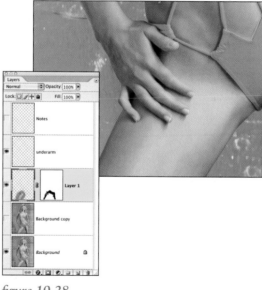

figure 10.28

The layer mask controls the transition between transformed and original.

© Shawn Gibson

figure 10.29   **BEFORE**

figure 10.30   **AFTER**

Watch Those Hands

The position and size of a hand can make or break the shot. If it is too flat it appears much larger than it really is (**figure 10.31**). If parts are sticking out or on someone's shoulders, the fingers look like little cocktail hot dogs, and if the manicure wasn't recent you may end up rebuilding every single nail and cuticle. To thin the hands (**figure 10.32**), I used the Pucker tool in Liquify as described here.

🌐⊅✂ **ch10_model_hand.jpg**

1. Select the hand with the Elliptical Marquee tool, Cmd-J/Ctrl-J to copy the active area onto a new layer and choose Filter > Liquify. The Pucker tool is a shrinking tool and its default settings are much too strong for anything except goofy effects.

2. Lower the Brush Density, Pressure, and Rate settings down to 1 and (preferably) using a Wacom pen, gently tap on the edge of the hands and centers of fingers (**figure 10.33**). Just tap, do not drag, as dragging the Pucker tool makes it work much too extremely.

Beauty Is in the Details

The folds of skin where the arms meet the torso are areas that all beauty retouchers are requested to remove, as seen in **figures 10.34** and **10.35**. Use the Patch tool and Healing Brush to carefully reduce or remove these folds of skin.

© Thiago Da Cunha

BEFORE

figure 10.31

AFTER

figure 10.32

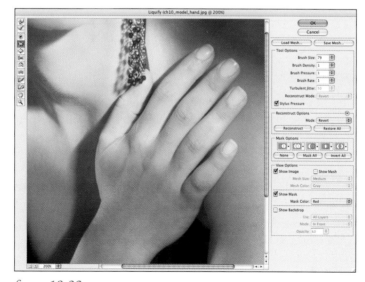

figure 10.33

Use the Pucker tool to narrow body parts.

© Thiago Da Cunha

figure 10.34

BEFORE

figure 10.35

AFTER

PERFECT SKIN

The key to retouching skin is to maintain the natural texture while removing blemishes, blackheads, wrinkles, and scars. Cloning and healing are used with great care to only conceal the very largest blemishes or beauty marks. Beauty retouchers work pore by pore—or, as I like to say, pixel by pixel—to create the perfect skin you see in glossy magazines and giant prints at cosmetic counters. In the following section, I'll show you three methods to retouch skin invisibly; practice all three on all of the skin samples provided to see which method creates the results that meet your quality and workflow needs. The techniques featured here take more than a few minutes to master and the secret is to work carefully and patiently, as every glamour face you see in print has taken hours and hours to perfect—pore by pore and pixel by pixel.

Neutral Layer Technique

All blemishes, wrinkles, and small scars are density differences of adjacent dark and light tones. The neutral layer technique enables you to lighten and darken on the same layer, which makes working with it very efficient. The example seen in **figures 10.36** and **10.37** shows how effective this technique can be.

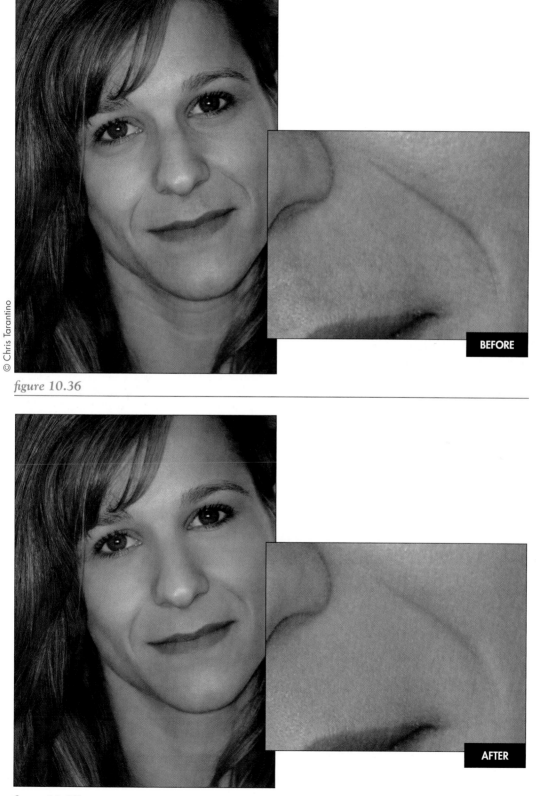

© Chris Tarantino

BEFORE

figure 10.36

AFTER

figure 10.37

ch10_neutral_skin.jpg

1. On an empty layer, use a hard-edged Healing Brush set to Sample All Layers to remove only the most obvious blemishes or birthmarks as addressed in the "Skin Blemishes… the Teenage Years" section of Chapter 9, "Portrait Retouching."

2. Option/Alt-click the New Layer icon on the Layers palette, change the Mode from Normal to Soft Light and click Fill with Soft Light-neutral color (50% gray) to create the retouching surface. Click OK.

3. Choose a 5-pixel, 50% hardness brush and change its opacity to 15%. Reset the color picker to the default black and white.

4. To conceal dark blemishes, paint with white and conceal lighter blemishes with black (figure 10.38). Figure 10.39 shows just the Soft Light layer.

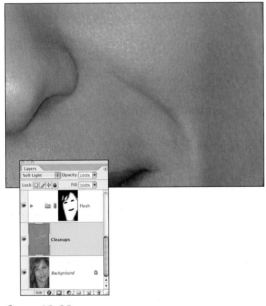

figure 10.38

Work at 100–200% zoom and patiently paint over the dark and light blemishes.

figure 10.39

Option/alt-click the retouch layer eye icon to see the layer.

5. To lighten larger areas, such as rings under the eye, or if you see any color shifts, sample the color from the person's skin and paint with that on the Soft Light neutral layer, as seen in figure 10.40, to offset any color shifts.

6. To soften visible transitions between the lighter or darker areas, use the Blur tool on the Soft Light layer to blur the transitions.

As Chris Tarantino explains, "All retouching can now be done on this one layer that is fully adjustable and undoable. The optimum opacity of the brush will differ for everyone. I find that when using white, I rarely go over 25%. However, when painting with black, I have gone as much as 90%. Sometimes when using black on a very light color, you may see a slight graying effect. If this happens, find and use a dark color that is the same hue as where the fix is being done and use that instead of pure black. You can find these dark colors on the hairline or in the nostril."

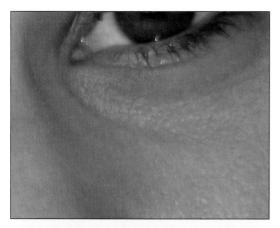

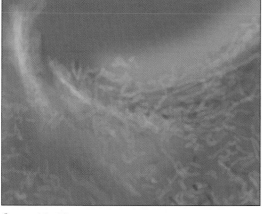

figure 10.40

Using lighter and darker skin tones helps to alleviate color shifts.

Dual Curves Technique

The second skin perfection technique uses two Curves layers—one that lightens the darker blemishes and one that darkens the lighter ones. This dual layer approach enables the retoucher to control the density adjustments in three ways: by adjusting the curve, changing the opacity of the Curves adjustment layer, and adjusting the density of the brush used to paint the correction, as seen in figures 10.41 and 10.42.

ch10_dual_skin.jpg

1. In the Toolbox, double-click the Quick Mask button and make sure the mask options are set to Color Indicates Selected Areas (figure 10.43).

2. Press Q to enter Quick Mask and use a small, 70% hardness, black brush to dab over a few representative darker spots (figure 10.44).

3. Press Q again to exit Quick Mask, which creates an active selection as seen in figure 10.45. Add a Curves adjustment layer and pull the center point of the curve until the darker blemish density matches the overall skin values, as shown in figure 10.46.

4. Use a small, soft, white brush with 100% opacity and the flow set to 10–20% to paint on the Curves layer mask to tonally blend the blemishes in as seen in figure 10.47.

5. Repeat steps 2 through 4, to create a separate curve for the lighter blemishes.

Carrie Beene from Otto Imaging explains, "I do all my skin retouching with two Curves layers—one to lighten and one to darken—and I go back and forth between them with a very soft brush with 100% opacity and the flow set to 10–20%. That way, I can make all kinds of adjustments along the way either to the mask or to the curve."

figure 10.41

figure 10.42

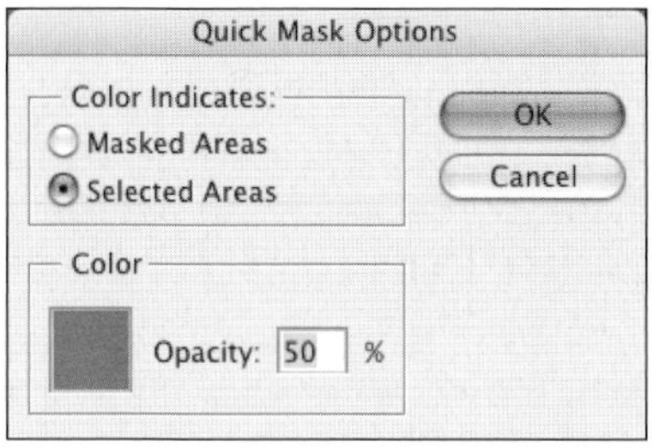

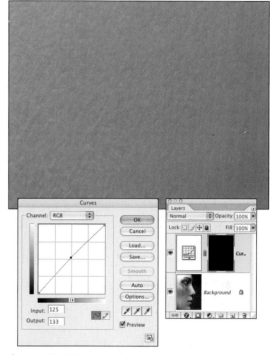

figure 10.43

Before entering Quick Mask, change the settings.

figure 10.44

Dab over a few of the dark spots.

figure 10.46

Adjust the curve to match the dark areas with the surrounding skin.

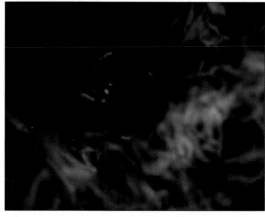

figure 10.45

The active selection may be very small.

figure 10.47

Painting in the Curves layer mask evens out skin density.

As **figure 10.48** shows, Carrie also improves the shading, shape, and makeup with multiple Curves and Selective Color adjustment layers, in which she uses this Quick Mask technique and her painting skills to refine high-end glamour shots for the most critical international clients. This will be explained further in the "Eye Makeup" section later in this chapter.

figure 10.48

Creating a separate layer for each change allows for tremendous control.

Evening Skin Tones

In glamour imaging the model needs to be perfectly perfect and the smallest dimple or shadow, which you and I wouldn't look at twice in real life, may look like a bruise in the photograph (**figure 10.49**). Use a lightening Curves layer on shadows by knees, necks, and hands to subtly lighten shadows, as seen in **figure 10.50**.

1. I used a 10-pixel feathered Lasso tool to select the darker tones by her knee and wrist, as seen in **figure 10.51**.

2. After adding a Curves adjustment layer, I pulled the curve up to lighten the shadows ever so slightly, which balanced out the shadows as seen in **figure 10.52**.

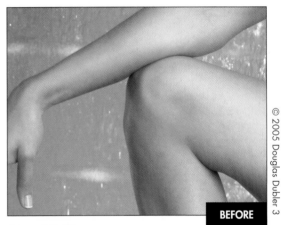

figure 10.49

figure 10.50

figure 10.51

Selecting the darker tones with a feathered Lasso.

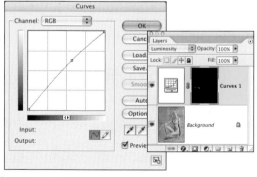

figure 10.52

The curve lightens the shadows and evens out the skin tones.

Heal and Restore Technique

I learned this third method of skin retouching from Andrew Matusik, who surprised me by using the Healing Brush to do the initial work followed with multiple passes of texture blending to create the beautiful skin seen in figures 10.53 and 10.54.

🌐▷< **ch10_heal_skin.jpg**

1. Duplicate the Background layer and use a small Healing Brush to painstakingly heal out all blemishes and wrinkles. Use a clicking mouse action rather than dragging to avoid a smeared look. Stay away from high-contrast areas such as eyelashes and lips, as seen in figure 10.55. At this stage, the skin will be much too smooth and look completely fake.

2. Add an Overlay neutral layer by Option/Alt-clicking the New Layer icon. Change the Mode to Overlay and select Fill with Overlay neutral 50% gray to create a surface for skin and grain structure. Click OK.

3. Select Filter > Noise > Add Noise and add 1.5 Gaussian Noise with Monochrome selected.

4. Use a 12-pixel feathered Lasso tool to select an area of the skin like the one in figure 10.56 and turn off the healed layer. Choose Edit > Copy Merged followed by Edit > Paste to paste the textured skin back into position, as seen in figure 10.57.

5. Reduce the layer opacity to 40% to allow the original texture to shimmer through. Use a soft-edged Eraser with 10 to 20% pressure to fine-tune the blending of the original texture with the smooth skin as seen in figure 10.58.

6. To double-check the blending, click the eye icon on and off. Adjusting the layer opacity gives you a tremendous amount of control over the final texture blending.

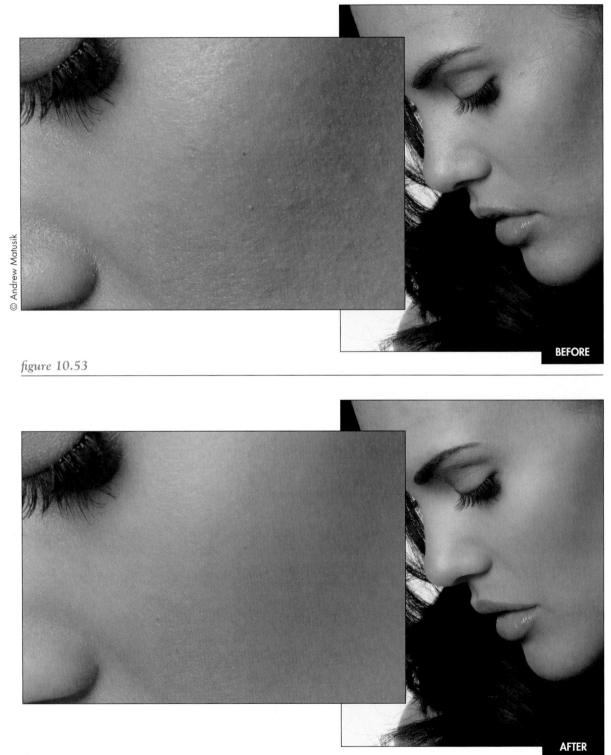

© Andrew Matusik

figure 10.53

BEFORE

figure 10.54

AFTER

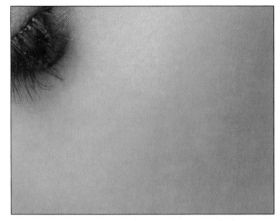

figure 10.55

Heal all skin texture away.

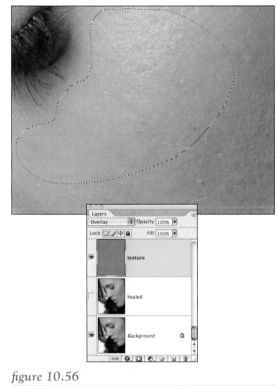

figure 10.56

Use a feathered Lasso to roughly select an area of skin.

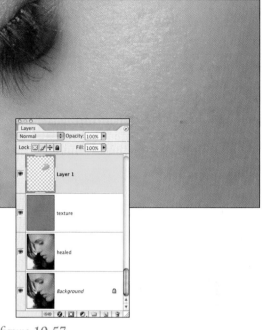

figure 10.57

Paste the original textured skin back onto the file.

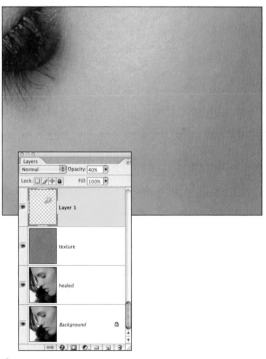

figure 10.58

Adjust layer opacity and erase to blend the textured and healed skin.

7. Andrew repeated steps 3 through 5 to create the multilayered image seen in **figure** 10.59.

Andrew explained to me, "Think like a makeup artist: the Healing Brush is the base makeup and reapplying the texture creates the illusion of reality. To avoid the over-retouched look, I make sure to leave one or two subtle imperfections, such as a small beauty mark. In an older person or a celebrity, keeping a hint of a wrinkle under an eye maintains the appropriate reality." In **figures** 10.60 and 10.61 you see a close-up that shows how effective Andrew's technique is, especially on fine hair by the nostrils and lips.

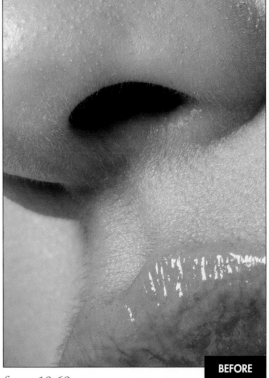

figure 10.60

© Andrew Matusik

figure 10.59

Use many separate layers to refine the texture exactly as needed.

figure 10.61

ENHANCING FACIAL FEATURES

Enhancing facial features includes refining eyes, slimming noses, making lips fuller, and repairing cracked or flaky makeup, to name just a few of the challenges you may face. The techniques shown in Chapter 9 are also used in the glamour industry and rather than repeating them here, I'll concentrate on highlighting new techniques and show some of the best retouching work being done today.

The Eyes

Eyes need to appear clean, clear, moist, symmetrical, saturated, and beautifully framed by eyelashes and eyebrows, as seen in **figures 10.62** and **10.63**. Andrew Matusik, who retouched this image, says, "Eyes are the 'hot spot' of the image, so they must be perfect." For more on retouching eyes, refer back to "Eyeball Fundamentals" in Chapter 9.

🌐▷※ **ch10_beauty_eye.jpg**

1. Duplicate the Background layer and name it *WIP*, for *Work in Progress*. Carefully clone out the red veins. Start in the area with the fewest veins near the iris and work outward, building up clearer and clearer eye whites as you progress (**figure 10.64**). When working in such a small area with the Clone Stamp tool, unselect Aligned so the clone source doesn't "follow" the Clone Stamp.

2. Add a new layer and use a hard-edged Clone Stamp to clean up any clumps in the mascara, specks on the skin, and distracting hairs around the eyelids, as **figure 10.65** shows.

figure 10.62

BEFORE

© Andrew Matusik

figure 10.63

AFTER

figure 10.64

Use a small, hard-edged Clone tool to remove each vein.

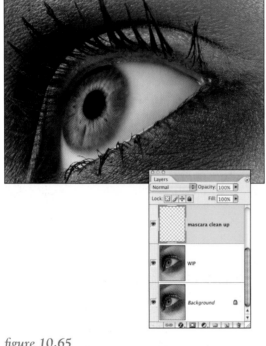

figure 10.65

Carefully clean up any clumps of mascara or flecks of skin.

3. To fix the gap in the eyelashes near the out-side corner, select one eyelash (**figure 10.66**) with a 2-pixel feathered Lasso tool and chose Edit > Copy Merged to copy all the visible information that makes up the eyelash, fol-lowed by Edit > Paste.

figure 10.66

Select one eyelash.

4. Use the Transform command to rotate and skew the eyelash into place. By changing the eyelash layer blending mode to Darken, the lighter areas become invisible (**figure 10.67**).

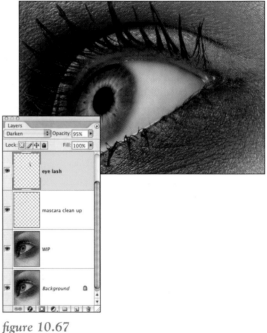

figure 10.67

The Darken blending mode ignores the lighter areas.

5. Erase away the unneeded areas around the eyelash.

6. Add a Hue/Saturation adjustment layer and boost the overall saturation by 15% to make the golden and blue tones pop beautifully (**figure 10.68**).

figure 10.68

Hue/Saturation lets the makeup glow.

Hollywood Eyes

When we're young, our eyes are larger in relation to our faces, which is why larger eyes insinuate youth and innocence. Enlarging and balancing eyes is an often-requested procedure as seen in figures 10.69 and 10.70.

 ch10_hollywood_eyes.jpg

1. Select View > Show Rulers and drag out guides to the top and bottom of the eyes as seen in figure 10.71 to check for balance and symmetry.

figure 10.69

BEFORE

© Thiago Da Cunha

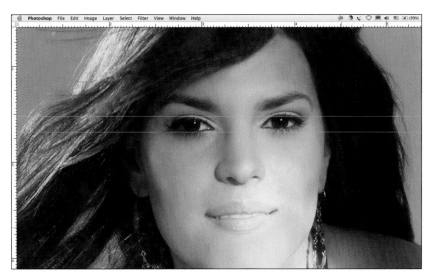

figure 10.70

AFTER

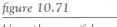

figure 10.71

Use guides to see if the eyes are level and the same size.

2. Use a 3-pixel feathered Lasso tool to select one eye and Cmd-J/Ctrl-J to copy the selected eye onto a new layer. Repeat with the second eye (**figure 10.72**) so that each eye is on its own layer.

3. Choose Edit > Transform to scale the smaller eye (in this example the camera-right eye) to match the larger eye (**figure 10.73**).

figure 10.72

Duplicate each eye onto a separate layer.

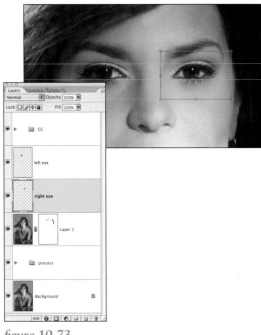

figure 10.73

Scale the smaller eye to match the larger.

4. Shift-click each eye layer in the Layers palette and select Edit > Transform to scale both layers together, as shown in **figure 10.74**.

5. Erase away any extraneous skin.

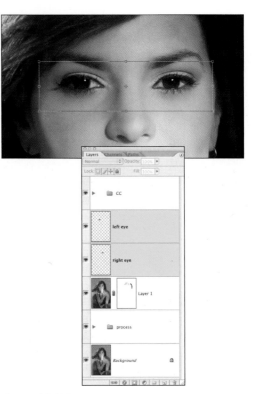

figure 10.74

Enlarge both eyes to approximately 102%

Scaling the eyes just a small amount has a large effect. On a similar note, if you need to make someone appear more important, make the head larger by just 1 or 2 percent. The "Focus and Sharpness" section later in this chapter will cover how to accentuate the focus of the eyes.

Size, Balance, and Shape

Figures 10.75 and **10.76** show how subtle yet effective the enlarged the eye can be. Andrew Matusik made the eye more important by extending the eyebrow and making the eye larger.

The very best aspect of this enhancement is that it is not noticeable until you see the comparison, but once you do see how effective it is you'll consider making eyes just a bit larger to give them greater visual presence and importance.

figure 10.75

figure 10.76

Refining Eye Makeup

To perfect the ornate eye makeup, Carrie Beene used numerous layers to transform figure 10.77 into the stunning image seen in figure 10.78. Carrie comes to retouching with a traditional background in painting and sculpture; she is an expert at removing distractions to reveal the true beauty of the subject. By using 22 separate adjustment layers Carrie is able to refine every single aspect of the eye.

figure 10.77

BEFORE

AFTER

figure 10.78

1. After duplicating the Background layer, Carrie very carefully used a hard-edged Clone Stamp tool and Healing Brush to minimize the most obvious wrinkles under the model's eye. Then she used the previously described Dual Curve technique to further conceal the wrinkles, as seen in **figure** 10.79.

2. To enrich the yellow eye shadow, Carrie added a Curves layer and boosted the contrast. She then inverted the Curves layer mask and painted with a large, soft-edged, white brush on the yellow eye shadow area to brighten it up, as seen in **figure** 10.80.

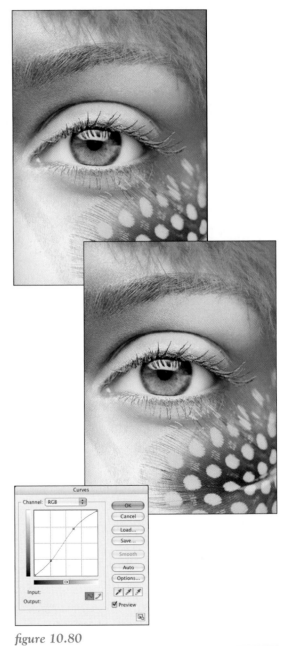

figure 10.79

Initial cleanup and wrinkle reduction.

figure 10.80

Brightening the yellow eyeshadow.

3. Adding another Curves adjustment layer, she darkened the eyebrows, which makes the yellow eye shadow pop even more (**figure** 10.81).

4. To make the yellow spots on the feathers stronger, Carried added a third Curves adjustment layer, reduced the blue channel (because it is the opposite of yellow), inverted the layer mask, and dabbed white on the yellow feathers to make them more dramatic (**figure** 10.82).

5. Next, Carrie duplicated the previous Curves layer and lightened the feathers. To insure that the lightening did not change the color of the feathers, she changed the blending mode to Luminosity, as shown in **figure** 10.83.

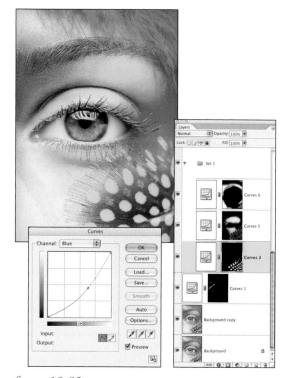

figure 10.82

Treating each element separately allows for essential flexibility.

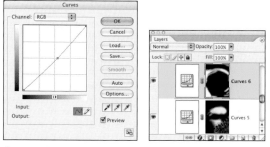

figure 10.81

Darkening the eyebrows makes the yellow seem even brighter.

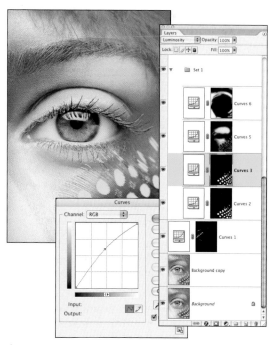

figure 10.83

The Luminosity blending mode negates possible saturation shifts.

6. To tone down the catchlight of the photographer's lighting softbox at the top of the iris, Carrie added a new layer and cloned over the catchlight. By lowering the opacity, the catchlight's importance is reduced without making the eye look non-photographic, as seen in **figure** 10.84.

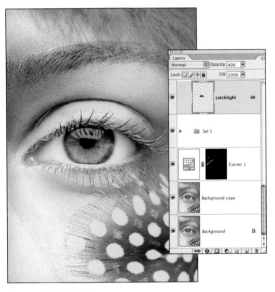

figure 10.84

Toning down the catchlight

7. Ever the perfectionist, Carrie noticed the slightly lighter area on the right side of the eye, which she reduced by selecting it with a 3-pixel feathered Lasso tool and adding a Curves adjustment layer to darken the area to match the rest of the eye (**figure** 10.85).

8. To add additional lashes, Carrie copied and pasted individual eyelashes and then erased away unnecessary information.

 T i p

After pasting a new lash into place, add realism by cloning a few details such as a small clump of makeup or a hint of sparkle from a real eyelash onto the new one.

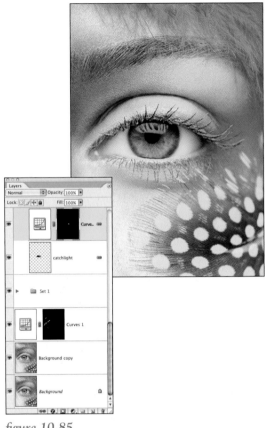

figure 10.85

The tiniest detail is perfected with a separate adjustment layer.

9. To define the eyebrows, Carrie merged all visible layers up (Cmd-Option-Shift-E/Ctrl-Alt-Shift-E) and chose Filter > Other > High Pass with a setting of 3. By changing the layer blending mode to Soft Light, the dimensional sharpness remains and the gray disappears.

10. Setting the Dodge and Burn tools to hard-edged 5-pixel, midtones, and 100% exposure, Carrie dodged and burned the eyebrows with black and white strokes as seen in **figure** 10.86 to add contrast and dimension to the eyebrows.

To add even more drama to the eyes and show how carefully a professional retoucher works, Carrie used four separate Curves adjustment layers to accentuate the shape of the eyes and eyelashes.

11. To make the lower lid white, she added a Curves layer, lightened the entire file, inverted the layer mask and drew in exactly where the skin needed to be a purer white, seen in **figure 10.87**.

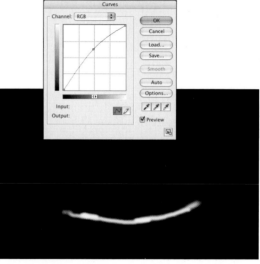

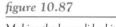

figure 10.87

Making the lower lid white.

12. To extend the yellow eye shadow, Carrie added a Curves adjustment layer and adjusted the red, green, and blue curves to create yellow. She then inverted the layer mask and painted the yellow eye shadow in perfectly, as seen in (**figure 10.88**).

figure 10.86

Dodging and burning dimension and contrast onto the eyebrows and feathers.

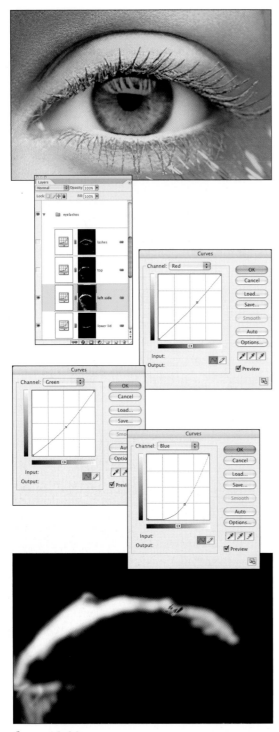

figure 10.88

Extending the yellow eye shadow.

13. The eye shadow needed to be a touch darker and richer. Carrie used Curves again to darken the green and blue curves, then inverted the layer mask and painted in the required color correction and shading, as shown in (**figure 10.89**).

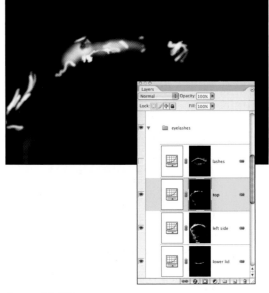

figure 10.89

Refining the density of the eyelid and eye shadow.

14. Finally, to darken the lashes and better define the eye, Carrie added a Curves layer, darkened the entire file down, inverted the layer mask, and painted over the individual eyelashes (**figure 10.90**).

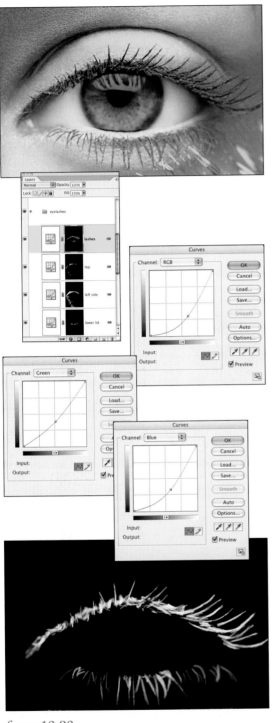

figure 10.90

Framing the eye with dark, dramatic eyelashes.

15. After seeing a printed proof, Carrie increased the overall contrast and darkened down the light area on the model's forehead to create the final image, as seen in figures 10.91 and 10.92.

figure 10.91

Before the final contrast tweak.

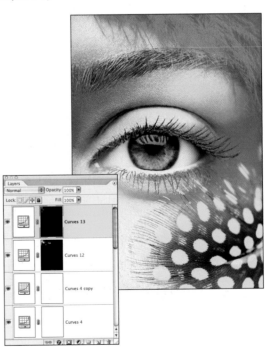

figure 10.92

After seeing a proof and making four additional contrast improvements.

The cosmetics industry has some of the most critical clients you'll ever face. It is an industry where perfection and color accuracy are the only acceptable options. Now that more photographers are shooting digitally, the skills of the make-up artist also need to be greater; as high-resolution digital capture also captures any unevenness in the make-up. Thankfully, the ability to see the test shoot on a 21-inch monitor often allows the make-up artist to inspect his or her handiwork and make corrections and refinements before the final shot is taken.

Luscious Lips

All lips have folds and crevices in them; if they didn't, we couldn't open our mouths to speak or eat. Lips need to be inviting without being so smooth that that they look fake. When working on lips, the issues to pay attention to are symmetry, contours of makeup, maintaining moisture, and reducing the natural wrinkles with either the Neutral layer or Dual Curves technique as used for skin retouching.

To add moisture and gloss to lips, Andrew Matusik showed me this technique. In the original photograph the makeup artist used a lot of care to create the super-moist lips and droplet (see figure 10.93). To enhance the cool feeling, Andrew knew that he would color the image blue and replace the background with some icy water, as seen in figure 10.94. But before he did that he would retouch the skin and make the lips even wetter.

1. To make the lips wetter, he generously selected the lips with a 3-pixel feathered Lasso tool and selected Layer > New > Layer via Copy.

© Andrew Matusik

BEFORE

figure 10.93

AFTER

figure 10.94

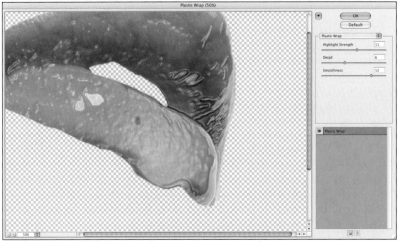

figure 10.95

Use the Plastic Wrap filter to create wetness.

2. To add the moisture, Andrew selected Filter > Artistic > Plastic Wrap and adjusted the filter settings as seen in **figure 10.95** to accentuate the highlights and smoothness while suppressing some detail.

3. By adjusting the layer opacity and refining the lips with a bit of cloning, he made the lips even moister and glossier.

Andrew says, "I don't use Plastic Wrap technique very often, but when the lips need to appear very moist and stylized it can be very effective."

Hair Is the Holy Grail

Every professional photo shoot has a dedicated makeup artist and hair stylist (**figure 10.96**) to make sure that each hair is in place. But during the shoot the model does need to move her head, which can require some Photoshop coiffing to add the finishing touch. When working with hair, the issues you need to pay attention to are exactly the same ones that the hair stylist pays attention to: fullness, closing gaps, removing flyaway hairs from face and background, color, and shine. The real challenge is to make the added or retouched hair blend in and look natural.

figure 10.96

Professional hair stylist at work.

In **figure** 10.97 and 10.98 you see how subtly the hair has been made thicker and the darker roots have been lightened up ever so slightly.

1. In this example, the fullness was added with the Liquify tool (**figure** 10.99) using a large, low-density, low-pressure Forward Warp tool brush.

figure 10.97

figure 10.98

figure 10.99

The Liquify tool adds volume to her hair.

2. To lighten up the roots, I added a Curves adjustment layer and pulled the curve up. I selected Image > Adjustments > Invert to invert the Curves layer mask from white to black and painted with a soft-edged white brush on the darker areas, as seen in **figure 10.100**.

figure 10.100

Lightening her roots with an adjustment layer.

More challenging is the example seen in **figure 10.101** and **10.102**, in which Andrew Matusik needed to close the gaps in the hair.

1. Andrew started by selecting a section of hair under her mouth and used Cmd-J/Ctrl-J to copy it to its own layer. After positioning the hair, he used a soft-edged Eraser tool to merge the hair with the existing hair.

2. To maintain consistency in lighting and hair structure, Andrew continued to duplicate, move, and blend in the similar pieces of hair to build up her hair. Working piece by piece and layer by layer, Andrew closed the distracting gaps with hair, as seen in **figure 10.103**.

BEFORE

© Andrew Matusik

figure 10.101

AFTER

figure 10.102

Andrew recently told me "Hair is the Holy Grail of glamour retouching. It is very critical and requires a lot of patience to do well. For me, rebuilding hair is solving a puzzle, as I look for and use the pieces that fit the best."

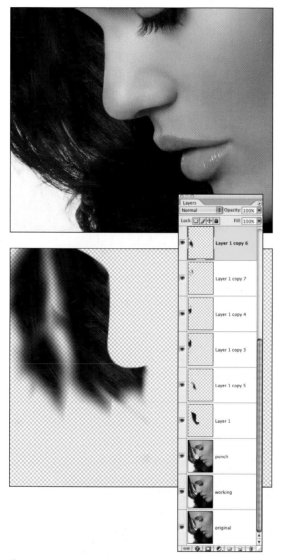

figure 10.103

The results and the isolated layers.

FOCUS AND SHARPNESS

The sharper part of any picture is always what our eyes will look at first and longest. After the retouching is done and you've sized the file for the printer, you should always sharpen the eyes slightly more than the rest of the image, as shown in **figures 10.104** and **10.105**.

1. Carrie clicked the topmost layer and chose Cmd-Option-Shift-E/Ctrl-Alt-Shift-E to merge all layers into a separate composite layer.

2. She used Filter > Other > High Pass with a setting of 4 to enhance the edge details. On your own images, try a setting between 2 and 5; look for edge detail, as seen in **figure 10.106**.

3. Often the High Pass filter maintains some of the original color, which has to be removed with Image > Adjustments > Desaturate.

4. Carrie changed the layer blending mode to Soft Light (**figure 10.107**) and Option/Alt-clicked the layer mask button to add a black layer mask.

5. Using a soft-edged, white brush, Carrie painted over the eyes, eyebrows, and—with a lower opacity brush—over the lips to sharpen these features more than the surrounding skin.

Note

When sharpening your own files, experiment with strengthening the effect, by either duplicating the High Pass layer or changing the layer blending mode to Hard Light. As with all sharpening techniques, you will need to see a print to evaluate the sharpening accurately.

figure 10.104

figure 10.105

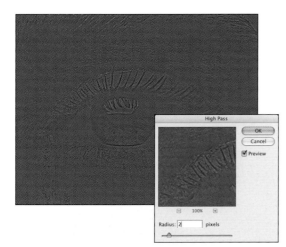

figure 10.106

Adjust the High Pass filter to create well-defined lines.

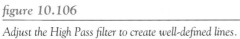

figure 10.107

The High Pass filter and Soft Light blending mode accentuate the edge contrast.

Beauty Glow

Although less frequently called for, adding a subtle glow is the opposite of sharpening a file. As with sharpening, you use a layer mask to control which areas are soft and which are sharp, as seen in **figures 10.108** and **10.109**.

 ch10_beauty_glow.jpg

© Allure Photography

BEFORE

figure 10.108

AFTER

figure 10.109

1. When working on a layered file, use Cmd-Option-Shift-E/Ctrl-Alt-Shift-E to merge all the layers into a new composite layer. When working with a flat file, duplicate the Background layer.

2. Used Filter > Other > High Pass with a setting between 2 and 5 until the edge detail is obvious.

3. Remove any of the original color with Image > Adjustments > Desaturate.

4. Change the layer blending mode to Overlay. As you can see in **figure 10.110**, the entire file is too sharp.

figure 10.110

Sharpening the file is the first step of softening it.

5. With the High Pass layer active, select Image > Adjustments > Invert, which softens the file and smoothes her skin wonderfully (**figure 10.111**).

figure 10.111

Inverting the High Pass layer softens the entire image.

6. Add a layer mask by clicking the layer mask button on the Layers palette. Paint with a 50% opacity, soft black brush over her eyes and mouth to bring them back into focus, as seen in **figure 10.112**. To lessen the softening effect, reduce the layer opacity or double the Overlay layer to increase the effect.

figure 10.112

Paint over the eyes to bring them back into focus.

GLAMOUR LIGHTING

Of course, photographers pay a lot of attention to lighting while taking pictures, but you can use Photoshop to fine-tune lighting to add a drama that draws the viewer's eyes deeper into the photograph.

Sculpting the Face

To enhance the dimension of the face, such as in **figure 10.113**, retouchers lighten the protruding areas of the face—forehead, cheekbones, and nose—and darken receding areas under cheekbones and lips (see **figure 10.114**).

figure 10.113

figure 10.114

To add the final polish and dimension, Andrew added a Curves layer to lighten the image and increase contrast. He then painted on the layer mask with a large, soft-edged brush to take the contrast away from the less important image areas, as seen in **figure 10.115**. Notice how the subtle use of contrast adds intriguing dimension to her bone structure.

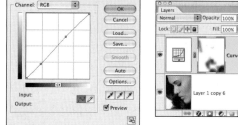

figure 10.115

After lightening the file, Andrew controls the tonal effect with a large, soft, black brush.

Contouring the Body

You can use shading to draw attention away from the less flattering aspects of a person and to sculpt a person's legs, arms, and abdomen to look more three-dimensional. Darkening and lightening contours adds contrast, which makes body parts seem shapelier and more toned, as shown in **figures 10.116** and **10.117**.

1. I used the Pen tool to outline her body and her bathing suit, creating the alpha channel seen in **figure 10.118**.

2. I made sure that the path and the alpha channel were not active and added a Curves adjustment layer, clicked OK without changing anything, and then changed the layer's blending mode to Multiply and lowered the opacity to 35% to darken the entire image, as shown in **figure 10.119**.

3. With the Curves layer active, I pressed Cmd-I/Ctrl-I to invert the layer mask, which turns off the darkening effect.

4. I duplicated the darkening layer and changed its blending mode to Screen (see **figure 10.120**).

5. I chose Select > Load Selection to load the alpha channel (**figure 10.121**) and clicked on the lower Curves adjustment layer, which contains the darkening adjustment layer from steps 2 and 3.

BEFORE

figure 10.116

AFTER

figure 10.117

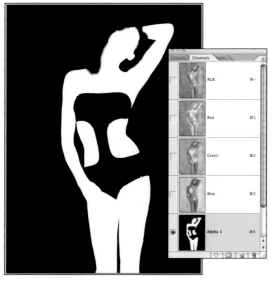

figure 10.118

The alpha channel.

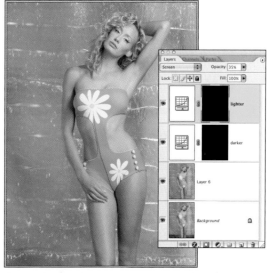

figure 10.120

Repeating the procedure, but this time to lighten the image.

figure 10.119

Darkening the image with the Multiply blending mode.

figure 10.121

The active selection.

6. With a very large, soft-edged, white brush, I painted along the edges of her thighs and arms, as shown in figure 10.122. This contours her body shape with slightly darker tones along the edges. For illustration purposes, figure 10.123 shows the Curves adjustment layer mask.

7. I used a smaller brush on the lightening Curves adjustment layer to draw down the center of her legs, contrasting dark with light, as shown in figure 10.124. To refine the lightening and darkening effect, I adjusted the layer opacity to 35%. Figure 10.125 shows the lightening Curves adjustment layer mask.

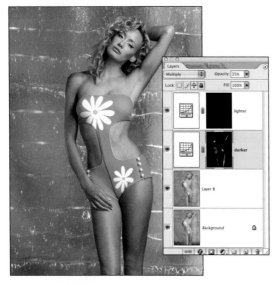

figure 10.122

Painting with white on the black layer mask enables you to selectively paint the darker tone onto the model's outer contours.

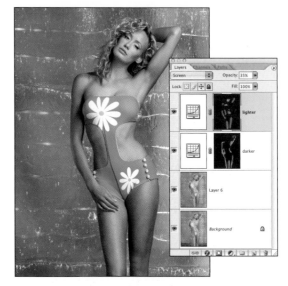

figure 10.124

Use the outer edges of a very large brush to add gentle gradations of tone.

figure 10.123

The isolated layer mask.

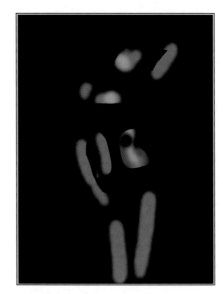

figure 10.125

The isolated layer mask.

Framing the Image

As shown in Chapter 9, vignetting the image with either darker or lighter values emphasizes the subject very effectively. In the first example, darkening the image backdrop brings more attention to the lighter parts of the image as seen in **figures 10.126** and **10.127**.

BEFORE

figure 10.126

AFTER

figure 10.127

ch10_dark_frame_jpg

1. Press F once to make sure you are working in full-screen mode. Add a Curves adjustment layer and pull the highlight point down to darken the entire image (**figure 10.128**).

figure 10.128

Darken the entire image.

2. Press D to reset the color picker to the default settings of black and white and press X to make white the foreground color. Select the Gradient tool; choose the White to Transparent gradient, as shown in **figure 10.129**.

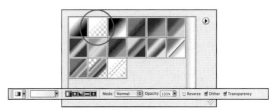

figure 10.129

Selecting the second gradient, foreground to transparent, is essential.

3. Zoom out so that you can start the gradient well outside of the image. Draw a number of gradients from the outside corners in toward the image center. It is better to build up the darkening effect with numerous gradients instead of trying to get it right with one perfect gradient pull.

© Thiago Da Cunha

4. Adjust the final strength of the edge burn by adjusting the layer opacity, as shown in figure 10.130.

figure 10.130

Multiple pulls of the Gradient tool create the delicate transition.

In figures 10.131 and 10.132 you see how lightening the image makes the darker information more prominent. As Jarkko Viljanen, who translates my books from English to Finnish, wrote, "I wanted to show you how I implemented what I have learned while translating. I shot this image last night and put an hour and half of Photoshop into it. Thanks." For me, this is exactly what this book is about: Look, learn, and explore new images and ideas. Enjoy the journey.

CLOSING THOUGHTS

I hope that the techniques you've seen here help you in a Photoshop sense, but also in a dose-of-reality sense. To maintain a healthy body and self-image, it is important to separate the reality from the illusion. More often than not, the perfect bodies and faces in the fashion magazines, cosmetic advertising, and swimwear calendars just don't exist—except as a collection of finely tuned pixels on a professional retoucher's hard drive.

BEFORE

figure 10.131

AFTER

figure 10.132

© Jarkko Viljanen

APPENDIX

CONTRIBUTORS

This book would never have been come to fruition without the generous sharing of images and techniques by these very talented professionals. I thank them all for their time, help, and insights.

ALAN
PhotoRescuer
Photo Restoration & Retouching
Maryland • (301) 873-3983
www.photorescuer.com • sales@photorescuer.com

KEN ALLEN
Image Conservator
Digitization consulting, catalog development, and photo-safe storage
New York, NY • (917) 853-0592
www.savethephotos.com • ken@savethephotos.com

JANEE ARONOFF
myJanee.com Graphic Creations
Adobe Certified Instructor, educator and author, freelance graphic art, and restoration
Bloomington, IN
myJanee.com • myJanee.com/contact.htm

MARK BECKELMAN
Beckelman Photo Illustration
Digital imaging, retouching services, conceptual and editorial illustration
Springfield, NJ • (973) 467-3456
www.beckelman.com • mark@beckelman.com

CARRIE BEENE
OTTO Imaging, LLC
High-end beauty retouching, silhouetting, and hair
New York, NY
(212) 995-1451 • (212) 658-9590
www.ottoimaging.com • cbeene@ottoimaging.com

SHAN CANFIELD

aka "Photoshop Mama"
Training, digital art and photography,
beauty retouching
Nashville, TN • (615) 228-5935
www.shanzcan.com • www.moidesignstudio.com
mama@shanzcan.com

RICK DAY NYC

Fashion, glamour, and beauty photography
New York, NY • (646) 279-7387
www.rickdaynyc.com • info@rickdaynyc.com

DOUGLAS DUBLER 3

Beauty, fashion, and fine art photography
New York, NY • (212) 452-2525
www.douglasdubler3.com • ddubler@mac.com

SHAWN GIBSON

Shawn Gibson Photography
Digital portraiture and classical portrait painting
Toronto, Ontario, Canada • (416) 603-0707
www.shawngibson.com • shotbyshawn@yahoo.com
shawn.gibson@utoronto.ca

H AND H COLOR LAB

Full-service professional photo lab specializing in
optical and digital services, digital and traditional
retouching/enhancement, and finishing services
(800) 821-1305 • Kansas City, MO
www.hhcolorlab.com
customerservice@hhcolorlab.com

ART JOHNSON

Memories in Minutes
Digital photography, restoration, and portrait
retouching
Albany, GA • (229) 888-7135
www.ArtPhotog.com • Memoriesinminutes@mchsi.com

W. ALAN JONES

Digital photography, wood lathe, and
woodworking
Milledgeville, GA • (478) 452-6859
Ajones@alltel.net

ANDREW MATUSIK

Digital Retouch
Fashion, beauty, and celebrity photography
New York, NY • (917) 779-8606
www.andrewmatusik.com • www.digitalretouch.net

JOHN MCINTOSH

School of VISUAL ARTS
Chair, Computer Art
New York, NY
www.svacomputerart.com • jmcintosh@sva.edu

SKYY STORM MCKENDRY

Conviction of the Heart Photography
Capturing the true beauty of my subjects
Kanab, UT • (435) 616-5463
www.betterphoto.com/gallery/
gallery.asp?memberID=105527
skyymckendry@hotmail.com

JASON NADLER

Nadler Photo Design
Digital photography, enhancement,
and restoration
Wading River, NY • (631) 682-3329
www.jasonnadler.photosite.com
nadlerphoto@optonline.net

RICH OASEN

U.S. Navy, Foto Ace
Chief Photographer for the Navy,
Digital Photography
Washington, DC; Fredericksburg, VA
(540) 371-4537
www.fotoace.com • rloasen@fotoace.com

PHIL POOL

Omni Photography
Digital portraiture and wedding photography,
image restoration
West Burlington, IA
www.omniphotobyphil.com • pep9454@yahoo.com

TERESA SETTERLUND

Designer Photo Imaging
Photo manipulation, portrait retouching,
image restoration
Minneapolis, MN
www.designerpi.com • ts@designerpi.com

CHRIS TARANTINO

Twisted Pixel
High-end beauty and fashion retouching,
color management
Connecticut and NYC • (203) 314-7924
Retoucherpro@mac.com

JARKKO VILJANEN

Pixelcom
Digital imaging, photography, and training
Vesilahti, Finland
+358-400-796 768
www.pixelcom.fi • www.studioamanda.fi
jarkko.viljanen@pixelcom.fi

JUNG AND NATALIE WI

Allure West Studios
Wedding and fashion photography
San Francisco, CA • (415) 513-5925
www.allurewest.com • contact@allurewest.com

JOSH WITHERS

Arthaus—TBWA \ Chiat \ Day
Retouching, digital art, and photography
Los Angeles, CA
www.joshwithers.com • josh@joshwithers.com

LORIE K. ZIRBES

Retouching by Lorie
Portrait retouching, image restoration, and
creative color tinting
Las Vegas, NV, and the Internet
(702) 648-4410
www.retouchingbylorie.com • ArtistLZ@aol.com

IMAGE CONTRIBUTORS

Thank you to these photographers, museums, and companies for allowing me to feature their images. Your generosity and understanding made this book possible.

Jose A. Basbus
Richard Berke
George Brinkerhoff
Thiago Da Cunha
Brent Davis
The Dallas Museum of Fine Art
Colin M. Dearing
Alyssa Duncan
Frank Eirund
Regan Ehrman
Pamela Herrington
JupiterImages
Eugene Larson
Elliot Lincis
Angie W. Lowe
Robert Malarz
Myke Ninness
Patrick O'Connell
Scott Seewald
Luanne Seymour
Barry Silverstein
Brent Shirk
Thomas T. Taber Museum
Cindy Reding
Stephen Rosenblum

Thank you to these families for allowing us to feature their family images: Allely, Beckelman, Berger, Bonham, Eckert, Eichhorn, Eismann, Holmes, Jackson, Knoll, McIntosh, Morgan, Palmer, Sampson, Shaw, Wheeler, and Wunn.

INDEX

D

Z